LAW, ORDER, AND EMPIRE

LAW, ORDER, AND EMPIRE

POLICING AND CRIME IN COLONIAL
ALGERIA, 1870–1954

Samuel Kalman

CORNELL UNIVERSITY PRESS
Ithaca and London

Copyright © 2024 by Cornell University

All rights reserved. Except for brief quotations in a review, this book, or parts thereof, must not be reproduced in any form without permission in writing from the publisher. For information, address Cornell University Press, Sage House, 512 East State Street, Ithaca, New York 14850. Visit our website at cornellpress.cornell.edu.

First published 2024 by Cornell University Press

Library of Congress Cataloging-in-Publication Data

Names: Kalman, Samuel, 1971– author.
Title: Law, order, and empire : policing and crime in colonial Algeria, 1870–1954 / Samuel Kalman.
Description: Ithaca [New York] : Cornell University Press, 2024. | Includes bibliographical references and index.
Identifiers: LCCN 2023020301 (print) | LCCN 2023020302 (ebook) | ISBN 9781501774041 (hardcover) | ISBN 9781501774058 (epub) | ISBN 9781501774065 (pdf)
Subjects: LCSH: Criminal justice, Administration of—Algeria—History—19th century. | Criminal justice, Administration of—Algeria—History—20th century. | Discrimination in criminal justice administration—Algeria. | Algeria—Colonial influence—History.
Classification: LCC HV9960.A44 K35 2024 (print) | LCC HV9960.A44 (ebook) | DDC 364.0890965—dc23/eng/20230823
LC record available at https://lccn.loc.gov/2023020301
LC ebook record available at https://lccn.loc.gov/2023020302

Contents

Acknowledgments vii

List of Abbreviations xi

Introduction   1

1. Agents of Empire and Crisis of Authority: The Professional, Racial, and Financial Reality of Policing in French Colonial Algeria   19

2. An Anticolonial Crime Wave? Policing Banditry in the Constantinois   53

3. Unlawful Acts or Strategies of Resistance? Crime and the Disruption of Colonial Order in Interwar French Algeria   83

4. Colonial Policing during Wartime: From Vichy to the Allies and Free French   117

5. Policing Colonial Politics: The Surveillance, Arrest, and Detention of Leaders and Members of the Parti du peuple algérien, 1944–1954   148

Conclusion   184

Notes 193

Bibliography 237

Index 249

Acknowledgments

First and foremost, this book was made possible by an Insight Grant from the Social Sciences and Humanities Research Council of Canada (SSHRC), whose help made possible research travel to France, Algeria, and England, as well as attendance at conferences and publications arising from extensive archival work. I also received generous funding from the University Council of Research at St. Francis Xavier University, which seeded the project in its inception, permitting me to seek a SSHRC award. The consistent financial and material assistance from the university has been both essential throughout my career and sincerely appreciated. I must also thank my colleagues in the Department of History at St. FX, whose ongoing support has made the task of producing this book much easier on all fronts.

Tremendous gratitude is further due to the personnel at various archives and institutions that made my research possible. Without their indefatigable efforts on my behalf, the investigation of policing and crime in colonial Algeria would have been infinitely more challenging. As always, Daniel Hick and the staff at the Archives nationales d'Outre mer (ANOM) in Aix-en-Provence not only facilitated the task of working through a literal treasure trove of documents but also pointed out essential yet previously undetected resources that greatly improved various publications. From the *magasiniers* to the *chefs de salle*, the CAOM team is unparalleled in its attention to researchers and expertise concerning their extensive collections. An equally large round of thanks is due to Naima Mehareb and the workers at the Archives nationales d'Algérie, who patiently guided me through the process of seeking permission to view key materials and graciously answered my numerous queries about multiple papers. Particular mention must be made of the archivists, whose encyclopedic grasp of the site's holdings permitted me to quickly find relevant evidence. In addition, the staff at the Archives nationales and Bibliothèque nationale in Paris, along with the Service historique de la défense, provided their habitual assistance and keen knowledge to aid my efforts in their collections. Finally, I must acknowledge the generosity of the team at the National Archives of

Great Britain, who went above and beyond to grant me timely access to various files and folders, given that I could spend only a week in London. It is a first-rate institution on all counts.

Of course, the book would not have been remotely possible without the wonderful editorial team at Cornell University Press, and particularly Bethany Wasik, whose precise eye for detail, superb suggestions, and constant support greatly facilitated the publication process. I was also extremely fortunate to have comprehensive, gimlet-eyed evaluations from the anonymous reviewers, whose excellent critique and ideas vastly improved the original manuscript. Various other publishers must be recognized for their willingness to allow me to reprint material that originally appeared in chapters and articles. Portions of chapter 2 are taken from "Criminalizing Dissent: Policing Banditry in the Constantinois, 1914–18" in the collection *Algeria Revisited: History, Culture, and Identity*, used with the permission of the editors, Claire Eldridge and Rabah Aissaoui, and Bloomsbury Press. Part of chapter 3 is drawn from the article "Unlawful Acts or Strategies of Resistance? Crime and the Disruption of Colonial Order in Interwar French Algeria," *French Historical Studies* 43 (2020), reprinted with the authorization of the editors and Duke University Press.

I owe a further debt to a large number of colleagues, whose expertise, advice, and rapport have informed the book and my enjoyment of the profession in equal measure. Sean Kennedy, Cheryl Koos, and Geoff Read are much more than fellow historians—they are tremendous human beings, whose friendship and support has been integral to my success from the beginning of my career. The late William Irvine and Wayne Thorpe continue to provide stellar examples of what it means to be engaged with the historical profession, and their spirit inhabits every page of the book. In the French colonial and postcolonial fields I am indebted to numerous confreres who have commented on and/or inspired my work: Rabah Aissaoui, Arthur Asseraf, Ben Brower, Cari Campbell, Partha Chatterjee, Sung Choi, Joshua Cole, Patrick Dramé, Carolyn Eichner, Claire Eldridge, Richard Fogarty, Ruth Ginio, Dónal Hassett, Norman Ingram, Peter Jackson, Eric Jennings, Ethan Katz, Laurent Kestel, Patricia Lorcin, Michelle Mann, Chris Millington, Kevin Passmore, Jen Sessions, the late Michael Sibalis, Martin Thomas, Sylvie Thénault, Michael Vann, and Louisa Zanoun.

Outside of the historical profession, I have been incredibly fortunate to have a tremendous number of friends, family members, and colleagues who have consistently proffered encouragement and support for my work, even if it meant listening to voluminous blather about all manner of things French and Algerian: Carl Adams, Lynn Chapman, Graeme Clyke and Nathalie Gagné,

ACKNOWLEDGMENTS

Patricia Cormack and Robert Kennedy, Michael D'Arcy, Hilda Dunnewold, Aaron and Tammy Farrell, Peter Ferguson and Erika Kato, Elena and Ralph Gould, Renée Filgarz and Alex Grassino, Chris Frazer, Yvon Grenier, Mavis Jacobs, Josh Judah and Conor Falvey, Ilana Keeb-Rich, Ron Kent, Joseph Khoury and Janet Becigneul, Ozlem Kizirnejad, Erika Koch, Jon Langdon and Liliona Quarmyne, Laurie Lemmond, Ron Loranger, Kuli Malhotra and Layla Khalil, Neil Mayers, Derek Neal, Diane O'Neill, Elvis Aaron Petrie, Shah Razul and Susan MacKay, Marion Rosen, Carole Roy, Cory Rushton and Sue Hawkes, Heather Shaw and Steve Schnier, Jane Stirling, Tara Taylor, Andrew Terris, Lori Ward, and Rob Wickham. An even greater expression of gratitude is due to my late brother, Ben, an incredible sibling, best friend, and constant inspiration, and my sister-in-law, Ashley, along with my father, Calvin, and late mother, Judy, for their unwavering encouragement. Most importantly, to my son, Josh, and my muse and partner, Brenda: I could never have written the book without you both, the most wonderful people in my life, and I love and adore you always.

Abbreviations

AL	Amitiés latines
ALN	Armée de libération nationale
AML	Amis du manifeste et de la liberté
AN	Archives nationales
ANA	Archives nationales d'Algérie
ANOM	Archives nationales d'Outre-mer
BM	Brigades mobiles
BN	Bibliothèque nationale
CF/PSF	Croix de Feu/Parti social français
CGQJ	Commissariat général aux questions juives
CGT	Confédération générale du travail
CRS	Compagnies républicaines de sécurité
CRUA	Comité révolutionnaire d'unité et d'action
DST	Direction de la surveillance du territoire
ENA	Étoile nord-africaine
FEM	Fédération des élus musulmans
FLN	Front de libération nationale
GGA	Gouverneur générale d'Algérie
GRM	Garde républicaine mobile
IGAME	Inspecteurs généraux de l'administration en mission extraordinaire
LICA	Ligue international contre l'antisémitisme
MTLD	Mouvement pour le triomphe des libertés démocratiques
NAGB	National Archives of Great Britain
OAS	Organisation armée secrète
OS	Organisation spéciale
PCA	Parti communiste algérien
PCF	Parti communiste français
PG	Police générale
PJ	Police judiciaire
PPA	Parti du people algérien
PPF	Parti populaire français

PRG	Police / Renseignements généraux
PTT	Postes, télégraphes, et téléphones
RNAS	Rassemblement national d'action sociale
SFIO	Section française de l'Internationale ouvrière
SHD	Service historique de la défense
SLNA	Service de liaisons nord-africaines
SOL	Service d'ordre légionnaire
STO	Service du travail obligatoire
UDMA	Union démocratique du manifeste algérien

LAW, ORDER, AND EMPIRE

Introduction

On 8 April 1926, the Constantine head of the Sûreté générale wrote to the director concerning an attempted robbery and murder weeks earlier in a *duwar* (tent enclave) in Fedj-M'zala, initially ignored by police but then belatedly investigated after his office contacted the administrator of the commune. A local man named Ramdane Fetouhi had been shot to death by a would-be thief on leaving his tent in response to strange noises. No information had been gleaned from the inhabitants, and the officers and their superiors concluded that the deed was perpetrated by outsiders, and thus closed the case. Another incident, on 22 January 1921, provides a stark contrast. That night, assailants attacked and robbed Paul Hierling, a European who managed a farm in Randon, outside Bône, with suspicion falling on Aissa ben Ahmed, a local Muslim. Quite unlike the administrative apathy shown in the Fedj-M'zala case, this time, the governor general personally traveled to the crime scene and offered all necessary assistance to the mayor, while two top detectives immediately began to reconstruct events. Their efforts revealed that Hierling, who suffered from tuberculosis, had gone to sleep early and woke up covered in blood after his head was struck multiple times with a machete, his attacker nowhere in sight. His wallet and watch were missing, and the weapon had been left at the crime scene. As for the alleged perpetrator, he had known the victim for two years, having migrated from the Territoires du

Sud, in the Sahara desert. A warrant was immediately issued and a comprehensive search began for the criminal.[1]

Why were the two crimes treated in such a diametrically opposite fashion? Both involved extreme violence and seemingly threatened the peace and order of rural territories in the department of Constantine, and the perpetrators could strike again, killing or maiming others. Moreover, the divergent responses were part of a far larger pattern: apathy toward violent acts committed against Arabs and Kabyles, yet desperate urgency whenever the victim was European. The answer to this contradiction can be found in the work of Florence Bernault, who observes that the imperial state continually engaged in "une entreprise de conquête interrompue. Conquête, c'est-à-dire une hégémonie incomplète et aléatoire, toujours en train de s'établir au gré des initiatives des gouvernements et des colonisés, de leurs rapports de force et intérêts respectifs [an interrupted attempt at conquest, that is to say an incomplete and uncertain hegemony, in the midst of being established at the behest of governments and colonizers, according to their respective power relations and interests]."[2] The French administration encouraged the construction and maintenance of a racial state by settlers in Algeria from 1870 onward, in which Arabs and Berbers lacked the rights and representation enjoyed by Europeans, including financial compensation for ownership of businesses and land. Concomitantly, the Europeans expropriated resources and territory, exploiting cheap labor while monopolizing government and the use of force. As a result, authorities in the metropole and colony alike also prioritized the mobilization of the army and police, the agents used both to enforce colonial laws and to uphold the entire hegemonic apparatus throughout the history of what settlers called *l'Algérie française* (French Algeria), simultaneously charged with law enforcement and repression.

This book provides a comprehensive overview of police and crime in the colony, including the organization and functioning of the police, and the challenges encountered by officers. Unlike the metropolitan variant, imperial policing was never a simple matter of law enforcement; instead, it engaged in the defense of racial hegemony and imperial rule. Officers and gendarmes waged a constant struggle against escalating banditry, the assault and murder of settlers, and nationalist politics—anticolonial violence that rejected French rule. Hence, it became synonymous with repression, its brutal tactics foreshadowing the torture and murder during the Algerian War of Independence from 1954 to 1962.

That police and gendarmes, along with judges and prisons, represented state or private interests is certainly no great revelation.[3] Officers necessarily function as both an instrument of political authority and the enforcers of social or cultural norms; police can (and do) use violence to exert social control, punishing deviance while upholding social and political order, whether authoritarian or republican in the metropole or racial in the colonial setting. This includes gathering information on behalf of the administration, acting as its eyes and ears on the street, producing daily reports, and providing patrols of gendarmes or *commissaires* to prevent crime on multiple levels, supported by an elaborate system of files, reports, and surveillance from the political police and support technicians dedicated to providing the needed intelligence to identify and prevent threat formation.[4] In the colonial setting, these factors combined to powerfully bolster European racial hegemony.

The ordinary methodology and practices of a criminal justice system, from investigations and arrests to interrogations and trails, all strictly regulated by laws and expectations, simply did not apply in the colonial setting. Officers indiscriminately arrested and detained the colonized, placed groups under surveillance on the mere suspicion of malfeasance—usually anti-imperialist activity—and went far beyond metropolitan law enforcement norms, engaging in what Taylor Sherman calls "bodily sanctions," from arbitrary detention and beatings or killings to collective fines. The actual pursuit of criminal cases became secondary to using the wide range of powers granted to individual officers or bureaus to ensure that racial borders were maintained and that European superiority was reinforced by public spectacle.[5] The constant push to defend and expand racial hegemony necessitated a police endowed with far greater powers than their metropolitan confreres, and this extended to a wide variety of indigenous auxiliaries and guards who together exercised a de facto state monopoly on violence aimed exclusively at non-European denizens.[6] Worse still for the colonized, the military often took the lead; in Algeria, the gendarmerie patrolled rural communes, empowered to use force against any perceived threat. Much like in the metropolitan force, in each colonial branch, rookie officers and soldiers jettisoned training instructions once on the job, prioritizing crimes and potential threats against Europeans, while investigating "indigenous" crimes solely to maintain the peace necessary to permit continued colonial exploitation.

Law enforcement also participated in the functioning of what Martin Thomas terms the "intelligence state," in which information gathering and threat assessments proved vital to the maintenance and continuity of colonial administrations. From government officials and experts to African and Asian collaborators, police, and soldiers, all attempted to provide needed detail concerning political, economic, social, environmental, and cultural factors that might prevent the rebellion of the colonized, provide justification for French rule, and ensure racial hegemony and imperial order. Algerian police were literally on the front lines of this effort, as representatives of empire and hubs of local and regional intelligence-gathering networks that were necessary because Arabs and Kabyles never accepted European dominance, and thus they combined information harvesting with the threat of violence and heavy-handed repression.[7] In this way, metropolitan practices concerning the surveillance of individuals, political parties, religious sects, and organizations, along with the management of agents and informants, and the collection of vast tranches of data, were combined with colonial violence in Algeria toward distinctly imperial ends.[8]

None of this was particularly novel in French Algeria, and from 1830 onward, officials in Paris and Alger (Algiers) responded to ongoing security concerns with various legal and judicial machinations designed to perpetuate colonialism and, most importantly, turned to policing, both an omnipresent symbol of Gallic domination and the primary instigator of the suppression of anticolonial dissent and crime against the growing settler population. Following the formal annexation of Algeria in 1834, the colony was placed under military control under Governor (and General) Thomas Bugeaud and the Bureaux arabes (Arab bureaus), who were charged with gathering intelligence concerning the inhabitants and terrain, politics and society, and religion and culture of the new possession. Personnel were further tasked with spreading acceptance of imperialism and establishing control over the Muslim population while policing anti-French sentiment, managing rural districts, and selecting local leadership. This included the orderly transfer or expropriation of land by Europeans and the maintenance of strict racial boundaries, including the removal of all nonassimilated individuals from local French life.[9]

Prior to 1870, law enforcement meant the gendarmerie. Attached to the army, they arrived from France to replace the Ottoman police, which had emphasized the fulfillment of local needs as opposed to an overarching system. Due to the immense territory under consideration, gendarmes required the assistance of Algerian adjutants and *gardes champêtres* (rural policemen), along with Spahis (African cavalry units). Their brief included everything from physically protecting Europeans from the local population to fighting cattle theft, yet they did not engage in military campaigns, which were the exclusive purview of the army; instead, they acted as police under the direction of the governor and the military. As French-controlled territory expanded, so too did the number of jurisdictions served by gendarmes, and by the 1850s larger centers had received brigades. Yet, this was only true of locations where the European population grew substantially; law enforcement existed solely to protect the colonizer. Algerians interested officials and gendarmes exclusively in cases where French aims could be furthered or where security concerns emerged involving "suspect" or criminal individuals or groups. Thus, brigades tended to appear solely in towns like Oran or Bône, rather than in the Tell or the mountains, and they ventured into the countryside primarily to search dwellings for arms or to root out anticolonial activity.[10]

Nonetheless, as the decades passed, their numbers increased dramatically, rising from 200 in 1830 to 708 in 1870, although staffing shortages proved to be a constant problem, with gendarmes transferring out or leaving the service due to poor barracks and food, the climate, and illness. The problem tended to be less acute in major centers like Alger, where four-man teams patrolled neighborhoods, with a fixed number also reserved for duty outside the town limits. However, as business and settlement expanded, so too did the need for gendarmes in smaller rural communities, particularly to protect roads and *centres de colonisation* (settler farming villages) in the Tell. The service also filled auxiliary roles, functioning as military police dealing with anything from desertion to disorderly conduct to theft and murder. Yet, in general, most brigades combined the duties of the Police générale (keeping order and enforcing civil laws) and the Police judiciaire, who investigated serious crimes, along with the function of the Police des moeurs (gambling and prostitution) and the Police de la chasse (hunting and grazing). In addition to this potpourri, gendarmes were expected to assist in the maintenance of peaceful relations between Europeans and Algerians, resolving disputes and criminal claims and preventing incidents between settlers, Jews, and Muslims, from brawls to arguments in markets and cafés. The latter duty proved especially problematic, due to the lack of Arab-language skills and a paucity of knowledge concerning local politics and society, making it difficult to press charges, locate witnesses, and keep order more generally.[11]

Complicating this picture, settlers and officials alike viewed Algerians as obstacles to the pacification and exploitation of the newly conquered territory, even after the surrender of Abd al-Qadir's forces in December 1847, which paved the way to uncontested colonization. As William Gallois states, "The local population were conceived of as a problem which would need to be solved, and it was plain that the burning and attacks on redoubts had become the tactics by which such goals could be achieved."[12] This became immediately apparent in 1832 under Governor Rovigo, the brutal ex-minister of police from the Napoleonic era, who ordered the murder of the entire Ouffia tribe for reportedly stealing goods from a pro-French notable in Constantine. The conclusion of General Pierre Boyer, the governor of Oran, represented the official line: "The law they need is that of the sword."[13] Despite the outrage expressed by an 1834 parliamentary commission of inquiry, which viciously excoriated the conduct of officials and was particularly scathing concerning summary executions without trial and massacres, rape, and looting, the authorities ignored the irate deputies, appointing a governor general responsible exclusively to the minister of war and capable of ruling by decree.[14] Thus, campaigns of terror were brought to their logical horrifying conclusion. Previously a ramshackle cavalcade of violence against Arabs and Kabyles under the guise of military campaigning, under Bugeaud's influence, looting and murder coalesced into organized razzias and massacres and the devastation of land and livestock, culminating in the mass asphyxiation of hundreds of Algerians who took refuge in caves outside Dahra in 1845, the ultimate expression of the general's *pénétration pacifique* (peaceful penetration).[15] By that time, sixty-five thousand soldiers lived and fought in Algeria, and brutality had become a fixture of Algerian life. When the Za'atsha tribes rose up in 1849, French troops eliminated the entire local population, and they did the same with uprisings throughout the 1850s and 1860s in a variety of locales.[16]

Decades of extreme colonial violence resulted in economic and social dislocation, extreme poverty, and resentment and anger toward the colonizer. Yet, settlement continued apace, and while Arabs and Kabyles seethed, settlers demanded self-government, which included control of policing and the judiciary. The "pacification" remained incomplete, accomplished by force of arms rather than providing benefits for Algerians, and thus the importance of accurate threat assessments and law enforcement increased dramatically. Crime and security became linked in a colony where anything from participating in a labor protest to joining a nationalist organization, assaulting a European, or taking to the hills became an insurrectionary act. All the while, environmental devastation, outbreaks of disease, harvest failures and insect infestations, and ongoing interclan conflicts further complicated the colonial tableau. Moreover, the increasing land seizures ruined many well-to-do merchants and farmers, leaving former notables penniless.[17] Not for nothing did Governor General Patrice de MacMahon, the future butcher of the Paris Commune and monarchist president of France, claim that during his 1864 to 1870 tenure Algeria "has been subdued, but has not submitted."[18]

Into this increasingly complicated picture came the end of military rule after 1870, with settlers occupying most official positions, and the formation of three French departments in Alger, Constantine, and Oran, formally binding the colony to the metropole. With the transformation came wholesale changes to government and law enforcement. This book begins in 1870 due to the shift in that year from military governors and policing to a civilian variant, and with it, completely different expectations, organization, and outcomes. The new administration included a governor general appointed by Paris, assisted by a *conseil général*, along with departmental prefects in imitation of the metropolitan system. Although the minister of the interior set the budget and the minister of war controlled the military (including determining the complement and mission of troops), the appointed figures controlled all other aspects of Algerian life, given their de facto control of the colony—including the police. However, they could not govern alone, and by the 1880s, each department elected two deputies (later increased to three) and a senator, to represent settler demands in the metropole. In addition, from 1898 onward, budgetary matters were the strict purview of the délégations financières, a financial parliament that was also dominated by European interests, granted two-thirds of the seats. The new administration oversaw a dramatic expansion of the European population, rising from approximately 20,000 in 1834 to 244,600 in 1872; it would reach almost one million on the eve of decolonization, buoyed by the 1889 decision to grant citizenship to Spanish, Italian, and Maltese inhabitants, along with Jews, who received the same treatment through the Crémieux Decree.[19]

Yet, the growth was almost entirely urban, particularly in certain coastal enclaves, for Bugeaud's vaunted "sword and plow" never truly materialized, having been replaced by city-based businesses and neighborhoods. However, this did not mean that Algerians owned land and operated farms. As early as the 1860s, Arabs and Kabyles increasingly became hired hands, despite Napoléon III's vaunted Sénatus consulte and its talk of protecting local interests. The July 1873 Warnier Law only hastened the transfer of property, allowing Europeans to trigger the sale of any nonprivate parcels, with 11.6 million hectares of the best land eventually seized by French interests. The *colons* (rural settlers) made a fortune, while the state crushed Algerians through the *impôts arabes* (Arab taxes), a second wealth-transfer mechanism, forcing the payment of 41 million francs in 1890 alone. Almost half of the taxes in all three departments came from Arabs and Kabyles, despite the massive income disparity.[20]

The resulting administrative reorganization divided the colony into *communes de pleine exercice* (full-function communes) and *communes mixtes* (mixed communes), corresponding to the population in a given region. Claude Collot refers to the former as "tools of European domination," comprising millions of seized hectares and run by a French administration, including a mayor and municipal council, and containing a substantial number of non-Algerian denizens. Naturally, these administrations prioritized beautification and infrastructure maintenance, much like the European neighborhoods in major cities along the coast, paid for by the *impôts arabes*. Only in 1944 did such communes allow even Muslim deputies to participate in their political life. Yet, the vast majority of Algerian territory was *communes mixtes*; fully five-sixths contained almost two-thirds of the Arab and Kabyle population, and they enjoyed few of the benefits of the European variants. They were run by administrators who combined the roles of mayor, justice, and banker and were vested with the authority of an officer of the Police judiciaire until 1931 in all matters deemed criminal. They routinely ordered beatings, house searches, and fines or jailings, assisted after 1919 by elected *djemâas* (tribal councils) in the *duwars*, which looked after administrative and financial matters (including tax collection), and the *caïds*, local notables appointed by the French administration to represent tribes before the colonial state.[21]

Moreover, law enforcement varied according to the status of the commune. In *communes de pleine exercice*, where a substantial European population lived and worked, various branches were created, from municipal cops to criminal investigators, in order to deal with quotidian and violent crime. Yet, given the expense of such resources, including everything from crime laboratories to police stations, *communes mixtes* with predominantly Muslim populations were primarily served by the gendarmerie alone. If a town within its borders contained sufficient inhabitants, a small local constabulary formed, usually with a few Europeans and various Muslim adjutants. Yet for the most part, the gendarmerie toured the vast areas in each *commune mixte*, investigating where pertinent or simply flying the flag by demonstrating the constant French presence in even the most remote villages. However, the clear disparity in resources and budgets meant that in practice, only predominantly European areas could rely on a continuous police presence.

Both administrators and police or gendarmes could act with such impunity due to the Indigénat, a series of regulations that pertained exclusively to Arabs and Kabyles, which provided discretionary powers to any colonial authority, from mayors to magistrates and police. Although it comprised only vague guidelines and never became an official legal code, punishments routinely included fines and jail terms, and the governor general alone decided the limits to applicable sentences. Moreover, various provisions demanded everything from work obligations to collective fines, and hard labor often was the preferred penal tool. As Sylvie Thénault concludes, "Avec le régime penal de l'Indigénat, l'État colonial reposait sur un appareil de coercitation, assurant l'assujettissement des populations et leur soumission à son autorité [With the penal system of the Indigénat, the colonial state rested on an apparatus of coercion, assuring the subjection of the local populations and their submission to its authority]."[22] Neither did Arabs and Kabyles meaningfully participate in the judiciary. From 1902 to 1931, *tribunals répressifs* (sentencing tribunals) without restraint jailed Algerians deemed criminal. Special Muslim courts lacked a jury system; instead, they were staffed by three European justices and two Muslims permitted to act only as consultants. The governor general possessed the ability to enact administrative detention, and any sentence of fewer than six months or fine of 500 francs or less could not be appealed. Even when the system finally changed in the 1930s, juries and justices were European, in a system described by one historian as "low intensity warfare."[23]

Thus, all Algerians were officially shut out of the new administrative model, with the exception of token *évolués* (literally, the evolved)—those considered "civilized" due to their education, command of the French language, and breeding. Termed *beni oui ouis*, they earned the hatred of those Arabs and Kabyles beneath them in the social hierarchy. Various fault lines quickly emerged, encouraged by the French authorities in order to bolster colonialism. The "Kabyle myth" that Berbers were superior to Arabs resulted in preferential treatment for that community in the late nineteenth century, which was abandoned only when the settlers loudly refuted the notion, insisting that both groups were equally inferior.[24] Nonetheless, divisions persisted, not least between the *Vieux turbans* (the descendants of the old notable families from the Ottoman era) and the small minority of upwardly mobile landlords, businessmen, and officials who combined a French education with Algerian beliefs and ideals. The latter frequently supported the Young Algerians movement in the early twentieth century, demanding secularism and reform and adopting European manners and dress. They further dominated non-European politics through the Fédération des élus musulmans (Federation of Muslim Elected Representatives) until the advent of anticolonial nationalism in the post-1945 era.[25]

However, perhaps the greatest conflict concerned Islam, with French officials co-opting spiritual governance from the late nineteenth century onward and seizing *hubus*, lands traditionally granted for religious use. The authorities purposefully left the religion backward and unevolved, shocking foreign observers as many leaders chose exile by the early twentieth century. Traditional schools were replaced by a weak and poorly funded Gallic system that resulted in widespread illiteracy; these schools were far different from the French institutions serving the children of skilled workers and professionals alike, with highly competent and well-paid staff.[26] Moreover, Islam itself specifically prevented Algerians from obtaining French citizenship, the gateway to rights and privileges and legal and political equality. According to the 1865 Sénatus consulte, Algerians could qualify only by renouncing the *statut personnel* (personal statute) that permitted them to be governed by Qur'anic laws. Citing concerns about polygamy and primitive customs, the administration systematically denied even enthusiastic applicants, and in any case, observant Muslims refused to abandon their religion.[27]

Clearly, Europeans owned the press, businesses, and farms, and they controlled every level of government and society.[28] With the transfer from military to civilian government, they required police and gendarmes to defend this new settler colonial and racial order. Initially, in the post-1870 period, law enforcement primarily focused on rural communes, protecting the *colons* from Arab and Kabyle encroachment as thousands of hectares were seized by European interests. Rural guards and brigades patrolled towns and villages, with soldiers supporting them during frequent rebellions. Policing in larger urban settings fell to a relatively small constabulary, and given that the preponderance of Algerians resided in the countryside, it is unsurprising that the Indigénat was overwhelmingly concerned with offenses such as illegal grazing, forest fires, and taxes owed at harvest time. Yet, by the 1920s, a combination of rural poverty and economic growth led to a rush to the cities, with *villages nègres* (negro villages) and shantytowns housing newcomers, while older neighborhoods like the casbah in Alger burst at the seams. A small but vibrant middle class emerged—made up of transport, hospital, and postal workers, small businessmen, and so on—but the mass of unemployed and menial laborers fueled European fears concerning revolt, especially given the huge demographic imbalance, with the Muslim population rising from four million in 1906 to nine million on the eve of the War of Independence.[29] As a result, by the 1880s, a long process of reform and expansion began for law enforcement in both towns and the countryside to simultaneously modernize and rationalize the branches charged with protecting *colons* and urban dwellers in all three departments.

The constant push to defend and expand hegemony necessitated a police force endowed with far greater powers than their metropolitan counterparts, along with indigenous auxiliaries and guards, and the gendarmerie in rural districts. Accordingly, this book will discuss the double standard inherent in Algerian colonial policing: that the assault, harassment, and/or detention of a "native" was both perfectly legal and an expected component of colonial law enforcement, in stark contrast to the treatment of Europeans, for whom the legal code of the metropole continued to be applicable.[30] The system rested on the stereotypical portrayal of the African or Asian as part of a "dangerous class," an "other" whose characteristics and attitudes were exaggerated, following Orientalist visions of the colonized—that is, they were deemed naturally criminal, duplicitous, and prone to rebellion.[31] Yet Algerians (and indeed, imperial denizens more broadly) were often far from passive victims of colonial violence and hyperrepressive policing. Thus, the book will also focus on the engagement of ordinary Arabs and Kabyles in anticolonial struggle through violent means, well before the ascent of nationalist politicians and movements. Such agency often manifested itself in behavior considered "criminal" by European authorities. If they did not engage in open revolt—which was almost impossible in a settler colony where the force of arms and technology favored the colonizer—they used a wide variety of tactics to foil French attempts to dominate individuals and communities. In certain instances, this involved what James C. Scott terms the "weapons of the weak," mobilizing everything from language (most French officials and police spoke neither Arabic nor Berber) to work slowdowns in order to resist domination. The colonized also used French institutions—refusing to testify, or falsifying evidence in police inquiries or official inquests, for example.[32] Yet, by the outbreak of the Great War, Algerians increasingly engaged in anticolonial violence, going beyond noncooperation to banditry, violent crime, and targeted counterattacks—including assaults and sabotage—against the perpetrators of domination. During the conflict, various deserters joined forces in the wooded and mountainous Constantinois to violently reject colonial authority. By the interwar era, group attacks in crowded spaces—football stadiums, for example—or violent criminal acts against Europeans such as armed robbery or murder in cities and countryside alike made it abundantly clear that despite the façade of colonial control, Algerians possessed agency and were not afraid to act aggressively toward their supposed superiors.[33]

Hence, as the following chapters demonstrate, police and gendarmes remained unconcerned by crimes committed by Arabs and Kabyles against their brethren, unless they were likely to compromise security. To be sure, they duly investigated such acts, yet without the level of interest and concern displayed when the victims were European. When the governor general expressed concern about a potential crime wave in Sédrata in July 1927, the administrator responded by happily noting that if incidents were up across the board, there was no cause for alarm: no Europeans had been victimized; no special measures would be needed beyond the usual repressive measures.[34] The colonial archives contain literally thousands of reports concerning serious incidents or killings in villages and towns every year, yet very few cases elicited comment, except for intertribal brawls or revenge murders that threatened to plunge a given region into disorder. Yet attacks against Europeans, no matter how small, if successful or left unpunished, threatened to strike a serious blow against French prestige and power—a demonstration that the colonized were not inferior, primitive, and helpless after all. The sole other exception, and then only after 1945, concerned politics, and particularly nationalism. The rise of the Parti de peuple algérien (PPA; Algerian People's Party), and demands for independence from French control, alarmed the population and government alike, seriously worrying officials and police in Paris and Algeria, who initiated a massive campaign to undermine, arrest and jail, and otherwise destabilize anticolonial voices. Even more than banditry or violent crime, organized demonstrations of separatist sentiment, whether in a sizable town or tiny village, could mushroom into a full-blown insurrection. Given the constant shortage of law enforcement personnel in all three departments, faced with patrolling, surveilling, and controlling a massive territory, it was deemed essential to strike quickly against any vestige of support for the PPA and decolonization.[35]

All of this makes for difficult research, not least because of serious gaps in archival and extant published primary sources. As Ann Laura Stoler has noted, such materials both reveal and obscure facts and truths about colonial life and administration, requiring careful gleaning and parsing by scholars, with the tacit understanding that the biases and aims of the author may taint the document altogether. Rigorous questions must be (and have been) asked in interrogating archival materials: What is the real purpose of the document? What did the author know or assume? What is the source of their information and what are the personal beliefs and judgements of the author, and how did they impact the assessment or conclusions contained therein?[36] Particularly in the Algerian setting, everything from the lack of Arab-language training or experience with local populations to xenophobia and key mistakes could (and did) impact police investigations and threat assessments. Moreover, certain prejudices or controversial subjects are either unspoken (the belief in Arab and Kabyle primitivism or inferiority, for example) or mentioned only euphemistically (references to "hard interrogations" rather than torture or extreme violence). Disciplinary or hiring files routinely reveal a double standard, while the language used in police files concerning crimes against Europeans always conveys an urgency that is lacking in lurid accounts of crime in Muslim districts. Even when the latter were prioritized after the emergence of the nationalist movement as a threat in the post-1945 era, rumor and supposition and errors and assumptions (often based on untrustworthy sources) frequently condemned policing efforts to futility.

Nonetheless, despite the temptation to examine only archives "against the grain," the grain itself displays much useful information. It speaks of the reality of empire, what officials thought and stated, and the omnipresent xenophobia that drove colonial police and gendarmes in every jurisdiction. As Stoler notes, archives are, at root, "transparencies on which power relations were transcribed and intricate technologies of rule."[37] For this reason, this book makes extensive use of them from collections in a variety of locales, from the Archives d'Outre-mer (Colonial Archives) and Archives nationales (National Archives) in France to the Algerian Archives nationales and the National Archives of Great Britain. If the narrators are not always reliable, they nevertheless reveal much about the aims, techniques, and consequences of colonial policing, along with the "shared beliefs" and prejudices that invariably mold accounts of events in empire.[38]

However, there are other challenges in using archives as the bulk of source material for the 1870 to 1952 period. First and foremost, Arab and Kabyle voices are often absent. Almost all police investigative summaries, arrest reports, and administrative overviews are written from a European vantage point, with only witness statements (themselves often coerced or deliberately falsified) consistently providing Arab and Kabyle testimony. In some cases, the Algerian press can be (and is here) used to supplement archival accounts, although far too often, these newspapers did not directly address law enforcement until the post-1945 era. Memoirs are less prevalent until the era of the Algerian War of Independence, when they are plentiful, yet beyond the scope of the present effort. Those that do exist (Hachemi Baghriche's examination of the pre-1940 nationalist movement, for example) are particularly effective at providing a contrapuntal perspective and contesting the official narrative. Of course, they can merely supplement official sources, due to their relative paucity—an extremely unfortunate reality that privileges European accounts. However, following Stoler's observations, I have attempted to read between the lines and rejected any facile or verbatim interpretations.

Yet another group is also severely underrepresented in the archives, and in the press and memoirs. Women are almost entirely absent from many accounts. When they are mentioned—in investigative reports, for example—they are either victims (European women killed or assaulted by Arabs or Kabyles) or a cause of insecurity (heartless Muslim Jezebels whose philandering and plotting caused intertribal conflict and internecine crime). This represents a blatant mischaracterization of the reality of gender in colonial Algeria. Although it is true that European women were precluded from employment in many professions, they nonetheless assisted on farms and with small businesses and worked as teachers, nurses, and volunteers with a wide variety of philanthropic causes.[39] Moreover, although the 1922 bill of rights failed to pass in the Senate, denying women full equality and the vote, they enjoyed rights and freedoms on a broad scale. Denied a full political and economic voice, they were the "inferior sex within the superior race," expected to police racial boundaries and ensure correct behavior.[40]

Arab and Kabyle women also faced obstacles, but these were not mirrored the official portrait as it regularly appeared in reports and summaries—that is, they were almost always painted as the cause of unrest and crime, by cheating on husbands, convincing male relatives to engage in subterfuge and underhanded dealings, and/or abandoning their families. They faced what one historian calls the "double discrimination of a colonial system that privileged masculine control and indigenous societies that privileged domestic roles."[41] The notion of the *femme d'harem* (woman of the harem) or the home-wrecker had been progressively dismantled by 1918, as Arab and Kabyle women began to take part in protests and joined the economic sphere through low-level employment in the service economy, from midwifery to artisanal shops. Moreover, while traditional Muslim leaders demanded the separation of the sexes, reformers like Ferhat Abbas and anticolonial voices like Messali Hadj viewed women's participation in their political struggles as essential. One of the unfortunate developments in later decades was that after they had played such a key role in forging independence, anti-European and traditional Muslim voices condemned them once again to second-class status.[42]

The police and gendarmerie were not gender-neutral spaces either. Instead, they were exclusively male and not inclined to feminism, and the archives reflect this attitude. Like administrators and businessmen, they worked in a very masculine space, and thus only in very rare instances (in reports concerning the black market during the Vichy era, for example) did female agency merit serious discussion. This is unsurprising in a colony where from the late nineteenth century onward, European authors and politicians lauded masculinity and violence, pitting the settlers as true and heroic men against both the effete and weak colonized and the incapable and soft metropolitan population in equal measure. Settler virility simultaneously kept supposedly primitive *indigènes* (a pejorative term for indigenous Algerians) at bay while conquering rough terrain. By the interwar era, the predominance of colonial Fascist groups in all three departments only deepened the influence of this doctrine, as hundreds of thousands flocked to meetings, read newspapers, and offered electoral support to the Croix de Feu / Parti social français (CF / PSF; Cross of Fire / French Social Party), the Parti populaire français (French Popular Party), Amitiés latines (Latin Friendship), and Rassemblement national (National Rally), whose leaders spoke openly of "Latin virility" and literally attacked perceived enemies. Although women played key roles in CF / PSF charitable organizations and as supporters, they were nonetheless expected to stay home and leave politics and the economy to Algerian men.[43]

Various historians have attempted to derive strategies for dealing with such omissions. Antoinette Burton, in particular, has successfully harnessed memory studies, using oral narratives and testimonies, and biographical or fictional works, to supplement official accounts. This proved tremendously successful in her project examining the household as archive.[44] Of course, this approach requires such sources to be attainable, and it is very unfortunate that no such extant material is available concerning policing and crime prior to the Algerian War of Independence, when Arab and Kabyle women played a major role and left multiple traces of their actions and thoughts.[45] The penal and legal control exercised by Algerian law enforcement were firmly masculine, echoing French trends and the entrenchment of the Gallic patriarchy. That the central goal was "la revendication de l'état à monopoliser la violence physique sur le territoire colonial [the demand that the state monopolize physical violence on colonial territory]," in the words of Emmanuel Blanchard and Joël Glasman, only served to underscore the highly gendered nature of colonial law enforcement, even in Algeria, where great numbers of women had emigrated by the interwar era.[46]

As a result, police and gendarmes prioritized the entrenchment of European racial hegemony and attempted to squelch crime, disorder, and potential revolt directed at the settlers. It is to this process that I turn in the first chapter, considering the evolution of Algerian policing, tracking the branches and personnel, the policies and problems, and the inner workings and internal dissent that characterized the service from the 1880s until the 1954 Algerian War of Independence. This includes a consideration of attempts (often unsuccessful) at modernizing, professionalizing, and expanding law enforcement from the late nineteenth century onward, detailing various branches, from the Police judiciaire and the Police administrative to the Renseignements généraux (political police), the gendarmerie, and the Garde républicaine mobile (Republican Mobile Corps). The chapter focuses on the realities and problems faced by each branch in the colonial setting. Although various services increasingly mobilized technology by the 1920s, modern investigative techniques were subverted for racial and imperial ends, from the use of photography and lineups to reinforce Orientalist clichés to the mobilization of informants to perform police work, due to a dearth of Arabic- and Berber-language speakers. In addition, constant personnel shortages, combined with dramatic European and Muslim population growth, led to gendarmes patrolling tens of thousands of kilometers, and insufficient urban policing to effectively combat crime, not least because metropolitan officials consistently underfunded Algerian law enforcement, despite an increasing threat to the French presence there. Recruitment procedures, courses, and candidacies proved equally problematic; the issues ranged from unsatisfactory housing and low wages to a blanket refusal to admit large numbers of Algerian candidates. A similar disparity persisted in promotion and discipline, with Arabs and Kabyles blocked from advancing in the ranks and subject to far harsher punishments than European officers for even routine breaches of regulations.

The questionable utility of the system was put to the test by a wave of banditry in the Constantinois region during the Great War (the focus of the second chapter), which began as a wave of protests against the recruitment and conscription of Algerians into the French army and subsequently evolved into an anticolonial struggle against imperial rule. Unlike nineteenth-century insurrections and revolts, which tended to be motivated by religion or economic malaise, the new banditry had a political bent that deeply worried officials and law enforcement, not least due to the lack of troops in North Africa because of the European conflict. The chapter discusses the pre-1914 unrest and French responses; rebellions were crushed by the military, often in spectacular and violent fashion against supposedly "inferior" and "barbaric" Arabs and Kabyles. This schematic is contrasted with the wartime reality that attempts to draw Algerians into the French army and metropolitan factories, combined with thousands of deaths in the continental theater, drove hundreds to desertion and noncompliance, joining criminals and prison escapees in gangs throughout the Constantinois. Together they engaged in campaigns of highway robbery and attacks, murders, and home invasions against European targets (state employees, police and guards, and settlers in remote areas), sowing panic and prompting official concern due to the isolation of the victims and the clear anticolonial bent of the bandits, who were assisted by the local populations out of fear of the gangs but also admiration for their stance against French rule. These efforts provoked a brutal police and gendarme response, including widespread house searches, patrols, surveillance, manhunts, and the capture, ambush, and/or murder of gang leaders and members. Although it largely eliminated banditry, the campaign did not succeed in staunching anti-French sentiment, which only increased due to the heavy-handed administrative response, evolving into a violent crime wave during the interwar era.

Thus, the third chapter examines anticolonial violent crime in interwar French Algeria. This was not simple malfeasance, but evidence of an emerging nationalism in embryo. Well before organized militancy and politics, individual Algerians frightened the local populations and officials alike by targeting Europeans. Much like chapter 2, this discussion adopts a subaltern approach, examining trends from below rather than prominent leaders on high, while seeking to frame through an evolving official lens the interwar anticolonial violence, from the acts of so-called barbaric primitives to an ongoing threat against the French presence in Algeria. The text demonstrates a conscious rejection of the increasingly tentative grip of the French Empire, by actors who were far from passive victims. Faced with European attempts at political, economic, and cultural hegemony, and battered by poverty, legal discrimination, and official and police intransigence, Algerians often committed criminal acts in an effort to destabilize and undermine French authority. More precisely, chapter 3 investigates the case study of the department of Constantine, where Arab and Kabyle inhabitants regularly engaged in anticolonial crime/violence, including burglaries of arms and explosives from government buildings or mines, train derailments, and football hooliganism. More seriously, certain "criminals" engaged in physical attacks, sexual assaults, and a constant spate of brutal murders against settlers. Various perpetrators also assaulted or killed police officers and administrative officials—the living embodiments of the colonial state and racial hegemony. In both city and countryside, the official response was brutal: violations of suspects' rights, excessive force in lieu of arrests, vigilante killings of suspects, and expulsions of the families of anyone deemed *hors-la-loi* (outlaws). In this way, administrators and law enforcement tried to restore European predominance, but the increasing prevalence of anticolonial crime effectively helped pave the way for popular nationalist movements in the post-1945 era and the Algerian War of Independence.

Prior to the advent of the nationalist wave, the end of parliamentary democracy and the start of the Vichy regime had a profound impact on Algerian law enforcement. The fourth chapter focuses on initial changes from July 1940 and further differences and reversals following Operation Torch in November 1942 and the US-led Allied occupation. In terms of personnel, few were purged initially except for a small number of Jews and Freemasons, as Europeans in Algeria had for decades been thoroughly permeated by the Extreme Right, which was reflected in the police and the gendarmerie. Chapter 4 examines in detail their changing duties, including mass surveillance of mail, telegrams, and telephones; the fight against smuggling, price fixing, and the black market; and finally a prioritization of the hunt for resisters, Gaullists, and Communists. These changes involved the creation of new branches: the Service spéciale de documentation (anti-Gaullist), the Corps civil des douairs (customs service and militia), and a Bureau économique (tasked with shutting down the black market). Yet, the same problems continued to impact policing, from a dearth of personnel to the prioritization of antisemitism and Gaullism over quotidian criminal investigations. Moreover, in light of the banditry and revolts during the Great War, officials evinced serious concerns about the growing Algerian nationalism, which was buoyed by high prices and shortages of staples that impacted Arabs and Kabyles far more than Europeans. Thus, by 1941 to 1942, the fight against the black market became a priority, and after November 1942 there were new law enforcement challenges, including violence committed by Allied soldiers and their participation in smuggling, and an attempted purge of pro-Vichy police and gendarmes, which faltered due to the ongoing pro-Fascist sympathies of the bulk of the European population.

However, that problem was quickly eclipsed from 1945, when Algerian policing priorities shifted from crime prevention to the criminalization of nationalist politics, and particularly the fight against the PPA and its sister organization, the

Mouvement pour le triomphe des libertés démocratiques (MTLD; Movement for the Triumph of Democratic Freedoms). Under the mercurial leadership of Messali Hadj, the PPA/MTLD experienced dramatic growth in the aftermath of the Sétif and Guelma massacres, as its thousands of members and tens of thousands of active sympathizers eclipsed other reformist movements, while younger and far more radical voices came to dominate the movement. The final chapter details efforts by law enforcement to combat these militants, for whom violence against colonialism and its agents was deemed necessary to end French imperial rule. This included thwarting PPA electoral success by underhanded means (including rigged ballots and the jailing of candidates), judicial bias against nationalists, and police campaigns against the press and propaganda. Yet, these law enforcement efforts only increased the movement's popularity with Algerians and cemented the position of the most radical members, culminating in the 1949 formation of the paramilitary Organisation spéciale (OS; Special Organization) under the leadership of Hocine Ait Ahmed and Mohammed Ben Bella and the renewal of anticolonial banditry in the Constantinois. Participants were given guerilla-style military training, including in bomb fabrication and communications, which were later used during War of Independence. For their part, the police mobilized a variety of tactics to root out the OS and extirpate the PPA/MTLD—terror campaigns involving mass arrests, violent interrogations in remote locations, and forced confessions obtained through the use of torture. Yet, once again, these actions only hardened nationalist militancy and engaged public sympathy, resulting in a far more widespread anticolonial war.

There was no great rupture in 1954 with regard police tactics and the Algerian refusal to accept European dominance, but rather a continuation of law enforcement practices and strategies, along with anticolonial doctrine and actions, progressively honed and expanded since the late nineteenth century. In all aspects of policing, from hiring and personnel to criminal investigations, the persistent double standard, in which preference was given to non-Algerian officers and each service prioritized the security of settler lives and property and often neglected Muslims entirely, became the norm. Naturally, this only fed Arab and Kabyle anger at the growing political, economic, and social inequality to encourage criminal and rebellious acts against *colons* and city dwellers alike. From the Great War onward, banditry and then violent crime became far more prevalent, culminating in the post-1945 nationalist surge that seeded the War of Independence. From a policing perspective, this process began with the organization, development, and exclusionary practices of the multiple branches of law enforcement in Algeria, the subject of the first chapter.

CHAPTER 1

Agents of Empire and Crisis of Authority
The Professional, Racial, and Financial Reality
of Policing in French Colonial Algeria

In an 1883 security report to the governor general, the unnamed author bemoaned the fact that the number of crimes proved to be considerable in Algeria, particularly noting thefts and assaults. Matters had become worse in recent years, and the complement of soldiers available—perhaps one thousand men in 195 brigades—had proved woefully inadequate and would in fact need to be doubled to keep pace. Troops faced the tasks of preventing rebellion, keeping roads clear, and ensuring public safety but were also drowning in paperwork and routine, from transporting prisoners to moving about on foot patrols, which seemed ridiculous in the age of the railroad. Most *duwars* (tent enclaves) and European centers required night rounds, and only in the largest towns, which employed police agents, could security be assured. Yet most of Algeria was rural and wracked by banditry, and if a new garrison appeared, it was likely staffed by Arab and Kabyle cavaliers, who had neither the time nor opportunity to patrol most markets and meeting places—*cafés maures* (Moorish cafés), for example. Only a dedicated Police spéciale throughout the colony, with officers in constant communication with each other and administrative officials, sharing information and investigations, could effectively tackle the problem, taking on criminal cases without delay or being hampered by tens of thousands of hectares of territory, in the manner of gendarmes and *gardes champêtres* (rural police).[1]

The report brings together a variety of concerns that predominated in policing policy considerations throughout the history of French Algeria. From insufficient staffing, logistical problems with huge territories, and a lack of transport to rising crime rates and a dearth of reliable information concerning suspects and communities, agents, guards, officers, and gendarmes constantly worried about their effectiveness. For their part, administrators vainly attempted to square limited budgetary resources with the demands of growing communities, particularly in burgeoning urban centers and with the intensification of agricultural production prior to the Second World War.[2] Security requirements in the imperial setting proved to be more onerous than in the metropole; crime and public security offenses were often twinned with anticolonialism and perpetrated by a hostile population that sought to remove the European presence on Algerian soil.[3] An enduring presence in cities like Paris and Marseille among immigrant and colonial worker communities, in the North African setting, racial animus formed the very basis of relations between police and gendarmes and Arabs and Kabyles, resulting in charges of physical and mental abuse, investigative bias, and the marginalization of subaltern Muslim officers and adjutants—ironically, those best positioned to glean valuable information from increasingly wary Algerians.[4]

The Professionalization and Expansion of North African Security Forces, 1883–1952

The immediate consequence of the report (and other similar verdicts) was the importation of the structure and organization of metropolitan policing, in an effort to professionalize and expand North African security forces.[5] An 1898 decree nominated the governor general to oversee the entire Algerian police operation through an intermediary—the Direction de la Sécurité générale (Directorate of General Security) from 1911 to 1941 called the Sûreté générale (General Security Department), whose heads and *contrôleurs* (inspectors) ran the state and local police, the Inspection des services administratives (Administrative Services Control), and the Inspection des Polices judiciaires (Criminal Police Control), with auxiliaries in each department. These contained multiple individual branches. In each locale, municipal police dealt with petty crime and public order beginning in 1884, while the Police administrative (Administrative Police) looked after permits and public morals, in addition to monitoring foreigners, attending to traffic violations, and providing service to jails. This proved somewhat problematic in fiduciary terms, as the police budget remained municipal, and the costs could be prohibitive, particularly wage increases and promotions. Yet there was a marked professionalization, with agents acting in concert with other services and considered *fonctionnaires d'état* (state officials), even if mayors paid and controlled them.[6] Moreover, the corruption endemic in municipal policing faced a reckoning. In Oran, *commissaires* (captains) and other government employees were fingered by investigators in October 1900, connected to an extortion scheme targeting Europeans in the city.[7] By the 1920s, dozens of agents patrolled the streets, engaged in surveillance of markets, monitored vagrancy, inspected train stations, and arrested those deemed suspect, both foreign and resident. As towns grew, so too did the municipal police, although the population growth frequently left commanders complaining about personnel shortfalls; in Marnia, in December 1947 the *commissaire principal* wrote to the mayor in desperation that the population had mushroomed and could no longer be protected, and public hygiene standards had fallen precipitously. Officers had been fired or transferred elsewhere, leaving fewer agents working horrendous hours that risked driving even more of them out of town, despite a wage hike the previous year.[8]

Municipal police were further expected to cooperate with the Police judiciare (PJ), launched in Algeria in December 1909 to investigate major crimes in urban centers, while coordinating with Brigades mobiles (BM; Mobile Brigades) and gendarmes in the countryside, and from 1927, overseeing police laboratories in major cities for fingerprints and photographs, along with tens of thousands of files on individual suspects and convicts. Although they were expected to actively work with mayors and judges, the PJ took orders exclusively from the governor general and prefects, and antagonism naturally developed between officials accustomed to exercising control through patronage and politics and *commissaires* who guarded their independence despite being paid out of local coffers. This service ran a network of informants and surveillance across each department, building a presence in every major center. In the department of Oran, for example, by the late 1940s, the PJ employed brigades well beyond the capital, branching out to Tlemcen, Sidi-bel-Abbès, Mostaganem, Mascara, Tiaret, and even the Territoires du Sud, each with a crime lab and database, and a full complement of motorized vehicles.[9]

These were distinctly lacking among gendarmerie units, which supported police efforts in rural and remote areas. This service proved essential, because as Benjamin Brower has noted, the colonial project was not equally apparent everywhere in Algeria, and various scholars have demonstrated that law enforcement in the countryside often was the sole representation of the state. *Gardes forestières* and *gardes champêtres* (forest guards and rural police) patrolled forests and fields on behalf of local interests, but gendarmes wielded colonial authority.[10] Their presence meant that it was no longer necessary to call in the army to quell disturbances. Beginning in 1908 in the metropole and Alger, and expanded in subsequent decades with the introduction of the BM in 1921 and a riot squad, the Gardes républicaines mobiles (GRM; Republican Mobile Squads) in 1926, their Algerian brief went far beyond the metropole to include investigating crime and arresting and detaining suspects and appearing in court, while also performing surveillance duties on local populations.[11] As a result, although the gendarmes were part of the army, their duties resembled those of the PJ, yet they were simultaneously charged with protecting the lives of *colons* in rural settlements while keeping communications open in the countryside. However, unlike their urban confreres, gendarmes suffered from the tyranny of distance, patrolling territories measuring tens of thousands of square kilometers (sixty-nine thousand per company by 1945), which meant that rounds could take up to a week in favorable conditions. Unlike the PJ and other units, gendarmes lacked vehicles, rendering patrols—on horseback or bicycle—even more difficult. As late as October 1946, responding to a demand in the commune of Renier, military authorities noted a severe shortage of cars and trucks. Finally, policing such vast districts entailed a huge amount of paperwork, from hundreds of reports to surveillance and intelligence updates concerning living conditions and popular opinion, and this led to anger and fatigue and fostered suspicion of and even violence toward Arabs and Kabyles, who were perceived as an enemy force. Ironically, in 1937 the BM and GRM merged, leading to fewer gendarmes in the field and declining reporting and data collection in the midst of an anticolonial crime wave (see chapter 3), at the very moment when the rise of nationalism produced a legitimate anticolonial threat.[12] Unsurprisingly, by 1949, they once again participated in gathering information, using a Vichy era law to amass intelligence concerning the nationalist Parti du peuple algérien (PPA; Algerian People's Party) and the Communist Party.[13]

In addition, the Renseignements généraux (RG) functioned as a political security force, gathering information concerning threats to the state, and particularly political organizations (Communists and Muslim nationalists were natural targets). This encompassed everything from public and private opinions to economic and social trends that might adversely impact Algerian sentiments toward colonialism. The RG sent regular reports to prefects and the governor general, particularly in the post-1945 era, when separatist sentiment emerged on a broad scale through Messali Hadj and the PPA. Data to be collated included police reports from across all three departments, and from 1943 the service provided personnel in each *sous-préfecture* (subprefecture) to coordinate these local efforts.[14] Finally, Vichy authorities inaugurated the Direction de surveillance du territoire (DST; Directorate of Territorial Surveillance) in September 1941 to police the black market and economic crimes, fight espionage, and provide border and frontier control and customs services.[15] The Algerian security services all answered to the governor general, but they were ultimately responsible to the minister of the interior in Paris, who could—and did—make recommendations or demands.[16] Finally, the French government occasionally sent in units of the Compagnies républicaines de sécurité (CRS; mobile police force), a metropolitan tactical squad designed specifically in 1944 to combat urban rioters or insurrectionaries. In June 1952, CRS units arrived in Oran to keep order during Communist- and nationalist-led riots there, using tear gas and heavy weaponry to subdue crowds, and they were also sent to the Moroccan frontier in January 1953 and June 1954 to patrol the border during times of potential crisis.[17]

Local police were gradually transformed into a Police d'état (State Police), beginning in May 1930 with Alger, and then Constantine, Bône, and Oran in 1936. This occurred for budgetary reasons, as most locales simply could not afford to maintain an adequate force by the interwar era, while physical and professional standards fell dramatically as wages stagnated. Moreover, nationalization of the police force countered a growing dependence on politicians and notables, who often used the municipal forces to advance personal interests, for example in Oran due to the growing influence of Gabriel Lambert, the leader of the virulently pro-settler and anti-republican and pro-Fascist Rassemblement national (National Rally). Like the RG, the Police d'état answered directly to prefects and the governor general, and continued to solve petty crimes while assisting the PJ and BM in major investigations in both urban and rural settings.[18] In the countryside, all worked equally closely with administrators and deputies, *caïds* (French-appointed community leaders), and village leaders, who often provided crucial information about the locale and its inhabitants unavailable to European police and even Muslim adjutants who did not live in the community.[19]

The colonial state harnessed non-Europeans across all three departments, subordinate to European officials and police but empowered to arrest Arabs and Kabyles, their mere presence deemed a deterrent to criminal acts and minor infractions. Originally, night guards provided this service in the nineteenth century, yet administrators complained that it had become outdated in the era of increasing European population and natural prejudices against the *indigènes*, who were treated as serfs and primitives.[20] Thus, the governor general and the *contrôleur-générale* of the Sûreté (director general of Security) focused on the formation of a paid force: the Brigades rurales, a cadre of guards in each commune, to replace the gendarmerie with a cheaper alternative. In 1904, after receiving the backing of the Délégations financières (Financial Parliament) and leading *colons*, they approached the minister of the interior, positioning the initiative as a supplement to the overworked and overstretched gendarmerie units that had resulted in a lack of security in European-dominated *communes de pleine exercice* (full-service communes). Brigades of four Algerians would be fed and housed by the state and shifted to locales depending on perceived need, to patrol villages, farms, and *duwars*, especially at harvest time when tensions became dangerous—thus they were armed and uniformed.[21] The first appeared in Constantine in 1905, and in the following year they expanded to Philippeville and Batna, where guards canvassed Arabs from outside the town, arresting those with false permits and monitoring those expelled from neighboring communities, while providing surveillance of local marabouts and mosques suspected of anti-French sentiment and watching forests, farms, and railroads. Their presence immediately lowered the crime rate, particularly fights and robberies during harvest time, and *bechara*, the theft of livestock by criminal gangs for ransom payments from the owner through a middleman, during the rest of the year.[22] Their success inevitably led to an expansion elsewhere, and the governor general's office regarded the scheme as a perfect antidote to problems in recruiting gendarmes from the metropole due to the length of tours, as well as the absences due to illness and vacations that eroded manpower. Candidates tended to be ex-army or police agents, or else cavaliers employed by villages to represent French justice in isolated regions.[23]

However, despite the "marvelous results" that had Europeans "sleeping well" across the department, with multiple districts noting French and Muslim satisfaction with the performance of the brigades, doubts began to emerge from 1908 onward. First and foremost, prefects in Alger and Oran refused to take part, rejecting the idea of armed Algerian personnel and questioning the utility of non-European law enforcement. Furthermore, the El-Arrouch brigade complained that the "indigenous character" pushed guards to form ties with local families and friends and encouraged favoritism and corruption. Few proficient men could be recruited in any case, and multiple operations, combined with tens of thousands of hectares to patrol, left the guards in much the same predicament as gendarmes, which meant that municipal police in towns were needed to fill the breach. Those few candidates who did make the cut worried about leaving family members behind to till the soil alone. Finally, communes were expected to pay a share of the expenses, but they proved delinquent in this regard, and prefects constantly harangued mayors and administrators. By 1910 the governor general attached the project to the Algerian budget, yet clearly, the long-term solution involved an expansion of the gendarmerie.[24]

As a result, a more informal system replaced the Brigades rurales (Rural Brigades), which had been suppressed in August 1910 by the governor general, with rural guards and cavaliers organized by *communes de pleine exercice* and *communes mixtes* (mixed communes) to provide an ancillary security service where the gendarmerie could not be present. They would still be paid, but they were designated by a mayor or administrator and no longer required to leave their town or *duwar* of origin.[25] Cavaliers received a broader mandate, including surveillance of all key points within the *village nègre*: cafés, baths, mosques, and other places regularly frequented by Algerians. They also patrolled forests and farms to prevent *bechara* and banditry, discreetly following visitors to ensure that they were not engaged in illicit conduct, and they combatted black market activity. Guards were more irregular, funded by either authorities or private interests in times of trouble, or forming goums—cadres of volunteers (sometimes paid a token sum) who patrolled roads and streets or forests and countryside to prevent banditry, theft, and rebellion.[26] By the interwar era, most communes retained four to seven cavaliers, with a brigadier in charge of the troop. Due to their temporary nature, goums were placed under the authority of *caïds* or *gardes champêtres*.[27]

Yet, problems persisted under the new system, first and foremost due to the voluntary nature of the goums. Simply put, Algerians often refused to cooperate, unwilling to patrol dangerous routes on a nightly basis for a token wage. The administrator in M'Sila reported in March 1921 that he had tried for over a year to form a unit, without success, and that cavaliers provided a superior alternative due to their permanent salaried status. In other cases, officials resorted to incentives to attract candidates, often offering firearm permits, only to find that they did not perform adequately due to age, lack of aptitude, or a dearth of funds in a bad harvest year. The Biban administrator referred to his crop as "cavaliers de parades" who fantasized about being police officers while shying away from the more somber and dangerous reality.[28] By the 1930s, officials openly worried that Arabs and Kabyles would not fight against their brethren in flash points of rebellion and crime like Kabylia, noting the rise of nationalist and "fanatical" (i.e., Islamic) sentiment and underscoring the need for European gendarmes in increasing numbers. However, the governor general rejected such views as alarmist and unreasonable, based on the false notion of Muslim locals as disloyal and untrustworthy: "Elles demeurent l'élément prépondéront du maintien de l'ordre public dans la colonie [They remain the principal element of law enforcement in the colony]."[29] The policy became even more pronounced during wartime. In August 1941 Vichy announced the creation of the Corps civils des douairs, Algerian militia units to patrol rural areas and urban centers and safeguard highways and coastlines in the absence of Europeans due to conscription, death, or prisoner-of-war status. The corps continued to receive administrative funding and priority as late as December 1945, with the governor general bemoaning a 30 to 35 percent decline in numbers for the PJ and Police d'état in the Territoires du Sud (Saharan territories), and even proposing arms and US military vehicles for all troops in that region.[30]

In theory, the existence of a varied group of police services, assisted by independent local guards and European and Muslim officials, ensured both efficiency and comprehensive coverage, with few stones left unturned as highly specialized agencies dealt with every conceivable aspect of colonial law and order. However, in practice, interagency cooperation remained a serious problem, particularly in rural settings, where gendarmes, the PJ, and municipal guards were expected to work together in solving cases. In March 1945, a gendarmerie colonel complained bitterly that in the aftermath of a spate of armed robberies and banditry, the local police had not bothered to call in the BM, leading a frustrated deputy prefect to lambaste negligent and shoddy personnel in Lamy. In July 1947, the minister of the interior dispatched a missive from Paris, dismissing RG, police, and gendarme claims that they were communicating regularly and acting according to protocol; either share intelligence and make investigations a team effort, he warned, or there would be serious consequences. For their part, gendarmes frequently complained that civilian personnel did not respect military authority, gave orders that could not be followed, and demanded their services in lieu of the local force in both cities and countryside, while prefects castigated officials and caïds who did not transmit detailed and timely crime reports.[31] Furthermore, they were expected to do the bulk of policing in Algeria, while civilian forces stole the credit. Administrators frequently countered that police and gendarmes undermined their position by refusing to respect their authority, whether the right to head an investigation or call on troops for assistance.[32] Despite continual appeals from civilian and military officials, and harsh criticisms and threats from ministers and the governor general, mutual suspicion and resentment plagued Algerian law enforcement through to the War of Independence.

Technology and Investigative Technique in the Service of Racial Hegemony and Settler Domination

Regardless of the service involved in a given criminal case, antinationalist initiative, or surveillance operation, law enforcement personnel used a variety of investigative techniques and strategies, some imported from the metropole and others distinctly Algerian, to maintain order and/or facilitate arrests. Technology proved particularly useful in this regard. Although not as quick as the metropole to embrace everything from police laboratories to the scientific gathering of evidence, by the interwar era almost every city and commune employed the latest methodology. The Service anthropométrique (Anthropometric Service) first appeared in 1903, yet the first police laboratory began operation in Alger only in April 1927. In addition to fingerprinting, it included facilities for detecting signs of forced entry, bloodstains and seminal fluid, and gunpowder residue, along with handwriting analysis. The facilities further housed databases including books of fingerprints, photographs, and records of physical characteristics (tattoos, scars, height and weight, hair, clothing, accent, voice), allowing for the identification of perpetrators in the absence of visual evidence or witnesses. They included state-of-the-art chemical laboratory facilities and darkrooms, and morgues complete with autopsy and forensics teams.[33] Of course, colonial investigations pursued a very different desired outcome, less concerned with crime prevention than the maintenance of racial hegemony, and photography, fingerprinting, and elaborate files all aimed first and foremost, at entrenching imperial order.

Photography perfectly encapsulated this set of priorities. As Roland Barthes notes, the camera operator or photographer frames and constructs their shot with a target audience or spectator in mind, which can obscure the authenticity of the subject by superimposing her or his own vision, producing objectification. This is particularly true in the unary variant, which seeks merely to transmit a message or incident with "no duality, no indirection, no disturbance." Through this process, the colonial police photograph carries within it a series of signifiers related to a racial and colonial system.[34] Further, as Michael Vann observes in a study of postcards depicting executions in French Indochina, the imperial photographic image carries the weight of authority, broadcasting a message for both colonizer and colonized, "communicating the colonial order of things" through the dehumanization of the *indigène* while "placing blame for white on non-white violence upon the native victim."[35] Thus during the trial of Arab perpetrators charged with the murder of a *muphti* (Muslim legal expert) on 2 August 1936 in a *café maure* in the Alger arcades, the judge demanded that the technical brigade from the police laboratory minutely reconstruct the crime. The report referred to the killers as "two Moors" (anonymous and typically *indigène*, perceived to be a threat to public order), and a series of photographs showed the murder scene, the positioning of the dead body in the shop where he died, and the steps taken by all of the principals, including key witnesses. Judge and jury thus entered the "other"

Algeria through the camera's gaze, a demimonde of winding back alleys and side streets behind the arches where Europeans did not tread, and the entire process simultaneously reinforced perceptions of exoticism and criminality.[36] In other cases, the reconstruction of the crime scene occurred publicly, providing a visual demonstration of French policing and justice. On 4 March 1937, the judge presiding over a trial for the murder of an imam insisted that the prosecutor and defense attorneys, perpetrators, and detectives head directly to the crime scene, to reconstruct the events with the assistance of police experts. They visited all of the areas related to the crime and questioned witnesses on the spot, including prostitutes from a nearby brothel. A photographer documented the entire visit, and local denizens witnessed the entire proceeding—a firm reminder to the Algerian public of both the consequences for criminal transgressions and the omnipresence of law enforcement and judiciary in non-European spaces.[37]

While photography functioned as a tool to preserve crime scene details and provide European access to Algerian neighborhoods and spaces, footprint and fingerprint analysis were far more widely used to identify perpetrators, particularly necessary due to a lack of reliable witnesses for many crimes. Usually, only the victims interacted with attackers, thieves, or gangs. A combination of fear of retribution and suspicion of police and administrators silenced urban denizens and country dwellers alike, loathe to cooperate with representatives of French rule even in optimal conditions let alone potentially handing over Arabs or Kabyles to foreign justice. Rural crime scenes provided particular challenges to technicians, as fingerprints and other physical evidence were often nonexistent. Thus, police often sought footprint matches from shoes or boots; in one robbery case in Batna, a knee-print contained traces of fabric used to identify thieves.[38] Fingerprints were more commonly lifted from urban crime scenes, particularly with European victims, from the robbery of a mechanic's home in Hamma to the double attempted murder of a French couple in Bougie, taken variously from the domicile and stolen items found in the possession of the three accused Algerians.[39] However, police reports complained about public interference with colonial crime scenes, lambasting overzealous cleaning that frequently removed valuable prints prior to the arrival of the police. In desperation, the authors of a 1929 annual report asked that a major newspaper such as the *Dépêche de Constantine* (Constantine Dispatch) run an article on the subject, educating the public about their use by the Police judiciaire.[40]

Colonial police themselves proved equally problematic when they used modern investigative techniques, particularly in the vast majority of cases that implicated Arab or Kabyle suspects rather than Europeans, and thus concerned them to a far lesser degree. In a June 1930 report concerning an attack on an automobile owned by a French local, a Philippeville gendarme described an identification lineup: "Je l'ai place parmi dix autres indigènes et les ai confrontés avec M. Jacquier [I stuck him in with ten other *indigènes* and brought them all in front of Mr. Jacquier]." Police made no attempt to find suspects based on physical resemblance, and to make matters worse, the Algerian arrested had an alibi for the evening in question—he worked a shift at the time of the shooting. Either the officer believed in the xenophobic trope that all Arabs looked the same, or he was solely concerned with making an arrest and simply selected an available and convenient suspect as the fall guy.[41] Even where law enforcement followed proper procedure, the lack of resources had a deleterious effect. Fingerprinting laboratories were available in major cities like Constantine and Oran, but nonexistent in communes and smaller towns, while even in larger centers, a paucity of trained personnel negated a facility's effectiveness. A lack of proper training also resulted in poor laboratory results in cities like Bône, and often, equipment was either badly outdated or entirely absent, leading to a delay of up to a full day while personnel waited for borrowed cameras to arrive, for example. In any case, metropolitan conveniences like telephone service did not appear in Algeria until 1932, and then only with Alger to Oran and Alger to Constantine lines, while smaller communities were still asking for Brigades techniques on the eve of the 1954 Algerian War of Independence.[42]

However, by far the largest impediment involved the noncooperation of community members in town and countryside in police inquiries concerning crimes involving Algerian suspects and/or victims. In a July 1934 report, Sûreté officers complained that Guelma inhabitants preserved complete silence when questioned about serious crimes by the gendarmerie, including murder, leading specialized investigators from their unit to force reluctant witnesses to come forward. Yet, for all their bravado, the latter often failed in equal measure to elicit any information. During a June 1923 investigation into the murder of an Arab farmer in Hamma during a botched robbery, locals remained silent in the streets, the market, and the vicinity of the crime, stymieing the efforts of two European officers.[43] Furthermore, when Algerians did offer assistance, it was universally deemed to be untrustworthy due to suspected ulterior motives. Relatives often supplied alibis for suspects, both in cases where the evidence clearly established guilt and in others where they faced arrest and imprisonment without a compelling rationale or the ability to consult a lawyer. Officers and officials found testimony concerning the culpability of a fellow Algerian to be similarly devious. The *administrateur* in M'Sila noted in June 1921, "C'est une machination countoumière aux indigènes . . . pensent qu'il était tout simplement d'articuler une accusation pour qu'elle soit acceuilie ipso facto comme une preuve [It's the usual *indigène* tactic . . . thinking that it's simply a matter of making an accusation and it will be taken ipso facto as evidence]."[44]

As a result, the governor general budgeted substantial sums to pay informants—a critical component of colonial law enforcement. The use of *les mouchards* (snitches) was far from unique to Algeria, and Gallic police had long mobilized a veritable army of snitches to support ongoing policing operations. The metropolitan RG relied on confidential paid informants, much as services in neighboring nations did, and *commissaires* depended on them to provide access to places that police could not patrol or keep under surveillance. All were recruited by a specific agent and attached solely to him, and received pseudonyms to guarantee their safety. Although their observations often lacked veracity, if they were successful in producing intelligence of any kind, the police retained their services. It was these sources who provided a window into the world of the Extreme Right, syndicalism, communism, and other movements deemed dangerous.[45] Yet, in the colonial context, informants served another, vastly different purpose. In times of budgetary constraint, when shortages of available personnel impacted the ability to cover vast areas in urban neighborhoods or rural communes, such shadow employees filled the gap, providing access to illegal or illicit doings in a given locale. Furthermore, the vast majority of European police and gendarmes spoke neither Arabic nor Berber, leaving them at a serious disadvantage. The colonial authorities understood only too well their inability to influence Algerians and their communities, and their failure to penetrate rural *duwars* and *mechtas*. They witnessed only what James C. Scott terms the "public transcript," a performance designed to placate the colonizer, and were not privy to the "hidden transcript" of private opinions that circulated in local communities through everything from humor to Arabic-language conversation.[46] Neither did European authorities fully trust subordinates, lower-level agents, and rural guards, whose loyalties remained suspect despite professions to the contrary.

Hence, informants provided a ready-made solution, with cash payments exchanged for details concerning the movements and activities of criminals and anticolonial activists. Initially, officials actively encouraged Muslim personnel to adopt the practice. From 1909 onward, prefects paid cavaliers twenty-five francs for information leading to the arrest of any criminal band.[47] However, by the interwar era, members of the public became the principal targets, and given the poverty and unemployment endemic in Algerian life, there was no shortage of candidates. In some cases, informants merely relayed information that led to the seizure of weapons or banned publications. Others provided both surveillance of illegal activities and information relating to major cases or notorious figures. In a *duwar* outside Sétif in July 1938, gendarmes employed a number of regular snitches to support raids on the houses of Muslim suspects involved in illegal arms dealing. A seven-man team drawn from the PJ and the BM then formed an operations plan based on the acquired information and raided the dwelling of a repeat offender named Guettaf, a supplier to Arabs across the region, and following a gunfight seized four rifles.[48]

These successes encouraged officials to pay hundreds of informants across all three departments, with money drawn from a "secret fund" controlled by the Sûreté. Initially pegged at hundreds of francs per annum for each town and commune, responding to literally dozens of municipal demands, the amounts mushroomed during the interwar era, reaching up to ten thousand per installment with the advent of communism as a threat to business and government and the interwar crime wave that adversely impacted settlers throughout Algeria (see chapter 3).[49] Snitches became employees in places like the southern oases, paid between ten and sixty francs depending on the utility of their information; assistance in solving murder cases or arresting gangs earned the informant 500 francs.[50] Given the vast numbers of Arab and Kabyle unemployed—fully 20 percent of the population by the 1950s—and the widespread starvation and misery, even for those in both rural and urban areas who worked during the interwar era, it is unsurprising that many agreed to assist the authorities.[51] For those unwilling or unable to emigrate to France in search of factory labor, a number that remained static at two hundred thousand until 1949, up to one-third of the eligible population were so malnourished and physically unhealthy that they could not meet the less than rigorous standards for conscription into the army.[52] By the 1950s, with the annual income of the vastly rural and small town population still below 17,000 francs per annum, and the advent of nationalist movements and the threat of decolonization looming, funding demands increased again, with the prefect supplying 150,000 francs annually to Oran-Ville alone. Yet even this was deemed insufficient by the RG, due to the prevalence of separatist sentiments. By that time, agencies also began to target members of nationalist organizations, labor unions, and even the Parti communiste algérien (Algerian Communist Party), and these cases proved to be even more expensive and required a longer-term commitment. As the police chief of Saïda noted in a letter to the Mascara *sous-préfet*, the difficulty in obtaining intelligence concerning the PPA/MTLD necessitated extreme measures, and a local snitch demanded a salary of 1,000 francs per month in order to even consider providing evidence of malfeasance.[53]

Colonial Threat Assessment, Recruitment/ Retention, and Budgetary Shortfalls

Such antagonism was not the only problem facing police and gendarmes. Recruitment and retention proved equally challenging, particularly serious challenges in Algeria due to chronic personnel shortages across all three departments. Towns and cities constantly complained that a combination of population growth, poor working conditions, and vacations or medical leave seriously compromised local security. In Oran, the director of departmental security wrote to the prefect in October 1926 to seek an additional police captain and various deputies, necessary to properly monitor the more than 150,000 locals and the thousands of visitors to the major, thriving port, which required passport control, visas, and medical authorizations. In February 1949, the Tiaret Security Commission similarly bemoaned the fact that the force was one-third of the necessary size—much smaller than comparable urban centers in the region.[54] In the years before the Algerian War of Independence, with the nationalist PPA increasingly visible and violent incidents on the rise, various municipalities reported having few agents or officers actually fit for duty. The Oran complement proved unable to clear striking workers from the docks in May 1951, due to a shortage of dozens of units throughout the department, and across the colony, there were many vacancies resulting from injury, illness, or transfers to other jurisdictions.[55] Neither was the shortage confined to the municipal police. In August 1949, the town of Oued Zenati in Constantine reported that for the fourth time in two years, the sole officer of the Police judiciaire had become the acting police chief—who would investigate major crimes under such conditions? Throughout the department, PJ officers were in short supply in the early 1950s, with vacancies reported in Sétif, Ain-Beïda, and Biskra, while Bordj-Bou-Arréridj and Djidjelli had no investigators at all due to unfilled positions.[56] In Oran, the RG similarly reported significant shortages in August 1948–a deficit of twenty-seven officers—and almost every urban center in the department required additional personnel. Two years later, the total shortfall in all three departments remained, with thirty-three vacancies overall.[57]

However, the worst shortages by far afflicted the gendarmerie. As early as 1881, a mere twelve gendarmes patrolled the entire commune of Tizi-Ouzou in volatile Kabylia, rife with banditry and livestock theft and containing 22,537 Algerians and 500 Europeans in a vast 2,332 kilometer expanse.[58] Almost three decades later, in September 1908, the brigade in Oued Zenati reported having only four men and one brigadier at their disposal, insufficient to patrol four markets and investigate myriad minor criminal cases, for impoverished Algerians frequently resorted to theft. Moreover, Europeans feared an attack if the economic situation of Arabs and Kabyles continued to deteriorate, and thus commanding officers recommended a minimum of two gendarmes to be posted in the potential flash point of Renier.[59] The entire Algerian complement on the eve of the Great War numbered 232, allowing one brigade for every 23,495 people. By the 1920s, vacations further wrought havoc with rural policing, and the Constantine squadron leader wrote to the prefect in October 1925 informing him that 47 out of 269 were on leave. All of this occurred in the aftermath of the war, which decimated the ranks, leaving only eight commissioned officers remaining by mid-decade. In any case, most Algerian commanders tended to be ineffective, falling back onto the nineteenth-century ideal of the armed forces merely bolstering colonial order in rural areas. The French authorities responded by authorizing the creation of twenty new gendarmerie brigades in 1930, yet as late as 1939, three of them remained unstaffed. In some cases, the deficits proceeded from a lack of housing, always a concern for Algerian law enforcement, with police in certain locations reduced to staying in hotels due to a lack of lodgings. Nonetheless, these were almost always temporary shortages, and they paled before the dearth of gendarmes. In January 1953, thirty brigades were missing from active duty because suitable barracks could not be provided, while budgets after 1945 contained no funding increase despite the clear need for additional soldiers due to population increases, a fact noted by the chief of staff in a report.[60] Despite promises from the minister of national defense that June, on the eve of the Algerian War, no new troops had arrived, and many gendarmes transferred out due to low salaries and the termination of the traditional housing allowance, not to mention having to patrol up to eighty-one thousand hectares, and the raw recruits taking their places in Algeria, lacking knowledge and experience with local conditions.[61]

As a result, security concerns remained across all three departments in the interwar and post-1945 eras. Towns and communes continually demanded gendarmerie garrisons or additional police officers to protect *colons* and urbanites from increasingly unruly *indigènes*, a "crisis of authority" caused by crime, disorder, and the absence of a French official presence.[62] In MacMahon, a village in the Constantinois, the municipal council reminded the prefect in November 1934 that they had survived an insurrection in 1916 and rioting in August 1934, and currently suffered from "indigenous agitators" throughout the region. Yet, the town's entire defense consisted of ten rifles and six hundred bullets, with no plans for a permanent presence to protect the town. At very least, they needed a detachment of soldiers from El Kantara and automatic weapons in order to defend the area until the arrival of reinforcements.[63]

In Biskra, the mayor wrote the prefect in June 1935 to similarly complain that the local Cercle de la jeunesse (a reformist movement opposed to traditional Arab and Kabyle elites) and its leader, Dr. Saadane, were a revolutionary force using rumor, the threat of violence, and Islamic fanaticism to sow the seeds of popular discontent—even among previously loyal Muslims—in a region with a mere five gendarmes patrolling 240,000 hectares of territory and a town with only one non-Arab brigadier.[64] Such accounts were echoed in subsequent decades by authorities across Algeria, with officials noting Muslim agitation and crime and criticizing the hesitation of the Paris-based ministers of the interior and war.[65]

The ministers provided a haphazard response lacking any centralized scheme and using disingenuous methods to avoid seriously increasing the Algerian law enforcement complement. As early as 1893, the governor general explored the idea of adding gendarmes in the towns of Colbert and Tocqueville, both in the department of Constantine, where local denizens requested a detachment to protect Europeans in the remote outposts. Additional requests arrived in 1898 and 1900, yet due to manpower issues, both were postponed; the Ministry of War had established a priority list, and both locales remained in the middle of the pack. By 1908 the local squadron leader joined the chorus noting a genuine security need, and finally in 1913 approval arrived from Paris for a five-man mounted complement. Yet, the troops never arrived, and again in 1920 and 1923 the municipal council and prefect formulated the same demand and were met with silence from the authorities, seemingly content to ignore their worries.[66] Where additional gendarmes were authorized, the rationale often puzzled local police, commanders, and officials. In June 1933, the minister of war approved a gendarmerie post in Bugeaud, outside Bône. That the town required assistance was beyond doubt; it had no regular police force, and hundreds of migrant workers arrived during the harvest season. Yet Bône itself remained short-staffed, with only twenty officers (only fourteen available at any given moment) patrolling a town with over 150,000 inhabitants, and this problem extended to the entire law enforcement complement, many of whom were illiterate or incompetent.[67] Although the administration did expand the GRM in response to serious deficiencies, adding three companies with almost four hundred personnel, these were split between three departments, and only in 1952 did authorities in Constantine unreservedly begin to create new stations and increase the number of police and *commissaires* in five cities and towns.[68]

One consistent rationale for government inaction concerned budgetary shortfalls, an omnipresent problem in every French colony. Spending in the empire never matched the level of metropolitan investment, despite official rhetoric concerning the critical position of colonies within "Greater France" and the exploitation of these markets for French goods, particularly in trade with Algeria. Colonial budgets were tied to economic development and performance, and the Depression thoroughly weakened North African mining, agriculture, and viticulture, while the metropolitan authorities did little to staunch the bleeding because of complaints from farmers and producers about unwanted competition from cheap imperial goods. Although Algeria was less deleteriously impacted than sub-Saharan territories, primarily due to its large settler population (over one million by the interwar era) and the incorporation of the three departments into the French political and customs system, the cost of maintaining public works, transportation, policing, and other services proved substantial in a colony divided between dense urban centers and isolated and/or depopulated rural communes. Moreover, taxes provided an inordinate percentage of the total allotment (alongside customs dues), with the *impôts arabes* (Arab taxes) contributing a disproportionate share despite the concentration of land and wealth overwhelmingly in *colon* hands. Although the total budget increased from 131 million francs in 1914 to 882 million in 1927, the amount proved insufficient, with the authorities resorting to bank loans to meet their obligations and still producing a shortfall of 486 million by 1936 and an ever-increasing deficit. Only drastic spending cuts and taxes unique to North Africa kept Algeria solvent.[69]

Hence, budgetary concerns often were the sole rationale for determining staff complements, and settler communities lobbied in vain for additional resources, their pleas almost always dismissed despite mounting security concerns. Already in 1906, the departmental council of Batna and the governor general's office requested the transfer of men from Tunis due to concerns about rebellion, only to be told by the minister of war that the number of available troops in North Africa was finite, with no funds available to increase the size of the gendarmerie, while money could not be procured for the necessary construction of barracks. In the mid-nineteenth century, when the Aurès was rife with rebellion, perhaps such an expense could have been justified, but that time had passed. The company commander in Constantine was even more blunt three years later, stating that any new squads would necessarily entail the suppression of others; if Gounod received a complement, then Constantine or Bône would lose an equal number of men, and this could work only if there was redistribution of the local workload.[70] Such demands increased in number following the Great War. In the aftermath of the Constantine and Sétif emergencies in 1934 and 1935, various communities viewed local Arabs and Kabyles as potential rebels, and smaller towns and villages in particular demanded additional police and/or gendarmes. In Jemmapes, Batna, Bugeaud, and many more areas, the requests were met with the same refrain—a limited number of available troops and a lack of funding for barracks. In MacMahon, in December 1934, these talking points were met with derision by local politicians: Could the allotted complement of ten aging rifles and six hundred bullets actually repel an uprising? Yet the governor general held firm, noting that the priority remained the defense of larger centers, with modern transportation to be used in the case of an emergency that required extra manpower. The Constantine *chef d'escadron* blamed the minister of war for the problem; directives specifically proscribed any further spending, and even brigades already approved in several locales months or years earlier had never actually arrived.[71]

Given this sobering reality, unsurprisingly, municipal governments paid for their own policing needs, with only the gendarmerie covered by the state through the army budget. As a result, constant quarrels erupted due to chronic budget shortfalls. In 1904 the Constantine municipal council voted to demand that Sûreté expenses be paid by the governor general, after they failed to economize sufficiently through other measures, from nominating police officers at lower ranks and reducing salaries to sending the hotel bills to the army when gendarmes stayed in urban centers.[72] When such tricks failed, municipal councils sought to eliminate local police altogether in favor of the gendarmerie, a tactic resoundingly rejected by the French government due to concerns over public safety, particularly in market towns.[73] Worse still, the governor general repeatedly cancelled or delayed planned increases in police and troop complements for fiduciary reasons, beginning in 1908 with seven Constantine locations. In August 1920, he further informed the prefect that brigades and detachments needed in Batna and Bélezma to decrease gendarme workloads and address the dozens of kilometers separating both locations from law enforcement could not be considered due to the cost.[74] Beginning in the mid-1930s, nationalization salvaged the situation, pushing urban police budgets onto the colonial side of the ledger, essential in the face of ballooning wage costs and material resource needs, in combination with shrinking or chronically underfunded yearly allotments, ranging from mere hundreds of francs for sparsely populated communes to 28,120 francs for Oran-Ville.[75] However, the shift toward state police did not occur in remote or rural areas, leaving those territories with the smallest budgets perpetually close to bankruptcy. In Sidi-Aïch, a commune with 110,000 hectares and 125,000 inhabitants in Constantine, the entire budget totaled 200,000 francs, a huge portion of which paid for three French and twenty-one Algerian rural policemen and ten Muslim cavaliers. Naturally, more police officers or further resources were unthinkable, despite the demonstrated need.[76]

Budgetary issues continued to plague colonial policing after 1945, revealing a seeming disconnect between the looming threat of decolonization and the administrative response. Despite the mounting danger to the French presence in Algeria from increasing militant activity and growing political opposition, the Finance Ministry consistently vetoed any fiscal increase, and lacking the required funds themselves, the Ministry of War necessarily followed suit. Journalists and deputies pilloried the Algerian budget as a massive resource drain, and the governor general from 1948 to 1951, Marcel-Edmond Naegelen, consistently reminded his Parisian colleagues that the vast majority of local inhabitants could not be taxed due to dire poverty, while the 89 million francs at his disposal barely covered the substantial administrative expenses of a colonial enterprise: "Si la métropole avait voulu ou pu engager dans ce malheureux pays le dixième des dépenses qu'elle avait consenties pour vaincre le rébellion . . . encadrée par la Tunisie et par le Maroc . . . la France eût abordé dans des conditions infiniment meilleures la révolte prêchée et déclenchée par le FLN [If the metropole had wanted to or could have deployed in this miserable territory a mere tenth of the expenses that they authorized for the defeat of the rebellion . . . guided by Tunisia and Morocco . . . then France would have tackled in infinitely better conditions the revolt preached and ultimately triggered by the FLN]."[77]

While the authorities continually issued official proclamations in defense of *l'Algérie française*, expecting a return to pre-1940 law enforcement norms, the growth of the PPA and the evident popularity of nationalism in both rural and urban districts further underscored the importance of police and gendarmes. Nevertheless, no help was forthcoming, with predictable results. Concerns mounted after 8 May 1945, when authorities were convinced (wrongly) that Messali Hadj and his lieutenants had provoked a mass rising in the Constantinois that resulted in the massacre of Europeans in Sétif and Guelma, and hundreds of members were arrested despite clear evidence that settlers and troops had in fact butchered thousands of Algerians.[78] In the late 1940s and early 1950s authorities used fraud to contest elections to counteract the participation of the group's political wing, the Mouvement pour le triomphe des libertés démocratiques (MTLD; Movement for the Triumph of Democratic Freedoms). Their fears were further stoked by the discovery of the Organisation spéciale (OS; Special Organization), a paramilitary wing dedicated to forcing decolonization.[79] From propagandists to newspaper editors, party members to leaders, the authorities regularly arrested dozens of Arabs and Kabyles, seeking to eradicate nationalism.[80] Given the prioritization of the PPA / MTLD threat, police services logically presumed a concomitant increase in budget allotments to staunch the threat, yet were instead confronted with fewer resources and talk of austerity.

In March 1949, responding to concerns that parts of Kabylia contained almost no European law enforcement, the governor general warned all three prefects that budget cuts announced by the minister of national defense would gravely impact security.[81] By October of the following year, the results became clear, as the chief commissioner of the Oran RG took issue with a directive from the director general concerning universal surveillance of nationalist North Africans. Such a strategy was simply impossible due to a lack of personnel, with the information and political movement sections understaffed in Muslim sectors—Sidi-Bel-Abbès had no agents whatsoever, despite being a stronghold of the Communists and the Union démocratique du manifeste algérien (UDMA; Democratic Union of the Algerian Manifesto). Neither could the security of the Algerian-Moroccan border be guaranteed, as it currently lacked any surveillance. Clearly, the government's financial situation had deteriorated, and the risk to French sovereignty grew stronger with each passing moment.[82] The situation became so dire in April 1951 that Colonel Morin, the commander of the Algerian gendarmerie, wrote to the minister of national defense to support local voices alarmed at the deep cuts to the gendarmerie, which had recorded a 30 percent troop deficit in recent years. Although his staff pulled out all the stops, requisitioning raw recruits and *gardes républicaines* from the metropole, reduced pay and the cancellation of vacations essentially nullified these efforts, driving away potential newcomers to North Africa. By 1952, officials from communes in all three departments besieged the governor general with demands for police and gendarmes, as well as motorized vehicles, yet only four towns received detachments, and prefect of Constantine reported that the total complement had been reduced from 952 to 720, to cover 88,000 square kilometers and 3.1 million people. No French presence currently existed in vast swathes of the countryside, and the force suffered from overwork, illness, severe heat, poor diets and housing, and a deficit of jeeps needed to effectively patrol vast territories.[83] Expectations were once again dashed in June, when the minister of national defense vetoed a project to create three new gendarmerie legions in Algeria due to budgetary shortfalls.[84] Administrators continued to acknowledge key vulnerabilities while sweeping matters under the fiduciary rug, promising unspecified future human and material resources and clearly hoping to avoid a large-scale revolt or emergency.

The complaints pointed to another major obstacle to increasing the number of police and gendarmes in Algeria: trouble with the recruitment process. In the metropole and colonies in the late nineteenth and early twentieth centuries, various branches sought ex-military types almost exclusively, demanding only that they were physically fit, passably disciplined, and moral. As a result, the quality of the candidates left much to be desired, and officials treated law enforcement as clients, a relationship only reinforced by low pay and questionable working conditions. With little to no professional training, police learned from colleagues or took voluntary basic courses offered in their municipalities. Only under the Vichy regime in spring 1941 were professional standards tightened in France, with the introduction of an *école nationale de police* (national police academy) in Saint-Cyr and regional programs for guards and municipal cadres, with *écoles supérieures* (institutes of higher education) and *écoles pratiques* (training schools) forming *commissaires* and inspectors, respectively.[85] However, these did not cross the Mediterranean until 1953, when an *école de police* opened in Hussein-Dey outside Alger. In the North African setting, police were instead expected to be team players; knowledge of the criminal code was less important than colonial law enforcement culture transmitted by fellow officers, few of whom has ever attended a metropolitan training course. Even after nationalization in the 1930s, relationships with local politicians and notables remained essential to recruitment and promotion.[86]

Thus, recruitment in Algeria was highly problematic, with excellent candidates vetoed by mayors or administrators if deemed insufficiently supplicant or unwilling to prioritize racial hegemony. Moreover, when (and if) funds became available, prefects tendered advertisements in France and North Africa for positions in Algeria, subject to meeting physical requirements (height, weight, fitness) and passing a concours, consisting of written and verbal exams including basic skills for municipal police to more advanced tests required for the PJ and RG. The exception was the gendarmerie, which adhered to the military formula of recruiting trainees meeting physical and moral standards, and making internal promotions based on performance and suitability.[87] Yet metropolitan posts paid far better than colonial ones, which also entailed higher risks to personal health and safety, fatigue, disease, and additional living expenses. Housing also tended to be filthy and unhygienic, lacking electricity and proper bathroom facilities, while local restaurants in one-horse towns consisted of what one squad leader called "une gargote qui débite une cuisine monotone peu appréciée par l'estomac européen [a greasy spoon that serves up a monotonous cuisine ill appreciated by the European stomach]."[88] Needless to say, metropolitan candidates in particular often fled home across the Mediterranean at the first opportunity, seeking transfers almost immediately on arrival. *Conseils généraux* (general councils) and the governor general were forced to offer substantial recruitment bonuses to attract gendarmes in the 1920s, for example, and post-1945 service vacancies can surely be partially explained by the fact that fully 686 of 700 barracks were deemed unsuitable by military authorities, while a further 774 had been approved but remained unbuilt. Given the billions of francs required to alleviate such burdens, in August 1950 Minister of Defense Jules Moch was forced to fund rental accommodations for gendarmes in order to lure recruits south.[89]

Arab and Kabyle Police and Gendarmes

This problem revealed a key paradox of criminal justice in the colonial setting. On one hand, officers and units provided a vital line of defense for French colonial interests and European settlers, fighting crime and anti-imperialism by coercive or even violent means if necessary. Not for nothing did Frantz Fanon observe that the frontier between colonizer and colonized is demarcated by gendarmerie barracks and police stations.[90] Yet, on the other hand, budgetary constraints consistently led to shortfalls in every branch of law enforcement, leaving gaping holes in urban and rural human and material police resources and forcing mayors, administrators, and deputy prefects to plead for resources on an annual basis. Of course, a natural solution would be the employment of Algerians in policing roles, more readily available and earning less pay, and such arrangments were a common feature in other empires, from India, where the British authorities mobilized the supposedly martial Sikh population and Muslims as constables under white officers, to Egypt, where rural police were exclusively "native," government outsourced law enforcement to locals.[91] Certain French territories acted in much the same fashion. A *garde indigène* patrolled Madagascar, while guards also provided the bulk of the force in parts of Africa like Dahomey and Cameroon, with the army taking up the role elsewhere. In strategic imperial possessions like Indochina and Afrique-Occidentale française (French West Africa), the models tended toward hybridization: French officers working side by side with Vietnamese or Senegalese subofficers or soldiers, almost essential given the minute French population in each territory.[92]

Conversely, Algerian authorities refused to seriously consider widespread adoption of indigenous policing. Although they served as adjutants or lower-level law enforcement in every branch (except the gendarmerie until the 1930s) and functioned as cavaliers and guards in rural communes, Arabs and Kabyles were mostly discounted from anything but entry-level police work. The notoriously xenophobic settlers would never accept any Muslim in a position of authority, and hence "native agents" worked under French superiors and officers and were paid far less than European colleagues, systematically denied promotion, and consistently harassed and disciplined by superiors.[93] In essence, they became trapped between the expectations of the imperial nation-state (the maintenance of colonial order, the arrest and detention of political agitators and criminals) and the reality of empire as a system of racial and socioeconomic subjugation (in which they were simultaneously authority figures and second-class subjects).

The recruitment process itself established a racial binary in Algerian policing. Entrance exams for the municipal force and the Police judiciaire demanded proof of literacy in French, with Arabic only an optional second language. A candidate would further necessarily demonstrate superior knowledge of French penal law, the judicial process, and the evolution of policing in the nineteenth and twentieth centuries. The history of France and its empire from 1715 and economic geography were also required subjects, and the test included a mathematics component, meaning that even an Arab or Kabyle who spoke French encountered a further bar to becoming a *commissaire*. Even a rural policeman could be hired only if literate. Moreover, physical aptitude tests included height and weight requirements and demonstrated skills at swimming, running, and endurance. Many Algerians were malnourished or overworked and could not possibly compete. Thus, the prefect of Alger in May 1928 lauded an Algerian prospect as capable of reading and writing French, in addition to being a *mutilé de guerre* (disabled war veteran) in excellent physical shape and being known for his irreproachable conduct. Moreover, for the Sûreté générale, charged with criminal investigations, the governor general personally approved all candidates, and thus Algerians would need to supply proof of loyalty to France, if not outright citizenship.[94] Of course, for the PM, PJ, and Police d'état, the jury overseeing the competition was exclusively European, headed by a police chief and assisted by ranking officers and distinguished, long-serving policemen.[95] Given the requirements, unsurprisingly, Europeans far outnumbered Algerians in many districts; in eastern Algerian cities like Constantine, Bône, and Philippeville, a quarter or fewer of the Police d'état were Muslims, who predominated only in the *communes mixtes*— rural areas with few Europeans, and the need to police tens of thousands of hectares.[96]

As a result, those Algerians who were hired tended to be *évolués*, the educated and assimilated elite deemed acceptable to the authorities and public—that is, the type of candidate who had attended French schools and could impress an all-white jury comprised of administrators and police drawn from the settler elite.[97] Thus, in February 1908, Taleb Serradj received approval for the position of auxiliary agent because of his blemish-free record, obedience to colonial authority, and ability to speak French fluently. Another file, from February 1942, for Mohammad Barkan, a police officer and candidate for an inspector vacancy, specifically referred to him as "assimilated" and thus acceptable; he was married to a French woman and thus no longer possessed "indigenous customs." This stood in sharp contrast to Zoubir Yahia, an unassimilated Muslim from Oran, who "ne semble pas remplir les qualités réquises pour faire une inspecteur secretaire [does not seem to have demonstrated the required qualities to earn the rank of secretary-inspector]."[98] Under Vichy, the situation worsened: candidates for superior positions now required sample case studies and arrest reports, an experience limited to European police.[99] In 1941 and 1942, the Pétainist authorities made racial requirements even clearer, with the inclusion of an essay on "the household" and barring Jews, Freemasons, and Communists applying for any position, requiring a certified statement of political and racial suitability in order for an application to even be considered.[100]

Moreover, entrance to the gendarmerie remained uncategorically barred to Arabs and Kabyles, as it had from the beginning, and even adjutant status proved difficult to obtain, despite constant promises by officials in both Paris and Alger to bring additional *indigènes* into the fold. In September 1926, the minister of war asked Premier Edouard Herriot to introduce a bill simplifying the recruitment process for Algerian gendarmes, allowing any candidate to serve who met the physical and moral requirements for the job and provided the required legal and administrative documents. Incentives included pensions and provisions for eventual promotion.[101] However, these ideas received strong objections from commanders. Algerian division head General Nogues complained that proposed recruitment strategies disserviced Europeans, who were subject to stricter physical standards and denied recruitment bonuses paid to incentivize Arab and Kabyle candidates. The latter had one year less of mandatory service and received all manner of exemptions, and they were mostly illiterate and therefore required extra training. Nogues's objections were nonetheless ignored by civil authorities, despite reflecting widespread distrust of non-Europeans by French commanding officers, as they were desperate to recruit career-minded Arabs and Kabyles into the gendarmerie due to their intimate knowledge of rural districts and relationships with local notables. The fight against communism (and later, nationalism) trumped xenophobia and preconceived notions in this instance. Subsequent instructions to recruiters demanded that serious attention be paid to the issue in all communes, using propaganda, bonuses, and tracts, along with job fairs and offices.[102] Nonetheless, Muslims were not permitted to ascend the ranks, even those with the designation *officier indigène*, and as late as November 1938, the minister of war continued to protest vigorously that *indigènes* did not understand the concept of military service and were physically inferior.[103]

Only after 1945 did the prioritization of Muslim hires lead to parity in certain urban districts, a result of wartime mobilization that shifted the previous paradigm. Police officers and gendarmes increasingly submitted to the draft as General Giraud authorized tens of thousands of soldiers for the Allied war effort, due to heavy losses during fighting at Bizerte and Tunis in April 1943, and in fall 1942 and summer 1943 Charles de Gaulle demanded the use of Algerian personnel among the Free French and the expeditionary force efforts establishing a continuing presence in African and Italian campaigns against the Nazis.[104] Suddenly, age and race ceased to matter, and Europeans over forty-five and Algerians thirty-six and older needed only to present a birth certificate and either a clean criminal record or a notarized statement of character in order to become a *gardien de la paix* at 2,600 francs per month.[105] Moreover, in the postwar era, the threat of Muslim nationalism increased exponentially following the events of 8 May 1945, when Algerian anti-imperial demonstrations disrupted Victory Day celebrations across all three departments. In Constantine, and particularly in the towns of Sétif and Guelma, police provocations turned peaceful protests into open revolt, while gendarmes and hastily improvised *colon* militias responded by massacring tens of thousands of Arabs and Kabyles. Unsurprisingly, there was increased interest in the PPA, along with its new sister organization, the MTLD, specifically designed to court electoral votes in municipal and regional elections, and Ferhat Abbas's Amis du manifeste et de la liberté (Friends of the Manifesto and Freedom), reformist but still explicitly disapproving of empire.[106] Not only were additional police desperately needed; Muslim officers, in particular, offered the illusion of Algerian governance while providing knowledge of communities and language skills sorely lacking in European personnel. In the department of Oran, only the Oran-ville RG had a sufficient complement of Arabic speakers, while every other community had either too few non-Europeans or no Muslim personnel at all. The governor general had initiated a bonus program for passing the language exams, yet it languished until the post-1945 era, when all agents and *fonctionnaires* working for the Direction de la Sécurité générale (Directorate of General Security) received an invitation to sit an examination in either Arab or Berber.[107] Certain services, like the Oran RG, actively began to recruit Muslims by late 1952, expressing alarm that only twelve "agents français mulmans" (French Muslim agents) had joined the service. Flash points such as Nemours and Sidi-Bel-Abbès, having none on the duty roster, petitioned for a distinct service without the educational requirements that prevented the necessary hiring.[108] The number of Muslim hires in certain locales dramatically increased as a result. In Constantine-ville the 1951 list of police force candidates writing exams included forty-eight Arabs and Kabyles and fifty-three Europeans, while the equivalent numbers for the November 1950 Police d'état Brigadier tests were fifteen and nine in Bougie, nine and seven in Batna, and twenty-four and nine in Sétif, respectively, while all four *gardien de la paix* candidates in 1952 in Bougie were non-European. Although the forces in other districts (Oran, Bône, and various smaller communities) were predominantly non-Algerian, Muslims were hired in vastly increasing numbers. Police d'état personnel numbers for 1947 included a preponderance in Batna, Biskra, and Ain-Beida, and fully 181 of 528 officers across the department of Constantine. Auxiliary agent numbers for March to April 1947 showed 156 Arab and Kabyle candidates and only 101 Europeans.[109]

However, despite much talk of the need for Arabic speakers and agents, the entrance bar for every branch remained too high for most Algerians. A July 1948 decree declared that candidates for the PJ and RG now could present either a recognized European degree, a *medersa* (Muslim school) certificate, or a secondary school diploma, yet few Muslims possessed such an education. Moreover, the curriculum and tests remained largely unchanged, emphasizing French law and policing, history, and similar subjects.[110] Candidates for police captain exams continued to necessarily be of French nationality and "robust constitution," and even lower-level officers required a superior diploma of the type required to enter the École nationale d'administration (National School of Administration), and to pass strict tests concerning penal law, investigative procedures, civil and criminal law, and constitutional and administrative regulations.[111] Hence, although Muslim candidates made strides at the lower levels of the police hierarchy, they continued to be stymied in attempts to penetrate the upper echelons of the security hierarchy. In 1952, all candidates for the *brigadier-chef* exam were European, while the *brigadier de 2e class* included ten Algerians and sixty-one non-Algerians (up from seven and seventy-one the preceding year), and in January 1953, every hire for the Police judiciaire was non-Muslim.[112] Thus, despite substantial gains in certain areas of law enforcement, the lack of Arab and Kabyle personnel persisted until decolonization.

The Racial Realities of Wages, Promotion, and Punishment

There was also a racially based double standard in the wages paid to successful applicants, and in promotions, with Arab and Kabyle police and gendarmes consistently passed over for advancement while deserving European colleagues easily cleared the necessary hurdles and passed exams. The fact that French officials and senior officers alone determined individual salaries and dossiers ensured an outcome favorable to the maintenance of colonial hierarchy. Moreover, discipline cases revealed a clear bias against Algerians, punished much more severely than European colleagues for the same offenses.

From the late nineteenth century onward, the governor general set pay scales for police by decree, with each service having a wide range of salaries, based on both rank and experience. Each rank further contained multiple classes of commander, officer, inspector, and guard, with concomitant salary adjustments. Colonial authorities regularly raised wages across the entire grid to reflect inflation and rising living costs, although disputes invariably arose concerning the amount of each increase. Nonetheless, with the expected career path (including promotions every two to three years), a trainee could earn thousands more in monthly salary by the age of retirement. An inspector for the Sûreté départementale (SD) in 1917 earned 2,800 francs per month, while a municipal policeman joining the force merited 2,800 francs (rising to 5,800), and a *commissaire central* in Constantine managed 8,500 francs, rising to over 35,000 for a similar position in the department two decades later. By 1936, police agents earned 8,000 to 10,500 francs per month, brigadiers took home 10,500 to 12,500, and secretary-inspectors took home 12,500 to 14,900 on average. However, these rates strictly applied to European personnel. Muslim "agents" earned considerably less: 1,400 to 1,900 francs in the SD in 1917, and 7,000 to 10,500 in 1936, still below their non-Algerian coevals, with no chance of promotion.[113] This policy was specifically sanctioned by chief administrators, with dual pay scales formally established by decree in July 1913, and although subsequent governors reduced the pay differences in subsequent decades, they were never completely eliminated. Administrators consistently rebuffed demands for pay equity. During an April 1938 meeting of the *conseil général* in Constantine, leading reformer Ferhat Abbas demanded that recruitment and wage standards be equally applied to both European and Algerian *gardes des eaux et des forêts* (water and forest guards), only to be brushed aside by the custodian. Although specific Arab and Kabyle ranks were phased out during the Vichy years, the lack of access to the upper ranks for such employees meant that the double standard effectively continued unabated. In May 1948, wage parity also became a reality for gendarmes, yet even here, Algerians could not receive metropolitan salary levels (unlike most French members), along with family allowances of 300 fewer francs per month.[114] For example, from 1913 until the mid-1920s, wages for an Algerian *commissaire de police* or Sûreté générale ranged from 2,700 to 8,000 francs per month, whereas in Le Havre, trainees alone earned 4,000 francs, along with a further 20 percent (plus housing adjustment) allotted in the Paris region.[115]

Additionally, attaining promotions proved very difficult for Muslims in various police services. Beginning in January 1909, the French government introduced annual data sheets for all Algerian policemen, combining service record information with a performance review, which determined employment status and promotions. All levels of superior could (and did) comment, with copies for both police chiefs and heads of service and the mayor, administrator, or deputy prefect in charge.[116] The latter often exercised undue influence, rehiring trainees who failed tests and acted unprofessionally, promoting favored municipal police, and agitating for the advancement or firing of those perceived to be disloyal to their office. The situation became sufficiently severe that in June 1935, the minister of the interior deemed it necessary to remind prefects that police were not municipal employees but rather representatives of central authority in situ, acting always in French interests, even if they were simultaneously empowered to engage in local surveillance or arrests.[117] Unsurprisingly, in the post-1945 era, the role of government officials was minimized in the decision-making process, as police captains filed *notes de service* scoring each candidate from zero to twenty in each category, with the results then considered by a departmental promotion commission. These were exclusively European, composed of the prefect (presiding), the local police chief, an RG or PJ chief of police, and union representatives, along with various officers from the region.[118]

Prior to 1945, all of the policemen receiving promotions were European, praised by superiors for their excellence, comportment, loyalty, and superior job performance. In 1933, a commission lauded successful candidates for advancement in the Bougie municipal police due to being married and having numerous children, along with a devotion to the profession. However, not all promotions were so positive. One candidate in Constantine received approval for elevation to *inspecteur 2e classe* despite being the subject of complaints from numerous "ingrates" (Muslims) in M'Sila, while others benefited from similar consideration despite being labeled as "mediocre" or "unsuccessful," or in some cases far exceeding the expected three or four years of service required for advancement.[119] As for Muslims, they faced consistently negative reports from commanding officers, preventing even a discussion of promotion. The author of a crime report for 1923 chided non-European policemen as lazy and deceitful, incapable of doing investigative work and lying under oath with stunning alacrity. An overview of crime and policing in 1928 similarly complained that all Algerian inspectors or agents were mediocre, occupying too many positions, and often ex-military types completely unsuited to the job: older, frequently illiterate, and lacking in professional attributes. A section concerning the BM chastised inspectors using the same language, characterizing them as a danger to public safety, with the exception of eight exceptional candidates whose zeal often surpassed that of their European confreres. However, their commendation led to no improvements in compensation or rank, and Algerian police were used only to support European colleagues, who always took the lead during investigations. Arab and Kabyle officers provided translations when required and directly interacted with locals to avoid the appearance of French domination (although few were fooled), but they were always in a subordinate position.[120]

The European trend continued in the postwar era, with such candidates consistently described as energetic, capable, and excellent in all facets of the job and quickly ascending the ranks if deemed sufficiently talented—or if they served colonial interests, often through violence. One European RG officer in Constantine, Yvon Bordier, who initially joined the Police judiciare in 1939 in Tlemcen, was an ex-schoolteacher with a high school diploma and an army reservist. Within a decade he had risen from trainee to *commissaire principal 2e classe*. Superiors universally supported his application for promotion to departmental police chief in 1949, noting his physical and moral aptitude, intelligence and judgement, and the authority and efficiency he brought to any leadership position. Adjudicators had previously singled out his role in the 8 May massacres (euphemistically called "events") and in leading "delicate" investigations into the actions of the PPA; an entire cadre of officers owed their careers to having similarly participated in colonial violence and antinationalist activity.[121] Yet Muslims never managed to reach the upper ranks in any service except the municipal police. Thus in 1951, dozens sat for the officer exams, but only three received promotions—two to *brigadier 2e classe* and one to *commissaire principal 2e classe*, a fraction of the Europeans rewarded. Numbers in the gendarmerie were similarly staggered, with test results as late as 1952 producing no Muslim officers; they never progressed beyond the adjutant level.[122] Moreover, the rare Algerians who became Sûreté inspectors in 1945 received promotion solely on the basis of having proven their loyalty during the Sétif and Guelma massacres by providing information that led to the capture of suspected "rebels."[123] Thus administrators created a public impression of Gallic control and Algerian subservience outside of Muslim districts; even in the countryside, French commanders were always the ultimate decision makers. To succeed, an Arab and Kabyle would necessarily participate in the repression of his own community.

Disciplinary cases employed a similar methodology to promotion decisions, with either European commanders or committees charged with considering evidence, hearing witness testimony, and rendering decisions concerning police misconduct at all levels. The sole exception remained the army, where superior officers subjected gendarmes charged with various offenses to military discipline and tribunals. For municipal policemen, minor cases often remained the purview of police commissioners, who issued warnings, reprimands, or fines, or required unpaid overtime. For more serious cases, particularly those that might result in lengthy suspensions, termination, or criminal convictions, the prefect convened a disciplinary council comprised of the mayor (presiding), four municipal councilors, the local chief, and several ranking officers, all of whom received a written report including the full case details. Guilty verdicts entailed a variety of punishments, from loss of vacation or six-month suspension to transfer, demotion, or firing. All of those charged appeared personally before the committee with a lawyer or fellow officer, answering questions and offering testimony.[124]

Europeans charged by the committee primarily committed criminal acts, including corruption and abuse of power. Although some were implicated in unethical behavior—taking unauthorized supplementary vacation time, for example—others received relatively minor admonishments for incidents perceived as quotidian, such as tardiness. One inspector in Ain-Beïda received a one-month suspension in June 1929 after being warned multiple times for insubordination. In certain cases, there were different disciplinary standards for abuses of power and corruption, depending on the race of the victims. In July 1951, a Kouba police officer faced accusations of extorting services from local European merchants, and prosecution witnesses included the mayor, several prominent municipal councilors, and multiple businessmen. Unsurprisingly, the perpetrator and several accomplices from the local force were found guilty of corruption and transferred to other posts, with letters in their files.[125] However, superior officers and committees ignored or minimized similar infringements on the rights of Muslim shopkeepers. When twenty-five Algerian merchants from Collo accused a local brigadier of malfeasance in March 1928, charging that he used his authority to force Algerians to patronize his shops instead of their own, the mayor intervened, writing the prefect to reject their story in no uncertain terms. He rhapsodized about the officers' zealous dedication to duty and professionalism, along with his friendly attitude toward *indigènes*, and sloughed off the detractors as a few malcontents who should be ignored. The case was summarily dismissed. Even more seriously, a committee in Bône threw out a January 1946 case of criminal negligence against Agent spécial François Savelli, accused of refusing to call an ambulance for a seriously ill Muslim. Once again, the police chief and deputy prefect both argued in favor of the defendant, agreeing that he had a severely problematic relationship with the local Arab population but demanding that the charges be ignored due to his meritorious service record and superlative performance. Only acts against

Muslims that resulted in criminal convictions merited disciplinary action. For example, a policeman in Sétif was fired for robbing drunks after receiving a six-month suspended sentence from a judge.[126]

Muslim police and guards, on the other hand, were held to far higher standards, fired or suspended for drunkenness (also applicable to Europeans if their behavior involved gross negligence or violent acts) and lateness. Discipline became the ultimate symbol of the dual nature of Arab and Kabyle law enforcement, empowered as colonial agents yet simultaneously facing precarious employment conditions and constant reminders of their subject status. The profusion of proceedings against Algerian police so incensed the governor general that he wrote the prefect of Alger in March 1947 to complain that the pursuit of non-Europeans over minor matters risked diminishing the authority of the disciplinary council.[127] The exasperation of such a senior official reflected a strategy that had been commonly practiced for decades. To be sure, certain cases were indeed serious and did not reflect capricious or xenophobic motives. For example, an agent caught asleep on the job during a crucial surveillance operation at the Italian consulate in Constantine in November 1935, during the height of the Second Italo-Ethiopian War, received a summons from the council, having already been administered several punishments for public drunkenness over the course of a fifteen-year career.[128] Yet such cases were rare, and most Muslim defendants received penalties that dwarfed those meted out to European colleagues for similar infractions. Another officer accused of drinking on the job, Mohamed Hansili, wrote to the mayor of Châteaudun-du-Rhumel in October 1926 vehemently denying the charge, which included the assertion that he chased after a suspect with a knife in his hand. The reality instead reflected a personal vendetta: Hansili angered locals due to his zealous intolerance of lawbreakers, and during the incident in question he had been assaulted by the son of a local veterinarian and a band of delinquents. Nonetheless, the mayor's deputies had been adversely impacted by the police, and thus a lengthy suspension was pronounced.[129] Dozens of similar cases resulted in firings or demotions, as drinking, improper conduct, or minor infractions merited severe penalties.[130] Perhaps the worst abuses occurred with respect to Muslim rural policemen, suspected of being habitually lazy and indolent. In October 1913, two such guards in Collo faced accusations of disobeying orders and received a fifteen-day suspension for failure to supply a needed horse and feed, with the press noting that such behavior had severe ramifications in an area rife with Algerian rebellion against gendarmes and officials. The guards were further accused of "mocking" soldiers by shirking their duty. Yet, depositions revealed a very different story, in which a minor matter was blown out of proportion by the colonial authorities and newspapers. Their only infractions involved confusion over where and when to deliver the needed mount.[131] European police in similar circumstances routinely received a warning or a fine, fired only for court convictions for theft, sexual assault, or physical violence, and even these often resulted in leniency. One *gardien de la paix* merited a mere suspension for attempting to blackmail his police chief, numerous assaults, and visiting brothels. Moreover, he had been convicted of theft in 1924 but received a full pardon on joining the state police a dozen years later.[132]

Conversely, complaints against Muslim police frequently reflected administrative enmity or xenophobia. Agent Ahmed Meflah in Tiaret was severely reprimanded in 1949 by the police chief for displaying a "impetuous character," yet the actual problem concerned claims of business dealings with members of the reformist UDMA and accusations of directing a planned campaign against the police and the mayor. Although various administrators acknowledged that the evidence was highly suspect (one deemed it "complete fantasy . . . totally unjustified") and a report by Meflah's superiors noted his unswerving loyalty, the inspector-general declared him violent and problematic and the author of several false reports. Unsurprisingly, he was severely reprimanded for rudeness and inappropriate conduct. Moreover, the deputy prefect demanded that he be transferred to another jurisdiction.[133] Similarly, Said Benider in Bône faced sanctions for insubordination in 1948, despite being married to a French woman, having been awarded the Croix de Guerre and the police medal of honor, and deemed the perfect *commissaire* in his reviews when promoted to *2e classe*. Benider had objected to his Muslim police officers being used to move furniture, paint the station, and plunge toilets rather than fighting crime, bemoaning the lack of supplies and medicine due to budgetary constraints. The chief responded with a profane xenophobic tirade, accusing the *commissaire* of being part of a "dirty race" and demanding that he immediately move elsewhere. The prefect accused Benider of lacking discipline and promptly transferred him to the tiny precinct of Khroub, refraining from sending him before the disciplinary council only because he was a "good Arab" and loyal to France.[134]

More often than not, the Arabs and Kabyles accused were charged with nationalist sympathies, particularly in the post-1945 era, as the PPA/MTLD emerged as the voice of Algerian separatism. Given the group's mercurial rise, French authorities—including the police—sought to squelch its influence and partisans across Algeria. In April 1947, Philippeville auxiliary gendarme Ramdane Bouzitoure was accused of nationalist sympathies due to the activities of his brother, and claims were made that he consistently insulted French police and administrators. The inspector's memo concluded that "la place de cet élément troublé n'est pas dans le corps d'élite de la Gendarmerie [the place for this disturbed element is not in the elite corps of the Gendarmerie]." His lieutenant-colonel dismissed the allegations following an investigation that revealed them to be completely false. Another auxiliary, Ahmed Zoubir in Tiaret, was forcibly transferred away from Alger "en raison de son attitude vis-à-vis des milieux nationalistes [due to his attitude concerning nationalist milieux]" in October 1948. The message was clear: employment with law enforcement agencies existed at the whim of both superiors and local officials, who resented the idea of Muslims being granted authority—even of the most limited kind.[135]

That racial bias existed within the ranks of police services and the gendarmerie in the colonial setting is hardly newsworthy. Throughout the French Empire, law enforcement reflected the priorities of the metropolitan administration: support for racial hierarchy, a strident rejection of nationalism or anti-imperial sentiment, protection of European settlers and businesses, and a suppression of local religious and cultural norms that did not serve Gallic aims. More surprising were the myriad budgetary constraints and abject refusal to even consider additional hires across the Algerian security matrix. Given the growth of nationalism from the 1920s onward, and the alarm evident in communications from local officials and even prefectorial offices, Europeans fully expected additional security personnel in both town and countryside. Yet, to the dismay of governors and the general public, additional human and material resources arrived only sporadically, and even the most urgent requests were treated as recalcitrant rather than urgently necessary. Similarly, officials in both France and Algeria paid lip service to the notion of Arab and Kabyle recruitment to resolve the problem, and yet settlers and security services alike staunchly rejected the notion of armed Algerians in their midst, even in a professional capacity. Moreover, the very criteria to enter the ranks of police and gendarmerie—examinations, physical fitness levels, education and experience—remained prohibitive to all but a miniscule and select assimilated minority. In any case, given the rampant xenophobia among Europeans in constabulary and army, from the prevalence of abusive behavior and pro-settler and Fascist politics to the clear double standards for promotion and discipline, it is unlikely that many would have found the prospect of such employment attractive. Relegated to menial work by European superiors, their authority proved illusory, consisting solely of repressing fellow Arabs and Kabyles to avoid the appearance of French impropriety toward the local population. However, cavalier attitudes toward Algerian discontent and the lackadaisical official response to gaping holes in the security apparatus opened the door to mass action against colonialism. Always a problem across North Africa, the coming of the Great War transformed banditry from an economic and religious phenomenon into a widespread anti-French revolt, binding together nationalism and criminality for the first time.

Chapter 2

An Anticolonial Crime Wave?

Policing Banditry in the Constantinois

In August 1915, the deputy prefect in Guelma, in the department of Constantine, sent his superiors a memo and attached report expressing frustration with the lack of results in hunting down local bandit gangs led by Younes Bennour and Khader Khellil, active in the *commune mixte* (mixed commune) of Souk-Ahras. Under his authority, gendarmes and guards carried out extensive searches in *mechtas* (tent camps) across the region, and they uncovered evidence of bandits staying in certain dwellings, yet never the suspects themselves. Frequent visits always yielded the same results, and surprisingly, not a single weapon (knife or firearm) was found in any habitation—even traditional Kabyle blades were absent. Surveillance proved no more successful, and locals simply refused to cooperate, despite clear evidence that many knew the bandits in question. Even the imposition of *surveillance spéciale* (exceptional surveillance), the forced removal of family members and friends to distant communes, provided no intelligence. In desperation at the lack of results obtained by six hundred Zouaves, sixty Spahis, and European law enforcement, the deputy prefect asked for permission to offer bonuses of 500 francs to any local who brought the offenders to justice, dead or alive.[1]

This was not an isolated case; in fact, it was the norm. From 1914 to 1918, the department of Constantine, and particularly the rural communes in Kabylia, experienced a sudden resurgence of banditry. Due to its mountainous and forested topography, the Aurès was the scene of anxiety and tension, exacerbated by the fact that most *malfaiteurs* (bandits) had evaded conscription during the Great War or deserted outright.[2] In almost every case, gangs received assistance from family members or neighboring communities and further benefited from harsh or impassable terrain in heavily forested and mountainous regions. Cooperation from sympathetic or intimidated locals, despite the threat of imprisonment or removal, combined with impenetrable surroundings to stymie official efforts to arrest or execute criminals or deserters. Moreover, police and military opinions on bandits changed during wartime. Previously perceived as either religious fanatics spurred on by radical Islam or merely criminals motivated to commit robbery by economic conditions—bad harvests or rampant poverty, for example—an unprecedented wave of banditry beginning in 1914 convinced colonial authorities that the new *malfaiteurs* evinced political motives, attempting to strike a blow against the French presence in Algeria, particularly in the Constantinois, where deserters fled press gang–style recruiters and government conscription, taking refuge in the mountains and forests.

Police and administrators worried that banditry in Constantine could inspire a full-scale rebellion against imperial rule across the countryside, but expressed the belief that the gangs contained a few deserters and petty criminals who would ultimately be brought to justice by superior French police and armed forces. However, as Emmanuel Blanchard and Joël Glasman point out, colonial police and administrative records tend to be euphemistic and prone to exaggeration, at once bureaucratic in tone and supporting brutal violence in order to bolster imperial rule.[3] Terms that were standard parlance in the metropole—police, order, crime, justice—took on a completely different meaning in Algeria. Moreover, Bradley Camp Davis observes that "for communities far from centres of political power, bandits (or, abstractly, banditry) signify naked force.... They connect the exclusionary logic of imperial projects to cultures of violence." As a threat to the state monopoly on the use of force, and a disruption to the "legal" framework of imperial domination, in the Algerian setting, such individuals or groups became targets for elimination.[4]

Furthermore, banditry represented more than a simple rejection of fighting in the trenches or working in a munitions factory in Europe, for the wartime brigands were not the *hors-la-loi* (outlaws) of previous decades. Although they used many of the same tactics as their predecessors (robbery, assault, looting, even murder), these actions took on an added significance from 1914 to 1918. Wartime banditry also appeared to be explicitly political, eschewing the rationale of prewar inhabitants who engaged in criminality for reasons of subsistence. The perpetrators were now armed deserters (soldiers who fled an army base rather than fight in the trenches) and *insoumis* (conscripts who refused to report for duty) rather than disenchanted locals, and they possessed rifles and ammunition stolen from the camps they fled.[5] Given the cultural and economic stultification engendered by French imperialism, bandits were no longer petty criminals or religious rebels: they directly engaged the colonial apparatus and were perceived by the population as powerful figures who struck a blow against repression and exploitation, and thus precursors to the nationalist movement of the interwar era.[6] Neither were they traditional Algerian *bandits d'honneur*, seeking to avenge a wrong done to themselves or their family. Yet they were not what Eric Hobsbawm termed "social bandits" either—peasant outlaws motivated by economic crisis, lacking a political program but eager to punish the state due to their poverty.[7] Rather, their refusal to accept army service represented a rejection of the demands of the colonial system and their subordinate position within it. Police and gendarmes, administrators and mayors were acutely aware that, as Raphaëlle Branche notes, "toute crise est en effet un moment de mise à l'épreuve du système colonial [every crisis is, in effect, a stress test for the colonial system]."[8]

Thus, despite the confident tone displayed in official correspondence, law enforcement officials unleashed a massive counterinsurgency operation, designed to simultaneously eradicate banditry in the region by any means necessary, while criminalizing political dissent, no matter how minimal. Fearful that Muslims viewed the Great War as an opportunity to end imperial rule, given the lack of military presence in Algeria, the authorities ramped up surveillance efforts, enforced strict censorship of Arab-language publications and soldiers' mail, and brutally repressed any signs of revolt, particularly a wave of outlaw activity in the Constantinois.[9] The colonial authorities understood only too well their inability to influence Algerians and their communities, and their failure to penetrate rural *duwars* (tent enclaves) and *mechtas*. They witnessed only what James C. Scott terms the "public transcript," a performance designed to placate the colonizer, and were not privy to the "hidden transcript" of private opinions that circulated in local communities through everything from humor to Arabic-language conversation.[10]

French Official Fictions and the Realities of Nineteenth-Century Banditry

Bandits had existed in Algeria for centuries and operated with impunity in many regions. Yet in the late nineteenth century, despite the appearance of unrest at various times throughout the area, none of the bands evinced openly political aims. Instead, they engaged in local risings, petty crime, and interfactional rivalry.[11] Of far greater import to French authorities were insurrections, which principally involved an individual who pronounced himself a holy warrior and urged tribes to attack their neighbors and/or French authorities in the name of Islam, usually under false pretenses. Regular features of Algerian life prior to, during, and after the French conquest, primarily in the Sahara region, they tended to combine religious dissent with anger at deteriorating economic conditions—trade, harvests, or even environmental devastation. Together, these factors produced a series of disturbances, most notably the 1849 Bu Ziyan rising, which represents the culmination of such activity in El-Arrouch and Touggourt, and a major 1861 rebellion involving the Ouled Naïl tribe at Djelfa, north of Lagaout.[12] Yet, if they carried the potential to unleash large-scale popular dissent, none of these insurrections actually threatened the French presence in Algeria, and troops succeeded in suppressing all manifestations of dissent, often through spectacular violence and property destruction. As a result, most were summarily ignored by the authorities post factum, seen as merely the cost of doing business in a territory prone to periodic eruptions of Islamic "backwardness" or insecurity produced by bad harvests and European land seizures.

All of that abruptly changed in 1871 due to a massive revolt across Kabylia that required a concerted alliance between settlers and soldiers to contain. The uprising began on 14 March and gradually broadened throughout the department of Constantine, following an appeal by a local Ouled and senior religious figures to wage a holy war against the French infidels. Previously a staunch ally of France in Algeria, El-Hadj Mohammed El-Muqrani objected to civilian rule, which portended bankruptcy and land seizures for Arabs and Kabyles, while talk of Islamic purification appealed to tribesmen. Although the response to the call to rebellion fell short of a full-blown rising, 150,000 men nevertheless agreed to fight on behalf of the Muqrani family and the predominant Rahmania Sufi brotherhood, holding out until June 1872, when the army and its settler allies crushed the remaining opposition at the cost of two thousand lives. A wave of punishment followed, with leaders and followers executed, interned, and exiled and 2.639 million hectares of land expropriated, while the total fines levied on the inhabitants of Greater Kabylia surpassed 36 million francs.[13] Previously somewhat passive, officials in Paris and Alger clearly realized the threat to Gallic control posed by large-scale rebellions, and such incidents became their preliminary focus, pushing aside concerns about bandit activity in the 1870s and 1880s in places like Kabylia.

This logic proceeded from the fact that Kabylia continued as the epicenter of revolt following the Muqrani campaign, particularly in southern regions bordering the Sahara beginning in April 1876, when a recently disgraced and imprisoned ex-*cheikh* (sheikh), Mohamed Yahia of Biskra, partnered with sympathetic local notables and presented himself as a *chérif* (noble) and attracted a following among several local tribes, including the prominent Bou Azid clan. He took advantage of a political vacuum after the death or imprisonment of local notables following the 1871 insurrection, which left the Ben Ganah tribe firmly in control of the region, yet beholden to the colonizer. By mid-decade the Bou Azid, a sizeable religious warrior tribe, rejected this arrangement under Yahia's influence, deepened by family connections with members and a partnership with a local dervish preaching holy war against the pro-French infidels. Other resentful tribes quickly joined a full-tilt revolt.[14]

Loyalist nobles and the local *caïd* (tribal leader) teamed with French troops in suppressing the rebellion with ruthless efficiency. A reporter for *Le Morbacher* noted that the government seized territory from all pro-Yahia owners in the El Amri oasis and Foughela in southern Constantine, excepting only those who fought with Gallic soldiers or had been absent on business.[15] Those deemed guilty were uprooted and moved to Mascara with their families (a total of 399 men, women, and children), and the state levied 194,000 francs in fines against the Bou Azid for "war taxes," representing the cost to the French army of suppressing the rebellion, along with an additional 45,000-franc penalty for the weapons used. Leaders also faced a trial before the *conseil de guerre* (war council), with punishments ranging from banishment to internment; many plotters had either died in battle or faced summary execution.[16] In the aftermath, officials blamed both the hot desert climate and "backward" religious fanaticism for the violence; marabouts and an Islamic oligarchy dominated the area, and they unanimously rejected Christian authority. Although the general in charge of the region assailed the settler press for abusing Arabs and Kabyles and recommended treating them as "children of France," he demanded a military solution to finish the conquest of the southern regions, with all "Muslim fanatics" forcibly removed. However, given the ease with which the army had crushed the rebellion and the lack of participation beyond the oases, officials expressed far less concern than during the Kabyle insurrection. Most perceived only unfortunate exceptions to otherwise orderly rule, while the deportations and imprisonments effectively pacified Biskra.[17]

A similar situation occurred only years later in Tébessa, along the Tunisian border on the opposite side of the department of Constantine. The root of tribal dissent was similar, buoyed by Mohammed Abderahmane, a notable posing as a *mahdi* (holy warrior and preacher), who assailed the French as infidels. Various communities killed *caïds* and attacked troops in Rebaa in early June 1879, murdering dozens before a senior officer arrived to restore order in the region, as the rebellion spread throughout the Biskra region and threatened the regional center of Khenchela. Several companies of Spahis working with cavaliers and goums together won back the territory using artillery and cavalry to outgun the opponents. Soldiers razed and burned large villages, including Hammam, and despite entreaties by a loyal *caïd* to the sergeant, others hunted down and killed tribesmen fleeing into the Sahara, where those who eluded patrols perished of thirst and starvation. Multiple suspects who surrendered were placed under arrest, including local leaders who participated in the insurrection, while Abderahmane fled to the village of El Habel under the protection of the powerful Bou Sliman family.[18] Prisoners became hostages to force his surrender—a common tactic in such cases—and many of the 188 detainees died of illness in cramped quarters; only in August did the remainder obtain release. A year later, the *conseil de guerre* once again tried the leaders of the rebellion (including Abderahmane) in June 1880, sentencing fourteen to death and thirty-one others to hard labor and prison.[19] The rebellious tribes received massive fines of hundreds of thousands of francs and had hundreds of firearms seized by the authorities.[20]

In a postmortem of the events, the general in charge of the counterinsurrection echoed a familiar refrain, blaming an innate "hatred of the Christian," a supposed constant in Algerian life. French officials had been fooled by the suppression of the 1871 rebels into thinking that the matter had been definitively settled, but they misunderstood the trigger for such events: bad harvests and dry weather, which increased volatility and transformed religious belief into holy war. Starving locals became easy targets for "fanaticism" in places like the Aurès, already unruly at the best of times. Hence, Islam and "le fanatisme et les sentiments de haine que tout bon musulman entretien dans son coeur [the zealotry and hatred that every Muslim keeps in his heart]" represented a clear threat to French domination, and only extreme vigilance could preserve the colonial project.[21] However, the officer noted that the noncooperation of the majority of local tribes was a major cause of the insurrection's failure, and others de-emphasized religious extremism in favor of financial exploitation and the expropriation of lands. A local official observed that the tribes owed massive debts to banks that purposely issued loans that could never be repaid, allowing the seizure of land and livestock, which further eroded Algerian farm ownership and contributed to a European agricultural monopoly.[22] For their part, the press echoed the conclusions of the official investigative commission, demanding an increased official presence in Kabyle territory. If locals were naturally rebellious and prone to the occasional Islamic insurrection, traditional tribal authorities and *caïds* were insufficient to keep the peace. Only the constant presence of French troops and officials sufficed to guarantee the maintenance of order.[23]

The contradictory explanations offered by officers, officials, and journalists should have provoked an examination of the complexity of Algerian attitudes toward the French presence in Algeria, echoing the conclusions of historians like Benjamin Brower and Jennifer Sessions concerning the "multiplicity of actors and relations of force" that propelled colonial violence, and particularly the perils of ignoring the "cultural and political logics embedded within violent actions."[24] French policies, settler attitudes, and traditional grievances, problems, and tensions within Algerian society all equally contributed to rebellions, while things as banal as the weather and droughts became a major factor. Yet the colonial administration possessed no such nuance, and thus officials and officers tended to reduce outbreaks of violence to Islamic fanaticism, primitive tribesmen, and bad harvests. As such, they showed little genuine concern once the military had quickly restored order, and if anything viewed the unrest as a reflection of Kabylia itself—ungovernable at the best of times, but far from the locus of Algerian power. Although insurrectionary activity elicited an official response and brutal military retaliation, such revolts were easily contained, never spreading quickly to heavily populated areas on the coast or in the Tell, or threatening French colonial claims in Algeria. Administrators and officers often seemed more annoyed than nervous.

The established pattern continued with each subsequent local crisis or revolt. Thus, the 1901 Margueritte affair became a cause célèbre throughout France and Algeria, not least because settlers in that tiny village in the Zaccar Mountains were not merely attacked but forced to convert to Islam by armed Arabs. Government and public brushed aside notions of an anticolonial rationale and instead followed the reasoning of Alphonse Masselot, the general secretary for indigenous affairs in the department of Alger, reducing the highly complex events to yet another example of religious fanaticism. They summarily ignored the existence of serious differences between settlers and locals over a variety of issues, from land seizures to loan payments, despite being reported by the administrator in Oued Mariel, the site of the rebellion. All of this was secondary to age-old European views of Islam and its practitioners.[25] The same pattern emerged in French reactions to banditry, which by the 1880s became a far greater concern among government personnel in all three departments. Instead of instigating tribal revolt, gangs of *malfaiteurs* now took advantage of the remote wilderness and mountainous terrain in places like Kabylia to foil attempts at capture and arrest by police and gendarmes, having escaped prisons or simply attempting to make a living through crime due to harsh economic conditions and bad harvests. Given the status gained by bandits through effectively outwitting the authorities, the fact that they operated in more populous areas with European settlers nearby, and the potential for recruitment into existing groups or copycat efforts in neighboring locales, administrators and prefects, police chiefs and gendarme and army officers, and even the governor general were actively involved in chasing them.

The first post-Muqrani case of large-scale banditry emerged in mid-1875 outside the town of Jemmapes, northeast of Constantine, where the Bouguerra gang operated with impunity, engaging in armed robbery and murder for two years following their leader's evasion of armed gendarmes after being sentenced to two years at Lambèse prison.[26] The gang terrorized farmers and merchants, stealing cash and livestock and killing both those who refused to cooperate and soldiers sent to capture the leaders. When police brought his wife in for questioning in March 1876, Bouguerra shot a Spahi as the man relieved himself outside the camp.[27] Although they managed to arrest certain members of his group, constant surveillance, house searches, and sweeps of the surrounding area yielded no trace of the key figures. Units of the Police judiciaire, Chasseurs d'Afrique, and Spahis arrived throughout 1876, but they made little progress, employing informants and dressing up as locals during patrols in a vain effort to trap the perpetrators.[28] Despite the arrests of friends and family and the removal of dwellings near the wilderness, the inhabitants of various *duwars* fed and supplied the gang, which melted back into the nearby forests and mountains afterward, making tracking extremely difficult.[29] The governor general reported that inhabitants who did not enjoy friendly relations with Bouguerra were terrified as the gang remained at large throughout 1876 and 1877, defying a growing number of police, gendarmes, and soldiers and continuing to kill and rob without restraint, leading frustrated pro-French voices to berate "Berber capriciousness."[30] However, it became apparent that administrative ineptitude and inaction was equally responsible for the failure to locate and arrest the bandits. Only in fall 1876 did police seize property from those suspected of assisting the gang, a reversal of the previous policy to solely raze or expropriate land held by the immediate family, placing pressure on acquaintances who clearly provided everything from sustenance to lodgings. Moreover, the prefect permitted the removal of complacent *caïds* and *chérifs* who had turned a blind eye to the actions of their neighbors. Most importantly, in October 1877 frustrated officials finally offered a substantial reward for the arrest or killing of Bouguerra and introduced cavaliers from outside of the region without tribal loyalties, leading to his capture mere weeks later in a *mechta* while dining with his brothers.[31]

The difficulties experienced by officials and police or soldiers hounding Bouguerra persisted from 1871 across Kabylia, as authorities chased a variety of *malfaiteurs* across *communes mixtes* in the Aurès. Yet, each time, a similar set of circumstances arose from the impossibility of effectively patrolling over 338,000 hectares of densely forested and mountainous terrain with almost three hundred thousand inhabitants. It was relatively easy for armed forces to squelch full-blown rebellions in more densely populated areas, given their superiority in firepower and technological capacity. However, in Kabylia, individual bandits and their gangs received assistance from admiring or coerced locals, effectively used the terrain to their advantage to elude police and gendarmes, and became folk heroes to Kabyles, who possessed a long-standing suspicion of authority.[32] All of these problems coalesced during a prolonged attempt to capture the most notorious bandit of the late nineteenth century, Arezki-el-Bachir, an ex-rural policeman who turned to crime in 1887 when he masterminded the theft of 30,000 francs from the safe in a European villa. He subsequently joined forces with a local outlaw band, engaging in a prolonged campaign of murder and robbery, controlling rural roads and killing enemies. A favored tactic was kidnapping wives and daughters of local tribesmen and holding them for ransom. By 1893 he organized cooperation among the various bandits in Kabylia, resulting in spectacular attacks against villages in the area.

The administration initially responded by sending troops into the region, yet local goums and cavaliers communicated with the bandits about police tactics, often because they received death threats, for while soldiers came from other communes, guards lived in Kabylia and thus they and their families were vulnerable to such intimidation. As usual, locals also assisted the Arezki gang, mocking and threatening gendarmes, providing cash, food, and supplies, and tipping off the targets when police arrived for an operation in a community. Demands for additional soldiers and reward money followed, in the belief that the Bouguerra scenario could easily be repeated for the right sum. Nonetheless, only five bandits were found and killed, a number termed "unacceptable" by the prefect, and attacks against villages and highway robberies continued unabated, which only fueled locals' perceptions of Arezki's invincibility. Moreover, he began to exploit the old insurrectionary trope of Islamic rebellion, proclaiming himself a prophet and stoking the "fanaticism" of tribesmen. By mid-1893, officials responded with requests for a massive troop complement of 250 men, including mobile teams and platoons headquartered in *duwars* to prevent locals from interacting with the bandits. In addition, an extensive intelligence service, with funds at their disposal for informants, would fine any villager found guilting of aiding and abetting. Unlike in the Bouguerra case, none of this produced immediate success, and soldiers were particularly hindered by torrential rains and major snowfalls.

However, gradually, a number of gang members arrived in *duwars* looking for food and supplies, only to be captured or shot by locals seeking to collect increasingly tantalizing reward money. Surveillance networks provided effective intelligence too, leading to further arrests by gendarmes and soldiers, with tents and cafés searched on a regular basis. Soldiers also used more coercive means to force locals to cooperate. These included the imposition of *surveillance spéciale*, the forced removal of relatives of bandits or villagers suspected of helping them to far-flung communes away from the Aurès. Various figures also leveled accusations of abuse, including violent interrogations and property destruction, which according to the prefect were necessary evils in order to ensure results. Matters became so heavy-handed that soldiers erected a cordon sanitaire around an entire village until the required information was provided, leading the deputy prefect to issue a decree in mid-December against the wanton destruction of tents and the abuse of villagers. By that time, daily arrests netted Arezki's lieutenants, and the leader himself was caught on 24 December and paraded in a public spectacle of French power through a convoy to the local prison.[33]

Much like the insurrections of the 1870s, both the administration and the press, which at the height of the crisis had spoken openly about a repeat of the Kabyle revolt, abruptly reversed course once the bandits were caught. Previously concerned about an epidemic of banditry, their worries dissipated once the military restored order. Moreover, although Arezki did not act as a holy warrior but rather as a highway robber, Bouguerra was a prison escapee, and the authorities continued to invoke Islam and to ignore the complex reality at work, including the anger over settler land seizures that fueled the folk hero status enjoyed by the *malfaiteurs* and the desire to evade the misery of colonial prisons.[34] Instead, they once again blamed religious fanatics for attempting to stir up the populace, and anyone in a *burnous* (burnoose) represented a potential menace. Administrators and jurists were more circumspect, but only in nonviolent, quotidian cases such as *bechara* (cattle theft for ransom), motivated exclusively by droughts or poor harvests rather than Islamic teachings or anticolonial sentiment. In any case, most bandits did not belong to large gangs engaged in robbery and murder against fellow Muslims or European settlers, and thus their actions became a purely legal formality. Police and prefects evinced far greater concern with urban criminality; vagrancy, public intoxication, or fraud rated serious attention, along with petty theft and indecency. A crackdown ensued, spearheaded by Prefect Charles Lutaud in imitation of Paris chief of police Louis Lépine, targeting the Alger casbah and utilizing racist discourse that came naturally in an era dominated by antisemitic notables like mayor Max Régis and street violence against Jews and political opponents.[35]

Bandit Gangs and Violent Crime, 1914–1918

With the coming of the Great War, officials could no longer afford to ignore banditry, which increasingly targeted the colonial enterprise in toto, rather than cattle theft or economic relief. Moreover, the problem increasingly twinned with a fight against conscription, as Arabs and Kabyles rejected the notion of armed service—and death, after 1914—to defend a country that inspired little loyalty, given its abuse of the North African population. Fleeing armed service was certainly not a new trend after 1900; evaders had long sought refuge from the French authorities in the mountains and forests of Kabylia, with banditry becoming an alternative to armed service. From 1830, Algerian soldiers served with distinction in the French army, even in the *métropole* during the Franco-Prussian War. Specifically colonial units such as the Zouaves, Spahis, Chasseurs d'Afrique, and Tirailleurs sénégalais kept order in various Algerian locales. Although senior officers were always French, a certain number of Muslims received promotion to junior ranks (the *lieutenants indigènes*), and entire families were recruited from Kabylia and the Tell (for the army regiments) and the Hautes Plaines and tent regions (for the Spahis, which proved particularly attractive to the sons of the elite). Local goums were also staffed exclusively by Arabs and Berbers. This recruitment pattern largely reflected the so-called Kabyle myth, wherein French commentators believed that Berbers were more talented and intelligent than Arabs and eschewed Islam in favor of western-style mores.[36] Those who rejected armed service either fled from recruitment or deserted their units, but they were not a central preoccupation for either the military or civilian authorities. However, in 1905, the insufficiency of the incoming class of North African soldiers, mainly the result of a reduction in benefits for indigenous troops, led to an increase in the term of service from one to two years. Necessity trumped regional preference, and all non-European candidates were accepted regardless of background. In 1912, a combination of plummeting recruitment (due to a reduction in benefits to volunteers) and German belligerence in the region, evinced during the Second Moroccan Crisis, led the government to adopt conscription and offer large bonus payments to attract recruits.[37] Previously viewed as a nuisance, evasion and desertion became a criminal offense and severely punished by colonial officials, resulting in prison terms and hefty fines.

The situation worsened measurably with the coming of the Great War. Controlling a global empire second only to Great Britain's, the French army did not hesitate to employ colonial human and material resources in the struggle against Germany. Metropolitan authorities expected that subjects would pay the "blood tax" in exchange for the French civilizing mission and the promise of eventual assimilation, and over five hundred thousand imperial denizens served on the front lines. Hailing from Indochina, West Africa, Madagascar, and North Africa, they were seen as cannon fodder by the high command, sparing white soldiers from the certain death that accompanied large-scale offensives on the western front. As one officer noted, the use of colonial troops would permit France to "economize, in future offensive actions, the blood, more and more precious, of our [white] soldiers." Unlike British officials, who displayed serious reservations about arming the colonized against a white enemy and primarily confined Indian troops to the Middle Eastern theater, French officers evinced no such concerns, throwing imperial soldiers into the fray from the Battle of the Marne in 1914 onward. Considered a martial race of courageous and expert warriors, Algerians were deployed under Gallic commanding officers and alongside European counterparts assigned to specialized tasks (machine-gunnery, cannons, telephony) that required skills thought to be beyond the capability of the "inferior" colonized. Hundreds of thousands from across the empire, including 78,556 Algerians, were drafted as laborers in metropolitan factories, charged with providing the munitions and material necessary for modern warfare. This placed a tremendous burden on Algeria, bereft of a substantial portion of the male population, and the threat of unrest and starvation (due to a lack of agrarian labor), along with German and Ottoman anti-French propaganda campaigns, prompted the governor general to issue stern warnings against potential disturbances or anticolonial activity.[38]

Yet the difficulties persisted, not least because of blatant corruption as recruiters desperately attempted to fill quotas and *caïds* and local notables often refused to hand over candidates. Moreover, the elite paid cash to replacements throughout the war, leaving the poor and unfit to serve. Once war was declared, the colonial administration instituted a lottery system to address accusations of unfairness but could do little to combat dishonesty and manipulation in the recruitment process. By fall 1914, desertions and outright refusals to report became common throughout the colony, and particularly in the Constantinois, where escapees were aided by the topography: high plains, voluminous mountain ranges, and lush forests whose pathways were well known to local denizens but not the authorities. Within months, as news filtered back about heavy casualties at the front, press-gang tactics were increasingly used to fill extremely high quotas—tens of thousands of soldiers at five francs per head, on top of the thousands of workers sent to French munitions factories.[39] Following the Battle of Artois in December 1914 to January 1915, where Algerian soldiers led the charge and died by the thousands, the need for recruitment became acute, worsened by local perceptions of the conflict as a war of attrition, with no end in sight. Worse still, official propaganda campaigns backfired; one emphasized that "there is no battle in which our Tirailleurs have not participated, not one assault on a trench in which they are not found in the first rank."[40]

As a result, from October 1914 onward, recruitment drives unleashed riots and violence that at once rejected conscription in an imperial army and lashed out at the colonial system that leveled such demands in the first place. Following earlier noncooperation in the department of Oran, during a drive that month in Perrégaux, commanders of the Brigade de cheval were so concerned that they sent two platoons of Chasseurs and heavily armed gendarmes to ensure a smooth operation. They seized five notables, to be arrested and jailed if the conscripts did not arrive. Despite these precautions, a pitched battle ensued, with rocks and gunshots volleyed at the troops, forcing them to withdraw and only increasing Algerian anger. The same reaction greeted soldiers in neighboring Mascara, with tribesmen fighting with French gendarmes and troops, while five hundred mothers prevented conscripts from arriving at the recruitment center, and marabouts led crowds in shooting at officials and pelting them with rocks. When the cavalry attempted to intervene, two of them were beheaded. Locals thus became convinced that fighting in the Great War constituted a death sentence, and recruiters were greeted with rioting. They also loudly berated the "infidel empire," and the deputy prefect reported that rumors of German victories and a pledge by the Kaiser to restore Algeria to Algerians provided the spark, which had gone unnoticed by local officials and police, who received stern reprimands for their ignorance. Although reports continued to describe Arabs and Kabyles as "idiots" susceptible to pernicious influences (especially religious), troops crushed the violence, and rioters received massive fines, while for the first time, officials openly acknowledged an anticolonial bent.[41]

The disturbances spread quickly to neighboring departments, with police in Alger and administrators from the surrounding areas complaining throughout 1915 about deserters perpetrating violence in towns and cities. Riots also continued to plague conscription centers and drives; as late as October 1916, the deputy administrator of Bordj-Bou-Arréridj in Constantine reported mass refusal to work in the metropole as "volunteer workers" unleashed violence, led by "agents hostile to the [colonial] administration" who convinced the Muslim population of French intentions to seize all males aged twenty to forty-five. Similar trouble greeted conscription officers in Barika and MacMahon in the coming months, and unsurprisingly parents petitioned openly that November against the departure of the class of 1917, while officials demanded the presence of a small squadron to ensure order on the departure date.[42] The metropolitan response was total conscription: all Algerians born prior to 1890 were to serve in the army or munitions factories. The authorities were so desperate that they eventually began to siphon troops assigned to protect North Africa into frontline duty in France. Yet there was little they could do to stop the flight: desertions ballooned from 237 in 1914 to 1,138 in 1916, and the conscription order created a full-scale rebellion in places like the Aurès, where entire tribes fled to the forest rather than submit to the French army.[43]

Whereas *insoumis* simply fled their *mechta*, deserters escaped from training camps and thus were armed with rifles and pistols they took with them. This was so prevalent that gendarmes and military police often faced a barrage of gunfire when attempting to arrest the missing conscripts. Some were brazenly shot and killed in broad daylight, as a warning to give the area a wide berth. To make matters worse, deserters joined up with prison escapees (violent offenders who also tended to carry weapons), and they came together in bandit gangs, sometimes with the participation of thieves operating in forests and hills throughout the Constantinois.[44] As a result, smaller criminal formations became both larger and better armed, and by 1915 permeated the department. In Sidi-Aïch and Akbou, the Kezzouli brothers held sway with a substantial bounty on their heads, along with the Lahlou gang, a group of deserters who engaged in a campaign of terror across the region, including seven murders from 1916 to 1918 and the attempted assassination outside Azazga of a *caïd* who had defied the band and whose goums and cavaliers (and European gendarmes) were marked for death. In the *commune mixte* of La Calle, the Younès and Rouchi gangs attracted dozens of deserters, while in Oued Marsa, a smaller gang run by deserter Berrane Aissa and the Amar brothers committed violent attacks, including murder. It was so well armed that it drew a plethora of soldiers to the region. In many cases, more experienced criminal leaders eventually split off from the mass of deserters, who were seen as a liability—careless, imprudent, and willing to give up their fellow bandits if caught to avoid jail time or worse from the *conseil de guerre*, the military tribunal that judged cases involving soldiers and frequently condemned them to hard labor or the death penalty.[45] This made the capture and detention of the leadership extraordinarily difficult, a task rendered far more troublesome by the trend of youth imitating the bandits in communities like Tarf and Blandon. Of course, there were also criminal gangs at work throughout Algeria from 1914 to 1918, thieves and brigands who forged alliances with deserters in order to form ever-larger organizations. Bandit chief Omar Guendouzi escaped from prison in September 1916 and connected with others who fled French justice, along with deserters and criminals already active in the Tizi-Ouzou region, including prominent figures such as Amar ben Lounés and Said Raich. In subsequent years, the gang engaged in a veritable campaign of terror against the local population, killing fifteen witnesses, robbing with impunity, and murdering anyone suspected of talking with police, while the Sûreté failed to ascertain their whereabouts.[46]

On the surface, and particularly considering the participation of thieves in certain gangs, the resulting crime sprees were technically simple matters for criminal investigation, no different from centuries-old bandit traditions in Algeria. Gangs frequently robbed merchants returning from the local market at gunpoint, stopping vehicles on main highways and taking cash or clothing from both Europeans and Algerians, or stole livestock and food from local farms belonging to both Algerians and Europeans. Most of the time, the motive was simple sustenance, as bandits required everything from blankets to *burnous* and could not obtain them in any other manner. One gang in Sidi-Aïch stole shoes and clothing, and in Lamy near Bône brigands took everything from pocket watches and guns to food and livestock. They attacked up to a dozen times a month in a given *duwar* or *mechta*, and administrators frequently declared a road or region dangerous as a result.[47] On 3 December 1914, eight well-armed bandits in the Soummam stopped six Muslim merchants from the village of Louta on the highway and threatened to kill them if they did not immediately hand over their money and merchandise. If they encountered resistance, either an attempt to flee the scene or a refusal to hand over money and goods, the aggressors often shot or stabbed one of their victims.

Of course, attacks against Europeans elicited the most concern from officials and administrators. The governor general demanded action during a wave of highway robberies in Maadid in October 1917 only when *malfaiteurs* attacked a M. Guidicelli and killed a European farmer; previous attacks and the murder of an *indigène* had elicited calls for guards on roads, but transgressions against Europeans and their property (including the Medjez post office) resulted in the arrival of soldiers and officers to restore order and apprehend the culprits.[48] Naturally, the same proved true for any spate of hijackings that provoked a European response. Writing in the *Dépêche de Constantine* (Constantine Dispatch) in January 1918, Achille Robert bemoaned the replacement of European drivers with Muslims in Sétif, which had allowed bandits access to schedules and departure times, enabling robberies across the region. Authorities responded with highway patrols and the cancellation of night routes, and the governor general subsequently noted the frequency of such attacks in the department. For his part, Robert demanded increased surveillance and regular permit checks on all travelers.[49] As usual, witnesses remained silent, fearing retribution from the gangs against anyone who assisted French law enforcement. Thefts of provisions and home invasions "terrorized" locales like Acif-el-Hammam and Biskra and overwhelmed the already overburdened authorities.

Not infrequently, attempts to loot dwellings led to violence, and the murder of the inhabitants.[50] In one such instance, ten armed bandits shot and killed a woman in the Aïn-Diss *duwar* during the theft of her brother-in-law's livestock. Encountering stiff resistance, the gang engaged in a firefight with the family inside the farmhouse and the victim was caught in the crossfire.[51]

In other instances, thefts had explicitly political overtones, reflecting Algerian anger over their political disenfranchisement and subordinate position in a colonial society. First and foremost, Europeans predominated not only as prefects and administrators but in almost every level of government, civil service, and professional life. Muslims were forced to pay exorbitant taxes, initially through the hated Indigénat and subsequently via a biased system that rewarded Europeans and penalized locals. Budgets were spent almost exclusively on public works, projects, and the bureaucrats who existed to promote settler growth. Many of the latter were appointed through patronage networks inaccessible to Arabs and Kabyles, and the massive salary discrepancy between Algerian and European workers and police, backed by European centers of power like the Délégations financières (Financial Parliament), infuriated Algerians.[52]

At certain times, primarily in the late nineteenth to early twentieth century, protests and denunciations by Muslims and Jews curtailed corruption and favoritism. Yet after 1903, political and economically exploitative behavior returned with a vengeance, buoyed by everything from French illiteracy (enabling Europeans to defraud or cheat Arabs and Kabyles) to access to political favors and capital.[53] With conscription and wartime dislocation only intensifying Algerian anger, it is unsurprising that settlers deemed official (foremen, government employees, et al) became targets, which resulted in acts such as the theft of a mail delivery, assaults on police officers and local guards, and attacks on specifically European targets—sometimes accompanied by death threats against *colons*. Hence in December 1914 a Seddouk postman was robbed and shot twice and his head smashed with a stone, in a far more lethal attack than others perpetrated in the same region at the time. In November 1915, six heavily armed bandits targeted European workers at the Aïn Taha train station near Souk-Ahras, threatening them with death and stealing their blasting powder. Naturally, robberies of European homes were also political in nature, and often included confrontations with the owners, who were threatened with death even if the gang did not successfully loot the dwelling. Such actions sowed panic among *colons* in isolated areas, particularly given the paucity of law enforcement during wartime, and the perpetrators were seldom caught. In the village of Lavasseur, thirty-seven kilometers from Chateaudun-du-Rhumel and guarded by a single cavalier, a few European police, and a small indigenous force, a large number of bandits descended on the community in

AN ANTICOLONIAL CRIME WAVE? 69

January 1917, overwhelming law enforcement and stealing thirty-eight ewes. As the males in the community were absent, serving on the front lines in Europe, the raid sowed panic among the remaining inhabitants (including an old man, ten women, and fourteen children).[54] A far worse fate befell the European population in the Aurès, who had been evacuated from the area due to a crime wave in 1916, only to face pillage and rape at the hands of the Beni-Bouslimane tribe on their return in March 1917, a gang of deserters who rejected both armed service and French imperialism in equal measure.[55] News of these events traveled quickly to neighboring settlements and across the department. In the absence of any real intelligence about bandit gangs, rumors were omnipresent, further fraying settler nerves.[56]

A much more explicit political statement, sabotage, seriously threatened European life and commerce in rural Algeria. Bandits frequently damaged water mains, a particularly dangerous act in regions with little access to potable supplies. Gangs also attacked work sites, cut and stole telegraph wire, and more seriously, lifted explosives from the Beni Himmel mine in 1917. One Sidi-Aïch gang attempted to load them into firearms, with disastrous results: one member dead, another losing four fingers on his left hand, and still another losing two fingers.[57] In each case, surveillance and additional guard posts were immediately authorized to prevent any future theft of company materials. Finally, bandits also attempted to derail trains, frequently resulting in the deaths of passengers. In each case, the chosen targets were tied to the imperial economy or settlements and thus carried extra weight.

The same was true of murders committed by bandit gangs, particularly the killings of Europeans in isolated rural areas, which were designed to instill fear in the *colon* population. To be sure, these were not unique to wartime, and police in all three departments reported violent incidents prior to 1914. In January 1907, for example, thieves committed multiple assaults against both Algerians and Europeans, alarming the mayor when they attacked a European at the Martel farm in La Chiffia.[58] However, the assaults increased in both frequency and malice after the declaration of war. Not content with burglarizing a farm in Duvivier in October 1915, one group systematically fired on the residents and murdered the owner only days after they attempted an armed robbery in Bouhadjar, during which members shot one victim and wounded another. Led by Lakhdar Laid and Maamar Khendi, the band distinguished themselves with a series of similar attacks in 1917 and 1918 "committed . . . in circumstances of exceptional cruelty," in the words of the administrator the *commune mixte* of Edough. The spree culminated in the April 1918 murder of the wife of a *colon* in Colombes and a subsequent home invasion and robbery and assault against a woman whose husband was away serving at the front.[59]

In other cases, not only did the perpetrators attack Europeans, they also explicitly and publicly stated their intention to rid communities of non-Muslims. In Aragonnès, a community outside Sétif, a 25 August 1917 home invasion included both armed robbery and a threat to the victims to leave the area or face severe consequences. Despite declaring the need to rid the area of Europeans, and the clear danger to local property, individuals refused to come forward, fearing reprisal attacks. What these might constitute was made frighteningly clear when the gang subsequently sexually assaulted an Arab mother while she tended to her three children at home.[60] Unsurprisingly, *colons* fled the countryside in droves throughout the war and in its aftermath, renting their land and dwellings to Arabs and Kabyles, which adversely impacted Algerian communities, now lacking buyers for their goods and employment (however menial) on European farms. As late as 1920, newspapers in Alger and Constantine continued to reference wartime banditry and its role in rendering country life unpalatable for settlers, who clearly understood the explicitly anticolonial rationale of the campaigns.[61]

More frequently, the victims were guards, who represented both law enforcement seeking to capture bandits and the imperial authorities who employed them to bolster the colonial order. Attempts to murder Spahis and gendarmes occurred on a regular basis throughout the war, particularly if they played a role in either the pursuit of a gang or the harassment of a local *mechta* or *duwar*. Having arrested Soummam bandit Chérif Otmane for the July 1915 murder of a young woman in Taourirt-Ighil, a rural policeman and three guards were attacked as they attempted to bring the prisoner to the magistrate in nearby El-Kseur. Shot multiple times by Otmane's gang, the policeman managed to reach a nearby guard post and survived the ordeal.[62] Needless to say, collaborators and informants received similar treatment, seen as working with the colonial authorities against local villages and their *insoumis* and deserters. *Caïds* were routinely victimized for acting at the behest of European administrators and recruiters. In Aït Malak and M'Zalla, gangs executed leaders who attempted to present names for conscription to the army, along with notables who assisted them in the task. That no arrests were made only worsened the situation, fueling the notion that bandits had outmuscled the French imperial government.[63] To intimidate police and their operatives, brigands also targeted informants working with the imperial authorities. In October 1915, two Sidi-Aïch men were executed by shots to the eye and nose, coups de grace designed to send a message to fellow villagers tempted to assist the police in tracking down outlaws. The victims had managed to infiltrate the Belkacem Chérif gang, participating in a variety of crimes and then providing information to an officer whom authorities feared would also be a target. In the aftermath, locals were afraid to leave their homes, and the authorities considered a variety of security initiatives, including the removal of all villagers to an undisclosed location for their protection.[64]

Police Actions, Military Reprisals, Executions, and Assassinations

In theory, prior to the Great War, criminal activity—including theft, murder, and sabotage—was dealt with in a routine fashion, whether the victims were European or Algerian. Police or gendarmes investigated the crimes, and in rare cases when gangs overwhelmed local law enforcement, reinforcements could be called in from neighboring communities. However, maintaining imperial order required tactics vastly different from the standard practices, which were often derived from metropolitan experiences. Thus, attacks against European targets were the highest priority, along with assaults against locals that might compromise security, either by instilling respect for the criminals or through exposing the colonizer as weak. In Algeria and throughout the French Empire, investigations were twinned with the maintenance of colonial hegemony, a task shared with urban personnel by the gendarmerie, rural police and village guards, and indigenous auxiliaries. They were assisted in this task by a variety of Arab and Berber employees, from interpreters and scouts to informants and clerks, who rarely appear in the colonial archives and yet were invaluable to the continued French domination of Algeria.[65] Moreover, unlike their metropolitan confreres, the army and police worked closely together in the colonial setting, with the newly formed Sûreté générale (charged with hunting down sedition) and its information bureau (a special branch attached to the Ministry of War and military intelligence) jointly monitoring local developments and preventing revolt. In this pursuit, they commanded indigenous forces of forest or farm guards and village beat cops. Further complicating matters, the police and gendarmerie were expected to issue regular reports to the prefects, governor general, and Ministry of the Interior, yet because they could not speak Arabic, they relied on their Muslim subordinates for all real intelligence, which could easily be manipulated at the behest of local notables.[66]

All these problems became readily apparent during wartime, when the colonial administration and gendarmerie and police officials evinced tremendous concern with the proliferation of bandit activity, noting the acquiescence of locals in feeding and hiding brigands and their staunch refusal to cooperate in the arrest and detention of suspects. Prefects and mayors also reported the lionization of deserters and *insoumis* and the concomitant perception that the French grip on Algeria weakened during wartime. Fearing that banditry unleashed nationalism and anti-Gallic sentiment, the authorities initiated a brutal crackdown across the department, criminalizing dissent and unleashing a campaign of intimidation, harassment, and state-sanctioned murder in order to staunch anticolonialism in rural *duwars*.

Given their inability to directly access the local population due to the language barrier and the clear refusal of relatives and neighbors to divulge the whereabouts of wanted bandits, administrators initially attempted to bribe Algerians, paying cash for information to aid the capture of gang leaders. The payments did convince some Arabs and Kabyles to turn in wanted men, leading to the capture or killing of leaders and gang members from the Constantinois to the casbah in Alger. Initially, these tended to be minimal, often 100 francs, but rose substantially if the case dragged on for months. The authorities often provided gun or café permits in lieu of cash, as these were notoriously difficult to procure for non-Europeans.[67] However, locals were often too intimidated to cooperate with authorities, more afraid of bandits than police or gendarmes, their fears stoked by regular episodes of retaliatory violence against anyone suspected of talking to authorities. Moreover, informants were frequently unreliable, and took advantage of the situation to settle grievances with neighbors. In Bordj-Bou-Arréridj in May 1918, an accusation against Ali Boubaya for highway robbery led to a search of his house by cavaliers, during which the interrogators broke household objects and "terrorized" his wife and daughters. The administrator subsequently admitted that the information had not been correct, and the entire affair was deeply embroiled in local family rivalries, including the complaints against the guards involved in the attempted arrest.[68]

Consequently, in most cases, the French military were dispatched to snuff out the threat. In certain instances, guard posts were deemed a sufficient palliative. Faced with heightened bandit activity throughout 1915, in November, foot patrols and surveillance were increased for villages and highways in the Soummam. Six- to eight-man armed squads were utilized in sensitive areas, primarily those where violent incidents had recently occurred, while in certain locations night patrols provided constant vigilance. Simultaneously, the local press and settlers in Bône-La Calle hurled abuse at officials and "indigenous scoundrels" for allowing crime to predominate throughout the region. In response, the *conseil général* and administrators not only authorized the mobilization of dozens of guards and cavaliers but also convinced the governor general to dispatch 380 soldiers to maintain order in *mechtas* throughout the neighboring *commune mixtes* and on regional roads, while the gendarmerie increased patrols in threatened regions and along the border to prevent the escape of bandits into Tunisia. In this way, local administrators sought to calm the "indigenous masses" while producing a show of force that demonstrated French strength and willpower in the face of rebel "criminals" and their local accomplices.[69] The prefects of Alger and Constantine extended surveillance exercises throughout Kabylia around the clock, in *cafés maures* (Moorish cafés), marketplaces, and places of business, while intelligence concerning bandits was shared with local and regional authorities across Algeria.[70]

Heightened security resulted in a dramatic increase in the responsibility and authority exercised by colonial administrators themselves. Faced with dozens of armed outlaws and agitated locals, mayors and their assistants in small towns and *communes mixtes* controlled the troops employed in the hunt against bandit gangs and wielded legal powers normally enjoyed by prefects. Charged with snuffing out banditry in Kabylia, Deputy Administrator Carayol for the *commune mixte* of Djurdjura organized and led a band of twenty-five to thirty goums, in tandem with police units across the territory, in order to apprehend the Kezzouli brothers. Any local who resisted this official effort, or worse still, aided or harbored a fugitive, would be sent on Carayol's authority to the *conseil de guerre* in Tizi-Ouzou and then incarcerated.[71] In the case of regional outbreaks, prefects took charge, due to their ability to more easily coordinate personnel and troops in their jurisdiction. Faced with a series of attacks in Alger and Constantine, in July 1915 the prefect of Alger (in tandem with his Constantine coeval) led a massive manhunt throughout the affected municipalities and surrounding forests. Local police had been seriously outgunned, culminating in the brazen June murder of a gendarme in Tizi-Ouzou by a bandit from nearby Acif-el-Hammam. Thus, the governor general charged both administrators with overseeing a combined effort of the army, Brigade mobiles, goums, and municipal administrations to capture the deserters.[72]

The number of troops deployed often far outweighed the actual threat. In response to a campaign waged in summer 1915 by approximately thirty bandits in Bouhadjar on the Algerian-Tunisian border, the local administrator arranged for three companies of Zouaves (six hundred men in total) and two platoons of Spahis to blanket the area for one month. The following year, the governor general ordered the entire Eleventh Battalion of Zouaves to Rousched in response to a letter of complaint from Senator Paul Cuttoli protesting the theft of four cows, two attempted burglaries, the sabotage of a water conduit, and a single murder over the course of two years. It was hoped that such a massive presence, including patrols and surveillance around the clock, would flush out the *malfaiteurs* and prevent them from being assisted by friends, neighbors, and relatives.[73] Administrators also frequently requested troops to quell "insubordination," a term used during wartime to connote desertion.

Sidi-Aïch sheltered hundreds of *insoumis*, necessitating dozens of reinforcements, while in Bougie, Zouaves were called in February 1917 after the assassination of a local *caïd*.[74] In certain areas deemed dangerous by commanders, mobile antibandit units were formed, mustering a number of officers with up to two hundred or more troops, specifically targeting mountainous regions or dense forests. This was the case in July 1915 in the Akfadou forest near Haut-Sebaou and Soummam, where bandits engaged in a crime wave that culminated in the brazen public murder of a gendarme, causing prefects to draft soldiers from the army and gendarmerie along with local police into a comprehensive unit.[75]

Once in the field, troops divided into two units. The first initiated searches of any suspect dwelling in a *mechta*, including locales known to house "criminals," which in practice included anyone suspected of anti-French leanings. Other squads went into the forest and/or hills to ambush the bandits or locate their hideouts, a very difficult proposition given the advantage enjoyed by locals who knew the area far better than the newcomers. Worse still, the terrain proved difficult to manage in favorable conditions, and utterly impassable in winter. In February 1915, the Brigade mobile abandoned the hunt for the Boukhasen-Arrighat gang from Tebessa due to snow and treacherous footpaths, giving months of respite to the bandits.[76] Administrators and commanders also complained of troops being withdrawn too quickly. The deputy prefect in Bône wrote bitterly to his superiors in January 1916 that prominent outlaws had evaded capture for precisely this reason. As a result, the military established sixteen guard posts in Edough, Tarf, and La Calle, each with up to thirty troops, including cavalry and Spahis. The area had previously been the scene of dozens of robberies and attacks, but the presence of troops instilled calm and security, while uncooperative villagers were removed from the region and sent to neighboring communities. However, the bandits themselves, the "notorious" Younès and Rouchi gangs, were never captured due to the impenetrability of surrounding forests. Their prestige among the area's non-European inhabitants grew immensely as a result, leading to increased desertions and prison escapes across the region. Thus, on 30 January 1917, a local administrator complained to the prefect about "l'état d'insubordination d'un nombre exceptionnellement considérables de jeunes indigènes [the state of insubordination of a considerably high number of young *indigènes*]," all deserters, forcing the local government to demand a platoon of Zouaves to hunt them down. In Sidi-Aïch, a colleague described the numbers arriving at boot camp as "disturbing," pointing out that bandits regularly attempted to assassinate *caïds* or Algerian agents assisting the colonial authorities in hunting *malfaiteurs*, which drove the local population to support their cause.[77]

Nonetheless, the operations did produce a certain level of success. Many bandits were captured and arrested—most often, prison escapees serving sentences for violent crimes, but in rare instances, an entire posse.[78] In September 1915, a massive manhunt resulted in the arrests of seventeen members of the Bouhadjar gang in La Calle and subsequent trials of deserters before the *conseil de guerre*, which meted out executions and harsh prison sentences for treason. Although few suspects were apprehended, a December 1915 sweep of the Akbou region, and a similar action the following month in Sétif, effectively drove bandits out of both areas. In direct communication with mobile units, local administrators pooled their resources, tracking the gangs day and night. In many cases, outlaws were tried and convicted by French courts, their sentences ranging from a short prison term to a life sentence of hard labor, and in extreme cases, to execution. One large-scale operation in Beni-Salah (Edough, La Calle, and La Séfia) led to numerous convictions at a December 1916 trial in Bône, resulting in two capital punishments and a variety of prison sentences and revocations of *droit de séjour* (right of residence) from five to twenty years.[79] The severity of the repression, along with the number of bandits jailed, effectively terminated outlaw activity in the region.

However, not all prosecutions were so effective. In September 1914, Moula Belkacem, the leader of a Kabyle bandit gang that included numerous deserters from the Tirailleurs, received a mere three-year sentence, while three bandits who robbed a courier and shot a train conductor in Akbou were jailed for one to three years, and ultimately freed on appeal. Similar cases were simply dismissed outright, and the administrator of the Soummam noted wearily in June 1918 that those regions with severe sentencing for banditry experienced a marked drop in criminal activity throughout the war.[80] Faced with such legal uncertainty, he (and many of his colleagues) petitioned for trial by the *conseil de guerre*, which had exclusive jurisdiction over deserters and *insoumis* and was not bound by the criminal code, routinely sentencing offenders to death or life imprisonment.[81]

Given that sentences were frequently lenient, even for the most serious crimes, police and gendarmes often dispensed with the legal system altogether. The authorities simply killed their intended target rather than arresting him, sometimes in a shootout, but on other occasions in more dubious circumstances. Denounced by informants in Le Sefia, the gang leader Mohamed Younès was assassinated during a December 1915 operation, the same month that Ouled Selim head Ali Boukharouba and his chief lieutenant were killed by troops in the mountains. In most such cases, no warning shots were fired, and troops or guards never attempted to arrest the bandits. Younès was lured to a meeting of restitution with a local notable whose livestock he purloined, only to be met by twenty-three soldiers in an ambush and killed by multiple gunshot wounds.[82] Whether in a direct confrontation or an ambuscade, a significant number of bandits confronted by French or Muslim police or gendarmes, were seriously wounded or killed in a variety of locales across the Constantinois.[83]

In most cases, the element of surprise was deemed necessary due to the lack of cooperation of locals, the supposed cowardice of most Algerian leaders and guards, and the well-armed nature of the opposition. Colonial authorities suspected *caïds* and goums of tipping off bandits and even providing money and food to gangs. In La Calle, the administrator demanded the revocation of the Bouhadjar *djemâa* (tribal council) for actively working to prevent officials from successfully capturing bandits by providing them with material assistance and lodging in certain *mechtas*. Similar charges were leveled against *adjoints indigènes* in Bône (for aiding the Boularés-Zidane gang), with the deputy prefect demanding far tougher and more loyal replacements. Guards also functioned as middlemen. In both Duvivier and Edough, for example, forest guards delivered provisions from notables to bandits living openly in *gourbis* in the forest. For their part, even if *caïds* refused material aid, they were perceived to be ruining investigations through inertia, neglecting to act unless threatened with dismissal by their imperial masters.[84]

Moreover, local populations refused to offer any assistance to authorities, leading to concerns that France would seem powerless if immediate disciplinary action was not taken. Brigands were believed to be sheltered with the complicity of neighbors, while parents acted to prevent military recruitment. Troops seeking to capture Abdelouhab Lahlou in January 1918 entered the home of close relatives only to find a crawl space stocked with fresh provisions and firearms. In another case, police discovered that Mohamed Younès had been hiding in plain sight in Ouled Azzaz with the aid of his parents.[85] Locals in Oued-Marsa and Lafayette also helped bandits, who lived openly and received food and provisions in what villagers considered a blow against the hated colonial authorities. Only the capture or execution of gang leaders restored Algerians' cooperation with French authorities and police. When soldiers finally nabbed the hated Rouchi band and shot its leader, other *malfaiteurs* in the Lamy-Duvivier region went into hiding until the troops left. Moreover, locals no longer paid the costs of occupation (food and lodging for soldiers, for example) and guard patrols, which lessened vocal anti-imperial sentiment.[86]

Faced with Algerian obstinance and unwillingness to assist in the search for suspects, not to mention the sheer number of troops in the field and the multitude of operations running at a given time, officials and officers often resorted to abusive behavior. As superiors demanded desperate methods to find and capture increasing numbers of bandits, who were seen as a serious threat to colonization during wartime, searches frequently devolved into violence against family members and property. Addressing concerns evinced by the governor general over allegations that soldiers abused women during a 1916 action in La Calle, the administrator denied the accusation, yet ultimately blamed the inhabitants for any unfortunate conduct or burdensome impositions: "A une situation exceptionnelle il a fallu opposer des mesures exceptionnelles [In an exceptional situation one must take exceptional measures]." Taking this notion to its logical conclusion, he demanded a "concentration camp" for persons assisting bandits, calling it "la seule mésure qui pourrait donner un promt [sic] et efficace résultat [the only measure that can provide a prompt and effective result]." Nonetheless, local inhabitants continued to send petitions, and official pressure on the administrator only intensified.[87] Others took his talk of "exceptional measures" quite literally—in an effort to force relatives of the Kezzouli bandits to talk, soldiers razed their houses to the ground, leaving the prefect to pay compensation and worry that such an overreaction would only encourage anticolonial sentiment.[88]

Faced with such abuses, many Algerians offered armed resistance to European encroachment on their territory, especially attacking police or military recruitment offices. In fall and winter 1914 in various communities, they banded together to block army trucks from departing, pelted administrative buildings with rocks to protest conscription, and physically attacked gendarmes. The most severe anticonscription action occurred in 1916 in the Sud-Constantinois, where rioting engulfed several communities, leading to numerous fatalities and widespread property destruction. The events began on 12 November in the Batna region, whose local tribes had a long history of rebellion, first against the Turks and then the French colonial administration, particularly in the 1871 Kabyle revolt. Various *communes mixtes* had experienced staunch opposition to recruitment drives in 1912, including a near riot in Mac-Mahon, and renewed opposition in the opening stages of the Great War, with one *caïd* bluntly stating that "on peut augmenter les impôts, nous prendre nos biens, mais nous ne donnerons pas nos enfants [you can increase taxes, and take our goods, but we will not hand over our children]." Unsurprisingly, numerous soldiers refused to report, and the situation devolved into open revolt in certain *duwars*, forcing the abandonment of the 1915 recruitment class. The trend accelerated in 1915 to 1916 throughout the region with the announcement of renewed conscription, and the resulting increase in banditry manifested in rising crime rates: theft, kidnapping, and murder in Aïn-Touta, Belèzma, Khenchela, Barika, and the Aurès. To restore order, four hundred troops arrived from Constantine to arrest *insoumis* and deserters and to halt a spate of killings of both *colons* and Muslims, including politicians in Belézma and Aïn-Beïda.[89]

The ensuing riots were a rejection of both military conscription and French colonial hegemony. By September 1916, fathers in local *duwars* refused to allow recruiters to leave with their sons, and desertion quickly spread throughout the Sud-Constantinois region. Repressive measures taken by the French military failed to contain the threat, as too few troops were available to maintain order, and Muslims perceived the authorities as weakened during wartime in any case. The climax came in November in the form of a full-scale insurrection, with armed bands preventing conscripts from departing in villages near Belézma, and the attempted seizure of Bou Meguer by horsemen destroying telephone wires, blocking roads, and demanding an independent republic.[90] Then on 12 November, the Ouled Aout bandit gang killed the *administrateur* of the *commune mixte* of Aïn-Touta (MacMahon) and the *sous-préfet* and then attempted to seize control of the largest town. Rebels pillaged stores, stabbed and beat inhabitants, and torched buildings. The arrival of a team of twenty Zouaves resulted in pitched battles in the streets between the bandits and law enforcement, and news of the events quickly spread to neighboring communities. In Tamarins, Muslims engaged in robbery and arson, killing a forest guard and causing local *caïds* to abandon their posts and flee the jurisdiction. By late afternoon, villagers had blocked roads and ransacked farms across the territory, and Europeans reported fires and detonations in various locales.[91] In the aftermath of the MacMahon riot, the prefect of Constantine and army commanders engaged in extreme repressive measures, including aerial bombardments, *razzias* (destructive incursions) against rebel *mechtas*, and crop destruction. When order was restored, more than one thousand accused were tried in Constantine and Batna and sentenced to imprisonment in open-air prisons, where 143 deaths occurred during winter 1916 to 1917, mostly from typhus. The destruction of area farmland and closure of markets also led to a severe famine.[92]

Moreover, the combination of local noncooperation, the failure to root out bandits in many locations, and the fear that both of these factors contributed to potential rebellion led to the implementation of ever-more draconian measures to restore colonial order. The favored tactic was *surveillance spéciale*, the forced removal of a bandit's family members and their imprisonment in a remote village. Officials justified such acts by pointing to the tremendous rise in violent crime, from murders to sabotage, since the declaration of hostilities, rendering entire districts almost uninhabitable. Additionally, with locals sheltering and aiding bandits, and house searches, patrols, and even the occupations of *mechtas* proving fruitless, actions against friends and family members represented a potentially more successful strategy.[93] This process often involved force, with parents of suspects being taken from their homes by police. In Bougie, the prefect demanded the immediate removal of seven villagers accused of actively assisting a gang of deserters who had committed a string of robberies and murders in Amalou, where the population worked together to prevent their arrest. They were interned in M'Sila, while Zouaves seized all arms in the *mechtas*, closed a popular *café maure*, and recalled all Muslim elected officials, while a new special armed force would be sent to Amalou in order to "make the *indigènes* understand." Once taken, villagers were held under military guard (often in the municipal jail) or deported to another commune, preventing all contact with their former locale, and authorities hoped that this "administrative detention" would force bandits to turn themselves in to the gendarmerie. Although rarely effective, administrators and prefects continued to use *surveillance spéciale* when searches failed and communities were perceived (often wrongly) to be working in concert to foil police investigations.[94] Only in May 1918 did the governor general finally end the practice, arguing that it had been used far too broadly and tended to punish individuals who refused to turn in bandits primarily out of fear rather than sympathy, given the fate of those who acted as informants to police, soldiers, or gendarmes.[95]

In any case, heavy-handed police tactics resulted in serious complaints by Arabs and Berbers to both municipal and regional authorities, and in severe cases, to the governor general's office. This was hardly unique to Algeria, as arbitrary arrest and confinement without regard to judicial process, and beatings administered to suspects, produced voluminous criticism in numerous locales, and particularly in the Syrian Mandate.[96] As in Syria, the Algerian authorities blamed duplicitous locals. When police demolished the *gourbi* belonging to an infantryman whose cousin was the bandit Djaïch Abdallah, authorities greeted his complaint by noting his relative's long rap sheet.[97] In La Calle, the administrator admitted that soldiers regularly harassed inhabitants of certain *duwars* throughout the *commune mixte*, even uprooting them on various occasions, but justified the actions by claiming that the persecution merely responded to the aid given to bandits. Responding to similar abuses in La Calle and Bougie, villagers petitioned the governor general to intervene. In Bougie, popular anger was so acute that a gunfight broke out between two agents and a suspect, during which two children were killed. Rather than express remorse, the deputy prefect blamed a family feud and claimed that the region's Kabyles were all trigger-happy. The administration particularly recoiled at "the reprehensible attitude of soldiers concerning women," who were repeatedly manhandled in the Chiebra *duwar*, although municipal and regional officials continued to use harsh tactics ranging from searches to *surveillance spéciale*. In most cases the governor general accepted his colleagues' official explanations of events, no matter how serious the complaints or the treatment of the *indigènes*.[98]

Post-1918 Violence

Banditry did not cease to exist with the end of hostilities in Europe. Well after November 1918, gangs continued to operate in the Constantinois, harassing Europeans and Algerians alike. It is tempting to link this fact with postwar political, economic, and social realities, which left the population in a dire state, battered by starvation, unemployment, and disappointment. Despite promises of rights and perhaps citizenship in exchange for fighting in the trenches, officials used the old canards of polygamy and attachment to Qur'anic law to nullify the bargain. When Governor General Charles Jonnart tendered a 1919 reform law, it privileged the *évolués*—the literate, educated, and business elite. Although 425,000 Algerian men (43 percent of the adult male population) could vote, they were restricted to a separate electoral college and received no path to naturalization.[99] Added to the severe disappointment was economic disaster, as prices tripled in the conflict's aftermath due to inflation and unemployment rose sharply due to the closure of war materials factories alongside slowdowns elsewhere caused by renewed French production of wartime Algerian substitutes. Moreover, bad harvests in 1919 and 1920 led to the horrifying reality of tens of thousands of Arabs and Kabyles literally starving to death or dying of typhus and similar diseases.[100]

Unsurprisingly, many of the postwar bandits engaged in *bechara*, the theft of livestock which were then ransomed back to the owner, or robbery to feed a growing black market in various towns across the region. Mountainous and forested terrain proved impossible to guard, and police officials demanded the right to issue arms permits to farmers in order to halt the criminals.[101] Food transport remained an issue in the departments of Alger and Constantine due to bad harvests and droughts, and in October 1920 General Deshayes de Bonneval wrote to the prefect concerning security arrangements, including a possible cavalry patrol.[102]

Yet, socioeconomic malaise was not the only cause of the violence, and many inhabitants of the Aurès—the epicenter of banditry—were less affected by economic issues, due to migration to France in search of factory employment, opportunities that increased dramatically due to economic expansion. Restrictions eased in the post-1918 era, and substantial numbers of men took advantage of the new opportunites. In Paris, the number of Algerian workers rose from fewer than 20,000 in 1923 to 70,000 seven years later, while 71,000 came to France in 1924 alone.[103] This trend certainly had consequences in the metropole. First and foremost, it gave rise to the Algerian nationalist movement, which will be discussed in subsequent chapters. It also mitigated some of the economic suffering in Algeria, and many bandits were not acting out of desperation when they continued the wartime pattern of joining gangs that engaged in assaults, murders, and anticolonial activities across the Constantinois. One particularly worrisome trend involved bandits acting as hitmen, subverting the French legal system by offering justice to locals without recourse to courts and imperial officials. Intertribal killings or attacks against rival families were nothing new in Algeria; vendettas between *mechtas* had occurred for centuries in all three departments. However, officials noted that the current *malfaiteurs* "constitute a sort of corporation . . . a veritable business," in the words of a rural policeman in Tigzirt, and they demanded immediate and forceful action against perpetrators and their families to preserve the French monopoly on policing and judicial proceedings.[104] Among the most notorious assassins, Said Mazreg ran a gang that terrorized the Akbou region, killing multiple victims and overwhelming the local constabulary ill-equipped to deal with a barrage of violent crime. Well after the war had ended, Mazreg's gang continued to benefit from the assistance of a number of deserters who remained in the hills in 1919 to 1920, fearing arrest and linking up with bandit leaders.[105] Officials once again noted that his band owed its success in no small measure to local assistance and the fear it instilled in potential informants. They bemoaned the lapse of the policy of *surveillance spéciale* and house arrests, and the local prosecutor called for the return of troops to prevent further attacks. A platoon of sixty *sénégalais* duly arrived in July 1919 and arrested twenty villagers for providing the *malfaiteurs* with food and firearms.[106] Yet Mazreg and his lieutenants remained at large, and with the end of the war, courts no longer treated accomplices with urgency, instead imposing lenient sentences or outright acquitting the accused. Hence the gang remained at large, frustrating officials into 1920 and beyond.[107]

In the final analysis, the success of administrative campaigns to end banditry in Constantine was decidedly mixed. Crime increased dramatically in the region after the declaration of hostilities, and the number of desertions and evasions remained high throughout the war. Although in many instances bandits engaged in simple robbery (frequently against Arabs or Berbers), the practice often escalated in attacks on European targets: murder, sabotage, or attacks against law enforcement. To be sure, many leaders were arrested, and a large number of criminals and deserters were hunted down by soldiers, gendarmes, and police. Yet, for all the efforts to criminalize dissent through the ruthless suppression of banditry throughout the region, popular dissatisfaction with conscription, police methods, and indeed, French imperialism in general, severely weakened the law enforcement campaign. Brigands remained active throughout the Constantinois, in no small measure due to the assistance of villagers and relatives, from the provision of food and shelter to a universal refusal to assist gendarmes in locating and arresting the culprits. In many cases, bandits lived openly in *mechtas*, symbols of the purported weakness of colonial power and the Algerian rejection of the metropolitan authorities. Although the officials adopted a stance of calm determination, writing in administrative correspondence about simple *malfaiteurs* who would be brought to justice, they fully understood that banditry during the Great War was explicitly political, stymying conscription efforts while encouraging rebellion in the *duwars*—and foreshadowing postwar Algerian nationalism. It is thus unsurprising that they resorted to increasingly brutal methods to snuff out the troublemakers and minimize popular dissent; they were fighting not common criminals but *insoumis* whose refusal to submit to the colonial system actively endangered it. By the interwar period, the government's worst fears were realized: banditry had evolved into a wave of violent crime whose actors were determined to strike back at the settlers, French administrators, and indeed the entire colonial enterprise.

CHAPTER 3

Unlawful Acts or Strategies of Resistance?
Crime and the Disruption of Colonial Order in Interwar French Algeria

On 18 January 1939, in the *commune mixte* (mixed commune) of Rirha, the residents of a *mechta* (tent enclave) threatened a European guard on his daily rounds. Gustave Taillentou came to the *mechta* to serve papers concerning a minor legal matter to a local resident, on behalf of the French authorities. When he arrived at the dwelling of the *ouakaf* (leader), Messaoud Mehenni, to ask for directions, he was brusquely told to return "chez toi" and threatened with violence if he did not comply. Attempting to explain the reason for his presence only worsened the situation; Mehenni began to yell menacingly, while almost instantly a crowd gathered and projectiles were thrown, with one irate denizen brandishing a firearm. Realizing the consequences, Taillentou beat a hasty retreat, yet lashed out at the aggressors with physical violence, and his inspector subsequently hypothesized that the tribe feared widespread tent searches for illegal goods, a common law enforcement tactic outside of major centers. The *ouakaf* and two inhabitants were ultimately arrested and charged with assault, while the guard returned to base unharmed. It is tempting to view these events as an isolated incident, in which a particular community objected to the actions of a solitary officer.[1] Yet the aggression tells a different story, one of anticolonial violence rather than a mere spontaneous reaction to a feared search and seizure. For one thing, assaults on guards became standard fare throughout the interwar era, as Algerians rejected their authority and French laws concerning grazing, forestry, and property.[2] Furthermore, it demonstrates how violence perpetrated by state agents, official suspicion (and concomitant intrusive searches), and the colonial and racial hierarchy permeated the lives of Algerian subjects. However, it also reveals a growing trend throughout the interwar era: assaults against settlers, officials, and police, manifested through criminal acts, from robbery and football hooliganism to assault and murder. This was not simply delinquency or sociopathic behavior. Instead, it is evidence that well before the emergence of popular nationalism in the late 1930s, elements within the Arab and Kabyle population began to reject French authority.

Anticolonial groups did not appear in a vacuum. Decades prior to the fight for Algerian independence, Arabs and Kabyles regularly demonstrated their displeasure with Gallic aspirations to hegemony, without recourse to any formal party structure or organized militancy. As Martin Thomas notes, such trends were duly noted by officials, who feared Muslim anger at European economic predominance, Islamic extremism, and a political uprising in equal measure.[3] To be sure, the majority of workers and peasants during the interwar era valued caution over revolt, believing politics to be problematic and ill-advised. Moreover, reformism held sway among educated and affluent Algerians until the end of World War II, with the so-called *évolués* demanding better treatment under French rule rather than independence and decolonization. However, as James McDougall writes, "Among a rapidly growing number of Algerians, dissenting demands expanded, loyalty began to attach to a new and larger sense of community, the patience of even the most cautious wore thin."[4] Plainly put, with no end to French domination in sight, rampant poverty and inequality, and the settlers' refusal to even consider changes to the colonial system, Algerians began to engage in demonstrable anticolonial dissent—often by violent means. If spectacular and widespread uprisings were few and far between, and the perpetrators were not political nationalists, officials, police, and the European population nevertheless worried openly about increasing incidents of disobedience and belligerent refusal, which demonstrated Algerian agency rather than passive acceptance.

Political Reformism and Subaltern Protest

The interwar era in French Algeria birthed the first stirrings of overt anticolonial unrest. As the population increasingly moved to cities from the countryside, spontaneous protests increased, from demonstrations in the Alger casbah to antisemitic riots in Constantine. Newer press organs in French and Arabic complemented the critical mood, while cultural productions in music and the-

UNLAWFUL ACTS OR STRATEGIES OF RESISTANCE?

ater began to openly espouse pro-Arab and -Kabyle leanings.[5] Much like their urban confreres, farmers and rural laborers engaged in new forms of rebellion, including tax revolts.[6] However, overt political nationalism did not emerge as a popular vehicle for Algerian grievances until the post-1945 era. Messali Hadj formed the Étoile nord-africaine (ENA; North African Star) in the late 1920s, but it was essentially confined to Paris, and when the group crossed the Mediterranean in the 1930s, the newly renamed Parti du peuple algérien (PPA; Party of the Algerian People) proved to have a limited reach. As Omar Carlier has demonstrated, the organization attracted young members and future leaders like Hocine Lahouel and Youcef Ben Khedda via schools, scout troops, and the streets. It provided a genuine political outlet for Algerian independence, broadening the clientele from émigré workers in Paris and urban labor in Algeria to incorporate skilled employees and shopkeepers, along with students and civil servants. Party candidates won seats in municipal and cantonal elections, and thirty-one sections were founded across Algeria.[7] Yet the PPA largely remained a Paris-based operation, with only 1,190 members in Algeria, overshadowed by the reformist Fédération des élus musulmans (Federation of Muslim Elected Representatives).[8] As a result, government officials and police easily dismantled the PPA in 1937 to 1938, and Hadj, Hocine Lahouel, and other leaders received two-year jail sentences on charges of illegally reforming the banned ENA and breaching national security.[9]

For increasingly impatient Algerians, there seemingly existed no other political outlet for growing popular frustration with French predominance on their territory. Competing organizations did not provide an effective alternative for challenging European rule. The Parti communiste français (French Communist Party) derided separatist groups as "national reformists," and after an initial flirtation with the ENA in the late 1920s, it backed away from Algerian anticolonialism altogether. Although the nascent Parti communiste algérien (Algerian Communist Party) began to slowly reverse the flow after 1936, its continued insistence that Messali Hadj and the PPA were Fascist agents and its prioritization of European issues, limited its appeal. Hopes were again raised after the victory in June 1936 of the Popular Front government, which featured noted reformers like Minister of Colonies Marius Moutet and Minister of State Maurice Viollette. Yet the socialist Section française de l'Internationale ouvrière (French Section of the Workers' International) offered disingenuous proposals: assimilation for the *évolués* through the Blum-Viollette bill, and the continued colonial presence of France in Algeria. Thus, many subsequently echoed the sentiments of *Le Populaire* (Of the People) editor Siegfried Bracke that talk of equal rights for Algerians "is just banquet and birthday speech blather."[10]

The only other options were reformist: in the 1920s, the Emir Khaled and the Young Algerians, who demanded citizenship rights and educational reform, and in the 1930s, the Fédération des élus musulmans, led by Mohamed Bendjelloul and Ferhat Abbas, the *évolué* partisans of negotiated reform within a Gallic-dominated Algeria. Although reformers enjoyed substantial popularity throughout the interwar era, and they were far from docile puppets of the colonial regime, they failed to accomplish much of substance and thus hardly provided a palliative for the worker or *fellah* (agricultural laborer) struggling under the colonial yoke.[11] They first and foremost looked to end the hated Indigénat, the 1881 legal code for Arabs and Kabyles that supplemented French penal law, creating new categories of crime and punishment to be enforced by administrators and their Algerian proxies—*caïds* (tribal leaders) and local councils. The code authorized exceptional powers, from individual and collective fines or the seizure of goods and produce to prison terms, house arrest, and deportation. Clearly an instrument of domination under the guise of public security, it demanded obedience to official decrees and orders concerning a variety of instructions specific to *indigènes*, and legitimized legal violence against the colonized by state agents.[12] Neither settlers nor authorities agreed to any substantial changes during the interwar era, and only the experience of world war and occupation prompted the French government in 1946 to abolish the code. Nor did the reformists have much success in abrogating citizenship laws, which according to the 1865 Sénatus-consulte demanded that Muslims renounce Qur'anic law and Islamic tradition in order to become French and thus be theoretically afforded equal rights and opportunities. The 1919 Jonnart Law allowed the administration to veto any applicant for citizenship, while refusing to reconsider the status quo, which disallowed the candidacy of practicing Muslims. Although the law did offer a separate electoral college for 425,000 voters with local and regional political representation, Europeans far outnumbered them and effectively blocked any Algerian demands. Reformers consistently fought for changes to this system throughout the interwar era, to no avail.[13]

Nonetheless, as McDougall notes in his recent history of Algeria, Arabs and Kabyles were not mere hapless victims of French machinations until the arrival en masse of nationalist cadres in the post-1945 era.[14] In his work on the resistance of tribal councils to official demands, Neil MacMaster correctly asserts that prior to 1945, open revolt against French rule did not come from above, but from below: "There has been a preoccupation with leaders in the upper echelons of military and state hierarchies, a belief that political ideologies and movements stem from urban and educated elites alone, and a conviction that illiterate peasant societies were devoid of political consciousness or agency."[15] Stathis Kalyvas observes that such action was not the exclusive preserve of urban elites (such as the Algerian *évolués*), and most actors eschewed strictly ideological motives and parties (along the lines of Hadj and the ENA/PPA), often defying categorization while acting independently of openly nationalist and reform movements.[16] This was not always a peaceful process, and many Arabs and Kabyles embraced anticolonial violence, complementing emerging political nationalism by physically challenging the notion of French economic, military, and territorial hegemony.

Demographic and Socioeconomic Preconditions to Anticolonial Crime and Violence

If they did not represent nationalism per se, individual acts of anticolonial violence were nonetheless designed to simultaneously destabilize the colonial state while protesting against the inherent injustice that the system perpetuated. This was certainly not novel in the interwar era. In addition to the mass insurrections and banditry discussed in chapter 2, murders and robberies perpetrated by Algerians against Europeans occasionally sparked fear and mistrust in officials and *colons* (rural settlers) from the 1850s onward.[17] However, these violent offenses were not regular occurrences and did not cause prolonged anxiety; rather, it was the threat of mass revolt that initially worried the authorities. The Muqrani rebellion in the Constantinois provided instances of physical resistance that threatened French hegemony and settlement; an isolated violent crime did not. Yet the rebellions proved unable to match Gallic firepower, and they eventually succumbed to military or police counterattacks after failing to spark a full-scale revolutionary war.[18] Banditry proved far more difficult to contain. No longer petty criminals or the *bandits d'honneur* of old, seeking to avenge their family honor, the new *malfaiteurs* rejected the demands of the authorities and their subordinate position. By 1916, the Constantinois in particular became embroiled in insurrectionary activity, with police and gendarmes engaged in widespread counterinsurgency operations, well aware that hundreds of rebels tested the strength of the colonial system. Despite their efforts, they failed to end a spate of robbery, sabotage, and murder across the region, abetted by the local population, who provided food, shelter, and other assistance.[19]

Yet, the vast majority of quotidian criminal acts in the pre-1914 era were not violent but rather defied the Indigénat, particularly regulations concerning everything from cattle grazing and the collection or use of firewood to pilgrimages and the nonpayment of taxes. By the 1870s, laws increasingly displayed a preoccupation with fines or imprisonment as a means to teach "primitive" Algerians a lesson and underscore European supremacy, combining the exercise of authority, coercion, and colonial law. A large percentage of dossiers from 1889 to 1914 involved minor offenses or perceived slights to European officials, with the rest primarily involving simple (nonarmed) theft, fraud, vagrancy, or, at worst, *bechara* (cattle theft). There were murders or assaults, to be sure, but not in unusual numbers.[20]

In the postwar era, individuals and communities similarly adopted a variety of aggressive tactics to undermine imperial order, from robbery and football hooliganism to assault and murder. If they did not join nationalist organizations, engage in mass protests, or secretly collude against the empire, Arabs and Kabyles nonetheless perpetrated acts declared illegal under the French criminal code, and under normal circumstances, deemed malevolent. If colonial violence bolstered the colonial regime (its institutions, agents, and goals), anticolonial violence sought to disrupt the workings of empire. Moreover, it did not have to be explicitly verbalized. Just as perpetrators of colonial violence often did not formally announce themselves, those who attacked the system of European control frequently did so anonymously. Hence by the interwar era, authorities began to reject the views of ethnographers, psychiatrists, and officials who from the mid-nineteenth century onward viewed Algerians as violent, primitive, and uncivilized, naturally prone to criminal behavior, motivated by revenge and lust, immorality and greed, or the dictates of jihad and Islam.[21] Instead, they considered various forms of criminal behavior as consciously anticolonial, designed to strike a blow against French domination. This led to increased surveillance and severe sanctions against any transgression in both town and countryside. Previously confined to stereotypes designed to perpetuate the myth of French superiority, after the Great War, the *indigènes* represented an authentic threat that underscored the need for what Stephen Legg terms (in the context of British India) "zones of privilege and partition," using racial policing and criminal justice in a "theatrical performance of sovereign power" designed to staunch anticolonial crime and violence. In this way, officials and police, and indeed, the population at large, came to understand certain categories of crime as a vector in what Ranajit Guha terms "dominance without hegemony," the messy reality of empire as a battle between "the alien colonialist project of appropriation . . . matched by an indigenous nationalist project of counter-appropriation."[22]

To be sure, not all victims of crime were non-Algerian; the archives are full of reports concerning Muslim-on-Muslim murders, assaults, and theft. Yet these offenses received little serious attention from police or administrators, for they did not trouble the established political and social order in the colony. However, criminal activity against settlers, businesses, officials, and sites of power conversely took authorities by surprise, revealing an embryonic yet growing anti-European sentiment. Unlike crimes committed in Algerian communities, which primarily settled disputes (assault, murder) or provided the means for survival (robbery, banditry), attacks against European targets represented what Jean-Pierre Peyroulou calls a "low-intensity war" against the colonizer, involving property destruction (both public and private) and extreme violence, often designed to underscore the precarious position of outnumbered settlers in both rural and urban communities.[23]

Nowhere was this pattern more clearly established than in Constantine, one of the three departments in French Algeria. While neighboring Alger housed the seat of administrative power and Oran boasted a sizeable European population approaching the number of Algerian residents, Constantine enjoyed no such advantages. In demographic terms, even its larger urban centers were profoundly imbalanced: in 1921, Constantine-ville was home to 49,081 Europeans and 576,162 Arabs and Kabyles, while Bône's numbers were 37,302 and 111,985, respectively. Moreover, much of the population lived in the countryside, unlike Alger or Oran, which became increasingly urbanized following the Great War. The majority of denizens inhabited the almost impenetrable Kabylia, Berber lands to the north that encompassed the northern Tell Atlas Mountains, vast forests, and the high plateaus, rendering entire regions like the Aurès impassable during much of the year. Unsurprisingly, crime proved far more prevalent there, and Europeans increasingly equated law breaking with anticolonial activity.[24] In any case, they tended to be quite nervous, faced with a much larger Algerian population and few resources in the case of rebellion. Gendarmerie units were few and far between, with small garrisons responsible for tens of thousands of hectares of territory, little access to needed automobiles and heavy arms, and a lengthy delay should reinforcements be required.[25]

In addition, Constantine, far more than its neighbors, suffered from economic dislocation during the interwar era. By 1914, the majority of Algerian agricultural holdings were smaller than ten hectares, as Europeans seized or purchased the best tracts of land. Eleven interwar harvests were blighted or outright disastrous, and livestock holdings decreased throughout the period. This was not simply a matter of horrible weather, for Europeans held the most fertile plots and used their access to credit to fund technological improvement, effectively combating frost and pests. They were also better able to weather global price fluctuations that battered wheat and barley markets at the height of the Depression, while avoiding numerous taxes, duties, and permit restrictions that applied exclusively to Algerians. In any case, most Algerians did not own land; they were reduced to working for a mere three or four francs for a twelve-hour workday, and thus poverty became endemic in Arab and Kabyle communities during the interwar era. Despite a growing interwar migration to cities, urban settings provided little relief: Europeans owned everything of value, from printshops and metallurgies to quarries and businesses. Algerians worked in cramped shops as artisans and craftsmen, or as labor earning pittance wages and living in squalor in segregated neighborhoods where disease and starvation resulted in mortality rates double the European average.[26] The alternative was work in the metropole, leaving family for the drudgery of Parisian factories and slums.

Arms Trafficking, Train Derailments, and Colonial Insecurity

Against this backdrop, Algerians increasingly resorted to criminality and violence. From the end of the Great War, one of the most worrisome trends was arms trafficking in town and countryside, a significant concern for both colonial officials and business owners, as Algerians purchased firearms from a variety of smugglers, robbed armories, and stole explosives from mines and construction sites. In some cases, smuggling rings provided the weapons. In Bougie, a customs official working the docks in August 1938 caught an African mechanic from a French ship delivering a package containing rifles and ammunition to a local merchant, Youssef Bouchebah, originating from a seller named Aissa, a Bougie native transplanted to Marseille. A scouring of the ship revealed more firearms and bullets, and house searches yielded letters alluding to a well-organized and long-standing operation.

Cases of individual dealers involved in illegal sales resulted in stores being raided by police, who uncovered dozens of unlicensed guns and a plethora of ammunition and charged the accused with a *flagrant délit*, a serious criminal violation carrying a mandatory prison sentence. Due to their access to guns and ammunition, many of the perpetrators were Europeans motivated by greed, benefiting from a hefty markup on illegal firearm sales. In February 1924, police charged a farmer outside Philippeville with selling twenty-five rifles to various Algerians, and he was arrested following a lengthy surveillance operation involving multiple informants. Specifically targeting non-European buyers at fall harvest time, when buyers had the cash to purchase a firearm, Antoine Dimeglio netted up to 150 francs per transaction. That he sold guns to Europeans under the table was of little consequence; armed *indigènes* alone represented a clear threat to French Algeria. The weapons in

UNLAWFUL ACTS OR STRATEGIES OF RESISTANCE? 91

question were subsequently used in attempted murder cases, which heightened the concern of the colonial authorities.[27]

By far the most spectacular case occurred in Saint Arnaud, outside Sétif, involving notable figures from across the region. A September 1930 police report noted that every day brought another surprise, including the arrest of prominent Europeans, from civil servants to wealthy landowners, all motivated by greed to sell arms to the *indigènes* despite the official prohibition. They included the railway chief of one town, two *colons* in Sétif, and railroad employees who transported the goods. Matters came to a head with the trial of a pharmacist who sold chemicals (saltpeter, sulfur) required for manufacturing ammunition in bags labeled "fertilizer"—he was convicted and sentenced to a three-month prison term, a sentence angrily denounced as far too lenient by furious locals. Police pronounced that "all the arrests are making a serious impression on the French population," shutting down both the illegal sales and official corruption. Yet settler anger did not sputter out, and the following June, an editorialist in the *Presse Libre* (Free Press) called for an official inquest from the governor general and *procureur général* (attorney general). Politics and favoritism were the only explanation for the lack of major convictions and sentences, the article seethed, and selling to any *indigène* threatened the very existence of the colony.[28]

Officials were equal alarmed by Algerians selling arms to their confreres, a far more regular activity. Unlike Europeans who engaged in illicit sales, Arabs and Kabyles tended toward limited and infrequent transactions, for they lacked the capacity to buy large quantities of guns and ammunition, and such activities risked raising suspicion. Nonetheless, police files include dozens of reports concerning the practice. Some cases involved Algerians who had taken up French citizenship and thus had access to licensed dealers. In December 1929, the Brigade mobile in Batna charged a railroad employee with eight pistol sales to locals over the course of several months. Others imported the contraband weapons from France. One Constantine hotelier told police that packages arrived from Lyon for non-Europeans, and a subsequent investigation uncovered a ring of Algerians in France who mailed guns under fake European names. Middlemen in the colony then moved the weapons by bus or car to the final recipients, which led to raids at depots and surveillance of mass transportation in various locales. Finally, Algerian shopkeepers dealt under the table, occasionally with sales permits that authorized transactions with Europeans alone. A police search of a Sétif storefront yielded records of eighty-three illicit gun sales to Arabs, along with dozens of bullets provided to the same clients.[29]

Police were concerned with such brokers because they provided arms to the colonized.[30] Officials and the European population deemed Arabs and Kabyles to be naturally violent and insurrectionary and thus denied arms unconditionally. A variety of official communiqués and legal prohibitions worked to squelch any and all weapons sales to the colonized throughout the interwar period. Until the postwar era, an 1851 law provided the only precedent, and it called for suspended sentences unless grave consequences could be demonstrated. Led by the *conseil général* (departmental council) of Constantine, lawmakers argued in the 1920s that the legislation was simply outmoded, as it considered only illegal sales to European buyers. Thus, minimum sentences gradually became the norm, combined with increased surveillance of armories and dealers. Police in Bougie and Collo reported that hefty jail terms led directly to a significant drop in offenses, while customs officials also became actively involved in order to terminate smuggling operations from the metropole. However, the problem never really disappeared, and officials became increasingly worried about an armed Algerian population. A small minority of Arabs and Kabyles received official authorization, yet non-Europeans in the countryside sought arms by whatever means possible, and the Constantine gendarmerie warned that "this trafficking has considerable influence on crime in Algeria."[31] As the governor general noted in a January 1932 memo concerning clandestine arms imports from the metropole by *indigènes* in Constantine: "Cette contrebande étant de nature à compromettre gravement la sécurité de la colonie [This contraband is of the type that severely compromises the security of the colony]."[32] Thus, handguns were banned by decree, and the police sought and received special powers to prevent illicit Muslim arms deals, including the authority to conduct random car and bus stops at police checkpoints and looser regulations on searches in villages and tent enclaves (*duwars* and *mechtas*) and indigenous business locations.[33]

Of even greater concern to police and population, Algerian operators across the department fabricated gunpowder to sell clandestinely at local markets. Using intelligence supplied by surveillance operatives, in September 1923, police seized eighteen kilograms of gunpowder in Bélezma, breaking up a three-man Algerian operation that sold the product in bulk to clients. Manufactured by an Algerian "specialist" and sold by his accomplices across the commune, his laboratory was uncovered using information gleaned from the interrogation of family members. Authorities took the crime so seriously that when the local court sentenced the perpetrators to one-year prison terms, the administrator complained that such leniency would merely encourage competing operations.[34] An even more ingenious team made huge purchases of blasting powder (ten to twenty kilograms) with an authorization from the prefect. Such permissions were to be granted only once, but the smugglers applied multiple times without noting the previous exceptions. This went on for years, until the clerical errors were discovered after an anonymous letter denounced the perpetrators, by which time, thousands of kilograms had been dispersed across all three departments.[35] As a result of mounting incidents, a decree in July 1934 banned the sale of most arms in an effort to provide a more effective penal deterrent. Nonetheless, despite dozens of arrests throughout the interwar era, the profitability of the trade ensured a steady stream of trafficking activity.[36]

Even more troublesome were the looting of armories and mines, which simultaneously provided military-caliber weaponry to Algerians while encouraging attacks on targets at the heart of the colonial power structure. The town of Constantine was particularly vulnerable; as the seat of imperial authority in the department, its government buildings were frequently burglarized by locals using false keys or filing barred windows. A successful theft at the local courthouse in April 1923, for example, not only netted high-powered rifles and revolvers with ammunition but very publicly mocked the notion of French administrative impregnability, as supposedly docile and inferior Arabs easily infiltrated a symbol of Gallic imperial control.[37] Even more disturbing in that regard, mines and factories were frequently relieved of explosive materials. Blasting powder could easily be converted into firearm ammunition, and administrators of *communes mixtes* and prefects worried about a profusion of such thefts in areas like the Constantinois that were subsumed by what one *chef de Brigade mobile* termed an "insurrectionary climate," in which guns were frequently used against official targets.[38] At the Gaultier warehouse in El-Milia, a gang operating in April 1931 stole two crates of dynamite and four thousand detonators, breaking into the powder keg through the front door in the middle of the night. This constituted the second successful theft in the region, and in both cases, the perpetrators exploited a lack of security and the fact that storage facilities were situated out of sight with badly locked doors. Both sites revealed traces of an inside job, meaning that employees of the companies had actively assisted in the crimes.[39]

However, these efforts paled before an August 1922 attempt to loot the Beni Falkai mine in Takitount. Thieves there not only pilfered a large percentage of the company's stock but also detonated the remainder, causing a spectacular explosion to cover their tracks. In the aftermath, authorities removed the local *caïd* for obstructing the investigation and the police arrested the guard, citing his "very suspicious attitude," yet no trace of the thieves or the loot could be found.[40] This was not unusual; in a letter to the administrator of Collo, the director of the Sidi-Kember mine lamented that tools and even explosives "magically disappear" all the time. The mine employed two hundred busy workers, and any one of them could easily steal items and sneak off to the nearby forest. Although the responsibility for storage and safety remained with a few Europeans, the actual work of blasting and transportation fell to Algerian workers.[41] The detectives' conclusion in the Beni Falkai case that the depot had been insufficiently guarded only heightened prefectorial concerns—how many other operations could be similarly dispossessed of explosives? The thefts were almost always inside jobs, with certain employees fleeing the district following major burglaries. Faced with a rash of theft and fraud, and the rise to prominence of nationalist movements by the late 1930s, the governor general barred indigenous employees from handling such materials on the job, and simultaneously banned the sale of explosives and blasting powder to any Algerian, or Europeans unaffiliated with a corporate concern.[42]

The police, officials, and the public at large understood the underlying message implicit in the raids and thefts: they provided the means to mount challenges to colonial authority, to strike at the foundations of the state—pillars of government, commerce, and the judiciary—while lashing out at the perpetrators of Algerian poverty and immiseration—settlers and bosses, police and administrators. Designed to hamper the colonial economy and transportation system, train derailments proved to be equally destructive, and they targeted the railroad: the ultimate symbol of European technology and power in the imperial setting. By 1927, the colonial administration oversaw the construction of 4,500 kilometers of railway lines, transporting passengers navigating the breadth of the urban coast and the fertile Tell and also millions of tons of agricultural produce from villages and oases to the ports in Alger, Constantine, and Oran. Trains disrupted traditional transportation networks and pushed aside camel and wagon trade in favor of expensive (and exclusively European) technology. Keith Neilson and T. J. Otte call this process "railpolitik"; trains provided the "path to empire," enabling the political and economic conquest of a territory and symbolizing the "modernity" of the colonizer in sharp contrast to the primitive condition of the *indigènes*. Given their centrality to Algerian life, the economic and human consequences of major railway disruptions were considerable, and derailments became a preferred method of rebellion against colonization. This was particularly true in the Constantinois, where trains disrupted the grazing patterns of animals, noisily disturbed local dwellings, and provided a daily reminder of European technological penetration of the Algerian landscape.[43]

Locals responded by consistently seeking to disrupt and damage trains and schedules. In certain cases, groups of villagers in remote areas moved massive boulders to try to force locomotives from the tracks. Their motivations variously included resentment at the economic exploitation practiced by industrial operations and commercial farms (and concomitant Algerian unemployment and bankruptcy), and revenge against local authorities. Rail workers themselves provided assistance to the saboteurs; in August 1926 in Bougie, a crew supplied the schedule, details about weaknesses in the tracks, and instructions concerning the placement of rocks in gaps between the rails. Many attempts were far more ambitious. In December 1920, attackers targeted an Algerian state railroad train in Sedrata, a symbol of colonial domination, simultaneously trying to cause the deaths of officials and the destruction of commercial goods. This attempted derailment provided the climax to a sustained campaign of anticolonial violence in the region, and the resulting manhunt involved police and Spahis performing house searches of the domiciles of local "dangerous Arabs," numerous arrests and internments, and a detachment of fifty *tirailleurs* sent to guard the railroad tracks. Local Europeans and officials applauded the forceful response, perceived to have restored order and racial hierarchy.[44]

Not all actions against trains involved derailment, and many attacks took the far more quotidian form of shootings. Such incidents often occurred along rural lines, avoiding guards and pedestrian traffic. A November 1925 attack on the Bône-La Calle line, in which multiple gunshots hit the train, occurred outside the village of Tarf, with two Algerians firing multiple times. Much more dramatically, a volley of shots damaged a commercial train in June 1919 on the Philippeville-Constantine route, but the cars carried only commercial goods and thus no injuries were reported. Nevertheless, the local prefect demanded a greater police presence to thwart future attempts, likely to produce significant casualties among passengers.[45] Yet, efforts to curb derailments through increased police presence and harsh sentencing (prosecutors demanded remand even for young offenders) came to naught, and attacks on trains remained a regular occurrence in the Algerian countryside.[46]

Football Violence as a Nationalist Enterprise

Although they frightened police and the local population, thefts of arms and explosives did not directly result in major anticolonial attacks during the interwar era—that would have to wait until the late 1940s, with the PPA's formation of underground militia units. Nor were train derailments permanently disruptive; tracks were quickly repaired and commercial losses minimal. Of far greater import were direct attacks against Europeans in public spaces that symbolized imperial power, which served to disrupt the traditional racial hierarchy and colonial order.

In this regard, Algerians often fought Europeans at sports stadiums, where the humiliation of being beaten by the colonized, along with the sabotage of officially sanctioned league sporting events, reverberated with French officials and the general public in equal measure. As J. A. Mangan notes (in the British context, but equally applicable to France), the authorities viewed sport as both "a means of propagating imperial sentiment" and "a significant part of imperial culture," constituting a repository of metropolitan values and "civilized" behavior. To be sure, sporting events operated simultaneously as spaces for negotiation and cultural encounter, among the only meeting places where both the colonizer and the colonized participated on the pitch and as spectators in the stands. Yet, sports were seen as a significant method for inculcating imperial values among the subject population, believed to encourage acceptance of colonial rule while bolstering settler self-identity.[47]

However, in the North African setting, football in particular became something altogether different for colonized populations, and particularly Arabs and Berbers in Algeria. From the 1840s, Algerians were permitted to attend certain sporting events, and by the interwar era, interest boomed in rugby and football, culminating in the 1901 formation of the Ligue algéroise de la Fédération française de football association (Algerian League of the French Federation of the Football Association). Teams were either European or Muslim by the 1920s, and both competed in departmental divisions. Matches regularly pitted the colonizer against the colonized, and with these competitions came crowd disturbances that often spilled over onto the field.[48] Football riots and racial attacks in a stadium symbolized something far more political than athletic. When perpetrated by Arabs and Kabyles against European spectators or players, such assaults in public spaces that symbolized imperial power served to disrupt the traditional racial hierarchy and colonial order, creating an enclave of nationalist identity and politics. Various scholars position football in particular as a nationalist enterprise; in colonial Algeria, teams were rooted in community and religion, with every facet of the competition echoing Muslim identity and rejection of colonialism. Clubs in the Bab-el-Oued neighborhood in Algers and Saint Eugène in Oran were exclusively European, for example, while over a dozen Algerian sides attracted Arab and Kabyle players and fans. Many sported uniforms adorned with Islamic imagery, especially the crescent and the five-pointed star, which traced back to the Ottoman era and the Qur'an, respectively. Club names underscored these associations. Several adopted the word *nasr* (victory) as a double entendre, referencing Muhammed's triumph over the infidels according to Allah's will. The Hamidia franchise similarly evoked the Turkish sultan Hamid II and the pre-French conquest era, while Mouloudia celebrated the birth of the Prophet, a traditionally nationalist celebration. Club names were thus deeply political, and they encouraged anti-European action on match days. Moreover, supporters explicitly understood the stadium to be a "political space," not least because it allowed them to enter habitually forbidden European spaces usually reserved for servants and assorted lowly workers due to the urban segregation practiced throughout the colony. In the words of Youcef Fates, football thus became embedded with nationalism and anticolonial discourse through slogans, chants, and disturbances: "Alors la competition sportive passe du stade géographique au plan nationaliste ou inter-ethnique [Thus a sporting competition moved from the locale of the stadium to the nationalist and interethnic plane]."[49]

Consequently, anticolonial violence became a regular occurrence at matches across the department of Constantine. One of the more spectacular incidents occurred on 24 November 1925 at the Stade Turpin in Constantine-ville, where the local football club squared off against a rival from Saint Arnaud. When a visiting European violently tackled an Algerian playing for the home side, the venue erupted, with hundreds of Arab and Kabyle spectators invading the pitch in an effort to attack the offender. The Algerian side judge told teammates that he would not leave the stadium alive, and only the intervention of an armed gendarmerie detachment prevented that outcome.[50] This proved to be far from an isolated incident, and by the 1930s, football matches were regularly twinned with anticolonial violence. At a match in March 1930 between Union sportive club de Constantine and the Stade olympique sétifien, police arrested twenty Algerians armed with razors, canes, and knives and charged them with menacing Europeans. Despite the arrests and police presence, a French player for the Constantine side struck an Algerian playing for Sétif, which prompted a pitch invasion and melee. This episode reveals a high degree of preparation prior to matchday violence. Muslim supporters' organizations frequently planned assaults and disturbances well in advance, identifying the stadium as a key venue for directly confronting French colonialism and European settlers in a manner otherwise impossible, as both leaders and participants could remain anonymous in a crowd of thousands. One incident in Blida illustrates both the planning and anonymity in equal measure. On 10 January 1937, the visiting Muslim Mouloudia Club Algérois took on the Football Club Blidéen (FCB) in front of three thousand fans, two-thirds of them Arab and Kabyle and five hundred of those from out of town. Insults and pitched battles in the stands occurred throughout the match, worsened by the fact that Mouloudia were completely outclassed by FCB, with the Europeans controlling the play despite being down two men, as proceedings degenerated into a boxing bout, according to authorities. The climax arrived in the second half, when a voice was suddenly heard screaming "On the pitch!"

from the grass embankment next to the field, a signal for hundreds to invade the playing surface and seek out Blidean players and fans. Only the presence of dozens of police and gendarmes prevented mass assaults, and the lead officer on the scene openly worried about security at future matches, given the organized nature of the violence, while FCB supporters interviewed in the aftermath spoke of a coordinated series of incidents orchestrated by the Algerian visitors.[51]

Local derbies in particular provided the occasions for assaults, often pitting European squads against Muslim rivals. In May 1934 the Union sportive squared off against the Algerian Club sportif team, and only minutes after kickoff, 350 Arabs and Kabyles brawled with 150 French and Italian fans, administering severe beatings to men and women alike. The latter were targeted with obscene gestures throughout the proceedings, and as Club sportif scored twice in the second half to pull ahead, the crowd became increasingly volatile, leading the concerned Europeans to concede well before full time. Writing to the prefect after the fact, the police chief recommended canceling future games: "In my humble opinion, matches that pit Europeans and *indigènes* against each other cannot be permitted in public, because for the latter it is not a question of sport but of race, which can cause serious incidents."[52] The violence was not confined to the stands; players themselves frequently boxed one another on the pitch during matches between European and Algerian teams. During a 28 February 1935 tilt between the French Association sportive Constantinoise and the Algerian Union sportive Constantinoise, forwards named Attali (an assimilated European Jew) and Omar (a local Arab) came to blows so forcefully that the official had no choice but to call off the match, fearing that both teams would engage in open fighting on the field.[53] This was a prescient move, for just weeks later, in Bône, the local side and the visiting team from Guelma fought so ferociously that a literal riot ensued, with all two thousand attendees invading the pitch. Muslim Bône fans and players attacked Guelma supporters and athletes, with European fans vigorously defending their end, including one with a loaded pistol. In the aftermath, the visitors were escorted back to their hotel, where they remained trapped as local youths prowled the streets looking to attack them. The police concluded their report by demanding more officers on match days and evenings to prevent escalating and uncontrollable criminal violence.[54]

Regardless of the venue or the teams involved, interracial matches often degenerated due to poor officiating. Referees were always European and consistently charged with bias against Muslim teams, who frequently had players sent off for supposedly violent conduct, while their French opponents rarely received similar treatment. After a particularly egregious display in Biskra in

March 1938, young fans attempted to physically attack the referee, who was quickly protected by several Europeans at match's end. The police officer in charge at the stadium thought it best to have the referee escorted to his car by one of his men, believing that the sight of a man in uniform would deter troublemakers, but the youths showered the automobile with rocks.[55] Arab and Kabyle players also attacked officials perceived to be biased in favor of European sides. At a March 1941 match in Boufarik against Mouloudia Club Algérois, the referee ordered a first-half penalty retaken after the European visitors failed to score. Following a series of similar "errors" in the second half, several Boufarik players punched him, forcing an early end to play before full time. On orders of the club's administration, the team came together under a flag at match's end, while fans hunted the streets for the errant officials, as gendarmes and police flooded various neighborhoods to prevent serious violence. As for the conduct of the officials, it was so blatantly biased that the French author of a police report bemoaned that quality football could be blemished by such horrible match oversight.[56]

The Boufarik case further reveals the overt anticolonialism and nationalism inherent in football violence. Administrators were all too aware of these implications, consistently worried about the potential for race riots, open revolt against the authorities, and the spread of separatist sentiment. In the 1920s, senior officials tended to delegate responses to subordinates charged with keeping order locally in all three departments. Following serious incidents in Biskra during a December 1928 match, Governor General Bordès asked deputy prefects, mayors, and administrators to do whatever they deemed necessary to prevent such acts in the future.[57] With the advent of political nationalism in the 1930s through the emergence of Messali Hadj and the ENA/PPA, who explicitly demanded decolonization, more severe punishments emerged, targeting clubs identified as nationalist hotbeds. In May 1931, the Muslim-run Mouloudia Club algérois received a suspension from league play due to fan assaults against partisans of Olympique the preceding year. By June, the governor general threatened to involve the local Fédération française de football delegate, while barring any club that permitted discord on its grounds. Several other teams faced lengthy bans in subsequent years, for fan possession of weapons or attacks against rival European supporters and match officials.[58]

Administrative sanctions did little to eliminate or even restrain nationalist sentiment and football violence at stadiums across 1930s Algeria. Among the most actively political clubs, the Jeunesse sportive from Djidjelli (JS) spent much of the decade facing bans or penalties related to fan behavior, and local officials tied them to rampant anticolonialism among local *indigènes*. The club's directors consistently attempted to foil the notorious "European player rule," which insisted that every side should have three non-Arabs or -Kabyles on their matchday side, and the president was openly accused of having a "phobia of Frenchmen." For their part, the crowd consistently engaged in violence against Europeans, showered visiting clubs with chants against the three-player regulation and France (dubbed "the slut"). Despite the fact that their rivals were run by a local notable from the Fascist Parti social français (French Social Party), the prefect chose to ignore this fact, instead evincing concern with the club's ties to the Islamic 'ulama, and in May 1938 he suspended matches between JS and their local rivals for six months.[59]

By the mid-1930s, the three-player rule became a flash point for almost every Muslim team competing in the Algerian league. Teams perceived to "always display a proper attitude" were granted exceptions to field squads exclusively composed of Arabs and Kabyles. Thus, the prefect of Oran lobbied the governor general to exempt the Union sportive musulmane d'Oran (USMO; Muslim Sports Union of Oran) on the grounds that their directors and fans were *évolués*—elite subjects who displayed pro-French tendencies, and hence performed important work developing youth and the community at large. The undersecretary of state in France further pointed out that the USMO were the premier North African football club, sending players to French League sides each year.[60] Conversely, the Union sportive musulmane blidéenne (Muslim Sports Union of Blida) annually lobbied for similar treatment, worried about unfair competitive advantages enjoyed by rivals like the USMO, only to be soundly rebuffed due to the "bad attitudes" of their fans and the omnipresent violence during their matches. League demands for the rule's abrogation met with the same response. When the Ligue d'Oranie de Football (Oran Football League) asked the governor general in August 1938 to personally rescind the three-player rule, and Muslim officials proclaimed the regulation "a taxing burden on young Muslim athletes," the administration remained unmoved, only deepening the anger of fans and team officials toward France and colonialism.[61]

In fact, French officials summarily regarded Algerian clubs as nationalist, promoting anticolonial behavior from both the boardroom and the stands. Police used informants to obtain comprehensive reports on club board meetings in all three departments, under a program dedicated to the "political surveillance of *indigènes*." Officers termed the Club sportive Constantinois an "anti-French propaganda club." Club president Benhammedi was identified in 1935 as a supporter of Mohamed Bendjelloul and the *élus*, a group dedicated to social and political reform in all three departments, while another board member named Lefgoun was declared "extremely francophobe." The club was so concerned about player suspensions and interdictions on the Stade Turpin that board members were forced to plead for bland and respectable fan behavior. Worse still for the authorities, in 1938, the incoming president and prominent lawyer Said Hadj was declared a staunch partisan of the 'ulama, while the sporting director supported the ultra-separatist PPA, and all worked to rid the club of European players, many of whom supported the Fascist leagues, a common stance in non-Muslim communities. Police further deemed that CC Biskra suffered from "Arab leanings," shorthand for nationalist, with Sporting Iqbal similarly "highly suspect."[62] Police could recommend only one solution to the racial and nationalist edge commonly displayed by Muslim football fans: reform, preferably with an eye toward an extension of economic and legal rights to Arabs and Kabyles. In April 1938, the police chief in Oran noted that the pattern of anger and assault in stadiums directly correlated to European-Muslim malaise. He observed that Spanish denizens, despite being relative newcomers to Algeria, received citizenship and privileges, while the original inhabitants—Arabs and Kabyles—were systematically denied status. This situation, he concluded, drove loyal Muslims into the waiting arms of nationalist organizations, embracing "treason and trouble."[63]

Football violence provided a venue for Arabs and Kabyles to physically engage the colonizer without fear of reprisal (due to the size of the crowds) and introduced the concept of mass action in the urban setting against the settlers. Much like robberies or violent crimes committed in the streets of various towns and cities during the interwar era, assaults in stadiums aimed to strike a blow against the colonial infrastructure and assail the prevailing racial and political orthodoxy. Moreover, with the emergence of nationalist organizations like the ENA/PPA, football matches provided an opportunity to construct an enclave in which fans bonded in racial and political terms, with youth in particular drawn by the prospect of rejecting colonialism in violent terms while striking a direct, collective blow to the supposedly superior colonizer. Although surely not a decisive blow against the French empire, football violence nonetheless played a substantial role in the formation and growth of cadres dedicated to Algerian independence.

Physical and Sexual Assaults, Real and Imaginary

Administrators were deeply concerned, and they became even more alarmed when attacks inside sports stadiums were twinned with a wave of violent crime in all three departments during the interwar era. Physical violence against settlers and officials, sexual assaults both real and imaginary, and a spate of brutal murders of Europeans by Arabs and Kabyles engendered panic both in the streets and in the halls of government. These comprised what Ann Laura Stoler terms "political crimes," carrying far more weight than a revenge plot or common criminal activity, correctly perceived as assaults against all settlers rather than on a specific target for profit or personal interest. Although far less frequent than quotidian thefts or threats, they nonetheless received a far more substantial official response, for the victims were European and the perpetrators Arab or Kabyle, and police and administrative documents reveal significant worries about assault and murder as predictive of widespread unrest throughout the Constantinois.[64]

In certain cases, this involved spontaneous assaults against the colonizer, avenging an insult or unfair policy, or being fired arbitrarily by a business or farm. In response to being randomly dismissed, for example, a mining employee in Boudjoudoun launched a rock at a European manager in August 1926. More commonly, theft provided the motive, usually premeditated and organized. On 12 April 1921, a gang in Lamy perpetrated an armed assault on a local bus carrying numerous passengers, simultaneously endangering highway traffic and sowing panic among the *colons* in the region. The culmination of years of criminal activity, the hijacking provided a clear example of the dangers facing isolated European farming communities surrounded by a far larger Algerian population deeply dissatisfied with imperial government and increasingly willing to engage in anticolonial violence.[65] Highways proved to be an equally popular setting for a wide variety of shooting incidents directed at specific European victims. In Collo, an assailant shot and wounded a local businessman behind the wheel of his car, in an incident arranged by a disgruntled ex-employee that prompted the institution of armed patrols on the autoroute around the clock.

Yet many of the most serious incidents occurred in the vicinity of European homes and on private property, and the perpetrators sought to harm the colonizers without a declared motive. One of these, a January 1920 assault in Bône, was so severe that the governor general openly worried about its impact on the European population in the region. Out hunting in Barral, a local bookkeeper and his son were ambushed by a local denizen who lunged for the father's firearm, and in the ensuing struggle, struck him violently with a rock, causing him to lose consciousness. Although he was only fifteen, the son shot at the assailant, who lived in a nearby *mechta*, and eventually struck him with the rifle butt and forced his retreat. Although the precise motive is not revealed in the official report, the governor general implies that the assault was part of a larger pattern of incidents specifically targeting *colons*, who furiously demanded protection and retribution. Europeans frequently intervened in judicial proceedings of suspects in assault cases, fearing that light sentences encouraged open rebellion and eroded their authority. Thus, the inhabitants of

UNLAWFUL ACTS OR STRATEGIES OF RESISTANCE?   103

Duzerville personally petitioned the governor general in November 1933 when two Muslim youths publicly thrashed a European and then struck the gendarmes who intervened to arrest them, forcing one to fire his revolver to restore order. When their municipal councilor father threatened legal action if they were jailed, the townsmen sought official intervention to ensure that a strong sentence restored colonial order.[66]

Far more terrifying, sexual assaults of European women fueled fear of Algerian males as potentially dangerous in both urban and rural centers. Settlers consistently worried about Muslim sexual desire for the female colonizer, a North African corollary to the "Black Peril" panic that swept sub-Saharan Africa during the new imperial era. The contrasting portrayals of the self-mastery of the civilized and bourgeois European and the primitive, unbounded sexuality of the predatory native provided a common link between the diverse imperial experiences of the colonial powers. Anne McClintock's diagnosis of British Africa could just as easily be applied to French Algeria: "In the colonies, black people were figured, among other things, as gender deviants, the embodiments of prehistoric promiscuity and excess." The protection of women and female sexuality was thus of paramount importance, to be enacted by violent means if necessary. The mere rumor of a "native" sexual assault unleashed the policing of female sexuality and constant vigilance toward the non-European population. As Jock McCulloch observes in the context of British Zimbabwe, the faintest possibility of an attack unleashed the European fixation on interracial sexual crime, which outweighed even the anxieties surrounding murder trials in its intensity. Although only handful of such assaults was ever reported in Algeria, much like in British Africa, police believed them to be widespread, and officials and *colons* alike thought that *indigènes* inherently wanted to rape white women.[67]

Unsurprisingly in Algeria, the mere suspicion of the potential violation of European women led to the criminalization of desire. An investigation into the May 1928 murder of a young woman in Philippeville turned toward an Algerian suspect, despite a lack of any physical evidence or witness testimony, solely because he was "connu à Saint-Charles comme cherchent à avoir des relations avec les jeunes filles européennes [known in Saint-Charles for seeking relations with young European girls]." Moreover, even a consensual interracial relationship provided grounds for suspicion. In June 1929, a young Algerian chauffeur from Batna who engaged in "improper relations" with a sixteen-year-old French girl was accused of kidnapping by her father, desperate to end the affair. In their report, police referred to her as a "girl of loose morals," terming the tryst "shameful," and they proceeded to jail the driver even though the girl had probably run away from home and nothing more.

The case twinned the common trope of policing female sexuality with a judicial and moral condemnation of Algerian sexuality.[68] Similar anxieties abounded concerning the possibility of rape at the hands of household servants. McCulloch notes a clear link between the proximity to white women of Africans employed in British homes and the burgeoning Black Peril panic in Zimbabwe.[69] Despite the fact that the French colonial archives contain records of only one such case—a gardener assaulted a Philippeville matron at knifepoint multiple times as she cooked the family dinner in a shed in July 1936—the language used by police suggests an omnipresent danger and concomitant public concern.[70]

Despite the fact that many accusations merely reflected racial animus and moral outrage, sexual assaults did in fact occur, although they rarely corresponded to the clichés parroted by police, press, and officials. More often than not, the motive was not sexual but political—a symbolic violation of the colonial system. In June 1935, a schoolboy confronted a pregnant European woman walking in Constantine's Place des Galettes and announced that African infantrymen wanted to sleep with her. When she responded, "Je suis une femme honnête et je n'ai rien à faire avec les sénégalais [I'm an honest woman and I want nothing to do with the Senegalese]," the youth violently kicked her in the stomach twice. Other cases involved soldiers and civilians acting in concert, publicly targeting white women in broad daylight, clear acts of anticolonial vengeance that broadcast an omnipresent threat that no European target remained sacrosanct. In Bône, a French waitress returning to her workplace in the company of friends in July 1935 was sexually assaulted by an Algerian co-worker; nearby *tirailleurs sénégalais* declined to arrest him and instead joined in, while her friends fled the scene.[71] Even more frightening for the European public were attacks that occurred in isolated areas, either in a rural setting or on the outskirts of towns and cities. One case, in a village outside Bône, involved a mother who had rented rooms locally as part of the treatment for malaria. She was attacked by a young man, dragged into an olive grove, and raped at knifepoint.[72] Although never very numerous, such incidents only heightened the ever-present anxiety over supposedly sexually aggressive Algerian males, particularly during the interwar era due to heightened tensions between the colonizers and colonized. As Stoler notes, "allusions to political and sexual subversion of the colonial system went hand in hand"; as subjects articulated greater demands for reform, the growing strength of anticolonialism manifested itself in allegations of rape and wanton sexuality, and more rarely, in cases of sexual assault meant to strike a blow against the sexual and political fabric of the empire. For this reason, the judicial response to any confirmed case was severe, involving lengthy jail terms or worse.[73]

Demographic Imbalance, Settler Vulnerability, and Murder as Anticolonial Revolt

Given the concerns evinced about physical and sexual assaults, it is perhaps surprising that murder was deemed the most serious crime committed by Algerians, due to the sheer volume of cases and the insurrectionary potential epitomized by the killings. By the interwar era, the European population in all three departments stalled for the first time, at one million, while the Muslim tally topped six million. The demographic imbalance was most pronounced in Constantine, which was decidedly more rural than Alger and Oran and contained the fewest non-Muslims in Algeria. In Kabylia, much of the Berber population saw very few Europeans at all other than gendarmes or officials. Given the demographic disparity, the isolation of many *colons* in far-flung *communes mixtes*, and constant worries about large-scale revolt, the killing of any settler reverberated throughout the community, a fact not lost on Muslims in the Constantinois.[74] Worse still, the tribe as a whole often participated in the planning and execution of a murder, clearly striking a blow against French predominance.

Consequently, a double standard quickly emerged throughout the department. Killings of Arabs and Kabyles by Europeans rarely resulted in prosecutions and certainly did not generate thorough police investigations and stiff prison sentences. Although gendarmes and policemen did examine cases of Algerians killed by their own brethren, in their 1929 annual report, the Sûreté générale referred to such homicides as a nuisance, as a disturbance of the peace that (if anything) underscored the need for security in order to maintain the docility of the native population. In any case, there were severe handicaps for European investigators charged with solving such killings. As there were no gendarmes stationed in Arab or Kabyle villages, law enforcement and the magistrate had to travel massive distances to investigate the crimes, arriving well after the events, a delay that permitted locals to destroy evidence or bribe witnesses.[75] Few investigators spoke Arabic, and thus they relied on subordinates or *caïds* to question witnesses and explain answers to the officers. Often, the word on the street substituted for actual information, and only rarely did an inhabitant cooperate; most rejected the notion of colonial justice altogether or sided with family or tribe over a rival band.[76] As a result, charges were often leveled against a convenient suspect, whether or not evidence of guilt actually existed.[77] Most such murder cases revealed crimes of passion or family (or neighbor) disputes. As no Europeans were involved, one report concluded, gendarmes and police remained apathetic: "Rarely is public security compromised by these attacks." Moreover, the bulk occurred in "backward" Kabylia, where officials claimed that the French could do nothing with the "rustic population with barbaric morals."[78] Only when the security of the colonizer came into question did authorities respond forcefully. In Sétif, a June 1929 homicide was deemed dangerous due to a major land dispute near a French town—the potential escalation of violence might threaten non-Algerian property and lives.[79] In contrast, when the victim was European, officials delegated police resources and demanded harsh penal sanctions for killings perceived to fundamentally attack the domination of the colonizers. After passing over dozens of murders committed in Algerian communities, the above report lamented eleven homicides of Europeans in 1928, highlighting the killing of a settler stabbed fifteen times by five Muslims in a remote village.[80]

The brutality of the killings testifies to a desire to foment violence against the colonizer, both in isolated areas and larger towns. In Souk Ahras, a town in the commune of La Séfia, three Algerians burglarized a house of hidden banknotes in October 1922, yet took the time to bludgeon a European woman to death and mutilate her child, found with face shredded and throat slit. A massive manhunt ensued, with tents and villages searched throughout the region. In a more urban setting, three Algerians stabbed sixty-year-old grandmother Thérèse Rolla to death in the major center of Sétif, stealing jewelry and valuables from her dwelling in the process. The autopsy revealed five severe hatchet wounds to Rolla's head, which the *commissaire de police* claimed to "demonstrate an uncommon brutality"—thefts were not usually accompanied by such mutilation. Moreover, the perpetrators tellingly struck while the victim's husband was at work, seriously unnerving the local population, concerned about attacks on their own families.[81] Only months later, in Bône, two Algerians murdered a widow during a robbery attempt on her bar and home, slitting her throat after administering a blow of such ferocity that she was almost decapitated, leaving her left ear impacted into the skull. Once again, the crime frightened Europeans, who presumed that the thief was not merely interested in pilfering valuables but instead wished to brutalize settlers, instilling fear while maximizing pain and injury.[82]

Of course, murderers did not solely target robbery victims. Many killings involved revenge, designed with justice rather than fear in mind. Typical was the case of a master mason from Bône, shot three times by Algerian colleagues whom he had recently fired, a punishment meted out to an official who had seemingly abused his authority and mistreated Algerian labor. A train station director in Oued Farah was similarly murdered as he left the station one evening, shot in the stomach by aggrieved ex-employees who resented both their arbitrary dismissal and the colonial authority that such decisions represented.[83] Attacks were more common in isolated agricultural regions, perpetrated by aggrieved farm laborers, unsurprising given the low pay and tenuous working conditions experienced by most Algerians in *communes mixtes*. Squeezed by falling produce prices, a mushrooming population with limited resources, disastrously low wages (one franc per hour by the 1920s), and rampant unemployment, many Algerians fled the countryside for Alger or Paris. For those who remained, their livelihood depended on capricious farm owners and managers, themselves buffeted by turbulent markets—the perfect recipe for violence.[84] When a Constantine landowner's son "snitched" about the misdeeds of a farmhand in February 1930, the accused stabbed him multiple times and seriously injured his wife in retaliation. The motive was revenge for the loss of livelihood. Smallholding farmers further resented the enforcement of property regulations that favored Europeans. Colonial law strictly prohibited any unauthorized grazing or collection of firewood on private land, but Algerians frequently ignored the restrictions, believing themselves to be the rightful proprietors of their own territory. Thus, in October 1930, the manager of a forestry reserve in Edough charged two local Arabs with trespassing, and the perpetrators shot him while he slept that evening.[85]

Most frightening for the settlers were unexplained murders, where Algerians attacked and killed Europeans for no apparent reason. The randomness of these crimes led to panic: Could any of the *indigènes* really be trusted to respect the authority of the colonizer? Were all Arabs and Kabyles merely waiting for a chance to kill any European they could find? When the manager of the Raffin farm in the village of Randon outside Bône was found covered in blood in January 1921, the governor general personally visited the scene and offered assistance to the town hall and investigating officers. He had been brutally attacked by a trusted Algerian worker, struck in the head several times with a machete. Although a minor sum had been stolen, the employee had access to the house and everything of value; there was no need to murder the notable in order to purloin 252 francs. Clearly, robbery was not the motive, and no mistreatment at the hands of his employer had occurred, meaning that it could not be revenge. It appeared to be a simple case of anticolonial violence, an attack against a European due to his position as a colonizer. Worse still, in the community's mind, the perpetrator fled the jurisdiction. Originally from the Sahara, it was unlikely that he would ever be found.[86]

Attacking the Agents of Hegemony and Repression

Whether Algerian or European, officials were often the main targets of anticolonial violence. They administered the Indigénat and justified the double standard by proclaiming that Algerians were subjects protected and governed by French administrators rather than citizens, despite the territorial unity with the metropole proclaimed in 1871. Officials represented the most visible presence of the despised colonial regime, and the purported hegemony and infallibility of the repressive system and assaults or murders symbolized armed revolt against the French occupation of Algeria.

In tents and villages, *caïds* were often assaulted when carrying out administrative orders. Appointed by the French authorities as trusted representatives, they managed local affairs on behalf of their superiors, collecting taxes, enforcing colonial law, and adjudicating disputes. When their authority came under duress, the administration grew openly concerned, for security depended on respect for French rule, and assaults against law enforcement and officials, crime and disorder, and infractions against the Indigénat invariably followed suit. In Briket, a number of residents in 1921 accosted the *caïd* and a guard attempting to mediate a water dispute, perceived by the deputy prefect as a veiled attack on Gallic authority. As they attempted to destroy a dam that interrupted the flow to neighboring villages, both were surrounded, threatened, and roughed up by a crowd of twenty Algerians, many of whom had previously done time for anti-French activities. The deputy prefect reserved the greatest concern not for the welfare of the *caïd,* but the rebellion against an official order tendered by the administrator of the *commune mixte*. Moreover, Briket had been a key flash point during the 1916 insurrection, in which French officials had been assassinated. Thus, maintaining Gallic prestige and authority and keeping order demanded that the rebels be given severe sentences, as an example to others tempted to defy French rule.[87] Other cases involved revenge, as *caïds* who presented outrageously high tax bills or assisted the administration in the capture of bandits or criminals became the targets of assault or attempted murder, perpetrated by irate villagers.[88] Regardless of the motives for the crimes, officials viewed the attacks as extremely prejudicial to Gallic interests. Tellingly, a September 1921 monthly report dismisses multiple murders of Algerians, focusing solely on the killing of a *caïd* in M'Sila: "Aucun de ces crimes n'intéresse la sécurité publique . . . sauf en ce qui concerne l'aggression dont a été victim le Caïd de Kessabia [None of these crimes impacts public safety . . . except the attack against the *caïd* of Kessabia]."[89]

An equally difficult situation concerned Arab or Kabyle law enforcement, similarly targeted as colonial emissaries who directly implemented the legal system that benefited Europeans and subjugated Muslims. In many instances, the assailants rejected the authority of Algerian guards and police to enforce the law. In June 1934, a soldier and two gendarmes attempted to seize sheep in Jemmapes as payment of a debt, only to be assaulted by sixty locals, who swarmed the officers with sticks, pitchforks, rocks, and firearms. Only police action involving all available officers and eleven arrests restored order and prevented a massacre.[90] Indeed, debt and tax collection proved so fraught throughout the Constantinois that guards were routinely roughed up when presenting bills to inhabitants. The tithes were often ludicrous; a *fellah*'s tent charged at the same rate as a settler's house, for example. Nonetheless, the state maintained a variety of mechanisms designed to maximize payments from non-Europeans, with exorbitant rates for "subjects" and discounts for "citizens."[91] Unsurprisingly, an attempt to collect taxes in Batna ended in a riot in 1937, with fifty people involved in a melee that ended with a guard punched twice in the face. Only the timely arrival of soldiers and government personnel prevented a worse fate, and the assistant administrator blamed the anti-French *djemâa* (tribal council) for whipping Muslims into a nationalist frenzy and preventing the payment of taxes across the region: only a paltry 2,000 francs had been gathered in the preceding year, as opposed to over 30,000 per annum in the past. Commenting on the case of a cavalier stabbed by an allegedly "lazy" Algerian he had been charged with bringing in for "straightening out," the administrator of Soummam echoed these sentiments, viewing the assault as indicative of an increasing refusal by the local population to follow orders. Not one villager had stepped forward to assist the injured party.[92]

European officials also proved to be frequent targets, because they often exploited impoverished Algerians for their own financial gain, a not uncommon occurrence in smaller towns. In April 1935, angry locals in the town of Tamalous shot and killed the railway chief, who had used his administrative position to engage in loan sharking, land acquisition, and shady commercial deals. His domination of the village economy and usurious business practices led to profound resentment and, eventually, murder. Unlike the assault and killing of Algerian officials, this case provoked the intervention of high-level administrators, two investigators from the gendarmerie, and the prosecutor's office, because the victim was European.[93] However, not all such attacks could be traced to official misconduct. An assault in Bougie in June 1936 pitted an angry Muslim against the mayor of Akbou and his guard as they promenaded in public. Although they initially believed that the assailant was drunk, officers soon realized that the attack was religious in nature, as the suspect carried a book of saints and spoke constantly of Allah and the insults of unbelievers, and expressed a desire to kill the mayor due to his Judaism.[94] Although the authorities demanded that he be committed to an asylum as insane, his real target appeared to be the non-Muslim power structure.[95]

Police and guards also bore the brunt of anticolonial anger; as visible targets across the region, their uniforms and job descriptions embodiments of the imperial state. Various historians have documented a correlation between policing in the empire and the maintenance of colonial order, going beyond merely upholding the law to bolstering hegemony and repression, their mandate far different from the law-and-order brief of the metropolitan force.[96] Moreover, Algerian law enforcement abetted the construction of racial boundaries through what Partha Chatterjee terms the "rule of colonial difference": the broad spectrum of political, economic, social, and cultural factors mobilized by the colonized to perpetuate white racial superiority.[97]

As a result, the inhabitants of villages and tents vociferously objected to any police presence, from guards on patrol to gendarmes conducting searches or arrests. When two agents arrived in El-Ksar in February 1923, looking for a murder suspect wanted for the killing of a night guard, they faced immediate hostility from the locals. Various voices yelled, "Maudit soit les français et leur gouvernment de merde! . . . Fils de cochon! [The French and their shit government are wretched! . . . Son of a bitch!]," while others peppered the police with anti-French insults and threats to "bugger your women." Eventually, the irate crowd began to gather clubs and rocks, and came perilously close to killing both men. A similar situation erupted in Châteaudun in June 1929, when police sought to interview witnesses to a murder and were confronted by a mob armed with sticks and clubs, led by a twice-convicted killer. Having managed to escape unscathed, primarily due to the threat of gunfire, they subsequently faced a "conspiracy of silence" as the women in question refused to testify.[98]

That such actions were explicitly anticolonial in nature is best exemplified by an attack against two gendarmes on 28 May 1925 in Bordj-Bou-Arréridj, a town in the hills southwest of Sétif. That afternoon, the officers spotted an Algerian racing into a ravine and gave chase. He fired in their direction and in the subsequent exchange, was seriously wounded. Parents and villagers almost immediately arrived on the scene and surrounded the officers, throwing rocks and declaring, "We're going to do the same to you as in Morocco," a clear reference to the Rif rebellion then occurring in that protectorate. The administrator noted in his report that the entire region was poor and the inhabitants furious at the colonizers, as this was the third recent attack against law enforcement from the Mansourah brigade. Needless to say, the crowd forced the release of the injured man, and no arrest or trial ever proceeded. The general in charge of the Constantine division raged at anti-French propaganda that blanketed the region and the need to force the "Arab territory" to respect Gallic authority, by violent means if necessary. Otherwise, revolt would threaten settlers throughout the area.[99]

Not all attacks on police were premeditated or mobilized to prevent arrest and detention. Routine patrols and duties proved to be equally dangerous for police officers and gendarmes, particularly in villages in an overwhelmingly rural department containing few Europeans and a preponderance of mountains and forests, and thus no possibility of reinforcements. This allowed inhabitants to assist anyone suspected of malfeasance, and they often displayed a violent hatred for law enforcement that betrayed a distinctly anticolonial bent. In June 1925, two gendarmes working in Mansourah, a desolate and sparsely populated area with rough terrain between Honda, M'Sila, and Bordj-Bou-Arréridj, engaged in a scuffle with an Algerian that ended in the shooting of one of them and the suspect, who was arrested by the uninjured officer. Locals from a nearby group of tents proceeded to attack that agent with rocks, administering a severe beating. In the aftermath, the deputy prefect complained bitterly that the Algerian population did not respect authority, engaging in anti-French and nationalist activity manifested in crime against European targets. Pointing out that one of the five men apprehended for the assault bluntly informed the local magistrate that he regretted not killing the gendarmes, the official joined the general commanding the Constantine division in demanding an "immediate and merciless crackdown" against anyone who either attacked a European or aided the perpetrators. Whether a direct assault or propaganda or material assistance, the commander thundered, all anticolonial activity undermined French authority and security and thus required a vicious response.[100]

Official and Police Responses to Anticolonial Crime and Violence

Facing frequent incidents of anticolonial violence throughout the Constantinois, police responded with a variety of tactics designed less to solve criminal cases than to bolster French imperial hegemony, including illegal searches, arbitrary arrests, and brazen murders of suspects. Official responses to the threat throughout the region reflected broad imperial security concerns during the interwar era, and increasingly draconian methods were used to staunch attacks against the European population. Colonial and municipal governments attempted to intimidate Algerians, forcefully terminating anticolonial violence through a campaign of arrests, harassment, and even assault and murder. In Bône, a January 1928 roundup led to 150 arrests, the "perpetrators" fingerprinted and photographed at the police station and eventually released after a lengthy delay. These strong-arm tactics yielded a mere handful of thieves, prostitution charges, and four illegal weapons.[101] Another occurred in Mansourah after unknown assailants beat and robbed a market inspector, hitting him from behind with a wooden stick and stealing 450 francs and a gold watch. Despite the fact that neither victim nor police could positively identify the perpetrators, the authorities gathered a group of fifteen "idlers" in nearby woods and drove them to the police station, where they faced harsh interrogation and arrest.[102]

House searches also routinely ended in violence and rights violations, despite clear procedural rules concerning the conduct of officers and the methods to be employed. The wife of a suspect in Edough testified that six agents had beaten her and her husband and purposely damaged household items while looking for a firearm in their tent during a January 1930 raid. The chief administrator rejected her story, yet the counterevidence proved weak at best: she claimed that she did not know the names of the officers responsible (who did not live in the village) and had no visible injuries during the interrogation. The deputy prefect urged his superiors to ignore the entire matter, a very common occurrence when such charges were brought forward.[103] In a similar case from Bordj-Bou-Arréridj in May 1928, where gendarmes were accused of illegally searching a home and beating the wife and children of an absent suspect, the captain accused the author of defamation. It was a matter of military honor, and the officers categorically rejected the claims as yet another attempt to smear law enforcement with ridiculous charges. The complainant, Ahmed Mani, should face criminal charges and lose his job as railway worker, he thundered.[104] Administrators were equally uninterested even when Algerians produced evidence of property destruction during police actions. When the owner of a cake shop in Kerrata accused a local rural policeman of wrecking his establishment—overturning tables and destroying food—and subsequently falsely arresting him, the administrator not only claimed that the entire story had been fabricated but also referred to the wrong name—Medjirad rather than Messaoud.[105]

Complaints involving intimidation, theft, and assault were routinely dismissed, with officials and police bluntly stating that Algerians could not be trusted, as they consistently levied false accusations. When a *caïd* accused a brigadier of using "the most reprehensible and foul language" during a search in Bibans, unsurprisingly local law enforcement rejected the conclusions and instead claimed that the *indigènes* were unruly and uncontrollable. Despite a constant stream of accusations leveled against officers, of illegal home searches and violence, the administrator refused to contradict the official account. Although he admitted that not all arms seizures were properly conducted and that one of the accused gendarmes should in fact be transferred, attacking the actions of the service invited an increase in criminal behavior—indeed, the *caïd*'s attitude actually incited the population to anti-French sentiment, a reflection of his long-standing antipathy to the officers in question. The deputy prefect, in contrast, defended him as a loyal republican and supporter—the most important factor in such an appointment—and chided the brigadier for his foul mouth, yet noted that the sheer volume of successful arms seizures made any transfer unthinkable, and thus "the end justifies the means." Security in the region remained the only goal of the service. Naturally, the Brigade was far more blunt: the tribal leader should mind his business and show the gendarmerie sufficient appreciation.[106]

However, the sheer volume of complaints belies any facile interpretation, as across the department, Arabs and Kabyles bitterly described numerous instances of police brutality. One case in Bône involved a policeman responding to a brawl in his district, and shooting and killing the aggressor. Although the officer was charged with murder, the European jury threw out the case but ordered the payment of 10,000 francs in damages to the mother of the victim, in an extraordinary acknowledgement of wrongdoing. The inability to obtain justice from the courts was not unusual, frustrating Algerians, who were forced to rely on a biased system. Petitions carrying numerous signatures attested to vicious behavior; in one case from Collo, twenty-six locals charged a brigadier with coercing the population to do his bidding or face arrest and jail. Naturally, most such complaints were ignored, invariably accompanied by the testimony of superiors concerning the accused officers' excellent character and superb arrest record, or countering that police could not function due to the high volume of false charges launched by complainants.[107] In other cases, they simply shot the suspects. In July 1921, two officers in Batna killed an armed robber and severely wounded his accomplice. Both policemen were ordered to stand trial but the judge found no fault with their actions per se, clearly the agents lacked sangfroid—some form of nonlethal pacification would have sufficed. Needless to say, the manslaughter case was summarily dismissed.[108]

Most of the police violence was quotidian rather than spectacular in nature. In both France and Algeria, officers regularly subjected suspects to the infamous *passage à tabac* (thrashing), a term derived from the word *tabasser* (to do over). Although its use receded somewhat in the metropole by the twentieth century, it proved to be far more durable in the empire, where police spoke openly of "vigorous measures" and "hard interrogations" designed to force confessions, often from those arrested without a shred of evidence. Police and gendarmes were no less brutal in public, in both the countryside and the city. One April 1939 case in the *commune mixte* of Oued Meriel involved a European forest guard who grabbed a middle-aged woman and struck her repeatedly with a riding crop, producing contusions and blue hematoma. He then unholstered his service revolver and fired in her direction. The cause of this mistreatment? The guard claimed that the woman had been illegally grazing cattle in the forest, a common and nonviolent misdemeanor.[109]

Such abuse was worsened by the unduly harsh treatment afforded to non-Europeans by the Algerian criminal justice system. Where the Indigénat had instituted harsh penalties for civil offenses committed by Algerians, by the interwar era the same attitudes infiltrated criminal proceedings, enforcing a growing gap between trials and sentencing for European and Arab or Kabyle felons. Legal precedents allotted vastly different punishments for the same crimes, based exclusively on racial grounds, reflecting both the perception of Algerians as inherently dangerous and the desire to bolster colonial hierarchy and authority. This included the imposition of a double standard, whereby a European convicted of drunkenness and assaulting an officer received a paltry few months in jail and a token fine, while an Algerian was typically handed years in prison for the same crime. Punishments for assault or armed robbery normally averaged three to five years and often carried an additional loss of rights, including the *droit de séjour*, permission to live in their village or town. For prosecutors saw the forced removal of "criminal elements" as an essential step toward breaking anticolonial resistance. In this regard, murder charges were the most serious and almost always warranted the death penalty; acting as an accomplice assured a sentence of twenty years hard labor.[110] Judges rarely granted clemency, and a merciful verdict meant the commutation of capital punishment to a lifetime of hard labor and an exorbitant fine, leaving the accused's family penniless.[111] Moreover, executions were public events, designed both to satisfy the European thirst for revenge and send a message to Algerians tempted to kill their colonial masters. While the authorities did not require attendance, large crowds arrived from villages nonetheless, unable to avoid the events as they occurred at the beginning of the workday, or simply attracted mourning relatives and numerous sympathizers from tight-knit rural communities.[112]

Perhaps the most nefarious penalty was the imposition of *surveillance spéciale*, the forced removal of community members or an entire village to a distant locale, either to coerce suspects into surrendering or to remove those deemed criminal from the region altogether. Again concerned with felonies and misdemeanors as anticolonial rather than mere criminal activity, officials implemented the practice on a wide scale to combat disorder or revolt, whether manifest through either violence or unruly behavior. French administrators including the governor general, prefects, and *caïds* routinely authorized the process, often sending the local police to find needed evidence.[113] In Barika, the newly arrived administrator of the *commune mixte* in March 1928 immediately used *surveillance spéciale* against suspected thieves and delinquents, acting on suspicion of guilt rather than proof or arrests. Another case in Biskra responded to a 1935 violent crime wave, resulting in numerous weapons and assault charges. There, the authorities focused on Mohamed Kheneddine, termed a dangerous criminal, his removal accompanied by prefectorial edicts replacing the local muezzin and the Postes, télégraphes, et téléphones auxiliary and closing "suspect" Moorish cafés.[114]

Surveillance spéciale was a common palliative for sudden increases in criminal activity in a given locale, used by officials to placate fearful Europeans in rural or isolated districts and to ward off the threat of insurrection by the colonized. In July 1921, the administrators of various *communes mixtes* complained about the "almost intact preservation of the ancestral mentality of these regions' inhabitants, characterized by the warrior spirit and a talent for plundering." Blaming the Algerian "mentality" for the local crime wave, and vociferously criticizing the nonecooperation of *caïds*, the officials forwarded a list of "dangerous *indigènes*" for deportation. Failure to act invariably raised the specter of *colons* pursuing vigilante justice or intimidating local officials and juries. The inhabitants of Duzerville personally petitioned the governor general in November 1933 when two Muslim youths publicly thrashed a European and then subsequently struck the gendarmes who intervened to arrest them, forcing one to fire his revolver to restore order. When their municipal councilor father threatened legal action if they were jailed, the townsmen sought official intervention to ensure that a strong sentence restored colonial order.[115]

The need to resort to such draconian measures underscores the tenuous grip of French imperialism in Algeria by the interwar era. Although the authorities had long abandoned any pretense to seeking consent in favor of armed coercion, their response discounted even the illusion of criminal justice. By invoking police brutality and judicial bias, the colonial state moved toward tactics that would be used during the Algerian War of Independence (principally assault, torture, and physical displacement), designed to intimidate and dislocate anticolonial resistance, no matter how insignificant. Thus emerged the consolidation of what Taylor Sherman has termed the "coercive network," an interconnection of institutions, laws, practices, and security arrangements harnessed by the colonial state to maintain domination. Of course, this proved illusory; if the state used violence against all vestiges of rebellion, it "tended to be vulnerable, fluid, and replete with tensions."[116] Nonetheless, the ordinary practices of a criminal justice system—the arrest of suspects, trials, and sentencing—did not apply to the empire, where indiscriminate detention, harassment, and physical coercion, not to mention collective punishments and brutal treatment, constituted the norm.

Of course, interwar Algerians were not merely passive victims of colonial violence and police brutality. If political leaders and nationalist organizations were not yet ready to spark a mass independence movement or foment armed revolt, Arabs and Kabyles throughout the Constantinois adopted a variety of strategies designed to simultaneously refute the French colonial state and destabilize its hegemonic pretensions. By the interwar era, nonelite inhabitants of town and countryside increasingly turned to anticolonial violence, from arms trafficking to murder. Where attempts at full-scale rebellion faltered previously, primarily due to the capacity of French military firepower, anticolonial crime during the interwar era promised limited immediate results, yet provided examples of the successful rejection of European invincibility and the power wielded by the colonial state and its official representatives. In this way, it represents a bridge to the political anticolonialism that emerged on a mass scale after May 1945 and the ensuing struggle between the state and a growing number of actors determined to end the French presence in Algeria, culminating in the 1954 to 1962 War of Independence. Yet before that could occur, there was the small matter of military defeat in the opening stages of World War II and the Occupation. How would the Vichy regime respond to anticolonial violence? Did the same crimes persist under authoritarian rule?

CHAPTER 4

Colonial Policing during Wartime
From Vichy to the Allies and Free French

With the end of the Third Republic came an entirely new form of government in both metropole and empire, and nowhere was this felt more acutely than in the various police forces and security services. The vote taken at the Vichy casino on 10 July 1940 effectively transferred power to Marshall Philippe Pétain and Pierre Laval, a decision backed unanimously by the Algerian group of representatives. Parliamentary democracy was summarily dissolved, replaced when the dust settled by a Nazi-occupied northern zone centered on Paris and a smaller southern territory, closely monitored by German authorities yet autonomous for the moment. Pétain and company attempted to construct the "new order" long demanded by the Extreme Right, an effort doubly hailed in North Africa, which remained in Vichy's hands, and where the settlers had long supported colonial Fascist movements perceived to bolster the imperial project and its chief European beneficiaries. The new governor general was Jean Abrial, whose team of prefects and officials were all, to borrow Jacques Cantier's phrase, "men steeped in the new ways."[1]

Abrial spoke openly of a "great cleansing," echoing the metropolitan line concerning democratic decadence and the need for moral and physical regeneration following the defeat. Thus, change came swiftly to Algerian institutions. Prefects in Alger and Constantine were summarily removed and replaced with loyalists.[2] The Délégations financières (Financial Parliament) and Conseil supérieur (High Council) disappeared, replaced by an advisory commission with a purely consultative role, its eighteen members selected on the basis of fealty to the regime—Far Right for Europeans and *évolué* for Muslims. The *conseils généraux* (departmental councils) were similarly suspended and their powers devolved to prefects and regional appointed committees dedicated to the "new order." Much like the national commission, these bodies attracted extreme-rightist stalwarts from the lawyer Paul Saurin to the Parti social français (PSF; French Social Party) mainstay Stanislas Devaud, and even Arab members maintained ties to Fascist leagues or conservative organizations. In the same vein, mayors who were extreme-rightists or ultraconservatives kept their posts—Albin Rozis in Alger and Lucien Bellat from Sidi-Bel-Abbès, for instance—while Vichy immediately replaced all socialists and republicans.[3] Thus the regime ensured continuity from July 1940 until the November 1942 Allied landing, even as Abrial gave way to proconsul Maxime Weygand in November 1941 and finally to Yves Châtel the following year.

All the Vichyiste trappings duly arrived in Algeria, from the Légion française des combattants (French Combatants Legion), with 101,000 members by June 1941, to the Chantiers de la jeunesse youth work camps. The Légion embodied the Pétanist credo of *travail, famille, patrie* (work, family, fatherland), which replaced the revolutionary credo of "liberty, equality, fraternity," while the Chantiers combined with a new leadership school to train one thousand future Vichy loyalists. These moves reflected another key component of the new regime—the Pétain cult, which reached its apex in late 1941, a fairly easy task in a region where settlers had flocked to the Algerian Extreme Right, including Amitiés latines (Latin Friendship) and Rassemblement national d'action sociale (RNAS; National Rally for Social Action), and to the metropolitan leagues, including Action française (French Action), Croix de Feu / Parti social français (CF/PSF; Cross of Fire / French Social Party), and Parti populaire français (PPF; French People's Party).[4] Posters and images of Maréchal Pétain were omnipresent, with sixty-three thousand sold in Alger alone, while government officials and *colons* alike consistently exhibited complete confidence and veneration for the Vichy leader. Increasingly evident in the metropole, support for the Free French languished in Algeria, yet unlike Europeans, Muslims did not buy into the propaganda. As one Arab veteran noted, "Quels que soient nos services militaires, notre conduit civile et notre amour pour la France, nous sommes toujours les 'ratons' [Regardless of our military service, our civic behavior, and our love for France, we are all 'ratons']."[5]

Given such quotidian racism, it is unsurprising that persecution also crossed the Mediterranean, with those deemed "enemies of the state"—Jews, Communists, Freemasons, and Muslim nationalists—purged ruthlessly from the civil service and various professions. Only French citizens were able to serve the new administration, and 7,266 government workers were removed by April 1941, including anyone deemed socialist or communist, republican, or merely disloyal, which could mean displaying an improper attitude toward Pétain and Vichy. Thus, hundreds of teachers were fired due to their political leanings. On 13 August 1940, all Freemasonic "secret societies" were dissolved, deemed to be pro-democratic and republican, impacting three thousand members in Algeria, who lost their rights and employment. Another law overturned the 1870 Crémeiux Decree that had granted French citizenship to the territory's Jewish population, while the Jewish Statute of 3 October 1940 withdrew jobs, educational opportunities, and rights for all but distinguished war veterans. Under the jurisdiction of the army, concentration camps were constructed south of the Tell for "errant" types, from Spanish republicans to foreign Jews.[6] All of these moves pleased the settler population, in keeping with their prewar pro-Fascism, even if implementation was occasionally delayed by wartime necessities. Certain Jewish civil servants retained their employment due to a dearth of replacements, angering Algerian xenophobes. Yet by October 1941, only 469 of 2,671 remained in their posts, along with a smattering of lawyers, while plans for Aryanization tabulated Jewish businesses and property for liquidation.[7]

These moves also placated Muslims, playing on their long-standing hatred of the Crémieux Decree, as Algerians disproportionately suffered due to the languishing wartime economy. Cut off from the metropole and prewar trade, the population across the Mediterranean endured shortages of everything from soap and cooking oil to coffee and meat. Over sixteen million tons of goods passed through Algerian ports in 1938, reduced to 2.7 million a mere three years later, due to the closure of shipping lanes and the Nazi occupation of European trading partners. Imports of everything from textiles and sugar to chemicals and steel abruptly ended, leading the Algerian Chamber of Commerce to speak of a death blow to the import-export trade. Algerian factories turned to local production to attempt to make up the shortfall, yet food continued to be exported to the metropole in fulfillment of existing contracts despite the dire situation in North Africa.[8] For Muslims facing the prospect of starvation, emigration to France was no longer possible, and the 1940 and 1942 harvests were disastrous, leading to extremely high prices and a burgeoning black market inaccessible to European workers, let alone *fellahs* and urban Arabs or Kabyles. With dietary staples like lamb and wheat completely unobtainable, poverty overwhelmed communities, and theft and unrest compromised security across all three departments. Worse still, German propaganda fueled potential rebellion, encouraging nationalism on the radio and in print. Attempts by Vichy to counter Nazi maneuvers proved futile—schools and speeches could not feed the desperate population. By winter 1941 to 1942, desperate crowds literally invaded towns to obtain food, while fuel shortages exacerbated the already deflated local agriculture and industry, for imports collapsed during wartime; fifty thousand tons of coal per month did not come close to meeting Algerian needs. Foodstuffs were exported by contract to France while locals starved.[9]

Such conditions made law enforcement absolutely essential, and no major purge occurred in the ranks of the police. In the metropole, many officers remained from the Third Republic days, and the regime did evince concern about their potential adherence to parliamentarism and opposition to Nazism. However, many of the newer recruits were completely loyal to Vichy, and even pro-Nazi in certain cases. Moreover, by October 1941, all were required to take an oath of allegiance to Pétain and regularly demonstrate loyalty to the state.[10] The retention of certain stalwarts from the pre-regime days seemingly provided the illusion that the work had not changed, yet the reality was quite different: antisemitism and xenophobia were omnipresent in both metropole and empire, while Jews, leftists, and Masons were all ultimately purged, albeit in somewhat limited form in Algeria, where few officers fell into these categories.[11] However, there existed another compelling reason for the lack of significant transformation in the police, Sûreté, and gendarmerie: the Algerian forces and brigades were teeming with supporters of the extreme-rightist leagues. Many members were deeply antisemitic and xenophobic, seeing a nationalist in every Muslim home, trained by senior officers who themselves supported colonial Fascism. Well before Vichy, they backed the settlers unreservedly in cities and smaller towns, alongside mayors and councilors. In places like Oran or Sidi-bel-Abbès, no policeman could survive without extolling Jules Molle, Lucien Bellat, or Gabriel Lambert, and no Muslim adjutant could keep a job without renouncing independence in favor of French Algeria and colonialism.[12]

Unlike in the metropole, extreme-rightist figures and groups dominated the Algerian political scene, with tens of thousands of members backing the imperial project, providing a natural fit for law enforcement whose brief included the maintenance of colonial order and hegemony, staffing riot squads and paramilitary units against Algerian nationalists, and engineering racial repression in town and countryside. Years before the Nazi military victory and the fall of the Third Republic, police met leftist demonstrations with extreme force, beat Jews mercilessly with the encouragment of commanding officers, and personally joined the PPF, CF, or RNAS. In fact, the governor general's expansion of the state force in Algeria specifically responded to Fascist police and gendarme violence from Blida and Mostaganem to Constantine. Matters came to a head during the Popular Front years, when Jewish socialist Léon Blum became the prime minister and the nationalist PPA began to flex its muscles, leading to severe crackdowns. The brutal campaign climaxed in January 1937, when the Garde républicaine mobile in Oran policed a demonstration with rifle butts and truncheons, wounding eighty-seven, including women and children, and the inspector general's inquest led to revelations of extreme-rightist sentiment throughout the brigades. Naturally, the final report blamed Arabs and Kabyles, an "insufficiently evolved race."[13]

Service Reform, Manpower Shortages, and Recruitment

Consequently, Vichy had no need to purge Algerian law enforcement. Nor could they have dispatched many replacement personnel, due to the large number of police among the prisoners of war languishing in Europe. By summer 1940, fully 1.5 million French soldiers had been captured, including 67,400 from Algeria, and documents from the era consistently make clear that numerous police and gendarmes were missing from various locales across all three departments. Moreover, despite constant promises about releasing the prisoners, only in June 1942 did any substantial number return home, and then only in exchange of three skilled workers per POW, with the exception of those who fell grievously ill or escaped.[14] Yet, the Vichy government did export metropolitan structural changes designed to meet its political, economic, and social priorities. Law enforcement agencies were expected to provide blanket surveillance of the metropole and the empire, reading millions of letters and telegrams and regularly monitoring telephone conversations. Arrests became a regular feature of the Vichy landscape, targeting shady operatives at train stations and black market profiteers, leftists, prostitutes, and others engaged in "immoral" behavior, and resisters of all stripes. Thus, the regime introduced a number of innovations that would remain in place well after the liberation. In addition to expanding state service to all towns of ten thousand inhabitants, the Groupes mobiles de reserve (Mobile Reserve Units, a forerunner to the postwar Compagnies républicaines de sécurité), policed large-scale disturbances and riots. Various new services also formed to enforce the regime's decrees against so-called enemies: the Brigades spéciales (Special Brigades) to deal with leftists and resisters, the Police des questions juives (for Jews), the Service des sociétés sécretes (hunting Freemasons), and the Service de police anti-communiste.[15] All of these agencies used intelligence provided by the Centre d'information et d'études (Center for Information and Research), and they operated alongside the prewar Renseignements généraux (RG; political police), Police judiciaire (criminal police), and municipal forces, which all served the regime's agenda after the June 1940 defeat, prioritizing it over fighting quotidian crimes. They joined the Brigades spéciales in investigating subversive propaganda and individuals, with obedience and loyalty the only important factors. The state regularly paid bonuses for success and sanctioned any agent perceived to be half-hearted, particularly following the summer 1941 German invasion of the Soviet Union, which boosted the resistance by voiding the Molotov-Ribbentrop Pact and turned Communists against collaboration. Last but certainly not least came the Brigade économique (Economic Brigade), which fought against the black market, and the Service des contrôles techniques (Technical Inspection Service), the branch dedicated to the surveillance of public opinion, searching for "antinational" elements in three sections: post, telegraph, and telephone.[16]

In Algeria, each service responded to specific local needs, beginning with the leadership. Appointed in October 1940, the first Vichy-era director of security, Ernest Chauvin, was a former administrator of various *communes mixtes* (mixed communes) in the 1920s who had worked his way in the 1930s through the ranks of the Directorate of General Security. Fluent in Arabic, he was replaced in August 1941 by Léon Muscatelli, another veteran official with experience in civilian and police administration. Similarly, the Bureau des ménées internationales (Bureau of International Intrigue) and the Brigade de surveillance du territoire (Territorial Surveillance Brigade) were staffed with anti-Gaullist and anti-British officers whose Pétainist loyalties were never in doubt, though both agencies were also tasked with disrupting Axis espionage in addition to engaging the usual suspects.[17] Under their diktat, specifically North African services emerged, including the Oran-based Service spécial de documentation (Special Information Service), charged with searching for Gaullists and Anglophiles, and the Corps civil des douairs—technically, a customs agency tasked with protecting the coast from Beni Saf to La Calle, but also charged with border patrols, antismuggling details, and even policing in certain towns.[18]

In theory, the plethora of police services, supplemented by the gendarmerie in the colonial setting in smaller communities and internment camps, promised to export Vichy's agenda to North Africa. Yet, a familiar problem consistently hampered the system's functioning—a lack of manpower in almost every branch. In March 1941, the Alger police commissioner wrote to the prefect complaining that positions had now been vacant in several arrondissements for one and a half years, with military service and retirements scheduled to wreak even more havoc. Although the governor general in April 1940 had proffered temporary replacements (French citizens aged twenty-five to sixty who were ineligible for military service and had no criminal record), they simply could not mimic seasoned investigators.[19] A similar problem afflicted the gendarmerie, buffeted by the losses to their ranks of killed and captured soldiers and the concomitant need to withdraw troops from locations that needed them. After the entire complement was removed in July 1941, the mayor of Souk-Ahras worried openly about being protected solely by a group of *tirailleurs indigènes*. Would they risk their lives for European settlers, particularly if the Algerian population rose up in revolt?[20] By that time, the numbers, already challenging in the pre-1940 era, had plummeted across all three departments. The gendarmerie urgently required more than one thousand additional soldiers in North Africa; the Police administrative needed 650 in Algeria alone. Thousands of positions remained unfilled in the other services, and armistice agreements prevented many candidates from even being considered. By November, complaints streamed in concerning uneducated and untrained Algerian agents utterly incapable of doing the job—even in major centers like Bône and Constantine, some unable to write or even understand basic orders.[21]

Worse still, the quotidian duties of a police officer were seemingly lost in the Vichy shuffle, as the regime prioritized xenophobia, anti-Resistance actions, and black-market prevention. Yet even these duties gradually succumbed to the reality of manpower shortages. In Constantine, the prefect wrote in frustration to the police chief in June 1942 concerning the lack of market patrols. Additional personnel must be recruited, he insisted, rejecting the chief's idea of using *douairs* (customs officers) as auxiliaries. Brute force could not beat the black market, and thus he demanded intelligence fieldwork from the local police, including an administrative report for the Brigade économique detailing everything from harvests and local food consumption to the current state of the fight against fraud. It was bad enough that the Police d'état and the fiscal branch could not see eye to eye, he concluded, without a lack of resources handing victory to criminals taking advantage of shortages.[22] However, the move to force local officers into the Brigade économique resulted in staff shortages for fighting crime. The head of the Oran RG complained of a net loss of almost one-third of his complement in a matter of years due to such transfers, worse than illness or retirement.[23] Even so, such patchwork measures had little impact, and well after US troops landed in November 1942, official laments continued to regularly appear. In January 1943, the governor general succumbed to the inevitable and demanded that all Europeans over forty-five and Muslims thirty-six and older be considered for positions as police trainees, at a starting rate of 2,600 francs per month plus the family bonus, if applicable. As for the gendarmerie, whose members were literally fighting the Nazis in Europe by 1943, superior officers bluntly stated that they would make do with smaller complements—three men must do the work of six. There would be no replacements, no matter the concerns of senior officers in vulnerable communities like Guelma, Souk-Ahras, and Villars.[24]

Police Actions against Resisters, Communists, and Jews

Regardless of the number of active officers in a given branch, they were expected to consistently enforce Vichy's security agenda. In the metropole, the hunting down of resisters was a clear priority in this regard. This proved to be less necessary in Algeria, not least because few supported Gaullism or the Left. Most viewed Pétain as a legitimate leader, and given the sheer number of supporters for Fascist groups among the general population, few Europeans were opposed to restrictions on Jews, Muslims, and Communists, and thousands flocked to join official organizations. Police spent far more time seeking out subversives in the local bar or on the street, grumbling about food shortages or the regime's inability to reduce prices, often while inebriated. Similarly, the authorities swooped in to arrest anyone manifesting dissent—by whistling during newsreels in theaters, for example.[25] Needless to say, Algerian officials copied their metropolitan counterparts in banning all political activity, from meetings and public gatherings to press and propaganda. Only extreme-rightist groups like the PPF were free to operate as usual, although somewhat constrained by the local administration.[26]

However, actual support for the Free French rarely appeared in any venue. In May 1941, Paul-Louis Bret, the regional director of the information bureau, approvingly noted that "General de Gaulle has practically no support." The sinking of the French fleet at Mers-el-Kébir by British ships on 3 July 1940 unleashed massive fury in both the metropole and colony, much of which targeted the Gaullist contingent in London, suspected as complicit in the attack.[27] This is not to say that no partisans existed in North Africa, but mentions of pro-British sentiment by police were purely theoretical, and the rare sightings of a V for victory or a Cross of Lorraine (a symbol of Free France) on town walls never coalesced into resistance groups or actions.[28] Moreover, much like across the Mediterranean, anger at the state increased dramatically only once the population felt the full brunt of Nazi control over France. In Algeria, the greatest manifestations of resistance were directed at the Service du travail obligatoire (STO; Compulsory Labor Service), which brought youths from the adolescent Compagnons de France movement to Germany for factory work. When a convoy departed from Constantine in October 1942, those selected belted out "La Marseillaise" and yelled "Down with the Légion!"[29] Yet in a matter of weeks, Operation Torch brought US troops to Algeria, and the notion of active resistance became a moot point. In any case, it had gathered steam across France only in the preceding months, due to the efforts of Jean Moulin and many other leaders from across the spectrum at building a united front, and programs like the STO peaked during the following year.[30]

As a result, police actions tended to exaggerate the impact of fairly minor truculence. In October 1941, officers in Constantine arrested a middle-aged seamstress for displaying an "improper influence on popular and military morale." What precisely was her crime? According to two police officers, she was overheard complaining about the markets, bemoaning the unavailability of basic foodstuffs and leaders who were simply not up to the task of feeding the local population. Clearly, she was not a North African Lucie Aubrac, subsequently claiming that the offensive remarks were casually uttered during a conversation with another woman in the street. Nevertheless, the *commissaire central* announced to the prefect that she would be tried for her "crimes."[31] Surveillance efforts also ensnared Muslims, with brigadiers and gendarmes keeping a watchful eye for any hint of dissent, particularly anti-French statements. In Aïn-M'lila, officers arrested a local Arab for uttering defeatist and slanderous statements, specifically decrying high indigenous tax rates. Rather than paying the collector, the aggrieved local promised to "beat him up." Witnesses confirmed the statement, which led his to arrest and a probable prison term.[32]

Although Gaullists and various metropolitan cells did not liaise with Algerian counterparts, one organization continued to actively oppose Vichy and the Nazis in the colony: the Parti communiste algérien (PCA; Algerian Communist Party), which in theory ceased resistance action when the Soviet Union signed the Molotov-Ribbentrop Pact, but remained active nonetheless, and directly engaged Pétain and company following the June 1941 Nazi invasion. After the August 1939 agreement, Communists were labeled traitors by the republican government, and the PCA faced dissolution in September 1939, with the party's elected officials in both France and Algeria stripped of their mandate in January 1940, and often arrested. Censorship of all leftist newspapers increased dramatically with the declaration of hostilities, and in North Africa this included dailies like *Alger républicain* (Algiers Republican), which sympathized with working-class Europeans and Arabs and Kabyles alike.[33] Letters streamed into police headquarters across Algeria denouncing suspected Communists. In May 1940 a waiter informed on a post office employee, declared to be a "rabid Communist," and demanded that the police arrest not only every party member and sympathizer but also those who protected them, seen as equally culpable. Most such communications proved unreliable, motivated by personal grievances rather than sound information, but they reflected an official intolerance of suspect party affiliations.[34]

The surveillance and monitoring of suspected Communist activity increased after the defeat and the subsequent emergence of a government dedicated to the eradication of national enemies. By August 1940, police placed European workers suspected of such ties under watch in towns across all three departments, while military authorities in towns like Miliana noted a renewal of interest in the party after the armistice. All militants, and particularly veterans of the prewar PCA, were to be followed at all times.[35] Naturally, the most worrisome were potential supporters of Algerian nationalism. Sersou gendarmes evinced considerable concern about Mohammed Essemiani, the ex-secretary of the Jeunesse musulmane (Muslim Youth), seen as a Communist of dubious morality and anti-French, raising the specter of independence and antisettler activity. Yet some of the accusations were more outlandish. Officials in Sersou also demanded the surveillance of a European café owner and Popular Front stalwart, a supporter of Algerian separatism and staunch opponent of the pro-settler municipal council. The administrator demanded that his business be shuttered immediately, as police considered it a potential meeting place for subversive elements.[36]

The following year, the regime moved from surveillance and harassment to outright repression in Algeria, with the reconstitution of the PCA under the leadership of Oran militant Thomas Ibañez, a veteran of both the international brigades in Spain and the rough-and-tumble of municipal politics at home. Much like the metropolitan anti-Communist campaign, hundreds of PCA members and sympathizers in all three departments found themselves restricted or interned even before the arrival of Pétain and Laval, but by fall 1940, a central committee and twenty-five local sections reappeared, along with hundreds of young militants.[37] However, the fledgling group fell victim to police infiltration almost immediately, with undercover police reporting in August that the party was in the process of rebuilding, and using the mass suffering in Algeria as a recruitment tool among workers. Although outlandish tales of violent insurrection and infiltration of the gendarmerie abounded, there was certainly truth to the notion that the PCA staunchly opposed the Vichy regime and waged an active propaganda campaign.[38] Once a sufficiently complete picture emerged, the police pounced, arresting almost the entire leadership and dozens of militants throughout 1941, using an August law to strike a military tribunal specifically targeting Algerian Communist activity. Throughout the colony, *commissaires* from the Police judiciaire and the RG had gathered intelligence, using searches and (often violent) interrogations, and surveillance. During the February 1942 hearing, the tribunal promptly handed out severe penalties, including six death sentences, nine verdicts of a lifetime of hard labor, and numerous jail terms and heavy fines.[39]

In the aftermath of the arrests, the governor general demanded the internment of any Communist leader, a ban on all party activity, and a complete report on anyone in any government ministry or bureaucratic department suspected of militancy due to their behavior, actions, or public statements. Workers, too, faced severe penalties, with prefectorial circulars urging police action to round up "agitators" attempting to foment dissent in workplaces, from ports to warehouses. As strikes and work slowdowns were illegal and leftist activity proscribed by law, officers were authorized to detain "notorious Communists" without probable cause. They faced mandatory terms in detention camps until sentenced to prison, and hefty fines (up to 5,000 francs), regardless of their actions. The prefect of Alger went even further, insisting on the enforcement of a ban on Communist songs and poems, to be seized from shops along with Communist or Gaullist newspapers.[40]

Much like its other official antiresistance campaigns, Vichy's repression of Communism was interrupted by the November 1942 troop landings. No longer agents of resistance, and decimated by three years of state repression, the PCA rarely entered into official thinking in the post-Pétain era in Algeria, replaced in government offices by serious concerns about Muslim nationalism. Hence, the North African Communist bogeyman transmogrified into the willing accomplice of Algerian independence movements, with the Comité nationale de libération (National Emancipation Committee) pushing for rights and reforms and receiving Arab and Kabyle support as a result. In a February 1945 letter, the British consul-general, John Carvell, lamented to US diplomat Duff Cooper that a mass rising could follow the departure of US and British troops, not least due to continuing shortages of food and clothing and black marketeering that battered Algerians far more than Europeans. In already volatile Kabylia, there was a growing and widespread belief that official and business corruption were the reason behind price hikes, as starvation and misery directly translated into hatred of France.[41]

Most Vichy functionaries were anti-Communists by rote, but the top priority for the regime in Algeria may well have been antisemitism. Officials and police despised Jews, and they became a key trope in the settler lexicon of xenophobia. Primitive and volatile Arabs and Kabyles were certainly to be mistrusted and never given the rights and freedoms enjoyed by French citizens. Indeed, in the minds of officials and police, Algerian nationalism continued to be the clearest threat to French sovereignty over the colony. Yet Vichy's belief in Jews as inherently pernicious and dangerous, working internationally to defeat Gallic interests and destroy the nation and its empire, echoed what Europeans in North Africa had long believed.

Although 1930s census data revealed a population of only 111,021 Algerian Jews, settler anger focused on the 1870 Crémieux Decree, which granted French citizenship to the entire community. They assimilated rapidly, adopting European dress, mannerisms, and education, and yet settlers refused to accept the new legal status. Algerian Jews received titular rights and freedoms, but they were unceasingly harassed and denied equal rights by officials and law enforcement. Beginning with the riots of the 1890s, when antisemitic politicians Max Régis and Édouard Drumont led campaigns of violence and newspapers promised to "water the tree of our liberty with Jewish blood," xenophobia steadily gained ground, culminating in the vast popularity of colonial Fascism during the interwar era. With tens of thousands of members and many more active sympathizers, groups like the CF/PSF, RNAS, and PPF were the largest political movements in the 1930s, and they placed antisemitism squarely at the forefront of their programs.[42]

Thus, Vichy broke little new ground in Algeria when it exported anti-Jewish measures, beginning in summer 1940 in the metropole and the empire. Promulgated in October, the Jewish Statute and dozens of subsequent decrees and laws deprived Jews of professions and jobs, education, and rights and freedoms. The Algerian community faced an even worse fate, for the regime annulled the Crémieux Decree, withdrawing Jewish citizenship in favor of the same legal status held by the Muslim population; the preamble to the pronouncement specifically referred to them as "indigenous" and thus rendered them stateless. In the metropole, the Commissariat-général aux questions juives (CGQJ; General Commissariat for Jewish Affairs) controlled the repression of French Jews and the deportation of foreigners to death camps in Poland, while its heads, Xavier Vallat and Louis Darquier de Pellepoix, partnered with Otto Abetz and the Nazi leadership in Paris. In August 1941, the CGQJ established a Service algérien des questions juives (Algerian Service for Jewish Affairs), and in March 1942 a local branch of the Union générale des Israélites (General Union of Israelites) de France spoke exclusively for the community with officials in Alger and Paris.[43]

It is somewhat surprising, then, that the Holocaust did not directly impact Algerian Jews—none were deported or killed, although this may reflect logistical difficulties rather than official wishes. Even in France, those deported tended to be foreign Jews, and roundups began in earnest only in summer 1942, mere months before the Allied landing in North Africa, which negated Nazi and Vichy planning. Nevertheless, they were singled out for particularly harsh treatment, with foreign Jews imprisoned at work camps in the southern territories, and even the suspicion of malfeasance resulted in the maximum application of police and judicial powers. Law enforcement presumed that Jewish businessmen were natural speculators and cracked down mercilessly on any involvement with black marketeering. In March 1942, when a consortium led by Alger merchants the Doulieb brothers was tried for fraud and illicit price fixing, thirteen defendants received fines ranging from 2,000 to 50,000 francs and the leaders were sentenced to four to five years in prison. These punishments far outweighed the gravity of what was a minor affair, and as Pierre Darmon writes, "Elle met en scene un fonctionnaire de police soucieux d'avancement qui invente contre des innocents des malversations imaginaires [It put into the spotlight a police officer concerned about promotion who made up embezzlement cases against innocent people]." Thus, careerism intersected with official racism, a not infrequent occurrence. Moreover, prominent members of the community were often harassed simply for being Jewish. In October 1940, former Ligue internationale contre l'antisémitisme (International League against Antisemitism) head Bernard Lecache, a regular target of settler and press ire before 1940, was imprisoned in a remote town without any stated rationale. Of course, quotidian racist incidents occurred most frequently, and the archives are filled with notices concerning assaults against Jews and the defacement of their property, often with swastikas.[44]

Surprisingly, despite official and police persecution, a large number of security files concern Jewish retaliation rather than victimhood. This was not a new phenomenon, reflecting the prevalence of antisemitism in Algeria from the 1890s. Beginning in the preceding decade, attacks against Jews began in earnest as members of the community entered politics, and the Dreyfus affair accelerated the enmity, with various politicians and press outlets using xenophobia as an electoral tool. The rise of Max Régis and his newspaper *L'Antijuif* (The Anti-Jew) in Alger and Émile Morinaud in Constantine resulted in mass antisemitic violence, and inevitably, counterattacks by Jews against racist neighbors. One such assault in May 1897 against cycling club members led to days of mayhem in Mostaganem, and the following year was characterized by a seemingly endless parade of riots, beatings, and even murders.[45]

By the interwar era, battles were fought on two fronts, against European settlers and Muslims. In the former instance, the preponderance of Fascist leagues and mass support beyond anything imaginable in France meant that from 1924, a renewed barrage of xenophobic speeches, tracts, press invective, and mass meetings led by the Amitiés latines and Action française in the 1920s and by the RNAS, CF/PSF, and PPF in the following decade. Yet, once again, Jews in all three departments gave as good as they got, resisting intimidation from the leagues and individual assaults in equal measure.[46] Many of the most deadly incidents involved Muslim-Jewish belligerence, as Arabs and Kabyles were increasingly furious about the Crémieux Decree, which denied them equal standing unless they rejected Islamic law and embraced European standards, all while meeting stringent criteria that disqualified the vast majority of Algerians altogether. Their resentment reached its apex in the 1934 riots in Sétif and Constantine, during which the perpetrators inflicted numerous casualties and destroyed a substantial amount of Jewish property. This event was enabled by European antisemites who riled up the Muslim population, which had frequently assaulted Jews during the preceding fifteen years, and Jews consistently fought back in all three departments.[47]

Given the decades of antisemitic politics and attitudes displayed by settlers across Algeria, and the constant stream of counterattacks, it is unsurprising that the pattern continued under Vichy rule. For the new regime was far more insidious than the local antisemitic politicians and Fascist movements that had been forced to answer to Third Republic authorities, for xenophobia was now state policy. Once again conflicts erupted in the streets between Jews and Europeans, with racial slurs and fistfights a regular occurrence in various centers, and self-defense groups appeared, dedicated to combating newly tolerated hatred.[48] Xenophobic European neighbors became primary targets, in retaliation for decades of abusive behavior and language. In May 1942, Constantine police intervened when a tenant returned home from a trip to Tunisia late at night to find his apartment barricaded by an armoire placed in the corridor. He proceeded to break it apart, waking up the other residents, almost all of whom were Jews, and screaming "You won't be here long!" Police files regularly mention attacks against Europeans accused of racist language and behavior in public spaces. In August 1942, soldiers who yelled "Down with the Jews!" at pedestrians in Constantine were beaten in broad daylight by a large group. Desperate to avoid the ramifications of an assault against official and settler antisemitism, the Police d'état officer charged with the file ignored witness testimony and instead concluded that the assailants had been angry because they were ineligible for army service. Naturally, only the attackers were arrested and jailed.[49] Yet exactly the same thing occurred only a month later, with the press furious at Jewish insubordination and more prison sentences levied—six months to two years on a prison farm. The situation climaxed with the Allied landings in November 1942, as Vichy's grip slipped away permanently. In December 1942, police in Constantine reported that eight local Jews attacked two police officers, chanting "Long live England! Long live America!" and then turning on the agents with fists and a chorus of "You are nothing but Germans!," a reminder that although the regime had ended in November, law enforcement agencies remained staffed by the same Pétain loyalists in the aftermath.[50]

In fact, police and gendarme troubles with Jews began in earnest after the Allied landings. Matters came to a head in Oran in September 1944, when youths working in a market stall reacted to soldiers proclaiming, "Dirty Jew" and "Long live Pétain" by attacking the offenders and proclaiming them Germans and Fascists due to be purged. The resulting brawl included fully four hundred participants and required scores of police and gendarmes to break it up. The incident report demonstrates the last remnant of a fading trend: officers siding with the xenophobes and refusing to accept racism as a criminal act.[51] Police and gendarme brutality against Jews had been common in the prewar era, and by the 1930s, reports about such abuses were so frequent that the prosecutor's office demanded action to stem the flow, resulting in the formation of state police units by Minister of the Interior Marx Dormoy, which took law enforcement out of the hands of antisemitic local politicians and officials.[52] With the occupation of North Africa by Allied forces in late 1942, the official sponsorship of xenophobia abruptly ended, and violent antisemitism and Fascist sympathies became anathema to the new authorities. Previously solely noting the quotidian beatings and insults hurled by Europeans while processing dozens of letters denouncing community members for any number of supposed crimes, agents slowly came to realize that revenge attacks occurred with mounting frequency as the Allies took full control of North African government and affairs. In October 1944, two French soldiers overheard in a café declaring that the Germans should arrive and kill all the Jews caused a massive riot, with youths fighting them inside and outside the establishment as insults flew back and forth: "The Jews are screwing with you!," "Dirty kikes!" Yet, despite a crowd of one hundred Jews and Muslims surrounding the soldiers, unlike in previous years, there were no arrests, and the police merely dispersed the crowd. Officers generally changed their tune rather quickly after the landing, and by 24 November a gendarme chiding soldiers for speaking kindly to Jewish youths ("You're nothing but a dirty Jew") found himself charged with verbal assault.[53] Officials proved slower to change, but even they succumbed to the inevitable as war turned against Germany in Europe and Africa. On 14 March 1943, French North African high commissioner Henri Giraud and his cabinet, including Vichy stalwart and career antisemite Marcel Peyrouton, repealed the regime's racial laws. Although they reaffirmed the abrogation of the Crémieux Decree in an effort to keep Jews from reclaiming citizenship, substantial pressure from US president Franklin D. Roosevelt and

British prime minister Winston Churchill led to its reinstatement in October by the Gaullist Comité français de libération nationale (French Committee on National Liberation).[54]

Managing Muslim Dissent and Combating Algerian Nationalism

The official excuse for retaining the abrogation related to Muslim anger, which had seethed for decades at the special status afforded to Jews. Giraud (and the Gaullists) were right to worry, as violent incidents between Arabs and Kabyles, and their Jewish neighbors, erupted following the eventual restoration of citizenship. Although certain scholars note that Jews and Muslims were not constantly sparring across Algeria and in fact frequently lived and worked together in peace, mounting incidents in the 1930s greatly concerned the republican administration, particularly the Constantine riots of 1934, during and after which Fascists and antisemitic officials encouraged the looting of Jewish shops and violence against local denizens. Metropolitan policy initiatives like the Jonnart Law and the Blum-Viollette bill, which offered limited electoral reform without any possibility of power sharing or rights for non-Europeans, only further divided the Algerian communities, not least because certain settlers exploited the special status afforded to Jews in order to further their own political ends. Muslim anger became a convenient flash point in attempts to abrogate the Crémieux Decree, which had provoked Arab and Kabyle fury at being refused citizenship from 1870. Even a simple misinterpretation or circumstantial act could be deemed provocative and result in the threat of violence.[55]

Government fears thus seemed justified in August 1943 when, as the government publicly mulled a course of action to resolve the Jewish community's plight, two Jews and a young Muslim came to blows in Batna, and a crowd of two hundred quickly formed as the former took refuge in a nearby home. Police eventually arrived to arrest the Jewish assailants and to break up the gathering of onlookers, but the crowd reassembled outside the station house. Various unreliable witnesses who stepped forward could not provide basic details of the assault, and the resulting fury led to patrols throughout the night. In his report, the local RG inspector mentioned an almost identical recent incident in Philippeville and demanded constant surveillance in Jewish and Muslim neighborhoods to keep the peace.[56] Matters were even worse in Oran, where in August 1944 a Muslim adjutant attacked two Jewish soldiers patrolling the streets, yelling "Down with de Gaulle! Down with the Jews!" and shooting and severely wounding one of them. A full-scale brawl ensued, the latest in a string of antisemitic incidents between Jewish officers and Muslim soldiers in the region.[57] As Joshua Cole observes in his study of the 1934 Constantine riots, such violence "betrayed the complex mix of assumptions built into the triangulation between Frenchness on one hand and the status of Muslims and Jews in Algeria on the other," a tendency exacerbated by the subaltern role of non-Europeans in the military and perceptions of Jewish privilege.[58]

For these reasons, too, Vichy officials had actively worked to suppress Muslim dissent, convinced that full-scale rebellion was always a mere riot away. Their concerns were twofold. First, they correctly suspected that Algerian nationalists had successfully reformed dissolved organizations and had begun to work once more against French control (these efforts will be discussed in greater detail in chapter 5). Second, police and governors worried about the impact of food shortages and high prices for staple goods in Muslim communities, and particularly viewed the black market and rationing as flash points for disturbances in various locales.

From the regime's inception, Vichy's Algerian agents wrote reports questioning Muslim loyalty to France. Concerns mounted about pro-German propaganda and their perception of the Nazis as saviors from imperial bondage. One popular song in Kabylia lamented: "Ô Hitler . . . La France nous deteste. . . . Il nous appelent encore 'bîcots.' . . . Nous sommes dans la misère [Oh Hitler . . . France hates us. . . . They still call us 'scum.' . . . We live in misery]." Thus, in June 1942 authorities compiled a list of Muslims to be watched, all suspected of nationalist sympathies and treason. Police employed a large number of informants, both within the community at large and suspect organizations, specifically charged with reporting daily activities and future plans, along with popular attitudes and shifting public opinion.[59] In addition to the usual nationalist fare, they determined that even after the Allied landing, Algerians continued to evince pro-German sentiments despite a public façade of support for the Americans and the British in both town and countryside. Agents in Constantine complained that in certain cafés and public spaces, all talk stopped entirely when a policeman entered. Their worst fears were realized in January 1943 when Nazis parachuted into Algeria, seeking to spark a Muslim uprising. Police arrested thirty-five Constantine residents for assisting the enemy and abetting German efforts to foment rebellion. The resulting penalties were so severe that when Italian troops attempted the same tactic in February, locals immediately informed the Sétif gendarmerie.[60]

Vichy administrators attempted to connect Muslim support for the Nazis with Algerian nationalism, and police services frequently singled out Ferhat

Abbas and Messali Hadj as potentially encouraging or participating in plans hatched by the Germans. Yet as their position weakened, the regime increasingly turned to violence to staunch even putative disloyalty. In certain instances, officials used legal recourse to punish offenders. When an Algerian employee of the house murdered two European girls in 1942, the offender was sentenced to death after a standard trial. More frequently, the authorities took matters into their own hands, with disastrous results. In the summer of 1941, in Boghari, in the southern portion of the department of Alger, a European rural policeman beat a young Muslim suspect to death, and local anger exploded, necessitating a major intervention by law enforcement. Yet perhaps the worst example of malicious administrative behavior occurred in Zeralda, east of Alger-ville, where the mayor restricted access at local beaches in summer 1942, prohibiting Muslims, Jews, dogs, and horses. Not content with this provocation at a time of popular discontent, in August, two dozen police rounded up dozens of Algerians (including women and children) in response to reports of thefts from European homes. They were eventually charged with everything from the illegal gathering of firewood to defiantly using the restricted beach. Placed in airless cells, twenty-five died, and as such horrors proliferated across all three departments, the head of the Constantine intelligence bureau wrote in September 1942 of a point of no return: hatred and anti-French sentiment had mushroomed among the Muslim population, who viewed the French as violent and useless.[61]

Yet, the colonial violence practiced by officials was not the only cause of Muslim anger. As noted in the chapter 3, Arab and Kabyle individuals and communities had been resisting such oppression for decades, often through armed resistance and acts deemed criminal by the French administration. One of the key triggers (among many) in the prewar era, poverty and food security became the focal point of disturbances during the Vichy years. A November 1941 police study found massive disparities in allotments, with Europeans receiving five liters of petrol and Muslims perhaps half a liter if truly fortunate. Even Jews obtained larger rations of sugar and gasoline. The *djemâa* (tribal council) of the commune of Bou-Saada complained to the administrator that entire ration cards were missing. However, the worst demonstrations postdated the Vichy years and targeted the Allies and the Free French. In Blida, a June 1944 gathering of three hundred Muslims demanded a greater amount of wheat and cereals, and a riot was averted only when the deputy prefect agreed to receive a local notable to discuss the matter. Ignoring this agreement, an even larger crowd appeared the next day, and panicked municipal councilors agreed to increase the amounts of semolina and barley. Constantine officials reported similar problems, and in Saint Arnaud, the local *commissaire* claimed that the entire Muslim population had become irritable and rebellious, regularly protesting to demand more food. The only winners, he declared, were the local nationalists, whose cause received a tremendous propaganda boost from the ongoing misery of the Arab population.[62]

Policing the Black Market

These assessments were not guided by mere suspicion and irrational fears. Shortages, price gouging, and a vibrant black market constituted a major headache for both Vichy and the Allied and Gaullist administrations. Matters were only exacerbated by dismal harvests and ruptured trade in 1940, which caused widespread scarcity in Algeria by spring 1941, with shortages of everything from wheat and oil to coffee and sugar. Muslims were literally starving because they could not afford to pay skyrocketing costs for basic staples by 1941 to 1942, and encouraged by German and nationalist propaganda, riots were not uncommon.[63] Even a relatively bountiful 1941 growing season proved to be illusory, as a fuel shortage that impacted machinery and agricultural production meant that cereal harvests plummeted from over eighty million quintaux in 1941 to slightly more than eleven million a year later. Imports remained a utopian prospect, with textiles in particular unavailable, a brutal problem during the winter months when warmer clothing was impossible to find. By that time, even Europeans began to complain bitterly about ration cards and the seemingly uneven public distribution of scarce items, and officials and shopkeepers were cast as incompetent and corrupt. Fights in long lines at shops in Alger were bad enough; in Oran and south of the coast very little was available at all, while Kabylia and the Saharan territories were completely cut off from supply lines.[64]

The result of all this was a thriving black market, particularly in major centers. In Algerian towns and villages, a piece of clothing could be priced at ten times a *fellah*'s wages. In cities like Alger, at least they could sell sugar rations to Europeans for top dollar. Nonetheless, lacking foodstuffs, clothing, and medicine, thousands died by 1942, and settler mortality rates also soared. Authorities also worried about public morale, particularly noting the long lines filled with housewives waiting for goods and the concomitant opportunity to castigate the authorities as responsible for poverty and shortages. Women managed the bulk of the household expenditures and also wielded great influence in the household, and their ire could easily impact great swathes of the community. Thus a June 1942 report in Bône bemoaned the fact that the town had only one retail market and demanded that owners undertake measures to eliminate large queues, while demanding vigilance mixed with patience from police, who were enjoined to respond with politeness and understanding no matter how angry or profane the public response.[65] Into this breach came various service branches, particularly the economic section, charged with warring ceaselessly against illegal trade and price gouging. Authorities tasked the Brigade économique with everything from the surveillance of suspect individuals and shops to inspecting markets and train stations to ensure that official prices were respected and no illegal goods could be purchased. In certain larger centers—Bône, for example—the Service de la voie publique et des marchés (Roads and Markets Service) assisted this work, their agents and gendarmes patrolling the city, seeking out offenders. In Bône, leadership divided the urban center into thirty zones to be routinely inspected, with even the most remote neighborhoods served by two-man bicycle teams.[66] That these bureaus were extremely busy is an understatement; by far the largest trove of archival material on policing from the 1940 to 1945 era deals explicitly with economic issues, from the black market to price fixing.

The sheer scope of their work in Algeria (and indeed, the metropole), in both the Vichy and Allied-Gaullist periods, proved to be staggering. From July 1941 to June 1942, the Constantine head of the Brigade économique estimated that his branch pursued well over one thousand cases. Some of these were routine, such as the 377 examples of transactions without tax. Yet the remainder involved the black market and price fixing, from illegal sales of ration cards or foodstuffs to retail manipulations. Seizures of goods also became a quotidian policing reality, with a haul worth over 36,000 francs in June 1942 alone, including almost three thousand kilograms of sugar and six thousand kilograms of oil, among other staples.[67] Similar figures for Oran in December 1942 included thousands of eggs and oranges and resulted in sanctions against 189 Europeans and 109 Muslims, the former more involved in price gouging and the latter more inclined toward black market sales of products typically consumed by Algerians—lamb, for example.[68] Police squarely blamed the miniscule rations for the high rates of illicit activity. Only one hundred kilograms of beef could be consumed per week in Oran, with some arrondissements doing without on a rotating basis, and clandestine abattoirs appeared throughout the region, charging an inflated seventy-five francs per kilo, particularly to anxious restaurateurs in European neighborhoods and individual Algerians seeking lamb for their own use. Officials lamented similar problems with everything from oil and rice to vegetables and sardines, as eggs fetched up to seven francs apiece on the black market.[69]

Neither was this only an urban problem. Gendarmes stationed in the *commune mixte* of Tébessa near the Tunisian border reported massive sales of goods illegally imported from their eastern neighbor or skimming from local harvests. In response, an eleven-man team specifically targeted economic activity in the region. In Kabylia, police launched similar operations, chasing smugglers using mules to move goods through the mountains and forests with the assistance of a local *caïd*.[70] Police also faced the quandary of the participation of wealthy European clients in black market sales. In March 1942, the Philippeville Brigade économique received anonymous tips fingering a local tailor who had already been heavily fined by authorities the previous December for massive price hikes on clothing and material. According to the informants, he moved into shady deals, selling to rich clients without demanding ration cards. Using a sting operation involving a disgruntled customer, the brigade unraveled an operation that engaged in substantial accounting fraud to hide evidence of steady activity and huge profits.[71]

The Allied landing in November 1942 provided little resolution to the ongoing shortages and illegal activity. If anything, matters became even more strained, with gasoline the hot black-market commodity. In June 1943, police seized over one thousand kilograms, along with a significant amount of coal, and copious amounts of foodstuffs—often of extremely low quality or literally rotten—continued to appear on the lists of agencies like Oran's Service de la répression des fraudes et de la hausse illicite (Service for the Suppression of Fraud and Price Gouging). In the following year, they charged increasing numbers of Algerians with crimes ranging from price gouging to clandestine meat sales.[72] This reflects an increasing tendency to blame the *indigènes* for the black market and price gouging, with Europeans no longer the sole focus of legal proceedings. To be sure, Muslim participation in economic crimes was hardly novel to the post-Vichy era. Although they arrested more Europeans per capita, the Brigade économique had broken up Algerian operations involved in everything from reselling illegal wool and meat to stealing and dealing *sauf-conduits* (safe passage papers) with forged signatures out of a Constantine café.[73] Smuggling in particular increasingly worried police and gendarmes by 1942, with informants providing intelligence concerning goods arriving in cities via mail coaches and even rented transport on several occasions.[74] Yet with the arrival of American and British troops, the matter took on additional urgency, as teams of thieves targeted military bases. In April 1943, French and British officers requested assistance from police in Le Khroub, resulting in a sweep of local homes, seeking stolen clothing and yards of material. The action resulted in eleven arrests, with the perpetrators referred to the Constantine military tribunal for trial.[75]

Consequently, in September 1944 the chief commissioner in Alger proclaimed that non-Europeans flooded the cities to make a living in the shadows.

They "encrusted" urban centers, refusing to do legitimate work in the countryside, instead choosing the greedy and criminal path of illegally selling anything they could find at exorbitant prices, particularly foodstuffs. He particularly excoriated the low fines for such activity, demanding the authorization to arrest any male between eighteen and fifty who could not offer proof of steady employment or professional activity. Only hunting down the "parasites" would resolve the issue, and he accused the nationalist movement of encouraging this "filth." The governor general agreed, proposing internment in work camps for those arrested under the provisions of a November 1940 Vichy-era law that allowed this treatment for economic criminals, with the exception of deserters and *insoumis*, to be shipped to the front lines in Europe. Police subsequently rounded up fifty men in Alger and sent them off, but difficulties hampered the effort, not least the utter inability of existing facilities to absorb the dozens of new arrivals and provide labor for them.[76] Individual raids proved more effective than sweeping legislation. In September 1944, over one hundred Oran police and gendarmerie, in concert with military police stationed there, descended on a flea market, inspecting in excess of 1,500 sellers and clients. The complement arrested over one hundred suspects, sixty-five of whom were deported to their communes. The goods seized included a sizable amount of food, equipment, and clothing stolen from US barracks and depots, all in the possession of one merchant.[77]

The growing market for US goods presented one of the most immediate problems for the economic branch from 1943 to 1945, with employees and civilians alike involved in trafficking operations, mostly undertaken by Arabs and Kabyles outside military bases. Allied authorities constantly complained of regular thefts and demanded surveillance operations to catch criminals looting anything from jam and sugar to petrol and tires. At a November 1943 press conference in Oran, US and British officials joined French police and gendarmerie chiefs from the Services économiques to pledge a cooperative effort. Although the Allied representatives acknowledged that US personnel were involved, they were unable or unwilling to seriously punish those offenders, which exacerbated the problem, while simultaneously the French refusal to crack down on Algerian thieves until late 1944 also prevented an effective resolution.[78]

Yet it was the status of the soldiers who sold the goods in the first place that truly complicated matters. In response to the call for joint action, the Brigade des fraudes (Fraud Brigade) in Oran tackled 494 cases in December 1943 alone, levying 410,000 francs in fines and making numerous arrests. Nonetheless, personnel complained of their inability to search military vehicles, non-prosecution agreements concerning soldiers, and even French and foreign troops purchasing goods on the black market. Rather than blaming police, the author of one report fumed, interested parties should truly penalize their own.[79] Vigorous protests finally resulted in concrete action in 1944, with police given the right to arrest US army personnel and conduct searches on bases. In March, Tébessa officers noted the presence of a military vehicle from Constantine purchasing oil and soap on the black market, leading the Police judiciaire to seize a substantial haul of contraband and to intern the suspect after he was caught red-handed selling the merchandise to fellow soldiers.[80]

By that time, sentencing regulations for both Europeans and Algerians also toughened dramatically, facilitating the fight against black marketeering and price fixing. Under Vichy, offenders traditionally received relatively light punishments ranging from suspended terms to mere months in prison; only house arrests tended to last for years. A June 1942 memo from a Philippeville police chief epitomized the prevailing spirit, arguing that first-time offenders in particular (both buyers and sellers) deserved leniency. A quiet word explaining the very real difficulties of losing a major portion of French territory, worker shortages due to prisoners of war and labor service in Germany, and transportation problems should suffice. Once the immorality of their actions was understood, it would prevent further involvement in illicit activities. Only recidivists deserved brutal treatment—they were genuine criminals.[81] Under the Allies and the Free French, notions of soft solutions completely disappeared. Courts sentenced perpetrators involved in the black-market resale of a ton of sugar to up to three years imprisonment and thousands of francs in fines. Moreover, in 1943 to 1944, the Oran prefect and the governor general both demanded on several occasions that all law enforcement agencies must combat any increase in illegal economic activity with intense surveillance and "ruthless repression." With the public all too aware of open markets selling illegal goods for a literal fortune and the press extensively covering the matter, police should arrest every possible suspect, deporting any foreigner, while courts should render ruthless judgements. A peaceful conversation with those involved clearly no longer sufficed. For his part, the Alger prefect was so determined to squelch the black market that he demanded 100,000 francs to combat the problem.[82]

Yet, a familiar problem hampered the regime's attempts to rein in economic malfeasance under both Vichy and the Allies and Free French: there were simply too few agents to effectively clamp down on the growing number of offenders. In August 1942 the chief inspector of the Alger *douairs* demanded additional men to staff his service charged with patrols designed to thwart black-market activity. The situation in Dra-el-Mizan in particular demanded immediate action, as the commune represented the hub of illicit activity. Convoys transporting oil openly traveled with armed Algerian escorts. Any agent who approached them would be shot, and with only nine in the region, it was impossible to overwhelm a criminal operation. One hapless raid on 20 August pitted fifty smugglers against six *douairs*, who found themselves literally outgunned when the shooting started. Although the prefect agreed to increase the local complement to twenty-one, the lack of gendarmes rendered local law enforcement vulnerable, a common problem across all three departments.[83] Matters were even worse in Oran, where most men who worked in the Service des contrôles des prix (Price Control Service) were not police but civil servants, mainly drawn from the customs or tax service. Although the Police d'état were supposed to handle the actual investigations, their unfamiliarity with economic matters and staffing issues left them unable to participate. Without their assistance, rumors abounded that the service's employees accepted bribes from Jewish merchants and worked against Pétain and Vichy, unsurprising in a prewar hotbed of extreme-rightist support. In his November 1940 response to such accusations, the prefect noted a severe manpower shortage because twenty-nine Jewish officers had been fired and multiple *commissaires* lacked physical fitness or had been called up by the military. He demanded evidence to corroborate the charges and underscored that only those directly involved with fiscal matters could effectively combat economic crimes.[84] However, the problem did not disappear, and efforts to deal with a dearth of qualified personnel continued following the Allied landing. In September 1943 the prefect of Constantine demanded that the Brigade économique intensify surveillance and arrests and promised reinforcements if needed. A top law enforcement priority, the renewed effort included hounding wholesalers, middlemen, traffickers, and any merchant holding back the best produce or overcharging the public, with results demanded in only one month.[85]

Even where trained agents were readily available, accusations and complaints from both an irate public and commanding officers steadily piled up. Merchants frequently bemoaned heavy-handed law enforcement tactics, from the presumption of guilt to the closure of markets for lengthy forensics investigations, keeping clients away for hours at a time. In December 1941 a number of Constantine vendors sent a bitter letter to the prefecture, claiming that the Bureau économique closed every stall during the morning rush so that each one could be interrogated, gutting the day's sales. Worse still, police made no arrests and uncovered no illegal activity, while customers who arrived had their ration cards checked and in some cases faced arrest or fines. At one fishmonger's stall, they were not permitted to leave and thus missed arriving on time to their jobs.[86] In other cases, superiors discovered that individual officers collaborated with illegal sellers, providing papers for Algerians involved in the black market, taking bribes from individual vendors to look the other way, and committing various other offenses.[87] Long after the Allied landing, complaints continued to pour in, including accusations of gross incompetence. In Bône, the *sous-préfet* added fourteen men to the Bureau économique in October 1943, yet their lack of proper training led to numerous seizures of goods without proof of any criminal activity. In one case, fourteen kilograms of butter were returned to an angry Algerian who had never offered it for sale but collected it over time for his family during celebrations.[88]

Drunken Brawls, Armed Assaults, and Police Action against Allied and Free French Soldiers

After November 1942, an additional worry beyond the black market and price fixing frequently overwhelmed official and police economic concerns: the misbehavior and violent conduct of Allied and Free French soldiers across all three departments. Most cases related to excessive consumption of alcohol, which often provoked assaults and profanity. In one typical example, in Tébessa in January 1943, four US soldiers crashed into a brothel, firing shots at the manager as she ran to a nearby police station. Military police eventually arrived, but only after the louts had caused 25,000 francs in damages, and the local *commissaire* complained that this was not the first such altercation. The chief had previously alerted US and British authorities to incidents in cafés and restaurants around town perpetrated by undisciplined and rowdy soldiers. Allied commanders subsequently established an MP office in the station, and their officers accompanied the regular constabulary on patrol.[89] Yet this did little to quell matters; by May, yet another drunken soldier physically attacked a police officer, ignoring a warning shot from civilian authorities and surrendering only when a number of guards from his base arrived on the scene.[90] Matters came to a head in Oran in September 1944, when the Police d'état reported daily assaults by inebriated sailors and the use of vile language ("the cops are motherfuckers!"). Moreover, the population exhibited fear of Allied soldiers, certainly not what the top brass wanted.[91] In response to mounting incidents, French authorities vainly asked commanding officers to confine their men to certain establishments close to a given base, particularly in summer, when sweltering conditions only worsened the misbehavior.[92]

Even worse, from a local perspective, attacks against local Muslims threatened to turn Arabs and Kabyles against the Allied armies and the French authorities in equal measure. Already extremely irate due to food shortages and continuing colonial repression, Algerians chafed even further at unprovoked assaults from military personnel. In Khenchela, two US soldiers robbed a local Muslim schoolteacher in April 1943, taking his pocket watch, and then for good measure, attacked a young hairdresser, beaten so badly that he lost his left eye. Police noted that the terrorized locals remained indoors, fearful of any contact in the wake of multiple "regrettable incidents."[93] Officers in Bône similarly bemoaned the destruction of private property and harvests, bivouacking in fields, breaking into houses to demand wine, and the harassment of women in *mechtas*, and he predicted bloodshed if the trend continued. There were even armed robberies and home invasions. In January 1944, US soldiers in a jeep terrorized Oran's Muslim quarter, breaking into dwellings with a submachine gun, supposedly seeking stolen army uniforms yet in reality beating up the inhabitants and making off with cash and valuables.[94] French soldiers were even worse, due to the colonial racism that infused any encounter with Algerians. A May 1943 report in Constantine cited one for yelling at the *indigènes*, "Arabs are all motherfuckers! I'll fuck you all!" His victims included several local notables and businessmen, and Algerians praised the US and British military police for acting quickly in the city, while the French did nothing, a continuation of prewar racist practices.[95]

Military authorities finally began to genuinely acknowledge a serious problem in March 1944, after a series of incidents that included murder and a threatened massacre. In Châteaudun, drunken British soldiers beat a local to death for no apparent reason, the latest salvo in a worsening situation that included reprisal attacks against an Air Force pilot. *Caïds* reported predicted imminent revolt, particularly as the noted reformist Ferhat Abbas was due to address the community within the next week. That officers from the nearby base openly spoke of using a machine gun to annihilate the entire village only fanned the flames of smoldering rebellion.[96] As usual, French troops found a way to outdo their allies during a brawl between sailors and Muslims at a *café maure* in Alger's Bab-el-Oued neighborhood. Interrupting an Arab music concert, they attempted to fight patrons and the manager, particularly irate that no alcohol could be purchased in a Muslim establishment. As the inebriates began to methodically destroy the place, young locals responded by launching rocks at the offenders from amidst the growing crowd, and the situation reached a crescendo when a Royal Navy patrol arrived. The officer leading the drunken perpetrators attempted to grab a patrolman's submachine gun and fire on the crowd, and it took a massive effort to immobilize the would-be murderer. Matters became so dangerous that the chief of police personally wrote to the governor general demanding a ban on European personnel patronizing Muslim establishments.[97]

US and British soldiers did not share the anti-Algerian leanings of their French confreres, and they also gleefully attacked Europeans, which tended to provoke a far less muted response from the general public and officials alike. Quotidian attacks against Muslims often attracted little attention, but the April 1943 beating of a European *commissaire adjoint* from the Constantine Chantiers de la jeunesse—a popular Vichy initiative in a colony known for lauding the extreme-rightist leagues—attracted a hostile crowd of angry settlers loudly proclaiming that the Allies should concentrate on defeating Germany rather than attacking innocent Frenchmen. When the GI slapped a police officer before being dragged away, it precipitated a near riot.[98] The perpetrator's arrest made little difference, as US soldiers proceeded to assault a policeman, a judge, and a schoolteacher in the following months. The attacks provoked few consequences, as the head of the US military police declined to press charges, deeming the slap harmless, despite the numerous eyewitnesses and the irate European community, and refused to follow up the second case, although it involved a loaded rifle to inflict multiple blows to the head that left the officer in a pool of blood on the street.[99] Yet the worst crime in European eyes involved the sexual assault of girls and women by troops. Multiple reports in June 1943 revealed a constant stream of lewd comments and groping directed even at young children, along with attempted and actual rape. The Constantine police chief soberly reported that US soldiers had gone so far as to kidnap the companions of two French counterparts, attempting to drag them into the woods by force and precipitating a massive brawl only days after a similar incident in Sidi-Mabrouk. In the latter case, a Frenchman who attempted to aid the stricken women was beaten with an iron bar and a gun in an attack that ceased only when his cries for help attracted public attention. The women in each case ended up hospitalized and severely traumatized, inciting public fury, and the prefect warned of extreme violence if another incident occurred.[100]

Purging the Extreme Right from the Police and Security Services?

By the latter stages of the war such dangerous incidents diminished in frequency, leaving only the difficult task for officials and police in all three departments of purging of the Extreme Right from both the station house and the street. Under Vichy, each branch had eradicated racial and political "undesirables," and the task of restoring republican order fell to new heads installed by Allied and, later, Free French interim ministries. Reports came flooding in about the behavior of individual police officers and entire services from the Phony War onward. In Oran, the epicenter of the interwar Algerian Extreme Right, "fifth columnists" from the PPF and the PSF had seized control from September 1939, and loyal republicans handed over lists of names to military authorities after the November 1942 landing. These reports were bolstered by testimony from double agents operating within certain branches on behalf of the Resistance, including the director of port security, who sabotaged shipments destined for Rommel's forces and delivered maps and artillery to US forces during Operation Torch. He became a chief inspector at war's end, having meticulously preserved the names and actions of pro-Vichy officers subsequently purged and punished by Free French governors.[101]

Various Oran reports, often provided by anonymous sources, described horrific practices. Details of torture emerged as each station employed a specialist in the use of water and electricity against anyone suspected of anti-Fascist activities or behavior. Enemies of Pétain or Laval were beaten with iron bars, and in each case, confessions were elicited that courts employed to hand down maximum penal or death sentences. Every policeman was expected to be equally ruthless. The Alger prefect issued specific instructions in October 1941 that rejected leniency. House arrests and fines could not be used against black marketeers or potential resisters; the senior official demanded that all "actions by bad Frenchmen" land the offender in a penal camp, with police facilitating the process. Only those who agreed to support "the new social order" could expect release and clemency, and even then, officers would engage in three months of surveillance to ensure their fidelity to Pétain and Vichy.[102]

However, one roadblock to purging the Algerian police persisted: the frequent defense of those accused by colleagues impregnated with settler ideals and unwilling to tarnish their confreres' reputations due to their own pro-Vichy leanings or actions in the line of duty. In Paris, police staged a wildcat strike in support of the liberation of France, proclaiming total (if belated) support for the Resistance and playing a key role in the anti-German insurrection. Yet the stain of collaboration remained, and a purge commission led by genuine police resisters spearheaded the removal of hundreds of officers across France and a significant number of custodial sentences.[103] Denunciations in Oran, conversely, led to Prefectorial testimonies that "good cops" were being tarnished and should remain employed. If the most serious offenders were indeed punished, he wrote to the governor general in December 1943, many outstanding officers now faced sanctions or dismissal simply for acting against Communists. How should a cop be punished for merely following orders without any ideological motive?[104]

Matters in Constantine were little different. When governor general and noted Gaullist Georges Catroux ordered seventeen police suspended pending investigations in October 1943, mayors and officials worked to undermine the decree from the moment it appeared. A good example of this can be found in the dossier of Lucien Fusero, a chief commissioner revealed to be a PPF member and staunch antisemite whose children belonged to the PPF's Compagnons de France chapter. He had certainly been an outstanding prewar officer when judged by his service record, decorated with a Croix de Guerre and several police awards. Speaking fluent Arabic and German, he rose steadily through the ranks. Yet he truly flourished under Vichy, winning a silver medal for courage and loyalty in January 1942 due to his actions during a flood. Although he had not participated in political actions, this undoubtedly reflected his tenure in Oran, where his beliefs and profile were far from abnormal, and his pro-Fascist and xenophobic beliefs did not conform to the republican / Gaullist norm. The prefect there transferred Fusero to the department of Constantine, where his openly antisemitic views and PPF sympathies provoked an internal move from Tlemcen to Batna and eventually his suspension. Even then, numerous mayors and councilors wrote letters vouching for his character and underlining his nonpolitical record, with some even denying his racism and affiliation with the Extreme Right.[105]

Excuses of all kinds were regularly used to excuse pro-Vichy behavior. When the new Oran prefect asked for a report on the gendarmerie's *adjutant-chef* in January 1944, due to suspicion of pro-Vichy acts, his chief responded by valorizing the suspect. He agreed wholeheartedly that the officer had good relations with leaders of the Légion française des combattants and sympathized with Pétain. However, these attitudes were purportedly espoused solely to please his Italian (and presumably pro-Fascist) wife. Not only had he never acted in anything less than an impartial matter in his professional life, but he personally denounced the excesses of the Service d'ordre légionnaire (SOL; Legionary Order Service) in fall 1942 when suspected Gaullists were rounded up without his participation. Naturally he had been compliant after the Allied landing and caused no consternation (although clearly this was due to the change of government and not his evolving personal views).[106] This is not to say that every officer impacted by the commission's findings won such a reprieve. Although certain notorious Vichyistes were initially merely transferred after November 1942, some were indeed fired. Despite being seen as a model cop and a decorated war veteran, the *commissaire central* for Aïn-Beïda, François Susini, ended up being forcibly retired when his administrative protectors were removed in 1943 by the governor general.[107] Yet this proved to be an exception, and in comparison with the metropolitan purge, only a handful of policemen in Algeria lost their positions.

Nonetheless, previously pro-Vichy stalwarts now found themselves doing Gaullist work, actively hunting down former arch-proponents of Pétain and Laval and assisting in the official removal of those deemed ultracollaborationists. Previously sympathetic with such organizations, branches now initiated surveillance of suspected SOL members. Having banned all Vichy organizations, authorities wished to ensure that no illicit activities or meetings continued.[108] Anyone believed to be an active member of a Fascist league also found themselves arrested and put on trial, from a notary in Oran to the ex-leader of the Tiaret PPF, who had waged a constant anti-republican propaganda campaign after 1940 and was responsible for repeated instances of violent conduct and arms possession.[109] All branches were also directed to reverse course in the streets, arresting or citing anyone found to be anti-Gaullist or anti-republican. In March 1944, officers in the department of Alger who had spent years sniffing out potential resisters performed an about-face, dragooning Europeans who proclaimed "Vive Pétain!" or demanding that those who had executed Pierre Pucheu face the same fate. They also faced fisticuffs between the many settlers who refused to abandon the Extreme Right and their previous victims now emboldened by the return of republican government. In Constantine, in September 1944, a brawl erupted between two inebriated groups—one Jewish, yelling "Down with Vichy!," and the other unrepentantly Pétaniste, responding with "Dirty Jews!"—with police who had only two years before harassed and assaulted "undesirables" restraining both sides.[110]

The ultimate consequences of changing official policy included the reintegration of any policeman or gendarme excluded due to their race, politics, or ideology. In July 1943, prefectorial circulars demanded the rehiring in every branch of anyone fired in accordance with the July or September 1940 laws. Signed by de Gaulle himself, the orders demanded full restoration at the lost rank and salary, with no loss of active service time for pensions of promotion eligibility. This included an abrogation of Giraud's attempt at upholding Vichy's antisemitic legislation. Dozens of Jews, Freemasons, and resisters found themselves once again employed, their disciplinary files removed from circulation. By March 1944, the governor general personally intervened to ensure that each candidate's status was revised, empowering a commission headed by the *directeur de la Sécurité générale* to attend to the matter.[111]

Thus, by the time of the liberation, policing in Algeria once again became somewhat normalized. Yet, for all of the professionalization of the force under Vichy, from the insistence on training to the increasing specialization in the duties assigned to each branch of law enforcement, the legacy of xenophobia and brute force did not disappear, particularly with regard to the Arab and Kabyle populations. Jews and Freemasons once again served in the local constabulary, and even Communists regained their political rights, while the Extreme right vanished for the time being. However, none of these factors reflected a permanent change in the European mentality. Settlers continued to back a strict policy of *l'Algérie française* and chafed at the possibility of extending rights and freedoms to Muslims, while the security services reverted to their prewar position—technically republican, but (like most officials) tacitly supporting the *colons* and using violence and brutality against Algerians on a quotidian basis. If they kept their heads down from November 1942 onward, this reflected only their desire to avoid being purged and the knowledge that Pétain and company had been replaced by foreigners and Gaullists determined to remove Nazism root and branch, at least in the short term.[112] Nevertheless, once hostilities ended, promised reforms gave way to state violence. Moreover, in a dramatic escalation of trends from the pre-1940 era, Algerians refused to consider a restoration of the status quo, and increasingly turned to a burgeoning nationalist movement and direct attacks against the imperial nation-state, foreshadowing the War of Independence. For police and gendarmes, fighting crime increasingly devolved into a political struggle. Under Vichy, this had meant the fight against resisters and undesirables; after the Allied landing, it entailed capturing collaborators. By mid-1945, a new enemy emerged: the vast Algerian majority of the population.

CHAPTER 5

Policing Colonial Politics

The Surveillance, Arrest, and Detention of Leaders and Members of the Parti du peuple algérien, 1944–1954

During the legislative election campaign in November 1945 in the *commune mixte* (mixed commune) of Renault in the department of Oran, the president of the local *djemâa* (tribal council) Mohamed Abdelsadok was accused of electoral malfeasance by the authorities. He had handed out ballots in an attempt to ensure that all residents could vote, a move that offered a clear advantage to candidates affiliated with nationalist organizations, and particularly the banned Parti du peuple algérien (PPA; Algerian People's Party). Although the PPA had long demanded Algerian independence and decolonization and threatened revolt, its leader, Messali Hadj, now looked to capitalize on non-European anger through the voting booth. The administration promptly unleashed a massive campaign mobilizing *caïds* (tribal leaders), police, and local officials to squelch the threat. In the Renault case, gendarmes demanded that the *djemâa* president cease distributing ballots immediately, and Abdelsadok resisted. During the ensuing struggle, they shot and killed two voters and charged him with attempting to start a riot when the crowd objected to their interference. Needless to say, the resulting fraud handed the election to the European candidate.[1]

This incident demonstrates a new trend that emerged in the aftermath of the Second World War: the criminalization of nationalist politics, and particularly the PPA as an organization. To be sure, Hadj's activities had always provoked the ire of officials, who pilloried his Communist-affiliated Étoile nord-africaine (ENA; North African Star) in the 1920s, banned its successor in 1939 for subversion, and jailed him during the war. Yet in the aftermath of World War II the Algerian political tableau abruptly changed, rendering the independence movement far more dangerous in the eyes of settlers. On the surface, the colony experienced an era of party politics, in which the Parti communiste algérien (PCA; Algerian Communist Party), Ferhat Abbas's moderate Union démocratique du Manifeste algérien (UDMA; Democratic Union of the Algerian Manifesto), and even the decidedly nonelectoral 'ulama joined the PPA and its sister political party, the Mouvement pour le triomphe des libertés démocratiques (MTLD; Movement for the Triumph of Democratic Freedoms), in attempting to win over Algerian voters, taking advantage of the new Assemblée algérienne (Algerian Assembly, replacing the old Délégations financières) and its increased allotment to non-Europeans. More substantial parliamentary representation in France gave further hope to nationalists and reformers that the moment of recognition had finally arrived.[2] To the various parties, this represented the culmination of wartime trends: Abbas's 1943 Manifesto of the Algerian People demanded an end to colonization (which he termed "slavery"), Arabic as the official language, and equal rights enshrined in a constitution. In the streets, schools, and workplaces, PPA stalwarts led by the indefatigable Lamine Debaghine worked tirelessly to successfully convince the people to support new and radical demands, preferring action to votes.[3]

Yet, there was a violent side to the postwar era that simultaneously worked against any political solution to the thorny question of Algerian independence. By 1945, food shortages and peasant anger over a lack of cultivatable land due to European seizures led to demonstrations, culminating in full-blown nationalist protests on 8 May, which quickly turned riotous in certain locations such as Sétif, Abbas's hometown and the birthplace of the manifesto. When police used heavy-handed tactics to suppress the crowds, a departmental insurrection in Constantine resulted, stretching from the Aurès to Bône, with brutal violence against Europeans and mutilated corpses in certain locales, provoking Governor General Yves Chatigneau to call in the troops. Fully ten thousand soldiers under the command of General Duval crushed the rebels, with B-29 air bombardments in Guelma unleashing so many bombs that the explosions could be heard as far away as Alger and beyond. European militias joined the fray in what Martin Evans terms a "settler insurrection," killing thousands of Arabs and Kabyles, almost all of whom were innocent—estimates ranged from six thousand to twenty thousand dead.[4]

Settler and police violence certainly encouraged nationalist sentiment, which became radicalized due to the impossibility of meaningful political solutions to Algerian demands. The newly unveiled French Union in 1946 theoretically included Arabs and Kabyles as equal partners, and in 1947 the Statute of Algeria promised a new assembly equally divided between European and non-European representatives, with a similar arrangement for their French parliamentary delegations. Yet settlers refused to ratify the deal, and their allies in the Chamber sabotaged any efforts at reform.[5] Worse still, official corruption and voter intimidation condemned UDMA and MTLD electoral efforts to failure. Abbas's party resonated with voters in 1946 contests, and due to a PPA boycott, scored major successes in all three departments, encouraging the nationalists to run candidates in November legislative elections through the MTLD, garnering a massive public response at polling stations and in the streets and electing five parliamentary deputies. In response, in 1947 to 1948, Chatigneau's successor Marcel-Edmond Naegelen ordered officials and police and gendarmes to stymie both parties by all necessary means, stuffing ballot boxes in favor of European candidates, denying voter access in MTLD and UDMA districts, and arresting candidates themselves, rendering them ineligible for election. Fully thirty-three out of fifty-eight Messalist nominees found themselves in custody in 1948 alone, with the nationalist hotbed of Kabylia the most frequently targeted region. Naegelen further engineered a PPA press ban and authorized constant police raids to destabilize electoral operations. Unsurprisingly, UDMA and MTLD successes vanished almost overnight, as their representation decreased from 18 and 33 municipal seats in October 1947 to 7 and 5, respectively, by February 1951, while the MTLD were completely shut out in both Algerian Assembly and parliamentary contests.[6]

Given that settlers rejected every conceivable legal avenue toward reforms, no matter how small, it is unsurprising that by decade's end, various leading members in the PPA/MTLD had abandoned the electoral path in favor of renewed militancy and preparations for armed struggle. As Mahfoud Kaddache notes, "Entre les deux communautés, le fossé était reel; aucun dialogue politique n'était possible entre les représentants de la majorité éuropéene, attachés à l'Algérie française et à la souveraineté française, garantes de leur privileges, et ceux de la majorité musulmane acquis à l'idée de l'indépendance, seule voie possible pour une emancipation [Between the two communities, the gap was real; no political dialogue was possible between the representatives of the European majority, bound to French Algeria and French sovereignty, responsible for their privileges, and those of the Muslim majority won over by the idea of independence, the only possible route to emancipation]."[7] Moreover, the PPA press derided elections as simply untenable given the climate of repression, and a younger generation of educated fighters fought openly with older working-class militants who favored incremental solutions.[8] The MTLD continued to stand in elections when possible, joining the short-lived (1951–1952)

Front algérien pour la défense et le respect de la liberté (Algerian Front for the Defense and Respect of Freedom), putting aside its feuding with the reformist UDMA and joining Abbas's party, the 'ulama, and the PCA, which overcame a pro-European stance in the aftermath of 8 May 1945 to expound a soft nationalist stance that courted Algerians rather than a European clientele. Yet the gulf could not be bridged between reform-minded movements, which envisioned an ongoing yet equal partnership with France, and the hardened PPA position, which rejected anything short of complete independence. When their partners refused to back a nationalist general strike in May 1952 to protest Messali Hadj's deportation, the electoral partnership abruptly ended.[9]

As a result of both settler fears of the nationalist movement after 8 May 1945 and the official efforts to preempt PPA/MTLD electoral success and it ever-increasing popularity, law enforcement unleashed a constant campaign of harassment and brutality, designed to extirpate the movement and concomitantly preserve *l'Algérie française*, with its ongoing European hegemony. The level of dedicated policing and administrative effort to snuff out the PPA was without precedent in the postwar era. That the group had been progressively devastated by arrests and detention, and increasingly splintered between proponents of electoral strategy and young militants in favor of clandestine subversion, was summarily dismissed by law enforcement and administration alike. Police and judges used surveillance, intimidation, and violence to eliminate the perceived nationalist threat to French Algeria.

Political Policing and the Growth of the ENA and PPA, 1926–1939

In the metropole, political policing represented what one minister termed "political meteorology," simultaneously monitoring public sentiment while rooting out subversive ideas in defense of the republic and its citizens. By 1939, almost one thousand *commissaires* and inspectors of the Renseignements généraux (RG; political police) trailed Communists, anarchists, extreme-rightists, and a host of others, filing reports, keeping copious notes, and running informants in all departments.[10] A nineteenth-century innovation, the branch existed as part of an increasingly bureaucratic surveillance state that itself became a political tool. As Clive Emsley observes, "To the extent that they are expected to enforce a code of laws and dominant conceptions of public order, the police cannot, in the broad sense, be anything other than political."[11]

In the interwar era and again after 1945, this meant the prioritization of anti-Communist and anti-Fascist surveillance and arrests. Yet the RG in particular also deemed Algerians to be a dire threat, not tied to a foreign power yet a potential fifth column inside the republic's borders. Thus, from the 1920s onward, colonial denizens in the metropole became the object of surveillance, with informants and infiltration of workplaces and movements, wiretapping and phone monitoring of community or political leaders, and rigid control of identity papers.[12] During the interwar period, police kept a growing list of leaders and groups suspected of anti-French tendencies, yet xenophobic officers regarded Muslims as quiet and not particularly prone to radicalism, and thus they continued to display far greater concern for European political extremists. Moreover, in Algeria itself, police faced the usual paucity of resources and therefore elected to ignore any threat that was not immediate. As racial hegemony could be maintained, there was little to be done about naysayers, whether *évolués*, religious leaders, or nationalists, as long as their numbers remained small. It was only when violence occurred against European targets, or a direct threat to settler interests appeared, that the police acted swiftly and decisively.[13] By the post-1945 era, dedicated police divisions followed individuals and groups in cities like Paris and Marseille, infiltrating *cafés maures* (Moorish cafés), mosques, and workplaces.[14] Various authors claim that similar measures did not appear in Algeria, and it is certainly true that budgetary restraints and shortages of human and material resources prevented any ongoing large-scale operation in the colonial setting. Yet, officials, police, and gendarmes did sharpen their focus on one party deemed to be a constant and dire threat to *l'Algérie française* and settler domination: the PPA / MTLD, whose sole goal was decolonization and the forging of an independent state free from French domination.[15]

The origins of the PPA can be found in the ENA, the first revolutionary nationalist group focused on Algeria. Formed in 1926 as an auxiliary of the Parti communiste français (PCF; French Communist Party), it gathered together young Maghrebi workers toiling in Parisian factories due to the unemployment and misery endemic in indigenous communities throughout the empire. During and after the Great War, the small cohort of *évolués*—the Arab and Kabyle elite of civil servants, businessmen, and professionals—effectively dominated non-European politics. From the Young Algerian movement to the Fédération des élus musulmans (FEM; Federation of Elected Muslim Representatives), leaders like Ferhat Abbas and Mohamed Bendjelloul argued in favor of cautious negotiations with the colonizer, envisioning an Algeria in which the local population received rights and freedoms within the imperial framework, the product of lobbying for political and social reform in Paris and Alger.[16] However, such ideas meant little to agrarian laborers who toiled for a few francs per day on land seized or purchased by Gallic settlers, and were further burdened by a series of regulations concerning everything from collecting firewood to grazing rights, and a variety of taxes and duties. All of these measures were enshrined in the notorious double-edged legal framework of the Indigénat, which laid out exacting duties and punishments for Arabs and Kabyles. For those in urban centers, a combination of European commercial predominance (non-Europeans in Alger and Oran earned pittance wages, similar to their rural brethren), police harassment, and cramped and squalid living conditions in deteriorating neighborhoods rendered life uncomfortable, contributing to emigration to the metropole.[17]

The thousands who left for France during the interwar era found themselves in similarly decrepit conditions, living (sometimes clandestinely) in aging barracks or buildings, or in rooming houses in "company towns" in the provinces, lacking lighting, heat, or at times even windows, flooring, or toilet facilities. Similarly, in Paris and its suburbs, Algerians lived in close proximity to employers like Citroën and Renault, primarily in hostels and *bidonvilles* (shanty towns) rife with filth and excrement. In both cases, multiple workers shared cramped rooms; in the notorious Les Grésillons slum, dwellings were comprised of "dormitory huts made of tarred cardboard or breeze-blocks" rented for fifty francs per month. Employed at 20 to 25 percent below European wages, primarily in factories, often in dangerous and filthy conditions, illness and serious injuries proved common, and xenophobia only encouraged European apathy toward their plight. They were seen as disposable, and denied employment during the Great Depression, for example, which caused serious distress in Algerian communities dependent on supplementary income.[18]

These living and working conditions provided fertile ground for ENA recruitment. Originally in charge of propaganda, Messali Hadj became the group's president in mid-1926, and proceeded to engineer a reorientation toward nationalism, tremendously popular with the largely Kabyle workforce in the metallurgy, automobile, and aviation sectors in Paris. By 1928, the ENA had attracted four thousand members, and its newspaper, *El Ouma* (The Nation), routinely sold thousands of copies, which led to a long, acrimonious split with the PCF, whose European base and leadership did not support Algerian independence.[19] With this success came official suspicion, as police engaged in the surveillance of cafés and residences, driving the ENA leadership into clandestine operations, which by the 1930s encompassed all of Algeria in addition to the metropole. PPA leaders were charged and convicted of anti-French acts, while the PTT (Postes, télégraphes, et téléphones) seized ENA newspapers and tracts, but neither action dulled the movement's growing popularity. On 14 July 1936, thirty thousand supporters marched with the Popular Front, shouting nationalist slogans, and on 2 August Messali Hadj returned to Algeria to address a packed Stade municipal in Alger, demanding the suppression of the Délégations financières (Financial Parliament) in favor of an Algerian parliament elected by universal suffrage.[20]

The ENA's success and radicalism hastened its demise. In January 1937 the Popular Front government banned the movement and considered the problem solved. Yet Hadj and his lieutenant, Embarak Filali, transformed the group into a legal political entity that March, the Parti du peuple algérien. It remained dedicated to Algerian independence, but it broadened the clientele from émigré workers in Paris and urban labor in Algeria to incorporate skilled employees and shopkeepers, along with students and civil servants. Increasingly, young members and future leaders like Hocine Lahouel and Youcef Ben Khedda entered the movement via schools, scout troops, and the streets. Party candidates triumphed in municipal and cantonal elections, and thirty-one sections were founded across all three departments.[21] Yet, despite a certain level of success, particularly in urban centers, the PPA remained largely a Paris-based operation, with only 1,190 members in Algeria, overshadowed by the reformist FEM and the Salafi 'ulama brotherhood. By 1938, rejected by the PCA and the Congrès musulman (Muslim Congress) and pilloried in the Muslim press, Hadj's organization failed to consolidate its gains, despite the respect afforded to the party leader.[22]

As a result, government officials and police presumed that a wave of surveillance and arrests would decapitate the PPA, and they proceeded in 1937 and 1938 to overwhelm local sections across Algeria. In his memoir of the era, Hachemi Baghriche recalls that during the ENA years, police entered meetings, shutting off the microphone and evacuating the room. Conversely, the PPA's formative experience included arrests and beatings at the hands of police, fingerprinting and identification cards, and (in Baghriche's case, in Constantine) illegal house searches followed by months spent in a filthy jail cell while undergoing interrogation in the Coudiat prison.[23] Dozens of party leaders in all three departments faced similar fates, while Hadj, Lahouel, and four others received two-year jail sentences in November 1937 on charges of illegally reforming the banned ENA ("reconstitution de ligue dissoute") and breaching national security ("atteinte à la souveraineté française"). Trials of Embarak Filali and others followed in February, by which time, Baghriche notes, "the organization's leadership had been removed," with sympathizers avoiding all contact with PPA members for fear of being detained themselves.[24] Authorities shuttered *El Ouma* in summer 1939, and the already fraught membership dwindled in all three departments.[25]

The Radicalization of Algerian Nationalism and the "Events" of 8 May 1945

Thus, on the eve of World War II, police presumed that the PPA had been effectively eliminated from Algerian political life. In any case, faced with a rash of anticolonial violence among the general population unaffiliated with Hadj's organization (as detailed in chapter 3), the authorities turned their attention elsewhere. Events in the aftermath of the war completely reversed this trend. After 1945, the PPA symbolized a singular threat to the French presence in Algeria, a movement to be forcibly extirpated in defense of the European settler population in both town and countryside. Previously a relatively insignificant presence across the colony, dwarfed by reformists in the FEM and the 'ulama, the PPA grew substantially in the postwar era, from mere hundreds to thousands of members organized in cells and sections in every corner of Algeria. Police and officials had previously confined their actions to sporadic raids and arrests, focused almost entirely on the party leadership, yet now engaged in an unrelenting campaign against anyone even remotely associated with Hadj and company. Political activity itself became criminalized; an Arab or Kabyle either supported colonialism or became a dangerous opponent to be arrested, jailed, or worse.

None of this was apparent in the opening stages of the war. Hadj and other PPA leaders were jailed for the duration of the conflict due to their refusal to cooperate with the authorities, and the party only very slowly reconstituted itself. Attempts to forge armed rebellion—by joining a January 1941 mutiny in Maison Carré, for example—failed miserably. However, the growth of "Messalism" in Algeria, viewing Hadj as a martyr and a heroic leader, combined with French military weakness, encouraged certain segments of Arab and Kabyle youth to form clandestine cells across the colony. At first, they merely sold tracts and portraits with assistance from scout troops and football supporters, but gradually a central committee formed, led by moderate Lamine Debaghine and youth stalwart Mohamed Belouizdad.[26] These newcomers were not like the older generation of PPA militants, whose nationalism was founded in Parisian factories and betrayed an intellectual and communist bent. The young cadres of 1942 to 1945 proved to be far more radical, professional militants willing to sacrifice their lives for Algerian independence, and far more disciplined and hierarchical than their predecessors. Whether university students like Benyoucef Benkhedda, *lycéens* like Hocine Ait Ahmed, or manual laborers like Belouizdad, they rejected the focus on working-class issues in favor of reaching out to illiterate *fellahs* in the countryside and urban *évolués* alike.[27] Moreover, by 1944 their militancy came to the attention of police, concerned about increased membership, activity, and propaganda, from the distribution of *Action algérienne* (Algerian Action) to recruitment drives at weddings, funerals, and cafés. Roundups invariably followed; in Oran, October actions netted newspaper vendors and PPA leaders.[28]

Rather than embracing the radicals, Hadj instead moved toward rapprochement with moderate Ferhat Abbas, a frequent visitor to the PPA leader's detention house in Reibell, where Abbas persuaded him to write an afterword for his 1943 Manifesto of the Algerian People. When the reformer founded the Amis du manifeste et de la liberté (AML; Friends of the Manifesto and Freedom) the following year, the PPA chief perceived a distinct advantage: collaboration with a seemingly mild initiative could potentially convince the administration of the party's moderation, preempting arrests or a renewed ban. Although the AML represented soft nationalism, arguing for increased rights and political participation for Algerians, it adopted a decidedly legalist framework. It also provided an opportunity for mutual growth, and by December 1944, hundreds of thousands had joined both organizations. Yet it soon became clear that the PPA dominated the AML, and police were alarmed at the emergence of hard nationalism, engaged in everything from attacks against Muslims drinking alcohol to threatening *caïds* across Algeria, which only heightened when the March 1945 AML congress acclaimed Hadj as the uncontested leader of the Algerian "nation." For their part, PPA leaders had little faith in Abbas's ability to negotiate with the authorities, instead viewing the AML as a mere vehicle from which to elect militants at the local and regional levels, a fact made abundantly clear in the pages of *Action algérienne*, their newspaper.[29]

Hence, in 1945 the legalist strategy quickly fell apart. Unfortunately for Hadj, the PPA's central committee remained in the hands of the young radicals, who proceeded to ignore the imprisoned and therefore helpless leader and demanded unconditional independence. Moreover, March elections thrust many of them into local and regional office, while an increasing number of demonstrations and newspaper articles featured openly separatist language and proclaimed Hadj Algeria's rightful leader. However, the violence reflected the starvation of the population rather than political aims, directed not by the PPA but incensed locals. Food riots on 13 February in Fejd M'Zala and Orléansville involved hundreds of *fellahs* and workers protesting a lack of grain, while the Constantine *conseil général* (general council) reported a marked unease among Europeans across the department given the paucity of available rations.[30] Nonetheless, by April, unsubstantiated rumors of a major uprising led Governor General Yves Chataigneau to order the arrest of any PPA member for even the most minor infraction. Messali Hadj had been under house arrest since April 1943 (he would remain in this condition until June 1946), and thus unable to effectively lead any anticolonial action. Under the direction of the group's nemesis, General Henry Martin, tens of thousands of troops fanned out across Algeria while police and gendarmes arrested dozens of leaders and militants.[31]

Both Chataigneau and Martin presumed that the PPA planned a revolution, arms in hand, against French colonial authority. Many histories of the era agree with this assessment, proposing that the party fully intended a popular rising, and that these plans had a major impact on what came next during the infamous events of 8 May 1945 in the Constantinois and their aftermath. However, almost all police communications prior to 1 May emphasize the distribution of the PPA press and concerns over the growing popularity of the organization, rather than armed revolt, and the one major protest, on 16 April, involved five hundred Arabs in Alger explicitly demanding rations.[32] Moreover, nationalism hardly emerged in a vacuum, but rather acted as the sole rationale for Muslim anger. André Nouschi and Benjamin Stora echo the concerns of colonial officials, that food shortages assisted the spread of anti-French sentiment, which was manifested in disturbances and provided fertile ground for PPA recruitment. The collapse of the wheat and livestock markets led to skyrocketing prices and starvation, while inflation and shipping delays battered urban industries. Furthermore, economic dislocation occurred at the very moment when Algerians rejected political reforms ostensibly designed to provide electoral equality but which maintained the personal statute and twin electoral colleges that tilted the balance decisively toward the European population. While none of these problems were particularly new in 1945—bad harvests were a hallmark of colonial Algeria from the beginning, and colonial politics consistently favored French rule—they coincided with the exponential growth of the AML and PPA, raising the specter of a belligerent challenge to French authority.[33]

As it turned out, the PPA had other plans entirely: to demonstrate to the US occupation authorities that the party alone constituted the legitimate leadership of Algeria. On 1 May, they ordered a series of peaceful demonstrations; only in Alger did matters turn violent, when police attacked marchers, bristling at banners proclaiming independence and demanding freedom for Messali Hadj. They baited the increasingly frenzied crowd and then shot their way past the demonstrators in response to what one officer termed "the persistently aggressive attitude of Muslims," killing two and wounding twenty-one. The administration used these incidents, the unsubstantiated rumors of PPA and AML lists targeting politicians and police for assassination, and the increasing strength of the party and its dominance of the AML as an excuse to arrest hundreds of militants, effectively weakening the organization.[34] By 8 May, both the administration and the public presumed that a PPA-led insurrection was imminent, and acted accordingly, even though the organization had been effectively crippled.

Hence as Mahfoud Kaddache notes, the "events" of 8 May occurred despite official communiqués from the PPA and AML demanding calm in towns and villages. The supposed insurrection did not impact great swathes of Algeria; fewer than a dozen locales are mentioned in official records—Sétif and Blida are the largest towns, and neither was a major population center. To be sure, thousands of demonstrators marched on 8 May in Alger, Constantine, and Oran, and police injured Algerians while suppressing the protests.[35] However, Muslim-led violence primarily occurred in the nationalist hotbed of the Constantinois, with days of spontaneous sporadic attacks against isolated rural settlers, police and gendarmes, and government property. In Sétif, a crowd of thousands turned violent after police opened fire, killing twenty-seven and wounding forty-eight. There was a similar outcome in Guelma. Minister of the Interior André Tixier responded by ordering the creation of hastily organized European militias, which massacred Arabs and Kabyles, and the army intervened with troops and air strikes, while hundreds of armed Muslims (many of whom were PPA members) attacked isolated European farms. By the end of the month, 104 settlers were killed and up to fifty thousand Algerians massacred at the hands of the military and militias. Thousands more went on trial before military tribunals empowered to dispense justice in the state of siege during and after the massacres, reflecting the military's central role in crushing real and imagined enemies across the department of Constantine.[36]

Police Raids, Military Tribunals, Prefectorial Bans, and Electoral Malfeasance

The administration's negative perception of the PPA and its overestimation of the party's revolutionary nous only deepened following the events of 8 May 1945. Various officials and European press organs ignored the mass murder of Algerians, instead echoing the verdict of future governor general Marcel-Edmond Naegelen that helpless French men, women, and children "were savagely murdered, at times after having been horribly mutilated," by those inspired by nationalism.[37] Yet, despite the government's insistence that they had engaged in a planned rising, the events took both the PPA leadership and militants completely by surprise, and given the mass arrests and surveillance initiated in April, the group had few resources to devote to 8 May.[38] A new wave of roundups and imprisonment scuttled plans to belatedly capitalize on the events and the ensuing public anger by sponsoring further violence later in the month. The PPA was summarily banned and the AML dissolved in response to European claims that Muslims (rather than militias and gendarmes) had engaged in mass killings in the Constantinois, while officials blamed nationalists, reformists, and the 'ulama for the events, and General Duval of the army spoke of assuring "peace for ten years."[39]

Nevertheless, police and administrators designated the group a grave threat. They pointed to the collapse of the economy, with seven hundred thousand fewer hectares in cultivation, a drastic reduction in livestock per capita, and continued meager food rationing entrenching poverty, starvation, and disease in the countryside. Despite official proclamations that the PPA was finished, they also feared the group's growing popularity among nonmembers, a product of the 8 May massacres and their galvanizing effect on Algerian antiimperialism. Before the official inquest even concluded, the governor general and chief prosecutor both declared that the PPA had initiated an insurrection, the end result of clandestine meetings, propaganda, and demonstrations designed to erode French security. However, if the administration's *Bulletin mensuel d'information* (Monthly Information Bulletin) noted their participation in the "events" as justification for a renewed ban on their activity, they simultaneously worried about scarcity: hungry Algerians might very well respond favorably to calls for nationalist-inspired revolution. Going further still, the gendarmerie commander in Sétif divined secret messages in graffiti, gleaned insurrection in rumor and work absenteeism, and claimed to have discovered a plot—unsubstantiated—by Algerian officers to kill the police chief, mayor, and deputy prefect in Batna.[40] Meanwhile, the European press and public portrayed 8 May as a full-blown revolution, during which Muslims raped, pillaged, and murdered *colons*. Completely ignoring the massacre of Algerians, the prosecutor general worried about military courts treating arrested Muslims too leniently and demanded that nationalists (a term used to describe most of those arrested and charged) face civilian justice and longer sentences. Groups like Secours populaire français (French People's Relief) countered that the jailed included women, babies, and the aged—hardly a public menace—and demanded justice for the tens of thousands tortured and murdered by soldiers and civilians.[41]

Much like the prewar anti-nationalist response, authorities initially decided to violently repress the PPA "danger." An anti-French political movement deemed responsible for belligerent opposition to the European presence, they were subjected to an administrative crackdown on militants and activity. In

June, the government and police initiated a massive search and arrest campaign to "decapitate" and "annihilate" the nationalist presence throughout the department of Oran. The Mascara gendarmerie claimed to have dismantled a nationalist cell with dozens of members, arresting forty-seven youths who worked in scout organizations and Qur'anic schools supposedly linked to campaigns of sabotage and assault, including the firebombing of the post office and town hall. Both officials and settlers approved of the campaign of severe repression aimed at cleaning out the "rot" that permeated local *duwars* (tent enclaves).[42] Police and soldiers seized thousands of guns throughout Kabylia and an entire printing operation in Bougie, while authorities in Alger and Constantine initiated a series of raids that placed hundreds of leaders and militants behind bars and subjected them to "rough" interrogation (beatings).[43]

Judicial proceedings were equally ruthless in the aftermath of 8 May, with military tribunals rather than civilian courts meting out sentences. Throughout fall 1945, hundreds of suspected PPA militants were variously charged with treason, belonging to a banned organization, or assault and murder. In October, the entire Djidjelli section received sentences of up to twenty years of hard labor, despite the fact that the accused unanimously charged police with physical and psychological abuse and fabrication of evidence. Almost all confessions were recanted in court, while the prosecutors portrayed the section as armed bandits who aimed to destroy French Algeria. A similar outcome in Oran included executions, the confiscation of property, and the loss of both the right to live in a given community (*droit de séjour*) and political and / or legal standing (*degradation nationale*). Although the National Assembly declared a general amnesty in March 1946, this did not apply to those deemed to be dangers to French security. Of these, only Messali Hadj himself was freed in June 1946, and then merely to subvert continued (and highly successful) efforts to portray him as an anticolonial martyr. The severity of the government response had little to do with criminal activity but rather aimed to appease the frantic European population, which despite the massacre of Muslims and the dismantling of PPA cells across Algeria continued to believe in a clandestine threat.[44]

Unlike similar police actions in the late 1930s, however, a decade later these maneuvers played into the hands of Hadj and the PPA leadership. He and his confreres fundamentally disagreed with youthful militants and wanted nothing to do with violent insurrection, instead viewing the PPA strictly as a nationalist political movement. Moreover, continued persecution shored up their position as martyrs to the nationalist cause and (in Hadj's case) the universally admired voice of the separatist movement. Throughout summer and fall 1945, he attempted to wrest back control of the PPA from younger, more radical voices, focusing squarely on an electoral strategy, with the group bulletin prohibiting militants from carrying arms or responding to provocation. Subsequently, it was the group's new political wing, the MTLD, which became the organization's centerpiece, a legal party that engaged in electoral politics and sidestepped the ban that rendered the PPA an illegal entity.[45] The new entity aimed to become the voice of the Algerian people, combating reformism and the supposed "good intentions" of French imperialism, and preparing the masses for independence through propaganda, organization, and the campaign trail. Elected officials went into local *duwars* in *communes mixtes* throughout their districts, installing a press and propaganda network that used any opportunity to sermonize, including weddings, funerals, and festivals. *Cafés maures* and Muslim shops hosted party meetings, while schoolchildren learned to recite lessons with nationalist overtones.[46]

Given that a legal PPA branch could not be muscled by police and gendarmes, by 1946 the administration switched tactics, increasingly censuring party propaganda. Meeting with all three prefects on 6 January 1948, Governor General Marcel-Edmond Naegelen demanded the prosecution of nationalist movements and press, calling the MTLD an illegal extension of Hadj's banned party, believed to already control a number of municipalities.[47] In the aftermath of 8 May, the party had consistently emphasized the martyrdom of Messali, the torture and murders committed by the government, and Algerian independence as the sole viable solution to the colonial situation. Posters in towns across Algeria proclaimed the need to "Free Messali!" in French and Arabic, and *Action algérienne* decried the poverty and resistance to reform that authorities feared would turn to public toward the nationalist cause.[48] One of the most popular tracts, titled "Frères algériens" (Algerian Brothers), lambasted imperialism as the root cause of the discontent, manifest in the brute force employed against nationalists, reminiscent of Gestapo tactics. Such language had the European population in an uproar, particularly in smaller communities, where the experience of 8 May left rural settlers feeling vulnerable and resulted in visibly strained relations with Muslim neighbors.[49] The emergence of the MTLD only worsened the official predicament, for after initially boycotting elections following the massacres and subsequently being officially barred from running candidates, in the November 1946 National Assembly ballot the new party elected five deputies, including Lamine Debaghine, Djamal Derdour, and rising star Mohamed Khider, and new press organs—*Nation algérienne* (Algerian Nation) and *El Mograbi el arabi* (The Maghreb and Arabia)—appeared in all three departments, replacing the clandestine PPA newspapers.[50]

Naegelen's arrival signaled a complete shift in the administration's willingness to tolerate such manifestations of nationalism, as his office unreservedly backed the notion that Algeria should be French and the governor general displayed a willingness to use any means necessary to preserve European hegemony. In this, he was quite different than his predecessor, whose talk of broad political and economic reform in favor of Algerians earned him the nickname "Chataigneau ben Mohammed," as settlers rejected any and all talk of change, no matter how minute. In the aftermath of 8 May, and facing the surging PPA/MTLD, they demanded swift action against any potential threat. To be sure, Naegelen did propose efforts to eradicate racism, poverty, and the dearth of Muslim education. Yet, he unleashed police and gendarmes against the nationalists with such fervor that the metropolitan broadsheet *France-Observateur* wondered aloud about the existence of a "Gestapo state" in North Africa.[51] Neither was this policy quietly mooted behind closed doors, as Naegelen announced in a 21 October 1949 memo that law enforcement should embrace "the use of force . . . [as] legitimate when necessary to restore public order." In the post-Indigénat era, the legal code would no longer provide the fulcrum for repression, with the ultimate goal of "civilizing" Algerians rather than oppressing them. Instead, PPA-style nationalism demanded a far tougher approach. Thus, on one hand, he talked of disciplining any officer or official who used excessive methods "unworthy of France," yet simultaneously turned a blind eye to tactics that obliterated legal boundaries and encouraged a variety of practices ranging from electoral manipulation to mass arrests.[52]

Police launched counterinitiatives across Algeria, a practice that had already been in evidence under Chataigneau without official sanction or approval. Prefectorial bans criminalized the distribution of tracts and posters in public spaces, and train station guards and officers aboard carriages were instructed to maintain strict surveillance and arrest "suspicious" Algerians. Couriers found with bags containing PPA literature or party newspapers received sentences ranging from a few months to years in prison, with similar penalties assessed in urban centers. The leadership responded with transport teams to overwhelm guards, but this had little impact. In May 1946, one such group in Alger offered a 10,000-franc bribe to a police officer and assaulted him when he refused the offer; the ringleader was eventually caught and charged with attempting to bribe an official and "la distribution des tracts de nature à exercer une influence facheuse sur l'esprit de l'armée et les populations [distributing tracts that exercise a pernicious influence on the public and military spirit]." Moreover, authorities increasingly reported successful raids. In February 1949, police uncovered 409 kilograms of brochures in a Seine-et-Marne port, while their counterparts in Alger discovered a printshop containing twenty-three thousand tracts.[53] They particularly targeted MTLD offices, attempting to link the party's activities to the banned PPA, and thus searching homes and offices, instituting identification checks, and seizing material deemed provocative. In Tlemcen, one April 1948 sweep turned up 2,500 tracts declaring that "the Algerian administration engages in new incitements," which were seized by police along with membership cards, electoral strategy documents (deemed roadmaps to voter fraud), and PPA newspapers.[54]

Nor did judges demonstrate leniency toward those convicted of offenses previously seen as minor, condemning distributors of political tracts to years in prison and tens of thousands of francs in fines. Even the mere possession of party literature—already a criminal offense, yet seldom enforced—was now to be policed vigorously, with perpetrators facing similar punishments to the propagandists themselves. This was often deemed a response to local conditions. In April 1946, police in Tébessa and Constantine reported political chaos, preferential treatment for pro-PPA customers by grocers and wholesalers, and European fury at PPA activity. The distribution of nationalist tracts fanned the flames, claimed the assistant prosecutor in Guelma, and despite a lack of evidence of popular mobilization, he maintained that brochures contributed to a potential regional riot. The commandant of the Batna gendarmerie similarly noted Kabyle discontent with Arab political encroachment in municipal-tribal councils in August, as "nervous" Muslims increasingly avoided gendarmes in public spaces and locals spread rumors of the French army killing Tunisians like dogs. The *procureur générale* agreed that the distribution of a PPA tract in the region was a principal cause of the unrest.[55]

The arrest of individuals for the mere possession of nationalist propaganda pointed to a clearly defined criminalization of Algerian anti-imperial politics, a fact made even more explicit by administrative machinations against party meetings and electoral campaigns. Authorities had long targeted group gatherings due to the interest they sparked in Arab and Kabyle communities, with informants recording any conceivably anticolonial or menacing statements. Muslim police agents also routinely attended meetings, recorded the proceedings, and, when necessary, arrested the PPA militants involved. Yet, the judiciary displayed little interest in prosecuting the offenders, whose sentences were often overturned on appeal. In any case, police frequently fingerprinted and questioned them, and then granted their release on the condition that they leave the jurisdiction immediately.[56]

However, in the post–8 May era, police and officials were far less lenient, charging militants and leaders with treason and/or assault. The Algerian *procurer générale* and administrators mandated harsh legal sanctions against anyone accused of anti-French public utterances ("dangerous to the colony," in the words of the Tizi-Ouzou deputy prefect), provided that witnesses were reliable and the cases airtight, to avoid unsuccessful prosecutions that would only increase the prestige of PPA/MTLD militants. The latter used both party gatherings and electoral rallies to violently critique French colonialism and the settlers in equal measure. Gendarmes and police frequently cited speakers for supporting Algerian independence, complaining vociferously about the wealth of *colons* and the relative poverty of Muslims, and urging attendees not to pay taxes.[57]

Authorities particularly targeted prominent PPA speakers, including party leaders and MTLD elected officials. In January 1948, an *adjoint de maire* and four municipal councilors in Bône were charged following what the group termed a "major protest meeting against colonialist provocations," which attracted a crowd so large that hundreds of attendees spilled into the street. After militants referred to 8 May 1945 and repeatedly rejected French rule in irate terms, police attempted to shut down the gathering, leading to shoving matches throughout the hall, the seizure of numerous weapons, and twenty arrests—all were charged with rebellion and assault. Only two months later, in Mécharia on 29 March 1948, Algerian Assembly delegate Boualem Baki declared to a crowd that France was scared of Muslims, and that Messali Hadj and the party would drive the colonizer from Algeria. Baki was duly arrested and charged with "atteinte à la souveraineté française" spreading false rumors, and electoral fraud, and sentenced to eight months in prison, effectively terminating his political career.[58]

Another electoral rally that month resulted in an eight-month sentence and a 15,000-franc fine for two speakers and jail terms for several others for inciting hatred—punishments that became standard judicial fare. The deputy prefect promptly banned all local meetings and arrested both speakers, as well as four chief propagandists in the region for good measure. By 1950, police consistently raided PPA gatherings, often acting on information from informants within local chapters, and searching those in attendance, seizing money and firearms, and issuing heavy prison sentences and fines.[59] Somewhat ironically, administrative sanction only enflamed an already volatile situation, with the military reporting that their actions caused children to jeer at police and adults to demonstrate a "merciless hatred to the French" of a type hitherto unseen. Official attempts to prevent Hadj from addressing public gatherings similarly backfired: in March 1947, a ban on a series of talks in Kabylia only piqued local interest and increased attendance when the gatherings were held in privately owned fields.[60]

Even where meetings were permitted, local authorities resorted to electoral fraud on a massive scale. Despite legalizing the MTLD (although the PPA remained banned) and freeing Hadj from house arrest, authorities acted at every turn to stymie party candidates and prevent their election. In some cases, this involved rigged balloting, which cost over forty nationalist candidates their districts in April 1947, while electoral fraud similarly prevented major gains in October municipal contests.[61] In *communes mixtes*, administrators fixed *djemâa* elections by forcing PPA members to resign, imprisoning uncooperative leaders, and appointing their own candidates. Police and prosecutors often embraced even more draconian methods. Potentially successful MTLD candidates were frequently arrested for campaign speeches, regardless of whether they met the threshold for treason or incitement. In each case, the charge was "atteinte à la souveraineté française," engaging in treasonous acts. A common tactic used to combat the PPA press and militants, its use traced to the 1935 Regnier Decree, which declared that any *indigène* organizing anticolonial activity or engaging in civil disobedience faced potentially two years in prison and up to five thousand francs in fines. Anyone suspected of PPA membership or activity also merited a charge of "reconstitution de ligue dissoute" (reforming a banned organization).

Using these tools, police and gendarmes, in tandem with local officials, engaged in a wave of arrests during the spring 1948 municipal electoral campaign, in which MTLD candidates dominated the first round of balloting. Following their triumph in the 1946 campaign, the nationalists ran a full slate of candidates that April across all three departments. However, Hadj's team promptly clashed with Naegelen, who proceeded to back Ferhat Abbas and his reformist UDMA and accused the PPA of sedition. Before the municipal campaign even began, he had thirty-two out of fifty-nine candidates arrested and ordered the police to attack MTLD voters. Officials stuffed ballot boxes, closed polling stations early, and packed the urns with names of Europeans either recently deceased or absent from the jurisdiction.[62] Throughout Constantine, police arrested potential voters and local notables for pledging themselves to either the PPA or the MTLD, sentencing even *adjoints de maires* and municipal councilors to months in prison.[63] Most notoriously, in Alger, in the *commune mixte* of Aumale, gendarmes claimed that six *indigènes* had been sent to interfere with voting by inciting disorder and threatening locals at polling stations. Despite the fact that witnesses (including the *caïd*) recanted their statements during the trial, stating that they were given under duress (i.e., torture), and the testimony of the cavalier on site contained several inconsistencies concerning dates and details, all nonetheless received substantial prison sentences and fines. Ironically, the accused men constituted one of many PPA teams detailed to prevent electoral fraud. Monitors were instructed to ensure that candidates and voters properly registered with authorities, that banned meetings took place in private homes and properties, that voting booths were made public and maintained standard opening hours, and that the ballot boxes remained untouched by *caïds* or police. Should clear evidence of fraud emerge, militants were ordered to break the urns, rendering the results null and void for pro-French and nationalist candidates alike.[64]

The robust PPA/MTLD press reported any evidence of malfeasance, deftly countering the pro-colonial narrative of the European papers, while underscoring the benefits of sovereignty as opposed to the reformist program preached by competitors like the PCA and Ferhat Abbas's new UDMA. Due to its success in terms of sales and influence, administrators and police launched unrelenting attacks as part of their attempt to criminalize nationalist politics. Although the PCA press and Abbas's daily *Égalité* (Equality) both suffered similar harassment, the clandestine nature of the PPA's *Action algérienne* (renamed *Nation algérienne* in 1946) and *El Maghreb el Arabi* stymied police and presented a particularly dangerous conundrum: Abbas and the PCA could be sued; Hadj and the hidden editors of the PPA press could not.[65] Nonetheless, in early 1948 the minister of the interior prioritized felony charges against the nationalist press under the 29 July 1881 statute, demanding arrests and prosecutions for provocation, slander, or fabrication and authorizing "special" regulations for cases deemed severe. All copies of PPA publications would henceforth be seized. The printing facilities dismantled, and surveillance initiated at the Algerian borders and for each branch of the postal service, with updates provided on a daily basis. Police and gendarmes executed a huge number of search warrants, arresting dozens of PPA news vendors and sympathetic merchants and seizing hundreds of copies at a time. When special French-language editions of *El Maghreb el Arabi* appeared in 1948 to 1949, the governor general personally noted that despite equally condemnatory articles in *Alger républicain* and other newspapers, repeated references to sovereignty and anti-imperialism rendered any trial moot without the PPA/MTLD in the dock. Unsurprisingly, when the paper went public, editor Zahiri Benzahar was immediately fined 100,000 francs and the publication suspended for three months. Subsequent proceedings resulted in fines for the PPA's weekly *Algérie libre* and the formation in February 1950 of a parliamentary commission chaired by Interior Minister Jules Moch to find ways for prosecutors to circumvent "indulgent" courts by condemning the tone and spirit of a publication rather than its articles.[66] Moreover, courts criminalized the distribution of the PPA press under the Regnier Decree, handing out dozens of lengthy prison sentences to persons convicted of printing or disseminating newspapers. Although the MTLD launched an official protest with the minister of justice in September 1950, and municipal councilors across all three departments introduced motions condemning seizures and arrests, authorities in Paris and Alger soundly ignored the complaints.[67]

It became increasingly clear that the real intention of administrative actions concerning press and propaganda, meetings, and elections was to single out the PPA/MTLD as a criminal enterprise rather than a nationalist political organization. In July 1947, the governor general banned all PPA meetings in any open locale, demanded forced residency in France for Messali Hadj, and ordered multiple arrests in all three departments to stop propaganda and clandestine activity in its tracks. The minister of justice further authorized the use of *flagrant délit*—the equivalent of an aggravated felony charge—for any misdemeanor involving the PPA/MTLD, as it guaranteed better conviction rates and severe sentencing. Both men were particularly concerned about the appearance of French weakness due to acquittals, which had recently resulted in cheering crowds inside and outside courtrooms in Aïn-Boucif and Fort National. The procureur général further instructed local prosecutors to order preventive detention based on police and *caïd* testimony to serve as an example (in addition to the *flagrant délit* charge) to the general public. All members, from Hadj on down, carried "moral complicity" by encouraging violence and anticolonialism, thundered the governor general in August 1950, and thus the MTLD should be summarily banned and all nationalists given severe prison sentences, even for publishing a tract or collecting dues. This reflected a change in penal and sentencing directives that broadened the culpability under the charge "atteinte à la souveraineté extérieure de l'état" (breaching the external sovereignty of the state), which had previously been difficult to prove, resulting in shorter prison terms and less substantial fines. The new guidelines made speeches, meetings, and even expressions of nationalist sympathy evidence of such a conspiracy, with concomitantly harsh sentences. In essence, the military verdicts rendered after 8 May 1945 could now be pronounced by civilian judges.[68]

PPA/MTLD Clandestine *Djemâas*, Banditry, and Paramilitarism

The goal of such draconian measures was clear: to eliminate the PPA/MTLD. At the very least, officials and police sought to minimize the influence of nationalism, and this meant preventing the party from attracting public acclaim and a sizable membership, not to mention negating their power at the ballot box. Yet the harsher the restrictions and the more draconian the police actions or judicial sentences, the more popular the party became with Algerians, who continued to experience the brutality of the colonial system and the xenophobia of the settlers on a daily basis. Moreover, in blocking off the legal path to independence—elections, press and propaganda, and the party's official presence in communes across all three departments—law enforcement unwittingly discredited Messali Hadj and the moderates, empowering radical voices within the movement. As the PPA once again eclipsed the MTLD by decade's end, banditry and paramilitarism trumped the ballot box and angry editorials.

Although the PPA was driven into hiding by waves of persecution and arrests from mid-1945 onward, it had 23,940 members in 1950 and did not lack for militants and supporters. Only in Oran did the group fail to take root, due to the sizable European population there; in Alger, Constantine, and the Sahara, the organization made substantial gains after World War II, with 2,150 in Kabylia alone.[69] In September 1946, the RG proclaimed that "the PPA is indisputably the most dangerous Muslim political party." The party continued to receive assistance from *djemâas* in *duwars* across Algeria because officials actively sympathized with the nationalist agenda and worked to circumvent French decisions on taxes and budgets. In addition, in March 1948 the governor general circulated a list of police and prison employees with suspected links to the PPA/MTLD, either because they had relatives in the group or reportedly made anti-French statements.[70]

Much more disturbing for officials in this regard, the PPA formed clandestine *djemâas* and courts in certain locales, funded by contributions from members and villagers. Messali Hadj had repeatedly called for such efforts in early 1947 to nullify the French authorities. They were especially popular in Kabylia, where the hatred of colonialism ran particularly deep, and members successfully badgered locals into joining the PPA despite the surveillance and arrests by gendarmes. Moreover, in May 1947, the Tizi-Ouzou council demanded a boycott of stores owned by Europeans or Muslims sympathetic to the colonizer, a campaign that ended in the arrest of the leader, a magistrate sentenced to five years in prison along with the local PPA leader.[71] Simultaneously, clandestine courts rendered judicial decisions on issues of civil and Muslim law, in a continuation of an age-old tradition updated for the colonial era to prioritize the negation of the French system. In Taher, Arabs and Berbers from El-Milia, Constantine, Sétif, and Bougie all arrived every Thursday to attend Larbi Kebbieche's "legal consultation practice" at a local café, while a *djemâa*-led court handed down verdicts and sentences for actual crimes. In other jurisdictions, notables supported the clandestine hearings, and officials noted that what had previously been reserved for religious disputes increasingly became a political vehicle due to PPA involvement. The hearings effectively eclipsed the French legal system, mirroring its practices by including a judge, a public prosecutor, a defense lawyer, and a jury. Gallic justices in various locales reported a steep drop in cases reported to their courts, as defendants were fined and imprisoned by their Algerian counterparts. Furthermore, police informants noted that PPA leaders forbade any collaboration with colonial authorities, deepening the reliance on the tribunals. Throughout 1947, the authorities arrested the militants involved for adjudicating cases involving land disputes, grazing rights, and felonies, but this had little impact on the growth of the parallel system.[72]

By that time, the focus of police investigations and judicial proceedings shifted to nationalist paramilitarism. Once again, Kabylia was the epicenter, long a source of anti-imperialist tension and violence against officials, gendarmes, and their informants. It also had been the focal point for banditry during the Great War, and it was this tradition that reemerged after 1945, in the service of the PPA and Algerian nationalism. Although gendarmes reported scattered incidents of assault and murder in the immediate aftermath of the war, an organized campaign first appeared two years later, rooted in PPA efforts to seize the region once clandestine *djemâas* and courts took over from their European counterparts. Emboldened by the thousands in attendance at meetings and their dominance in *mechtas* and *duwars* across the region, leaders announced a new rash of initiatives, from fines for any Algerian patronizing a European café to armed patrols. In March 1947, a speaker in Bordj-Menaiel told his audience to prepare for war, and attacks against *caïds* and Muslim officials began, along with public disobedience designed to provoke a response while simultaneously demonstrating the powerlessness of the colonizer. Gendarmes attempted to arrest the offenders, but they faced the usual barriers: witnesses refused to speak out, and the few members that were apprehended did not deter the growing illicit *djemâa* movement or the ongoing boycotts of European establishments.[73]

In November, the *sous-préfet* of Tizi-Ouzou reported a major escalation of violence that culminated in the assassination of two men in Bordj-Menaiel in broad daylight and the killing of the PPA regional chief in a shootout with gendarmes while wielding a submachine gun. The latter incident was so sensational that the European press weighed in approvingly on the deadly police raid, listing the purported criminal activities of the deceased. However, it had a negligible impact on the situation on the ground, as gendarmes reported being constantly watched by locals, while death threats against *caïds* increased and emboldened PPA activists continued to shoot, beat, and intimidate any Kabyle refusing to support the movement. The group's opponents retaliated in kind, and police reports by year's end noted the use of firearms by the unaffiliated when pressed by PPA stalwarts. Worse still, by December, the targets included Europeans, cavaliers, and *gardes champêtres* for the first time, as the PPA broadened its efforts across the region.[74]

Perhaps unsurprisingly, by 1948 the scourge of banditry returned to the Constantinois, with the hills and forests once again providing cover for bands of PPA members and sympathizers, as nationalists joined forces with criminals and deserters. They were also armed with rifles and submachine guns, making them doubly dangerous as they robbed the inhabitants of *communes mixtes* in order to survive. Although gendarmes did capture certain gangs, others persisted, stealing hundreds of thousands of francs, guarding PPA meetings and attacking political opponents, and engaging in arms dealing. They were protected by the party's clandestine *djemâas*, which stood by while *caïds* and officials became targets. Even after the arrest and internment of the Kabylian MTLD chief Bellounès and bandit leader Ali "Monsieur le Président" Galleze in May, maquis activity continued unabated.[75] The Tizi-Ouzou prosecutor's report resorted to the same old excuses: mountainous and forested terrain made capture almost impossible, and the "temperament of the Kabyle race" naturally encouraged revolt. Yet these were not the vendettas of old, or even the desperate anti-French *insoumis* of 1916 or 1944, and officials admitted that most of the bandits were PPA and MTLD operatives, assisting in everything from elections to political killings. Matters were worsened by the availability of firearms, most of which had been abandoned by the Allies or were stolen from army bases in the waning days of the last conflict. Moreover, with precious few officers available in Kabylia, the Brigades mobiles were outmanned and outgunned, and required immediate assistance from the army to effectively combat the bandits in the hills.[76]

Given the advantages enjoyed by the PPA and their bandit allies, police and gendarmes fell back on the playbook developed after 8 May 1945, relying on brute force to staunch the threat. Facing a potential Kabyle insurrection in October, the *sous-préfet* unleashed a massive operation involving almost two hundred law enforcement personnel, aimed at arresting and/or killing PPA "terrorists" and their deserter, fugitive, and criminal allies.[77] By July 1948, the dragnet managed to restore calm to the region, with the exception of party enclaves in Bordj-Menaiel and Haussonvilliers, which were viewed as beyond the reach of colonial authority. Describing Kabylia as "a nerve center," police and gendarmes arrested suspected murderers, seized arms caches (including machine guns), and apprehended PPA stalwarts, including the notorious Benai si Ouali, the party's Lower Kabylian leader. The interrogation of such major figures led to details of assassination campaigns against *caïds* and notables loyal to France, resulting in a wave of arrests.[78]

However, on this occasion, banditry and quotidian violence were secondary problems for the colonial police and officials. It was the Organisation spéciale (OS; Special Organization), a clandestine paramilitary wing of the

MTLD / PPA, whose formation represented the ultimate response to the government's years-long effort to criminalize the party and its anti-imperial politics. Although it boasted barely one thousand members, the OS came to symbolize the "new" face of the PPA: ultraviolent and bent on sparking insurrection among the general population. As younger, less doctrinaire voices rose to prominence within the nationalist movement, the older Messalist wing agreed to a compromise at the party's February 1947 Belcourt congress: the MTLD would continue to seek independence through legal and electoral means, while young militants led by Lamine Debaghine strove to go beyond the clandestine organization of the PPA to direct attacks on the colonial order. Until April 1948, the moderates continued to enjoy predominance, driven by electoral success in regional and municipal contests. Yet when the authorities successfully stymied MTLD candidates that month, while partnerships with the UDMA, the Confédération générale du travail / PCA, and others broke down, the OS emerged to force independence by other means, under the leadership of Mohamed Belouizdad, a former worker who now assisted Augustin Berque, the directeur des affaires indigènes (director of indigenous affairs). Fueled by post-May 1945 young recruits uninterested in political ideals or the Islamist rhetoric of the 'ulama, and slightly older leaders with military experience, the clandestine organization did not rely on educated members—most lacked even the *brevet* (school diploma). They were "shock troops," and many ended up in the Comité révolutionnaire d'unité et d'action (CRUA; Revolutionary Committee for Unity and Action) during the opening stages of the Algerian War of Independence.[79]

The organization's greatest success came after PPA central committee member Hocine Ait Ahmed replaced the seriously ill Belouizdad at the end of 1947. It was his attention to training manuals and insistence on subsuming pro-independence Kabylian bandits into the OS that proved decisive, under the sponsorship of Secretary-General Hocine Lahouel, who feuded with Messali Hadj and the moderate wing. Rejecting the disastrous full-blown fighting of 1945 and the idea of terrorist attacks in equal measure, in his memoirs Ait Ahmed instead spoke of a guerilla war specifically tailored variously to city or countryside. This form of warfare infused OS training and preparation, with its emphasis on practice fighting in forests and hills with pistols, submachine guns, and grenades.[80] However, the operation remained dependent on the parsimonious PPA, which refused to release funds needed for anti-French operations. Hence the decision to fund the OS via armed robbery, most notoriously the 5 April 1949 holdup at the Oran post office, which netted over 3 million francs. Internal politics eventually led to the replacement of Ait Ahmed, who was implicated in the Berberist crisis, threatening a schism within the PPA with the more reliable municipal councilor and Oran leader Mohamed Ben Bella, and the plans continued apace. The goal remained the construction of a secret organization with arms, equipment, and training to conduct a civil war. There were to be no extant documents to trace the OS's activities, and no participation in regular PPA/MTLD functions.[81] Of course, there remained links between the two organizations, and central committee stalwarts like PPA parliamentarian Mohamed Khider worked both sides of the aisle, recruiting "des surs, durs, et purs" (the reliable, tough, and righteous) for the OS and participating in clandestine activities while protected from legal consequences by parliamentary immunity. Moreover, although the party refused to supply unlimited funds, they eventually did release thousands of francs on a monthly basis for weapons and training.[82] The former came from established networks that had long supplied the PPA and other opponents of the regime with firearms and explosives, including submachine guns and pistols (including ammunition), to grenades and dynamite from Tunisia, the Territoires du Sud, and the metropole, along with numerous dealers in Kabylia and Alger personally known to Ait Ahmed and his lieutenants.[83]

Although technically the OS was run by a steering committee, its true organization remained local and regional. Ten *wilayas* (districts) throughout Algeria were run by *chefs*, and each one contained two to four *dairas*, or groups (depending on the *wilaya* size), run by leaders who formed a council. The *dairas* themselves were also headed by appointed leaders, and each comprised two to six *kasmas* (local organizations). At the base, *kasmas* were divided into five cells run by appointed heads. However, each level had no contact with those above, below, or lateral, and thus the chances of a successful infiltration by police remained slight, and even if an informant emerged, he could not betray the entire OS, since he was only aware of his own *kasma* or cell. Superiors were hooded during meetings with liaisons or squad leaders, keeping their own identities secret. It is significant that police only cracked the operation in March 1950 due to a botched assassination attempt, which resulted in the capture of key personnel due to their own incompetence and negligence rather than any official planning or action.[84]

Given its mission to disrupt the colonial system and eventually forge independence, the OS further contained a variety of specialized sections, each designed to maximize the organization's potential to attack a wide range of targets. Under Orléansville member Mohamed Arab, the munitions section fabricated detonators, bombs, and incendiary grenades and taught the skills required for the trade. The devices were quite basic, usually involving only iron pipe and gunpowder, and the recipes were gathered together in a training manual. Even so, a shortage of the required materials prevented practical exercises, despite a substantial budget ranging from 9,000 to 15,000 francs per month. The funds were laundered through an import-export shell corporation, through which Arab and a thirty-man team accessed needed cash and planned the destruction of bridges, railroads, and buildings.[85] They were joined by a signals corps under Ramdane Asselah, which trained recruits in the art of radio and communications to monitor and intercept government and police messages. Those selected tended to possess experience in the field or to work in a related sector, including PTT employees, electricians, radio technicians and operators, and mechanics.[86] Finally, an assistance section aided militants and *maquisards* (Maquis partisans) caught by police, providing legal help for any OS member arrested and imprisoned and hiding those on the run.[87]

Regardless of the section, the OS heavily recruited men with military experience, believed to be the most capable of successfully navigating participation in a clandestine paramilitary unit. Ex-soldiers were particularly prized, and recruiters sought those whose records included promotions and/or facility with weapons, along with those who had fought against the Germans in the metropole or the colony. Following his arrest in spring 1950, Maklouf Bouaziz told police that he had been a resister during World War II, fighting the Germans in France before returning home in November 1948 and joining the MTLD the following year. Given his wartime role, Bouaziz easily became a squad leader.[88] Others came from prison, like Mohamed Benmahdjoub (aka Krim), whose six-month stint in the Orléansville penitentiary for contempt of court brought him to the attention of the local OS chapter. He became the head of the assistance section, hiding fugitives and recruiting like-minded members across the region.[89] Wartime internment camps also provided many of the organization's stalwarts, including one member arrested in Berroughia at a 1945 nationalist demonstration. Converted to the party doctrine during his six-month incarceration, the member eventually migrated from the MTLD to the OS, and then went through basic training to hone survival skills learned during his sojourn in the penal system.[90] Once selected, recruits were required to attend an initiation ceremony with a hooded local leader, sworn to secrecy by taking an oath on the Qur'an. Superiors threatened any recruit who attempted to leave with death.

The PPA's target member tended to be young, typically between seventeen and twenty-five, and in peak physical condition, although even then a certain proportion could not tolerate the rigorous training in the mountains and forests that provided needed cover. Most were workers from communes across all three departments, although certain leaders were professionals— pharmacists, teachers, and even municipal councilors. On the formation of a completed new cell, the members received military training that included memorizing a French army manual, and exercises in weapons deployment, armed combat, and living as a guerilla in the countryside, under the strict supervision of an ex-military supervisor. One arms specialist recalled that a standard course included the use of rifles and ammunition, submachine guns, hand-to-hand combat, property destruction, and even rudimentary bombs.[91] Beyond firearms and explosives, OS members received instruction on topography, police techniques, coding, espionage, disguise, and establishing safe zones. The instruction manual further noted that candidates were expected to develop nerves of steel, the physical capacity to withstand extreme temperatures, and the ability to to live off the land. Once training had been successfully completed, a member would still be expected to participate in maneuvers every fifteen to twenty days and regular cell meetings. Moreover, they were required to provide monthly donations to the party and organization—up to 200 francs, often gathered from family members or neighbors pressed to contribute by armed recruits. In certain cases, the section would also act to keep the local population in line, with certain Kabyle OS outfits antagonizing the French authorities and threatening all non-PPA Algerians, while *caïds* and *djemâas* looked the other way. Naturally, a given *mechta* or *duwar* refused to reveal the organization's cell to the police or gendarmes, acting much as they had in previous decades.[92]

This conspiracy of silence had functioned quite well in defending bandits in 1916 and obfuscating the perpetrators of interwar attacks against Europeans. However, the hidden transcript could not protect the OS against poorly planned operations, which ultimately proved to be the organization's undoing. Despite talk of a clandestine army tens of thousands strong, the OS never managed to recruit more than one thousand to fifteen hundred fighters, often badly trained and unsuited to armed revolutionary struggle.[93] Nonetheless, the small size actually helped to conceal the group. It was not until 1949 that the governor general wrote to the minister of the interior about a terrorist "secret army" preparing to liberate North Africa. That June, gendarmes in Jemmapes had accidentally stumbled on a group of five Muslims undergoing military training, their instruction manual combining military documents and excerpts from the PPA militant handbook, and a cache of ammunition.[94]

However, only in March 1950 did the Police judiciaire (PJ) in Bône finally begin to arrest OS members, slowly unravelling an organization that had spread to all three departments across a diverse array of locales.[95] Assigned to murder a member suspected of becoming a police informant, a five-man assassination squad arrived in Tébessa and proceeded to botch the hit, with the police tipped off to their presence as a result. On 18 March, gendarmes set up barricades on roads throughout the department, and the commandos were stopped in Bône with guns and ammunition in their vehicle. Five were subsequently arrested, and their interrogation revealed the local operation and its arms cache of hunting rifles and training manuals. Twenty-eight OS members were detained within a matter of hours, beginning the dismantling of the entire network, which was finished in a matter of weeks. The European press gleefully followed the subsequent raids and interrogations, professing shock at each hidden submachine gun and grenade. Naturally, the PPA/MTLD denied any link to the OS, even as the dragnet widened throughout the department of Constantine to Philippeville, Bône, Guelma, Souk-Ahras, and beyond. Police arrested dozens of additional suspects and uncovered hundreds of weapons with thousands of rounds of ammunition.[96] Unfortunately for the organization, a cache of papers also revealed the structure and functioning of the vast conspiracy across all three departments, which by spring 1950 had grown to include everything from anti-tank divisions to intelligence units tracking the number of police, gendarmes, and armed forces personnel in certain locations, along with the names of prominent leaders such as Mohamed Ben Zaim in the Bône region; the Police judiciare quickly broke entire *wilayas*— Condé Smendou, for example, by the end of the month.[97] Official panic dissipated as the truth about the size and scope of the OS emerged. The training and recruits did not meet expectations. One Philippeville cell consisted of an ex-Muslim scout and a reserve sergeant, neither of whom possessed combat training, the Bougie group had been gutted in 1949 by the arrest of participants on unrelated charges, and the Bône operatives were later arrested in October 1950 following a bungled kidnapping.

Algerian Law Enforcement Confronts the OS

However, gendarmes and police did not rely solely on documents seized during raids of houses and businesses. Captains and officers spoke of interrogations as a key method they used to break the OS within weeks, particularly useful for obtaining the names of leaders like Mohamed Khider, along with links to the PPA-affiliated bandits that had hounded Kabylia for years. Although many armed OS leaders were killed outright by law enforcement during military-style raids, others wound up in custody. Along with the seizure of caches of weapons, dozens of supporters in all three departments thus became fodder for police violence.[98]

As discussed in previous chapters, police brutality against suspected criminals, and indeed the outright killing of bandits during the Great War, were everyday events in the Algerian setting. Yet the use of torture as a common interrogation device coincided with the emergence of the nationalist threat and the desire for independence expressed by the ENA and MTLD/PPA and its leadership. Faced with the prospect of an anti-French armed insurrection, or even the threat of a political secession, the colonial authorities responded with their own campaign of terror, presaging the tactics utilized by police and paratroopers during the Algerian War of Independence.[99] Accusations of torture by the police first surfaced in the aftermath of the 8 May 1945 massacres, when PPA members on trial before a military tribunal accused *commissaires* from the RG of using electricity, submersion in ice baths, whipping, and other techniques at the DST headquarters in Fort de l'Eau, where interrogations took place for those accused of killing Europeans. The accounts proved shocking (and plausible) enough that newspapers like the *Dépêche algérienne* (Algerian Dispatch) prominently covered the story, despite a stream of denials from law enforcement agencies. Officials did not help matters by claiming that defendants absent from trial were in hospital, supposedly recovering from "hernias."[100] Writing in the left-wing newspaper *Alger républicain* in January 1946, Gaston Mesguiche elaborated upon the story, detailing forced confessions (regardless of the facts of a case) extracted from suspects in Oran through savage beatings that resulted in broken teeth and profuse bleeding, whipping with belt buckles and cattle prods, threats of murder at gunpoint, and the notorious *baignoire* (bathtub), involving forced submersion in an ice bath until the victim almost drowned.[101] In later cases, suspects in custody asked for a doctor after undergoing interrogations only to be confronted with a European on the police payroll. Naturally, the physicians declared no sign of violence to be present.[102]

Unsurprisingly, the OS network provided the opportunity for a pre-1954 crescendo of police brutality. Almost immediately, calls emerged on the Left and in the Muslim press for a parliamentary inquest into abuse during searches of dwellings allegedly occupied by network members. Hundreds were arrested in April 1950, sequestered in undisclosed locations with no access to family or legal representatives, and regularly beaten, subjected to electricity and the *baignoire*, and rectal torture. Even before arriving at an interrogation house (the Bordj-Ménaiel gendarmerie used the Chateau Germain, owned by a wealthy settler, for example), a suspect who demanded to see a warrant or otherwise questioned police was assaulted in their home, along with wives, mothers, siblings, and children. Many were released for lack of evidence up to a week after their arrests, and they shared stories of intimidation and violence during questioning, their accounts confirmed by medical examinations. In other cases, they immediately retracted their confessions, claiming that their signatures were forcibly obtained. Although members of the Assemblée algérienne took up their cause, the administration refused to admit that any violence had taken place, pointing to signed confessions as proof that the perpetrators were guilty. When suspects were brought to the courthouses for preliminary hearings, all reporters were barred from entering, presumably to prevent evidence of beatings and torture from being spotted, which led to suspicions of police malfeasance, even from European newspapers.[103] As late as 1952, appeals hearings continued to feature claims of torture by officers of the PJ and staunch denials from prosecutors and law enforcement, while judges ignored the evidence and imposed stiff sentences. Of course, PPA meetings turned the entire debacle into separatist propaganda, with speakers bluntly stating that only one palliative existed for police abuse and violence: independence.[104]

The language used in police reports makes it clear that the real target was not the OS itself; it was a poor excuse for a covert militia, with fewer members than expected and no concrete means to turn ambitious plans into action. Rather, the PPA was the object of official malice, their politics a criminal act to be punished, in order to preserve *l'Algérie française* by any means necessary. The governor general set the tone in his August 1950 postmortem of the OS, denouncing the "fanatics" running the operation, whose sole goal had been civil war and murder, and implying that every PPA leader had precisely the same agenda in mind.[105] The authorities responded to any legal challenges with absolute fury, with one RG officer declaring, "On ne doit plus parler d'un parti politique, mais d'un gang ou d'une bande de cons penale [We can no longer call them a political party, but rather a criminal gang]."[106] Accordingly, police reports adopted the language of war to describe operations. The Tlemcen OS had not been dismantled but "annihilated," according to one PJ officer, defeating the attempted "liberation of Muslim national territory by violent and revolutionary methods."[107] Moreover, police action could not be limited to breaking up the current cells, for those arrested would inevitably become martyrs, and thus only constant vigilance and police and gendarme action could successfully prevent the end of French Algeria. Although the present OS had been "decapitated," as one officer noted, others would surely rise to take its place, like the mythical Hydra. Only a state of permanent repression and police violence could ensure the end of the PPA and its "fanatical" goals.[108]

As a result, officials wanted the OS trials to unanimously return guilty verdicts, with draconian sentences designed to ward off future nationalists tempted to strike an armed blow against the French presence in Algeria. All members were charged with "atteinte à la sécurité extérieure de l'état," and the dragnet widened to include propagandists and newspaper vendors, perceived as assisting paramilitary recruitment. Thus alongside hardened militants in Constantine, even persons simply in possession of PPA tracts netted one- to two-year prison terms along with fines of up to 300,000 francs. Yet judges did not ignore the clearly forced confessions and violent interrogations, and in those cases they tended to be more lenient. Following the trial of the Oran branch, the forty-seven convicted faced up to six years of incarceration simply for belonging to the organization, but defendants usually faced a fraction of that, and demonstrators loudly protested the entire affair outside the courthouse until police intervened with batons.[109] Unfortunately for officials and prosecutors, the local court overturned the convictions of eighty-three OS stalwarts in Bône, voiding five outright and dramatically reducing the sentences of seventy-one others (which had included fines of up to 1 million francs) due to illegal search and seizures by police and the confinement of suspects for days without access to attorneys; the presiding magistrate called the procedure "indisputably irregular."[110] Blida prosecutors succeeded in jailing the entire local OS chapter only by closing the courtroom, combined with a press campaign that emphasized the confessions of the accused and the exclusion of witnesses who might reveal details of an interrogation. Even then, the highest-ranking leaders were absent—Mohamed Khider, Hocine Ait Ahmed, and Mohammed Ben Bella all escaped from custody and eluded sentencing. The rest received punishments ranging from suspended terms to two to six years in prison, 120,000-franc fines, and the loss of civil rights for five to ten years.[111] It was only with the introduction of the concept of a state of emergency and the Inspecteurs généraux de l'administration en mission extraordinaire (IGAME; Administrative General Inspectors on Special Assignment) in 1955 by the Edgar Faure ministry and subsequent special powers under Guy Mollet the following year, during the War of Algerian Independence, that judicial repression of the harshest type become the standard. With military courts ignoring torture and violence committed by paratroopers or soldiers and civilian courts consistently taking a hard line with real and imagined Arab and Kabyle suspects when cases went before a judge, justice became what General Raoul Salan called an "effective counterrevolutionary weapon."[112] In the prewar era, with no direct threat to French hegemony posed by the skeletal OS, sentences were not certain to deter future nationalists, and once inside the Alger prison, members promptly displayed defiance, constantly harassing guards and making a racket that could be heard in the casbah nearby. Apprised of the situation, the governor general openly worried about a mutiny and demanded the transfer of gendarmes to restore order.[113] In this he was quite correct, as prisons effectively became training grounds for future Front de libération nationale (FLN; National Liberation Front) fighters.

Nonetheless, in the short term, the police campaign against both the MTLD and PPA intensified following the wave of arrests and trials, with members arrested in all three departments and local headquarters raided by law enforcement. Having been used with unfortunate effectiveness against the OS, "hard" interrogations and torture became regular tools of the Algerian law enforcement trade.[114] The party continued to issue tracts to militants, reminding them of the daily struggle, softening its stance concerning physical violence and instead emphasizing propaganda and political activism, from demonstrations and solidarity with prisoners to recruitment and fundraising.[115] Yet law enforcement personnel perceived any nationalist initiative as a direct threat to French Algeria, and acted accordingly. They were particularly concerned with the shift in 1950 from mass meetings and propaganda to secret sessions that precluded intelligence gathering. Police could use surveillance to track attendance, yet the actual proceedings remained a mystery, leading the deputy prefect of Tizi-Ouzou to demand a joint initiative of the local officers and the RG, with the SLNA (Service des liaisons nord-africaines d'Alger; North African Liaison Service in Algiers) supplying needed information about PPA activities, in order to form a network of informants in every public space frequented by nationalists, who would concomitantly be denied basic services like public transportation.[116] The conspiracy of silence was likewise noted by administrators in Lavigerie, Aumale, and Aïn-Bessam, all of whom bemoaned the growth of PPA activity and influence in the aftermath of the OS arrests and trials.[117] Gendarmes and police also reported that the new militants tended to be younger (between fifteen and twenty years of age) and managed by senior PPA organizers, greatly concerning Europeans in smaller communities.[118] The press fanned the flames of settler rage with exaggerated headlines—"À Souma, 1200 individus du MTLD insultent la France [In Souma, 1,200 MTLD supporters offend France]," screamed the *Journal d'Alger* (Algiers Journal) in May 1951, quoting the local mayor's accusation that police had let the PPA run wild, despite clear knowledge of where to find the anti-French locals. The *Dépêche quotidienne* (Daily Dispatch) upped the ante with an article describing hundreds of supporters running amok, "terrorizing the population" until gendarmes arrived hours later.[119]

As a result, the pre-OS sentencing guidelines and police procedures were replaced by harsh prison terms and raids designed to squelch growing nationalist sentiment in all three departments. In April 1951, police in Rélizane detained all the Algerians on an Oran-Alger train, taken to the station, and questioned before being released with one exception—a wanted MTLD militant traveling with a group of nationalists due to attend an appeals court hearing.[120] Regular harassment of real and suspected nationalists in some locales also occurred, particularly in smaller communities perceived to be susceptible to violence against *colons* or officials. In Affreville, in May 1951 the gendarmerie compiled a list of PPA militants, including the local delegate to the Assemblée algérienne, several municipal councilors, and a prominent lawyer, along with one "dangerous militant." All met regularly in a café, leading police to suspect secret decisions and plotting—again, evidence of the hidden transcript at work—and thus to act against suspects across the department. Throughout the Souma region, unmarked police cars and trucks arrived in towns carrying thirty to forty gendarmes to patrol the streets and search houses, and to prevent nationalists from accessing electoral polling stations. The local MTLD and PCA chapters in Blida complained of a law enforcement campaign to prevent an electoral victory, with the subtext of encouraging Europeans to engage in anti-Muslim racism or assaults while suppressing any PPA demonstrations with extreme force.[121]

Intimidation quickly morphed into mass suppression by force, with searches and arrests across Alger and Oran in late 1951 and 1952 that often involved vast numbers of personnel from several agencies. In Aïn-Témouchent, a December 1951 operation to arrest PPA members accused of starting a riot was twinned with what the *commissaire chef* termed the "permis de purger le village musulman de tous ses éléments suspects ou dangeureux et de créer un autre climat psychologique [license to cleanse the Muslim quarter of all suspect or dangerous types and to develop a new psychological climate]." The action involved hundreds of police and gendarmes encircling the *duwar* while armed commandos searched every house, removing all men aged fifteen or older. Those whose names appeared on a list of suspects circulated by the town hall to officers of the Compagnies républicaines de sécurité were then transported into town in trucks provided by local settlers.[122] Almost identical operations took place in the Alger casbah in May 1952 and in the city at large in January 1953, with the latter operation netting prominent members including Hocine Lahouel, and in Oran, Guelma, and other locales during the same month. In each case, police and gendarmerie commanders proclaimed the PPA/MTLD menace finished, with "loyal" Arabs and Kabyles once again satisfied, and Europeans feeling safe and content. The Oran commander in particular noted that the arrested members were completely docile, understanding that they had lost their grip on the "healthy population."[123] Officials then established lists of criminals to be arrested on sight, including the PPA Haussonvillers and Bordj-Menaiel chief Rabah Oumrane (convicted of attempted murder in absentia), Dra-el-Mizan maquis leader Belkacem Krim (accused of murdering a *garde champêtre*), and other regional heads charged with possession of firearms and armed robbery.[124]

The conclusions drawn by police and officials concerning the demise of the PPA once again proved to be stunningly naïve, not least because the brutalization of Arabs and Kabyles that had been a regular feature of colonial life for decades reached its apogee under the Vichy regime and during and following the 8 May massacres, and yet the organization only became stronger. Official and police repression did not have the desired impact on the party's fortunes; if anything, it was infighting within the movement that threatened to replace the focus on elections with an anticolonial hard line. For all of the bluster spouted by law enforcement about the weakness of the nationalist movement and its leaders, authorities consistently reported steady membership across all three departments along with the availability of funds for political and militant initiatives.[125] Moreover, despite the dismantling of the OS, all of those involved in that organization became folk heroes among Algerians, and its advocates actively challenged the political old guard for control of the movement. Under Messali Hadj and his lieutenants, the political struggle had yielded very little, in the minds of younger militants, who saw only decades of futility. If Ben Bella, Aït Ahmed, Boudiaf, and Khider had fled their homeland one step ahead of the authorities, by 1954 the PPA leadership faced an increasingly stiff challenge in city streets and rural *mechtas* alike.[126] Police began to report a new trend: nationalist cells, schools, and propaganda, all directed by a younger and rawer generation of militants. Weapons charges also reappeared in various jurisdictions, with the PJ reporting the reemergence of armed cells in all three departments.[127]

By mid-1954, the PPA effectively split into two hostile camps, with the Messalist political wing clinging to the idea of the electoral sphere as the vehicle for change, in the face of a growing militant wing demanding an armed solution to colonial occupation. Officials and police were both eclipsed as the enemy, sidelined witnesses to a fratricidal skirmish that made gatherings and discussion virtually impossible. The PPA general secretary, Hocine Lahouel, played a last desperate card to keep the two sides together, sponsoring the creation of CRUA, but the new committee clearly tilted toward unity as a precondition for armed struggle. The impasse could not be bridged, and in July the CRUA disbanded, leaving militants to plot a new strategy and organization, a coalition of ex-OS members, hardened young recruits, and older hands tired of staid political rhetoric that became the FLN, the group whose insurrectionary declaration in November 1954 launched the War of Algerian Independence.[128]

Clearly, attempts to squelch nationalism, and particularly the PPA, utterly failed in the long term. Again and again, the colonial authorities concluded that the party was defunct—"decapitated," "annihilated," and so on. Prior to World

War II, police closed the nationalist press, broke up meetings, and arrested and interned Messali Hadj and his colleagues. Again in May 1945, following the massacres perpetrated by the army and settlers, officials criminalized all political activity deemed "anti-French"; under the leadership of Governor Generals Chataigneau and Naegelen, police, troops, and judges engaged in mass detentions and sentenced substantial numbers of Algerians for "subversive" activities. Yet again in 1950, after the dismantling of the OS network, European observers commented on the docility of loyal Muslims, declaring the threat extinguished. Each pronouncement involved a dramatic misreading of the reality of nationalist implantation in Algeria, along with missed opportunities for reforms that might have quelled dissent, at least temporarily. Thus, for example, the postwar anger at unfulfilled French promises of political reform, quotidian colonial violence, and economic misery were greeted with such brutality from officials that it caused a redoubling of Arab and Kabyle fury. The subsequent dismantling of the PPA press and electoral machinery—after Hadj had successfully regained control over young radicals, no less—only made violence far more likely.

This further resulted from the changing PPA membership and the post-1941 emergence of younger cadres of militants more interested in decolonization by any means necessary. The Messalist idea of a political solution was gradually eclipsed by an all-or-nothing push to remove the French colonial presence root and branch. It was this new strain that culminated in the formation of the OS and the preparation for armed activity. Although the organization was dismantled fairly quickly, the die had been cast. Meetings and communications were kept secret following the 1950 trials, and the revolutionary cells model gradually overtook Messalism as the primary thrust of nationalist planning. After all, if elections and newspapers had been violently suppressed by the colonial state, what was left for youthful militants? If mere membership in the PPA was a serious crime, how could youths be expected to seek compromise with the colonial apparatus? Thus, hatred and fury replaced accommodation, the nationalist road to the 1954 insurrection beginning with banditry and the OS, clandestine *djemâas*, and official and police repression reaching its logical conclusion.

For police and gendarmes, the post-1945 fight against nationalism irrevocably altered Algerian law enforcement. Politicians and law enforcement had long been preoccupied with maintaining imperial and racial hegemony in place of the investigative and judicial standards that characterized (in theory at least) metropolitan criminal justice, and in the aftermath of 8 May 1945 and facing a revivified nationalist challenge, they embraced corruption, violence, and ultimately torture. Fearing an insurrection after the events in Sétif and Guelma, settlers and soldiers were permitted to kill with impunity, arresting thousands of real and imagined suspects, while military tribunals sentenced the survivors and stripped them of political and civil rights. The rise of the PPA / MTLD and its potential for electoral success engendered rigged contests that guaranteed victory for parties that agreed to maintain French rule. When that proved insufficient to staunch the rising tide of support for Algerian independence, police and gendarmes resorted to campaigns of aggression that culminated in the mass searches and arrests in the wake of the discovery of the OS and its plans. Previously used only in the face of anticolonial mass protests and attacks on and after 8 May 1945, torture became a central component of investigations and interrogations, with attempts to stamp out the PPA / MTLD and its press, membership, and electoral candidates replaced by an all-out campaign against anyone suspected of involvement in subversive activities. Thus, Algerian politics itself became criminalized, with any oppositional actor treated as an enemy to be eradicated. Moreover, approving of the most extreme measures, the French authorities laid the groundwork for the widespread abuses and murderous conduct that characterized military and civilian policing against the FLN during the Algerian War of Independence. The torture and killing during the Battle of Algiers and the judicial and legal exceptionalism promoted in both Paris and Alger flowed directly from the campaigns against the PPA / MTLD in the preceding decade.

Conclusion

The violence and repression instituted by various branches of colonial law enforcement in Algeria reached a crescendo during the 1954 to 1962 War of Independence, when torture, murder, and massacre became routine aspects of policing and all Arabs and Kabyles became suspects, regardless of their political affiliations. From the fateful attacks of 1 November 1954 by the fledgling Front de libération nationale (FLN; National Liberation Front) onward, the French response was brutal and immediate, as the state attempted to staunch the threat by force of arms. However, the FLN did not disappear, and its actions galvanized the public. In April 1955, Governor General Jacques Soustelle declared a state of emergency and imposed martial law. Police and the army declared "collective responsibility"; henceforth, every Algerian was declared responsible for the anti-French struggle. As workers and peasants began to tacitly or actively support FLN actions, in some cases fighting alongside partisans, French soldiers and police officers responded with massacres and killings designed both to demonstrate the superiority of their tactics and weapons while bullying potential recruits into submission. Yet many FLN leaders and members were veterans of the Organisation spéciale (OS) and had no intention of relenting, having endured torture and beatings in French prisons, and completely rejected the compromise solutions of reformists like Ferhat Abbas or nationalist stalwarts in the fashion of Messali Hadj, and prioritized the Armée de libération nationale (ALN; National Liberation Army) rather than its civilian adjutant. By 1957 the ALN became the center of all rebel activity, run by the uncompromising Abdelhafid Boussouf, Lakhdar Ben Tobbal, and the OS bastion Belkacem Krim. With twenty thousand fighters and operatives and assisted by civilian governing institutions—the *djemâas* (tribal councils), for example—they steadily made inroads into the countryside in Kabylia and the Oranais while gaining popularity in major urban centers like Alger.[1]

The state of emergency increased police power dramatically, with prefects and the governor general demanding rigid control of vehicle and pedestrian traffic, the institution of security zones in communes and cities, the closure of restaurants and cafés, and a ban on armaments and public meetings. While the Police judiciaire (PJ; criminal police) handled these quotidian matters, the Renseignements généraux (RG; political police) became a de facto antiterrorism unit, liaising with the Bureau psychologique (Psychological Bureau), which spearheaded counterpropaganda initiatives, and the Service de coordination des informations nord-africaines (Coordination Unit for North African Data, the successor to the Service des liaisons nord-africaines d'Alger [SLNA]), a branch dedicated to providing intelligence and surveillance. Officials tasked the RG with penetrating FLN and ALN cells or using informants to glean information about meetings and actions, which led to arrests by the PJ and gendarmes, in tandem with metropolitan contingents of the Direction de la surveillance du territoire (DST; Directorate of Territorial Security) and the Sûreté nationale (National Security).[2] Moreover, five additional units of the Compagnies républicaines de sécurité (CRS; mobile police force) arrived in Algeria in 1954, and more followed in subsequent years in all three departments, often participating in joint operations with the military and the gendarmerie, although by 1955 confined to larger urban centers, protecting buildings and engaging in ordinary crime prevention while patrolling the streets seeking FLN operatives. These counterterrorism patrols became even more frequent as the military took over operations, with parachutists teaming with CRS agents on a daily basis and in larger operations such as the Battle of Algiers in 1956 to 1957 against the growing insurgency there.[3] Interagency cooperation became the new mantra, and the RG gradually became a liaison bureau, an adjunct to the DST charged with wiretaps, snitches, stakeouts, and postal intercepts. As the FLN assassinated officers and police officers, an atmosphere of war descended on station houses in city and countryside.[4] Unsurprisingly, by the end of 1956 there were 8,928 police and 12,000 gendarmes in Algeria, supported by Groupements mobiles de polices rurales (Mobile Units of Rural Police, the successor to the old goums). The latter number in particular represented a massive increase from the hundreds of troops available in the understaffed rural divisions during the 1930s and 1940s, when a handful of men might be expected to patrol entire regions on their own.[5]

Despite French military victories during the Battle of Algiers in 1957 and the return to power of a surprisingly reform-minded Charles de Gaulle the following year, the FLN rejected anything short of complete independence, and thus redoubled its military efforts. However, its numbers had been reduced by continuous French military pressure, and the notorious Challe offensive in 1959 came perilously close to destroying the ALN and its commanders. Yet, despite factional infighting, the tactical nous of its leader Houari Boumediène enabled the rebuilding of the force throughout the year.[6] Hence, while de Gaulle considered the possibility of peace terms, the Algerian police were once again reorganized. The RG received further reinforcement, with more manpower and thus a larger array of intelligence-gathering capacity. In addition, the CRS no longer served simply as an urban police force. Following the infamous January 1960 "barricades week," when a coalition of settlers and army officers banded together to oppose the "treasonous" de Gaulle and defend French Algeria, the CRS became a "mobile unit for law enforcement" fighting on two fronts—against the FLN and dissident Europeans. Violent crimes and terrorism now became the brief of three Brigades spéciales attached to the Police judiciaire—still understaffed, considering the needs of the units, but better prepared to respond quickly to government demands.[7] Moreover, by year's end, newly appointed prefects of police could appeal for assistance from the army. By that time, they also fought the insurgent pro-*Algérie française* Organisation armée secrète (OAS; Secret Army Organization), as CRS and police teams conducted nine thousand apartment searches, seizing thousands of weapons and arresting hundreds, although law enforcement itself was purged of pro-OAS officers.[8]

Police and gendarmes were more frequently involved in assisting army units in the extirpation of the FLN and ALN, which invariably included criminal actions such as torture and murder. For officers in branches like the RG and PJ, which had been assigned to squelch Algerian nationalism and paramilitary wings like the OS, this did not involve a massive leap into unknown territory. For decades, so-called hard interrogations had included severe beatings of suspects, and after 1945, the *baignoire* (bathtub), electricity, and sexual assault were employed regularly during the questioning of suspects, often in abandoned or secluded locales where detainees were held for days in tiny cells without adequate heat, water, and food. Violence against Arab and Kabyle "criminals" was the ultimate expression of the xenophobia and European hegemony embodied by French officials and police and embedded in colonial politics, economy, society, and culture. It began with the fight against banditry during the Great War, continued apace during the interwar era, and reached a horrifying crescendo with corruption, arbitrary arrests, legal-judicial manipulation, and ultimately, assault and torture of suspects during the fight against nationalism in the post-1945 era. When confronted with an armed struggle for independence, police assisted paratroopers and soldiers in mobilizing the same treatment against suspected FLN partisans. Moreover, by the 1950s, most police and gendarmes had served in the military and then engaged in lengthy tours of law enforcement service in Algeria, where they quickly learned the necessary tools of the colonial trade, aided by colleagues who had transferred from Morocco and Tunisia after they won independence. Unsurprisingly, law enforcement personnel proved to be eager participants in *ratonnades* (xenophobic attacks against Algerians) during the War of Independence, engineering anti-Arab and anti-Kabyle assaults under the guise of crime prevention or antiterrorism, and on certain occasions killing or wounding dozens of victims.[9] It was the culmination of long-established practices and attitudes across all branches of Algerian law enforcement.

These tactics received official sanction in March 1956, when the Mollet government suspended civil liberties in Algeria, making it legally possible to use any means necessary to eliminate nationalists and enemy combatants, with the widespread torture of suspected FLN or ALN members (and Communist sympathizers) a standard tool for law enforcement. This, too, represented the logical conclusion to official policies that had held sway since the nineteenth century. Beginning with the Indigénat and the blind eye turned to the killing of suspects during antibandit campaigns, prefects and administrators (along with the governor general) regularly ignored legislation and established norms that interfered with their attempts to squelch dissent and anti-French attitudes. Mollet's decree simply made official what had long been practice, from the rigging of elections to the denial of Algerian legal rights during the battle against the PPA/MTLD prior to the outbreak of the War of Independence. In January 1957, Jacques Massu and his Tenth Paratrooper Division arrived to lead the Battle of Algiers and, more broadly, policing in Algeria. Under his guidance, selected civilian officers participated in the Détachements opérationnels de protection (Operational Defense Detachments), performing dirty work, with the PJ providing support for arrests and detentions, if not directly involved in the most brutal manifestations. In addition, Colonel Roger Trinquier's Muslim informant units provided a stream of information that led to the arrest and interrogation of 40 percent of the men living in the Alger casbah. In May 1958, the authorities made clear what Algerians had known for a long while: the army was officially in charge of law enforcement. Colonel Yves Godard became the head of the Algerian Sûreté nationale, with the absolute power to completely override legal rights and provisions.[10] The struggle became a total war—economic, social, political, psychological, and armed—and a horrifying exercise in population control at all costs under the auspices of a massive police operation.

Torture and summary execution became the chief tactics used in everyday law enforcement. General Allard demanded that the Constantine division use "the most brutal methods" against any rebel caught with a gun or committing an act of violence, which in practice meant shooting all suspects from mid-1955 onward.[11] Any assault, ambush, or murder against French soldiers or police involved the forced evacuation of entire populations, especially in trouble zones like the Aurès, where troops burned thousands of houses and *mechtas* to the ground or bulldozed entire villages. Reprisals for the 20 August 1955 Constantine rising proved particularly brutal, echoing (and amplifying) the aftermath of 8 May 1945, but this time, they were perpetrated by the army. The FLN attacked dozens of men, women, and children, their bodies mutilated, tortured, and killed, and soldiers responded with mass murders of entire villages, the number of victims surpassing twelve thousand according to Algerian sources.[12] Much like a decade earlier, the French army's tactics caused Arabs and Kabyles in ever-greater numbers to turn against the colonizer. The goal of ridding the territory of the FLN and ALN therefore depended on strategically identifying and eliminating militant cells and armed brigades, hence the shift toward Massu's squads and law enforcement regulars. This involved the widespread use of torture.

Well before the arrival of the Tenth Division, law enforcement *chefs de service* advocated for brutal methods of interrogation, particularly the *baignoire* and torture by electricity, and they received tacit assent from the governor general and the minister of the interior. Prior to 1957, this merely echoed the strategy utilized during the OS campaign, itself an intensification of practices long used by colonial police to break difficult suspects. However, with the military came new methods previously used in Indochina: starvation, mass roundups, and group torture techniques. Troops and police flooded the streets of a given town or city, often at night and particularly targeting *cafés maures* (Moorish cafés), arresting hundreds at a time for interrogation. Massu instituted forced entry into private homes, echoing the 1930s practice instituted for violent criminals. Taken together, public performances of violent authority achieved little beyond pacifying nervous Europeans. Yet the roundups and assaults proved that the military was now firmly in charge, with the police as an auxiliary to paratroopers.[13] Moreover, in 1957, Massu authorized the operation of hundreds of torture centers across all three departments, to be run jointly by the army and civilian authorities under Governor General Jacques Soustelle. The destruction of the FLN and ALN by all possible means became the new goal, echoing one colonel's dictum that "si on veut rétablir l'ordre, il faut agir sans pitié. Quand on a de la gangrène, il faut tailler toute de suite dans le vif [If we wish to reestablish order, we must act without mercy. When gangrene appears, it must be cut out as quickly as possible]." Whereas a pre-1940 house search often involved property destruction, threats, or assaults of the inhabitants, during the War of Independence, if a platoon discovered arms in a house it must be burned down and the rebel's family placed in detention. Worse still, survivors recounted hundreds of incidents of rape and murder, from suspects being thrown out of helicopters to naked women and children attacked by trained dogs, their villages, livestock, and crops decimated by napalm.[14]

However, torture was used primarily on an individual level, during interrogations of suspects designed to break the FLN/ALN network. The tens of thousands arrested and placed in camps suffered the same horrifying practices used during any rebellion that threatened the French colonial system, from Madagascar to Indochina, not to mention the Gestapo during the metropolitan wartime occupation.[15] A memo from Inspector-General Roger Guilhaume to Soustelle on 2 March 1955 outlined four distinct types of torture to be used against potential or actual FLN members. These included blows from fists, batons, or whips, the *baignoire*, the *tuyau* (water torture involving liquid being forced into a suspect's mouth with tubing until suffocation), and the use of electricity on extremities, nails, and/or the anus. Not only soldiers, but all gendarmes and police from the PJ and RG were to use these methods. Again, none of these were novel during the War of Independence; all were used by police in Paris and Algeria after 1945 against suspected nationalists or perpetrators of anti-European violence.[16] Whether at the hands of police before 1957 or paratroopers during the Battle of Algiers, interrogations typically lasted through the day and night, or even longer in severe cases. In addition to physical torture, police and soldiers subjected detainees to sleep deprivation (often with pincers holding open the victim's eyes) or suspended them upside-down, sometimes covered in petrol. As time wore on, beating a prisoner's feet, followed by forced walks, led to crippling injuries, and binding practices often led to shoulders being forcibly ripped from sockets.[17]

Clearly, such tactics did not produce the desired result, and the events leading up to the end of the war, culminating in the July 1962 French authorization of Algerian independence, demonstrated both the strengthening of the FLN/ALN and increasing support for their aims among the Arab and Kabyle population. Yet their employment represents both a culmination of practices that dated from the 1830 conquest and the only possible outcome of such tactics. As Raphaëlle Branche notes, a direct line can be drawn between Bugeaud's "peaceful penetration" and the regime of the Indigénat, quotidian colonial policing practices throughout the empire, and specific strategies used to enforce racial hegemony and bolster European interests in all three Algerian departments.[18] For the racial hegemony desired by settlers and officials could only be constructed and maintained through the use of force. In this regard, police and gendarmes manned the front lines of an ongoing struggle to enforce the second-class status of the colonized and their adherence to French laws and demands while suppressing and stultifying any manifestation of dissent, no matter how seemingly insubstantial. After 1871, multiple branches of law enforcement were dedicated to intelligence gathering and threat assessment, quotidian surveillance and crime prevention, and the arrest and detention of any Arab and Kabyle deemed suspect.

This meant that crimes against Europeans were prioritized by officials and officers at all levels, especially if the perpetrators were Muslims. To be sure, police did investigate in *mechtas*, *duwars*, and non-European urban neighborhoods, and often solved those crimes. Yet, in notes, reports, and annual summaries, a consistent pattern emerges: only assaults, murders, robberies, political rallies perpetrated by Arabs or Kabyles represented matters for genuine concern. They alone caused insecurity, due to the prioritization of settlers over Algerians. Muslim victims became problematic only if the crimes threatened to cause trouble in *communes mixtes* (mixed communes), where intertribal rivalries or personal vendettas could escalate into more severe and widespread violence. Otherwise, police and gendarmes prioritized their overarching mission—enabling colonization and conquest, and subsequently the exploitation of human and material resources for the benefit of settlers and metropolitan businessmen, government personnel, and French, Italian, and Spanish denizens. This involved a monopoly on the use of force, which officers and gendarmes did not shy away from using on a regular basis. Whether in the extirpation of bandits, the fight against anti-European violent crime in the interwar era, or attempts to squelch nationalist movements after 1945, all branches utilized colonial violence as a tool of their trade, alongside investigative methods and techniques more common to the metropole.

It is thus no surprise that once the War of Independence began, police and gendarmes joined the armed forces in an attempt to restore colonial order by any means necessary. As David Arnold has written about British India (yet equally applicable to Algeria), "The police . . . serve as a metaphor for the colonial regime as a whole." The more the colonial state was threatened, the more willing authorities were to mobilize extreme measures, and thus "much of the impact of the police lay in their unlicensed petty tyranny, their corruption and brutality."[19] Moreover, the lines between criminal and political policing quickly became blurred; in a setting where any organized opposition or even questioning of the regime could quickly devolve into open rebellion, officials and police and gendarmes perceived no difference between an illicit and explicitly violent act and a call for independence (or even reform). Yet, in an ironic twist, although this strategy could pacify a population in the short or medium term, through the threat of armed retaliation and daily surveillance, in the long term, it actually gave rise to the very thing colonial law enforcement was designed to prevent—open revolt. For as Martin Thomas makes clear, "repression [was] inherently self-defeating," eventually creating or perpetuating the very mass resistance it was designed to eradicate.[20] Hence well before the emergence of the PPA / MTLD and the FLN / ALN, Algerians exercised agency against the colonizer, heading to hills and forests in the Constantinois as bandits fighting against the French Empire, and attacking and killing Europeans during the interwar era to strike a blow against racial hegemony. Moreover, they increasingly sympathized with or joined reformist and nationalist organizations after 1945 despite massive pressure from police and officials. In short, they refused to accept French domination, and repression or colonial violence only increased their stridency.

Viewed from this perspective, the War of Independence was inevitable, the only avenue left once officials in Paris and Alger refused to genuinely share power with Arabs and Kabyles, and with it came the logical conclusion of colonial law enforcement, a return to the tactics of imperial conquest in the 1830s to 1840s—massacres, torture, and indiscriminate violations of Algerian bodies. Inseparable from the colonial project itself, physical manifestations of colonial violence had always been quotidian, twinned with structural violence that prevented the intrusion of Arabs or Kabyles into European spheres of power and cultural violence designed to negate the voices and traditions of the colonized, those facets of Muslim life deemed most likely to promote rebellion against the empire.[21] The ultimate failure of these policies nonetheless left scars still in evidence in Algeria today, evidenced in a plethora of literary and cultural efforts grappling with the past and its dark legacy in the metropole and the former colony. Needless to say, the French response has been incomplete at best. In 2005, educators were ordered to teach the positive aspects of empire for imperial subjects (a directive ultimately rescinded by President Jacques Chirac), while subsequently Nicolas Sarkozy explicitly rejected the notion of acceptance and repentance during his presidency. Only recently did President Emmanuel Macron acknowledge certain Gallic atrocities during the Algerian War of Independence, particularly referencing the murder of Ali Boumendjel, the lawyer and FLN member tortured to death in February 1957 by General Paul Aussaresses in Alger.[22] Yet, a report tendered by a government-sponsored commission on memorialization, led by leading historian Benjamin Stora, fell short of admitting to ongoing violence and repression throughout the colonial era, and no apology was offered to the innumerable victims of French rule. In any case, the authors barely scratched the surface of the pre-1954 era, despite calling for action: "Plutôt que de 'repentance,' la France devrait donc reconnaitre les discriminations et exactions dont ont été victimes les populations algériennes: mettre en avant des faits précis [Rather than 'repentance,' France must acknowledge the discrimination and exactions that victimized Algerians: bring to the fore a factual account]."[23] It remains to be seen whether such a program will emerge in coming years.

NOTES

Introduction

1. Constantine B / 3 / 360, Constantine, 8 April 1926, Chef de la Sûreté générale, "Rapport special"; Constantine 93 / 20040, Bône, 25 January 1921, Gouverneur générale d'Algérie (GGA) to Chef de la Sûreté générale.

2. Florence Bernault, *Enfermement, prisons, et châtiments en Afrique: Du XIXe siècle à nos jours* (Paris, 1999), 62.

3. For a detailed discussion of works dedicated to this theme, see Dominique Monjardet, *Ce que fait la police: Sociologie de la force publique* (Paris, 1994), 7, 9–19, 198–199.

4. Jean-Louis Loubet del Bayle, *Police et politique: Une approche sociologique* (Paris, 2012), 8, 22–36, 41, 50–64, 73–74, 97, 171.

5. Taylor Sherman, *State Violence and Punishment in India* (New York, 2010), 5–8. Although Sherman writes about British India, the argument can equally be applied to French Algeria, or almost any other colony or protectorate in the nineteenth to twentieth centuries.

6. David Anderson and David Killingray, eds., *Policing the Empire: Government, Authority, and Control, 1830–1940* (Manchester, UK, 1991), 8; Emmanuel Blanchard and Joël Glasman, "Le maintien de l'ordre dans l'empire français: Une historiographie emergente," in *Maintenir l'ordre colonial: Afrique et Madagascar, XIXe–XXe siècles*, ed. Jean-Pierre Bat and Nicolas Courtin (Rennes, 2012), 12–14, 17.

7. Martin Thomas, *Empires of Intelligence: Security Services and Colonial Disorder after 1914* (Berkeley, CA, 2008), 2, 4–6, 28.

8. On the metropolitan use of information gathering, see Jean-Marc Berlière, "A Republican Political Police? Political Policing in France under the Third Republic," in *The Policing of Politics in the Twentieth Century*, ed. Mark Mazower (Providence, RI, 1997), 39–44.

9. Thomas, *Empires of Intelligence*, 52; Abdelmajid Hannoum, *Violent Modernity: France in Algeria* (Cambridge, MA, 2010), 18, 30–31.

10. Damien Lorcy, *Sous le régime du sabre: La gendarmerie en Algérie, 1830–1870* (Rennes, 2011), 29, 34, 40–47, 57.

11. Lorcy, 59–71, 212–216, 240–249, 264. Only in 1860 did authorities approve the Corps des auxiliaires indigènes (Indigenous Auxiliary Corps) to support gendarmes incapable of speaking Arabic or Berber. See André-Paul Comor, "Implantation et missions de la gendarmerie en Algérie, de la conquête à la colonisation (1830–1914)," in *Gendarmerie, État, et société au XIXe siècle*, ed. Jean-Noël Luc (Paris, 2002), 188.

12. William Gallois, *A History of Violence in the Algerian Colony* (New York, 2013), 2.

13. James McDougall, *A History of Algeria* (Cambridge, UK, 2017), 55–56.
14. McDougall, 57–58.
15. McDougall, 52. For a comprehensive account of Bugeaud and the army's terror campaigns, see Benjamin Claude Brower, *A Desert Named Peace: The Violence of France's Empire in the Algerian Sahara, 1844–1902* (New York, 2009), pt. 1.
16. McDougall, *History of Algeria*, 73–76. For a full account of the 1849 revolt and its aftermath, see Julia A. Clancy-Smith, *Rebel and Saint: Muslim Notables, Populist Protest, Colonial Encounters (Algeria and Tunisia, 1800–1904)* (Berkeley, CA, 1994), chap. 4.
17. Clancy-Smith, *Rebel and Saint*, 85–89.
18. McDougall, *History of Algeria*, 102
19. McDougall, 101–107. On the Crémieux Decree and its impact on Jewish-settler relations, see Sophie B. Roberts, *Citizenship and Antisemitism in French Colonial Algeria, 1870–1962* (Cambridge, UK, 2017), chap. 1.
20. McDougall, *History of Algeria*, 86–98; John Ruedy, *Modern Algeria: The Origins and Development of a Nation* (Bloomington, IN, 2005), 90–91.
21. Claude Collot, *Les institutions de l'Algérie pendant la période colonial (1830–1962)* (Paris, 1988), 39–41, 93–97, 101–108, 126–130.
22. Sylvie Thénault, *Violence ordinaire dans l'Algérie colonial: Camps, internements, assignations à residence* (Paris, 2012), 40–43.
23. Ruedy, *Modern Algeria*, 88–90; McDougall, *History of Algeria*, 120–129 (quote on 127). Courts further assisted the seizure of land through rulings in favor of Europeans concerning the default on titles.
24. On the Kabyle myth, see Patricia M. E. Lorcin, *Imperial Identities: Stereotyping, Prejudice, and Race in Colonial Algeria* (London, 1995).
25. Ruedy, *Modern Algeria*, 99–105.
26. Ruedy, 124–126.
27. McDougall, *History of Algeria*, 120–129.
28. McDougall, 102–106.
29. McDougall, 135–139, 143–145.
30. On this point, see Martin Thomas, *Violence and Colonial Order: Police, Workers, and Protest in European Colonial Empires, 1918–1940* (Cambridge, UK, 2012), 49–51; Martin Weiner, *An Empire on Trial, Race, Murder, and Justice under British Rule, 1870–1935* (Cambridge, UK, 2009).
31. Thomas, *Empires of Intelligence*, 77–78. On the notion of Orientalism as a driving force in colonialism and its political, economic, social, and cultural representations, see Edward Said, *Orientalism* (New York, 1979).
32. On this phenomenon, see James C. Scott, *Weapons of the Weak: Everyday Forms of Peasant Resistance* (New Haven, CT, 1987); Blanchard and Glasman, "Le maintien de l'ordre," 36–40. In this regard, it is also critical to avoid a reliance solely on urban settings and a concomitant rejection of rural communities. In order to provide a comprehensive account of policing and crime, I wish to echo Stathis Kalyvas's call to move beyond an exclusively town and city approach, while also eschewing the study of elites and a top-down narrative and instead seeking out subaltern cases where possible. Kalyvas, *The Logic of Violence in Civil War* (Cambridge, UK, 2006), 40–48.
33. For a detailed analysis of these acts and their consequences, see chapters 2 and 3.

34. CAOM Constantine 93 / 20332, Sédrata, 2 July 1927, Administrateur de la Commune mixte to Préfet.
35. This effort will be discussed in chapter 5.
36. Ann Laura Stoler, *Along the Archival Grain: Epistemic Anxieties and Colonial Common Sense* (Princeton, NJ, 2010), 2–4.
37. Stoler, 20.
38. Stoler, 186.
39. On European women in Algeria, see, variously, Julia Clancy-Smith and Frances Gouda, *Domesticating the Empire: Race, Gender, and Family Life in French and Dutch Colonialism* (Charlottesville, VA, 1998); Martin Thomas, *The French Empire between the Wars: Imperialism, Politics, Society* (Manchester, UK, 2005); Caroline Campbell, *Political Belief in France, 1927–1945: Gender, Empire, and Fascism in the Croix de Feu and Parti social français* (Baton Rouge, LA, 2015).
40. Thomas, *French Empire*, 151–152.
41. Thomas, 351.
42. Thomas, 159–162.
43. Samuel Kalman, *French Colonial Fascism: The Extreme Right in Algeria, 1919–1939* (New York, 2013), 7, 27, 45, 63, 111–112; Martin Evans, "Towards an Emotional History of Settler Decolonization: De Gaulle, Political Masculinity, and the End of French Algeria," *Settler Colonial Studies* 8 (2018): 219. On the Algerian CF / PSF and gender roles, see Campbell, *Political Belief in France*.
44. Antoinette Burton, *Dwelling in the Archive: Women Writing House, Home, and History in Late Colonial India* (Oxford, UK, 2003), 21–22.
45. For an example of scholarship on this phenomenon, see Sylvie Thénault, "Baya Hocine's Papers: A Source for the History of Algerian Prisons during the War of Independence," *Historical Reflections / Réflexions historiques* 46 (2020): 110–127.
46. Blanchard and Glasman, "Le maintien de l'ordre," 13–14; Michael Vann, "Sex and the Colonial City: Mapping Masculinity, Whiteness, and Desire in French Occupied Hanoi," *Journal of World History* 28 (2017): 397, 403, 407.

1. Agents of Empire and Crisis of Authority

1. ANOM GGA 8H / 10, Report—"Sécurité" (1883).
2. On the increasing urbanization of Algerian Muslims and European denizens, see Thomas, *French Empire*, 141–142. For rural developments, including rampant land expropriation and development beginning in the 1880s and the intensification of agricultural production during the interwar era, see McDougall, *History of Algeria*, 96–99; Johan Hendrick Meuleman, *Le Constantinois entre les deux guerres mondiales: L'évolution économique et sociale de la population rurale* (Amsterdam, 1984), 38–57, 183–193.
3. Policing duties and expectations in the metropole are discussed at length in Jean-Marc Berlière and René Lévy, *Histoire des polices en France: De l'ancien régime à nos jours* (Paris, 2013).
4. A discussion of metropolitan policing practices toward immigrant and colonial populations can be found in Clifford Rosenberg, *Policing Paris: The Origins of Modern Immigration Control between the Wars* (Ithaca, NY, 2006); and Neil MacMaster, *Colonial Migrants and Racism: Algerians in France, 1900–62* (New York, 1997).

5. For a detailed examination of metropolitan police services, see Berlière and Lévy, *Histoire des polices en France*.

6. ANOM Constantine 93 / 5301, Alger, 20 February 1904, GGA to Préfet.

7. ANOM Oran 2F / 69, Oran, 31 October 1900, Commissaire central—Memorandum.

8. ANOM Constantine 93 / 1750, Constantine, 31 May 1929, Police municipale de Constantine—répartition de personnel, and Oran 1F / 79, Marnia, 1 December 1947, Commissaire principal to Maire.

9. ANOM Oran 1F / 72, Alger, 8 January 1910, GGA to Préfet; "Police judiciaire et Sûreté urbaine," *Echo du soir*, 29 October 1949.

10. Brower, *Desert Named Peace*, 6–7; Bat and Courtin, *Maintenir l'ordre colonial*, 27–28.

11. Jean-Marc Berlière, *Le monde des policiers en France* (Paris, 1996), 61–65; Thomas, *Violence and Colonial Order*, 92–95, and *Empires of Intelligence*, 204; Clive Emsley, "Police Forces and Public Order in England and France during the Interwar Years," in *Policing Western Europe: Politics, Professionalism, and Public Order, 1850–1940*, ed. Clive Emsley and Barbara Weinberger (Westport, CT, 1991), 159, 167–168.

12. Thomas, *Violence and Colonial Order*, 96–110; Edouard Ebel, "Gendarmerie et contre-insurrection, 1791–1962," *Revue historique des armées* 268 (2012): 5–7; André-Paul Comor, "Implantation et missions," 183–193; Constantine 93 / 6863, Constantine, 5 October 1946, Lieutenant-Colonel Bobillon, Commandant le groupement de gendarmerie du département to Préfet. The GRM made an exception with regard to vehicles. By a January 1938 ministerial decree, three units in each department were motorized. See ANOM GGA 3R / 18, Paris, 28 January 1938, Ministère de la défense nationale et de la guerre to Colonel commandant la gendarmerie de l'Algérie.

13. ANOM Constantine 93 / 1308, Constantine, 26 October 1949, Préfet, "Circulaire."

14. ANOM Constantine 93 / 1308, Constantine, 17 June 1949, Commissaire principal, Chef de la Police des Renseignements généraux to Préfet, and Oran 1F / 81, Alger, 9 February 1943, GGA to Préfet.

15. SHD 1H / 2859, Report—"Organisation centrale des services de la police en Algérie," Commissaire principal, Police algérienne to Direction de la Sécurité générale de l'Algérie; ANOM, Constantine 93 / 5301, Alger, 24 February 1911, GGA to Préfet.

16. "À Oran, un contrôleur général et dix-huit commissaires dirigeant les services de police," *Echo du Soir*, 25 October 1949.

17. ANOM Alger 1F / 439, "Decret du 8 décembre 1944"; Oran / 2577: Oran, 28 June 1952, Préfet to GGA; Alger, 23 December 1952, GGA to Préfet, "Patrouilles de reconnaissance / CRS-janvier 1953"; and Oran, 24 June 1954, Préfet, Memo.

18. ANOM Alger 1F / 422, "Police d'état d'Alger / Historique"; "À Oran, un contrôleur général"; "Le gardien de la paix: Policier en uniforme," *Echo du Soir*, 31 October 1949. Concerning Lambert and the formation of the state police in Oran, see Samuel Kalman, "*Avec une brutalité toute particulière*: Fascist Sympathies, Racial Violence, and the Municipal Police and Gendarmerie in Oran, 1936–37," in *The French Right between the Wars: Political Movements and Intellectual Trends from Conservatism to Fascism*, ed. Samuel Kalman and Sean Kennedy (New York, NY, 2014). The pervasiveness of the Extreme Right in Algerian policing will be fully discussed in chapter 3.

19. ANOM, Constantine 93 / 20332, Alger, 11 September 1925, GGA to Préfet. *Caïds* were French-appointed officials tasked with running a given community. They acted as both liaisons with the colonial administration and imperial representatives to the local population.

20. ANOM Alger 1K / 37, Alger, 28 December 1900, GGA to Préfet.

21. They would receive monthly salaries, necessitating a 200,000-franc annual budget. See ANOM Constantine 93 / 5323, Alger, 29 January 1905, Controleur-général des services de sécurité, "Gardes ruraux indigènes-Projet."

22. ANOM Constantine 93 / 5323: Alger, 17 January 1906, GGA to Préfet; Alger, 19 October 1906, GGA to Préfet; and Batna, 14 November 1908, Sous-préfet to Préfet. The *sous-préfet* believed that the effectiveness of the brigades lay in their mobility, not in serving a community where they might be corrupted by local interests. They could also effectively take the temperature of denizens on everything from taxes to administrators.

23. ANOM Constantine 93 / 20109, Alger, 19 July 1907, GGA to Préfet; ANOM Constantine 93 / 5323, Bougie, 6 June 1908, Sous-préfet to Préfet, and Bougie, 1 August 1908, Sous-préfet to Préfet.

24. ANOM Constantine 93 / 5323, November 1908, Reports from Philippeville, Guelma, Sétif, Bougie, and Conde-Smendou brigades; ANOM Constantine 93 / 20010, Collo, 3 June 1909, Commissaire spéciale to Préfet; ANOM Constantine 93 / 5319, Constantine, 23 June 1909, Préfet to Maire, and Constantine, 13 July 1910, Préfet, "Arrête." Quotes are from ANOM Constantine 93 / 5323, November 1908, "Rapport—Brigade d'El Arrouch."

25. ANOM Alger 1F / 37, Alger, 31 August 1910, GGA to Préfet.

26. On cavaliers, see ANOM Constantine 93 / 20010, Batna, 3 August 1909, "Rapport de l'administrateur détachée sur le fonctionnement de la Brigade rurale—juillet 1909." For a discussion of guards, see ANOM Alger 1F / 37, Médea, 14 March 1909, Sous-préfet to Préfet; ANOM Constantine 93 / 20059, Medjana, 22 December 1921, Administrateur de la Commune mixte de Bibans to Préfet.

27. ANOM Constantine 93 / 20059, Alger, 24 February 1921, GGA to Préfet; ANOM GGA 9H / 32, Alger, 19 June 1929, Préfet to GGA.

28. ANOM Constantine 93 / 20059, M'Sila, 18 March 1921, Administrateur de la Commune mixte to Préfet," and Medjana, 19 March 1921, Administrateur de la Commune mixte to Préfet."

29. ANOM Constantine 93 / 5357, Batna, 6 September 1934 and 7 February 1935, Sous-préfet to Préfet, and Alger, 16 April 1935, GGA to Préfet.

30. ANOM Oran 1F / 70, Oran / 11 August 1941, Controleur / Service départemental des douairs to Préfet; Oasis / 50, Alger, 7 December 1945, GGA to Préfet. The latter document noted Lyautey's maxim that the best way to avoid using armed force is to ensure that it is omnipresent, especially in "nerve centers."

31. On military-civilian contretemps, see ANOM GGA 3R / 18, Alger, 4 June 1935, Préfet to GGA, and Alger, 7 January 1936, Colonel Lavigne, Commandant la Gendarmerie et la Garde républicaine de l'Algérie to Général commandant le 19e corps de l'armée. On interagency noncooperation, see ANOM Constantine 93 / 1308: Bône, 8 March 1945, Colonel Monniot, Commandant la subdivision to Sous-préfet; Bône, 12 March 1945, Sous-préfet to Maires and Administrateurs; and Paris, 4 July 1947, Minister of the Interior to Prefects. As late as July 1954, conflict persisted between the

PJ and the gendarmerie. See ANOM Oran 92/2438, Oran, 22 July 1954, Préfet to Colonel commandant la Légion. Concerning crime reports, see ANOM Constantine 93/1308, Constantine, 23 November 1933 and 6 February 1934, Préfet, Circular.

32. Thomas, *Violence and Colonial Order*, 101–103; ANOM Constantine 93/20332: Bordj-Bou-Arréridj, 14 September 1925, Administrateur de la Commune mixte to Sous-préfet; Sétif, 6 October 1925, Préfet to Sous-préfet; and Alger, 5 October 1925, GGA to Préfet.

33. Georges Giraud, *Notice sur l'organisation et le fonctionnement de la Police scientifique en Algérie* (Alger, 1928); ANOM Constantine 93/5301, Alger, 5 February 1904, GGA to Préfet; Constantine 93/20072, Constantine, 30 April 1923, Commissaire de la Sûreté générale, "Rapport spécial"; GGA, Direction de la Sécurité générale, *Bulletin de la Police criminelle*, 1 August 1930.

34. Roland Barthes, *Camera Lucida: Reflections on Photography* (London, 1981), 9–14, 41. To be sure, Barthes would have rejected the colonial police photograph much as he dismissed its use in advertising, for refusing to either challenge the status quo or offer a surprising or spontaneous element. Yet, he acknowledges the propagandistic or journalistic usage of the medium according to the same operator/spectator dichotomy.

35. Michael G. Vann, "Of Pirates, Postcards, and Public Beheadings: The Pedagogic Execution in French Colonial Indochina," *Historical Reflections/Réflexions historiques* 36 (2010): 40–42.

36. Archives nationales d'Algérie 16E1/03/02, Alger, 11 March 1937, "Rapport—Laboratoire de Police scientifique d'Alger, Brigade technique."

37. Archives nationales d'Algérie 16E/1, "Reconstitution du crime."

38. ANOM Constantine 93/5332, Batna, 5 May 1923, Commissaire chef de la Brigade centrale, "Rapport"; Constantine 93/5382, Sétif, 8 September 1930, Inspecteur Olivieri to Directeur de la Sûreté générale.

39. ANOM Constantine 93/20072, Constantine, 30 April 1923, "Rapport spécial"; ANOM Constantine 93/20074, Constantine, 25 September 1924, Commissaire chef, Sûreté générale to Directeur de la Sécurité générale; ANOM Constantine 93/5384, Bougie, 30 August 1934, "Rapport spécial."

40. ANOM Constantine 93/20182, Constantine, 1 January 1929, "Rapport d'ensemble."

41. ANOM Constantine 93/5382, Philippeville, 16 June 1930, "Rapport spéciale–Brigade mobile."

42. ANOM Constantine 93/20182, Constantine, 1 January 1929, "Rapport d'ensemble"; ANOM GGA/3R/19, Alger, 2 April 1931, PTT to GGA; ANOM Oran 1F/79, Oran, 30 October 1953, Préfet to GGA.

43. ANOM Constantine 93/5332, Constantine, 8 June 1923, Sûreté générale, "Rapport spécial"; ANOM Constantine 93/20163, Guelma, 26 July 1934, Sûreté général, "Rapport spécial."

44. ANOM Constantine 93/20063, M'Sila, 28 June 1921, Administrateur de la Commune mixte to Préfet; ANOM Constantine 93/5379, Bône, 3 November 1929, Chef de la Brigade mobile to Préfet.

45. Berlière and Lévy, *Histoire des polices en France*, 318–320.

46. Scott, *Weapons of the Weak*; James C. Scott, *Domination and the Arts of Resistance: Hidden Transcripts* (New Haven, CT, 1990). *Duwars* were tribal tent encampments organized into family units; *mechtas* were small villages.

NOTES TO PAGES 30-33   199

47. ANOM Constantine 93/5319, Alger, 24 April 1909, GGA to Préfet, Constantine.

48. ANOM Constantine 93/5346, Sétif, 19 July 1938, Brigade mobile, "Rapport special."

49. The Communist threat particularly worried Oran officials, resulting in demands for further allotments. See ANOM Oran 1F/81, Oran, 19 July 1928, Préfet, "Arrête." Archives contain entire folders filled with demands for ever-larger tranches of money to be paid to informants. See, for example, ANOM Oran 1F/81, letters from Commissaires and officials to Sous-préfets and Préfets.

50. ANOM Constantine 93/20322, Constantine, 17 July 1933, Chef de la Sûreté départementale to Préfet; ANOM GGA 3R/22, Alger, 24 June 1933, GGA to Commandant militaire des oasis, and Ouargla, 5 May 1931, 28 August 1933, and 17 February 1939, Capitaine Estèbe, Commandant militaire du Territoire d'Oasis to GGA.

51. Daniel Lefeuvre, *Chère Algérie: La France et sa colonie, 1930–1962* (Paris, 2005), 81.

52. Lefeuvre, 87; Ahmed Henni, *Économie de l'Algérie coloniale, 1830–1954* (Alger, 2018), 78.

53. Lefeuvre, *Chère Algérie*, 86; ANOM Oran 1F/81, Saida, 9 December 1948, Commissaire chef to Sous-préfet, Mascara, and Oran, 6 September 1950, Préfet to Receveur principal des finances; CAOM Oran/1F/82, Commissionaire divisionnaire, Police/Renseignements généraux (PRG) to Préfet; CAOM Oran/2438, Oran, 8 November 1950, Commissaire principal to Préfet.

54. ANOM Oran 1F/70, Oran, 12 October 1926, Chef de la Sûreté départementale to Préfet; ANOM Oran 92/2421, Tiaret, 26 February 1949, Sous-préfet to Préfet.

55. ANOM Oran 92/2422, Oran, 13 March 1950, Commandant principal de la paix to Commissaire divisionnaire; ANOM GGA 3R/262, Oran, 24 May 1951, Préfet to GGA. On the low numbers and their causes, see ANOM Oran 1F/82, Oran, 18 January 1952, "Situation des effectifs de la Police d'état d'Oran"; and ANOM Constantine 93/6878, "Police d'état de Constantine: Situation numérique des effectifs/novembre 1953."

56. ANOM Constantine 93/1110, "Rapport mensuel sur la situation politique et économique se l'arrondissement de Constantine," August 1949; CAOM Constantine 93/6878, "État d'effectifs" (various locales), 1953.

57. ANOM Oran 92/2438, "Effectifs de la PRG d'Oran—10 Août 1948," and Oran, 14 November 1950, "PRG d'Alger, Oran, et Constantine."

58. Comor, "Implantations et missions," 183–193.

59. ANOM Constantine 93/20109, Renier, 10 September 1908, Maire to Préfet.

60. Thomas, *Violence and Colonial Order*, 92–95; ANOM Constantine 93/20332: Constantine, 9 October 1925, Chef d'escadron Mea to Préfet; GGA 3R/262, Paris, 2 January 1953, "Note pour l'État-major combine des Forces armées"; and Alger, 10 January 1953, Colonel Boulard, Directeur du Cabinet militaire, GGA to Lieutenant-Colonel, Chef du Secrétariat permanent à la défense nationale. Boulard petitioned for forty-four brigades immediately to ensure territorial security, along with four additional squadrons of the Garde républicaine. On shortages of housing for police, see, for example, ANOM Constantine 93/5394, Alger, 18 September 1930, GGA to Préfet; ANOM Oran 92/2423, Oran, 20 February 1951, Préfet—memorandum.

61. ANOM GGA 3R/212, Blida, 16 July 1948, "Rapport du Chef d'escadron Intartiglia"; ANOM GGA 3R/262, Alger, 17 March 1953, "Rapport du Général Morin, Commandant la 10e Légion," and Alger, 28 September 1954, GGA to Minister of the

Interior. Morin continued to lobby for additional personnel from 1952 to 1954, rejecting ministerial talk of a four-year wait for needed reinforcements. See ANOM GGA 3R/262, notes of 22 August 1952, 20 June 1953, and 24 September 1954.

62. ANOM Constantine 93/5357, Jemmapes, 31 August 1934, Administrateur de la Commune mixte to Sous-préfet, and Khenchela, 18 January 1935, Administrateur de la Commune mixte to Sous-préfet (Batna).

63. ANOM Constantine 93/5357, "Extraits du régistre des deliberations de la Commission municipale," 26 November 1934, and MacMahon, 26 December 1934, Administrateur de la Commune mixte to Sous-préfet.

64. ANOM Constantine 93/5357, Biskra, 1 June 1935, Maire to Préfet.

65. Jean-Pierre Peyroulou, "Rétablir et maintenir l'ordre colonial: La police française et les algériens en Algérie française de 1945 à 1962," in *La guerre d'Algérie (1954–2004): Fin de l'amnésie*, ed. Mohammed Harbi and Benjamin Stora (Paris, 2004), 93; ANOM Constantine 93/5357, "Rapport présenté par M. Cussin," n.d. (1930); ANOM GGA 3R/212, Oum-el-Bouaghi, May 1948, "Délégation générale du plan—rapport bimensuel"; ANOM Oran/2438, Oran, 18 January 1951, Commissaire principal, PRG to Préfet.

66. ANOM Constantine 93/20109: Constantine, 13 December 1893, Letter from Colbert denizens; Alger, 14 November 1898, Général commandant le 19e corps to GGA; Alger, 27 December 1900, GGA to Préfet; Sétif, 27 August 1908, Chef d'escadron Guillemard to Préfet; Alger, 24 June 1913, GGA to Préfet; Richa, 20 May 1920, "Extrait du registre des délibérations de la commission municipal"; Constantine, 20 March 1923, Préfet to Sous-préfet.

67. ANOM Constantine 93/5357, Constantine, 20 February 1933, "Rapport du chef d'escadron Vallon, commandant la 3e cie du la 19e Légion de gendarmerie"; CAOM Constantine 93/1742, Bône, 8 June 1935, Sous-préfet to Préfet. The former report explained that the unavailability of six officers proceeded from their duty to frequently testify in court.

68. ANOM GGA 3R/18, "Garde républicaine mobile de l'Algérie"; ANOM Constantine 93/6919, Constantine, 4 June 1952, Préfet to Sous-préfet.

69. On budgets and public spending, see Thomas, *French Empire*, 103–113; Henni, *Économie de l'Algérie coloniale*, 98–104; Lefeuvre, *Chère Algérie*, chap. 2, 90–93.

70. CAOM Constantine 93/20109, Paris, 24 August 1906, Minister of War to GGA, and Constantine, 17 February 1909, "Rapport du Chef d'escadron."

71. ANOM Constantine 93/20032, Auribeau, 16 August 1934, Conseiller général Pierre Cusin to General Kieffer, and Constantine, 2 February 1935, "Rapport du Chef d'escadron Vallon"; ANOM Constantine 93/5357: "Extrait de délibérations de la Commission munciipale d'Ain Touta"; MacMahon, 26 December 1934, Administrateur de la Commune mixte d'Ain Touta to Sous-préfet; Constantine, 20 February 1935, Général Richard to Préfet; Constantine, 22 February 1935, Préfet, Constantine to GGA; Constantine, 28 February 1935, Préfet to GGA and Préfet to Général commandant la Division; Alger, 16 April 1935, GGA to Préfets; and Sétif, 30 April 1935, Chef d'escadron Perree to Préfet.

72. ANOM Constantine 93/5301, Constantine, 13 February and 21 July 1904, Maire to Préfet, GGA, and Alger, 26 January and 6 August 1904, GGA to Préfet; ANOM Constantine 93/20109, Guelma, 21 May 1908, Maire to Préfet.

73. For examples of such rows, see ANOM Constantine 93 / 1345, M'Sila, 23 November 1927, Administrateur de la Commune mixte to Sous-préfet, and Sétif, 10 December 1929, Sous-préfet to Préfet; ANOM Constantine 93 / 1742, "Séance de 12 août 1935 / Extrait du régistre des délibérations du Conseil municipal-Chateaudun-du-Rhumel," and Bordj-Bou-Arréridj, 1 October 1935, "Extrait du régistre des délibérations du Conseil municipal."

74. ANOM Constantine 93 / 20109: Alger, 26 February 1908, GGA to Préfet; Batna, 17 July 1920, Sous-préfet to Préfet; and Alger, 17 August 1920, GGA to Préfet.

75. ANOM Constantine 93 / 1742, Alger, 31 December 1935, GGA, "Arrête."

76. ANOM Constantine 93 / 20322, Sidi-Aïch, 17 February 1936, Administrateur de la Commune mixte, Soummam to Préfet.

77. Marcel-Edmond Naegelen, *Mission en Algérie* (Paris, 1962).

78. Jacques Simon, *Le PPA (Le Parti du peuple algérien) (1937–1947)* (Paris, 2005), 179–185; Annie Rey-Goldzeiguer, *Aux origines de la guerre d'Algérie, 1940–1945* (Paris, 2002), 228–245; Mahfoud Kaddache, *Histoire du nationalisme algérien* (Paris, 2000), 625–675.

79. Simon, *Le PPA*, 208–229; Rey-Goldzeiguer, *Aux origines de la guerre*, 326–356.

80. These campaigns are fully discussed in chapter 5.

81. ANOM GGA 2R / 122, Alger, 14 March 1949, Préfet, Alger to GGA, and Alger, 24 March 1949, GGA to Préfet, Alger.

82. ANOM Oran 92 / 2438, Oran, 23 October 1950, Commissaire principal, Renseignements généraux to Directeur générale de la Sécurité générale, and Oran, 18 January 1951, Commissaire principal, RG to Préfet.

83. ANOM GGA 3R / 262: Alger, 15 April 1951, Colonel Morin, Commandant la 10e Légion to Ministère de la défense nationale; Constantine, 5 March 1951 and 25 February 1952, Préfet to GGA; and Alger, 21 March 1952, GGA to Préfet, Constantine.

84. ANOM GGA 3R / 262, Alger, 6 March 1952, Vice-président du Conseil, Ministre de la défense nationale to Général commandant la 10e Légion.

85. Berlière and Lévy, *Histoire des polices en France*, 409–414, 424–446.

86. Peyroulou, "Rétablir et maintenir," 102–106.

87. Gendarmerie and GRM units required candidates to be twenty-one to forty years of age and a minimum of 1.64 meters tall, and to possess minimal reading, writing, and math skills. See ANOM GGA 3R / 18, "Garde républicaine mobile de l'Algérie," n.d. (1936).

88. ANOM GGA 3R / 212, Constantine, 26 November 1949, "Rapport du Chef d'escadron Goulard."

89. ANOM Constantine 93 / 20109, Conseil général, Constantine, "Séance du 21 avril 1926"; ANOM GGA 3R / 212, Alger, 12 July 1950, "État de renseignements sur les casernements de la 10e Légion de gendarmerie," and Paris, 4 August 1950, Jules Moch, memorandum.

90. Frantz Fanon, *Les damnés de la terre* (Paris, 1968), 7.

91. Thomas, *Empires of Intelligence*, 39–40; David Arnold, *Police Power and Colonial Rule: Madras, 1859–1947* (Oxford, 1987), 25–26, 40–51. This trend predominated throughout the British Empire. See David Anderson and David Killingray, *Policing the Empire: Government, Authority, and Control (1830–1940)* (Manchester, UK, 1991).

92. See the articles by André Dia, Nicolas Courtin, Romain Tiquet, and Bénédicte Brunet-La Ruche in Bat and Courtin, *Maintenir l'ordre colonial*; and Patrice Morlat, *La*

répression coloniale au Vietnam (1908–1940) (Paris, 1990), 40–49. The Belgian Congo also mobilized a hybrid system, with nonwhites policing municipalities. See Thomas, *Violence and Colonial Order*, 305–324.

93. For a discussion of settler xenophobia in Algeria, see Kalman, *French Colonial Fascism*.

94. ANOM Constantine 93/7471, GGA, "Recrutements des commissions de police en Algérie"; ANOM Constantine 93/6889, "Cours d'instructions/destiné aux GDP, stagières de la PE"; ANOM GGA 9H/32, Alger, 10 May 1928, Préfet to GGA; ANOM Constantine 93/6829, Alger, 13 July 1913, "Arrête."

95. ANOM Alger 1F/439, "Reglement des services de la Police d'état d'Alger."

96. ANOM Constantine 93/6783, "Arrondissement de Bône: Effectif à la date du 30 juillet [1948]"; CAOM Constantine 93/6888, "Personnel titulaire en fonctions au 1er mai 1947"; Constantine 93/7447, "Liste des candidats inspecteurs de Sûreté stagières/18 octobre 1951"; Constantine 93/20322, Sidi-Aich, 17 February 1936, Administrateur de la Commune mixte de la Soumamm to Préfet.

97. McDougall, *History of Algeria*, 130–131; Jonathan K. Gosnell, *The Politics of French Algeria, 1930–1954* (Rochester, NY, 2002), 105.

98. ANOM Oran 2F/69, Oran, 17 February 1908, Commissaire central to Maire; Constantine 93/6791, "Notice individuelle d'un candidate à un employ d'inspecteur secrétaire de la Police d'état."

99. ANOM Oran 1F/76, Minister of Interior/Direction de la Sûreté générale, "Programme du concours/Commissaire de police," 1920; ANOM Constantine 93/7471, GGA, "Recrutement des Commissaires de police en Algérie"; ANOM Constantine 93/6791, Constantine, 16 February 1942, Préfet to Sous-préfet; Constantine 93/6789, "Rapport d'enquête," Police entrance exam, 1941.

100. ANOM Constantine 93/6791, "Dictée," February 1942; ANOM Constantine 93/6789, Constantine, 7 May 1941, Préfet—memorandum.

101. ANOM GGA 3R/12, "Décret du 7 septembre 1926/Recrutement des indigènes Algériens." Candidates were to be bachelors, eighteen to thirty years of age, and judged by military doctors to be morally sound and physically fit. They also had to have a legal certificate acknowledging their clean record from the mayor or administrator of their place of residence. Although gendarmes could leave the service during their term and later return, spots for non-Europeans were limited, and thus Arabs and Kabyles who had been promoted risked being readmitted at an inferior rank.

102. Thomas, *Violence and Colonial Order*, 104–106; ANOM GGA 3R/12, General Nogues to Parès, June 1933, and Instruction pour le recrutement des militaires indigènes de carrière, January 1935; ANOM GGA 3R/244, Alger, 13 May 1952, "Note pour les directeurs et chefs de service."

103. ANOM GGA 3R/244, Alger, 23 October 1935, "Analyse," and Paris, 23 November 1938, Ministère de la defense nationale et de la guerre to GGA.

104. Rey-Goldzeiguer, *Aux origins de la guerre*, 127–133; Julian Jackson, *A Certain Idea of France: The Life of Charles de Gaulle* (London, 2018), 267–268, 284–285.

105. ANOM Constantine 93/7023, Alger, 10 January 1943, GGA to Préfet.

106. On the Sétif and Guelma massacres, see Jean-Louis Planche, *Sétif 1945: Histoire d'un massacre annoncé* (Paris, 2006); and Jean-Pierre Peyroulou, *Guelma, 1945: Une*

subversion française dans l'Algérie coloniale (Paris, 2009). On the growth of the PPA / MTLD after 1945, see chapter 5.

107. ANOM Oran 92 1F / 77, Oran, 10 November 1953, Préfecture d'Oran—"Circulaire"; ANOM Oran 92 / 2438, Oran, 26 February 1954, Commissaire principal, Chef de la Police des RG to Préfet. The lack of Arabic speakers was par for the course in Oran; in the same communication, the head of the RG complained bitterly about a lack of typewriters in various headquarters, not to mention the lack of motor vehicles for police outside major cities.

108. ANOM Oran 1F / 83, Oran, 10 December 1952, Préfet to GGA.

109. Constantine 93 / 6888, "Personnel titulaire en fonctions au 1er mai 1947," and "Application de la loi de 10 mai 1946"; Constantine 93 / 7447, "Liste des candidats gardiens de la paix, 11 octobre 1951," and GGA, "Arrête," 22 May 1951.

110. ANOM Constantine 93 / 6888, GGA, "Arrête," 9 July 1948; ANOM Constantine 93 / 6889, "Cours d'instructions—Stagières de la Police d'état," 1949; ANOM Constantine 93 / 7448, GGA, Direction de la Sécurité générale, "Recrutement des commissaires de police stagières en Algérie," 1952.

111. Constantine 93 / 7447, "Recrutements du commissaires de police algérienne" (1948), and "Note relative aux conditions d'admission et d'emploi d'officier de police stagière" (October 1949).

112. Constantine 93 / 7447, GGA, "Arrête," 22 May 1951; Constantine 93 / 7448, GGA, "Arrête," 17 July 1952 and 19 January 1953.

113. ANOM Constantine 93 / 20322, Département de Constantine, Budget 1917; ANOM Constantine 93 / 1742, Département de Constantine, "Police municipale / Effectif budgétaire—1936"; ANOM Constantine, 93 / 6829, GGA, "Arrête," 31 July 1913 and 28 February 1919. Literally dozens of other examples can be found in the relevant cartons in the colonial archives.

114. ANOM Constantine 93 / 6829, GGA, "Arrête," 13 July 1913, 4 March 1926, and 10 February 1930; ANOM Constantine 93 / 1740, Constantine, 27 June 1938, Conservateur des eaux et des forêts to Préfet; ANOM Constantine 93 / 6864, "Rapport au Conseil général—Situation des militaires et gendarmes d'origine musulmane," 1950, and Conseil général, "Séance du 25 octobre 1950."

115. ANOM Constantine 93 / 6829, GGA, "Arrête," 31 July 1913 and 28 February 1919; Christian Chevandier, *Policiers dans la ville: Une histoire des gardiens de la paix* (Paris, 2012), 314–315.

116. ANOM Oran 1F / 72, Alger, 11 January 1909, GGA to Préfet.

117. ANOM Constantine 93 / 5353, Paris, 22 June 1935, Minister of the Interior to Prefects. This was not a specifically Algerian problem, and French officials were included in the communication.

118. ANOM Oran 92 / 2422, Oran, 31 October 1950, "Décision"; ANOM Constantine 93 / 6919, Alger, 5 November 1953, GGA, "Note de service."

119. ANOM Constantine 93 / 5779, "Commissaires de police: Avancements, 1er semestre 1930"; ANOM Constantine 93 / 5353, "Arrondissement de Bougie—État de propositions d'avancement, 2e semestre 1933," and "Police municipale de Constantine, Avancements 1934." In the case of the *commissaire* who did not perform well on the exam, the suggested remedy was a second sitting.

120. ANOM Constantine 93/20182, Constantine, 1 January 1924 and 1 January 1929, "Rapport d'ensemble."

121. ANOM Constantine 93/6886: "Propositions exceptionnels d'avancement—15 octobre 1945"; Constantine, 12 October 1945, Commissaire divisionnaire to Préfet; and *Bulletin individuel de notes*, 1949; ANOM Oran 1F/71, Oran, 24 August 1945, Préfet to GGA. Bordier also received the Médaille de la Reconnaissance française.

122. ANOM Constantine 93/6975, Alger, 29 July 1946, GGA, "Arrête"; ANOM Constantine 93/7440, "Personnel des commissaires de la police algérienne—Tableau d'avancement/1951"; ANOM GGA 3R/262, "10e Légion de Gendarmerie: Tableau récapitulatif des sous-officiers," 1952.

123. ANOM Constantine 93/6886, "Tableau des propositions d'avancement a titre exceptionnel," 25 September 1945.

124. ANOM Constantine 93/5371, "Ville de Bône, Police municipale—Reglement administrative," 1929.

125. ANOM Constantine 93/1345, Ain-Beïda, 8 June 1929, Police municipale to Maire; ANOM Constantine 93/6880, Constantine, 6 July 1951, Préfet to GGA.

126. ANOM Constantine 93/1345, Collo, 18 March 1928, Petition to Préfet, and Collo, 6 April 1929, Maire to Préfet; ANOM Constantine 93/6891: Bône, 12 December 1945, Letter to Maire; Bône, 10 January 1946, Commissaire central to Préfet; and Bône, 14 January 1946, Sous-préfet to Préfet; ANOM Constantine 93/6875, "Conseil de discipline, séance du 27 mars 1951." An acquittal spared a non-Muslim officer, regardless of the severity of the charge. A Jewish officer named Slimane Akouka, who had been suspended for killing a Muslim rioter in the line of duty, rejoined the force following a not-guilty verdict, despite the fury of the local Algerian population. See ANOM Constantine 93/5371, Ain-Beïda, 27 August 1935, Maire to Préfet.

127. ANOM Alger 1F/500, Alger, 6 March 1947, GGA to Préfet.

128. ANOM Constantine 93/1742, Préfet, "Arrête," 1 November 1935.

129. ANOM Constantine 93/1345: Chateaudun-du-Rhumel, 30 September 1926, Maire adjoint, "Arrête"; Chateaudun-du-Rhumel, 1 October 1926, Maire to Préfet; and Constantine, 27 October 1926, Mohamed Hansili to Maire.

130. Two serious examples can be found in ANOM Constantine 93/6888, "Demande de révision de peine disciplinaire," 1946, and "Situation administrative", 1948.

131. ANOM Constantine 93/5310, Collo, 6 October 1913—Depositions, and Philippeville, 15 October 1913, Sous-préfet to Préfet.

132. ANOM Constantine 93/6888, "Demande de révision de peine disciplinaire," October 1945, February 1946, November 1946.

133. ANOM GGA 3R/303: Oran, 3 February 1949, Commissaire divisionnaire, "Rapport"; Tiaret, 10 August 1949, Sous-préfet to Préfet; and Sous-préfet, memo, Oran, 24 November 1949. Meflah was also accused of being a best friend to the nationalist secrétaire of the Tiaret court, who was alleged to be the *chef camouflée* of the local PPA. Once again, despite surveillance and the use of informants, no proof was forthcoming, which those involved blamed on Meflah's "guarded" disposition. See Tiaret, 13 January 1949, Sous-préfet to Préfet.

134. ANOM Constantine 93/6887: Châteaudun-du-Rhumel, Benider to Préfet, 22 December 1947; Alger, 18 January 1948, Préfet to GGA; and *Bulletin individuel des notes*, 1951. This was not the first time that Benider had been charged with insubordination and na-

tionalist sympathizing. In July 1947, he was accused of impropriety in the arrest of a perpetrator defacing buildings with pro-nationalist graffiti. Rumors circulated that he too was a nationalist and sympathized with the accused, attempting to downplay the investigation and writing an error-strewn report that he never turned in. When reprimanded he purportedly responded by screaming "Je vous emmerde [Fuck you]," and the *commissaire central* demanded official charges. However, nothing came of the scathing indictment. See ANOM Constantine 93 / 6887, Bône, 1 July 1947, "Rapport—Commissaire central."

135. ANOM Constantine 93 / 6863, Philippeville, 11 March 1947, Inspecteur de la PRG to Préfet, and Constantine, 29 April 1947, Lieutenant Colonel Bobillon, Commandant le Groupement de Gendarmerie to Préfet; ANOM GGA 3R / 303, Alger, 7 May 1949, Directeur-général de la Sécurité générale to Préfet; ANOM Oran / 92, 2421, Mostaganem, 21 November 1948, Sous-préfet to Préfet.

2. An Anticolonial Crime Wave?

1. ANOM Constantine 93 / 5327, Guelma, 13 August 1915, Sous-Préfet to Préfet.

2. Due to the centrality of the region to banditry from 1914 to 1918, a fact reflected by the overwhelming percentage of documentary evidence devoted to the area, the chapter focuses solely on the department of Constantine. To be sure, the Aurès edged into the department of Alger too, but almost all of the extant material focuses on the neighboring department.

3. Blanchard and Glasman, "Le maintien de l'ordre," 12. Unfortunately, the same sources are often the only extant record of banditry in the colonial context. Clearly, reports and dossiers cannot be read literally; they must be vetted for euphemistic language and exaggeration. However, many unwittingly contain details about local conditions and subaltern voices, and certain authors recount gruesome details without any attempt to obfuscate events or meaning. Thus, despite their evident bias, official documents can be quite useful in reconstructing cases of banditry, providing that the reader exercises caution.

4. Bradley Camp Davis, *Imperial Bandits: Outlaws and Rebels in the China-Vietnam Borderlands* (Seattle, 2017), 9–12. Unlike their Algerian confreres, Vietnamese bandits tended to terrorize locals through campaigns of murder, rape, and enslavement, often motivated by ethnic nationalist rivalry or class conflict. Moreover, they were frequently co-opted by the state as agents of imperialism. Although this did not occur in Algeria, the connection between power, colonial violence and exclusion, and banditry was present in the North African setting.

5. The term "deserters" refers to soldiers who flee military service, usually from a base camp or training ground. By contrast, *insoumis* are those who refuse to report for service, evading conscription or recruitment.

6. Gilbert Meynier, *L'Algérie révélée: La guerre de 1914–1918 et le premier quart du XXe siècle* (Paris, 1981); Abdelkadar Djeghloul, "Hors-la-loi, violence arabe et pouvoir colonial en Algérie au début du XXe siècle: Les frères Boutouizerat," *Revue de l'Occident musulman et de la Méditerranée* 38 (1984): 55–63. As Daniel Branch relates, in Algeria, "colonialism drove a logic of extremes, obliterating the possibility of a meaningful, moderate nationalism." Branch, *Defeating Mau Mau, Creating Kenya: Counterinsurgency, Civil War, and Decolonization* (Cambridge, UK, 2009), 19.

7. Jean Déjeux, "Un bandit dans l'Aurès, de 1917 à 1921," *Revue de l'Occident musulman et de la Médeterranée* 26 (1978): 35–54; Eric Hobsbawm, *Bandits* (London, 2000), 13–22.

8. Raphaëlle Branche, "'Au temps de la France': Identités collectives et situation coloniale en Algérie," *Vingtième siècle* 117 (2013): 209.

9. Thomas, *Empires of Intelligence*, 79.

10. Scott, *Weapons of the Weak*; Scott, *Domination and the Arts of Resistance*.

11. On the Kabyle rebellion, see Ruedy, *Modern Algeria*, 77–79.

12. On the 1840s revolts, see Clancy-Smith, *Rebel and Saint*, chap. 4. On the Djelfa rebellion, see Brower, *Desert Named Peace*, chap. 4.

13. Alain Mahé, *Histoire de la Grande Kabylie, XIXe–XXe siècles: Anthropologie historique du lien social dans les communautés villageoises* (Paris, 2000), 190–201; Charles-Robert Ageron, *Histoire de l'Algérie contemporaine*, vol. 2, *1871–1954* (Paris, 1979), 10–16. However, Ageron further posits that the Muqrani defeat ushered in a complete capitulation by Algerians until the 1930s, a thesis clearly rejected by this author.

14. ANOM GGA 2H/87, Alger, 7 June 1876, GGA to Ministers of War and Interior, and Biskra, 12 June 1876, Caïd to GGA.

15. "Arrête," *Le Morbacher*, 12 June 1876.

16. ANOM GGA 2H/87, Constantine, 9 June, 29 June, 26 July 1876, Général commandant la subdivision to GGA, and Alger, 28 September 1876, Directeur général des affaires civiles et financières, memorandum. Authorities gave the tribe until 31 December to pay the fines. On the punishments and ultimate fate of the Bou Azid tribe, see Thénault, *Violence ordinaire*, 146–152.

17. ANOM GGA 2H/87, Alger, 7 June 1876, GGA to Ministers of War and Interior, and Alger, 12 June 1876, Général Chanzy to GGA.

18. ANOM GGA 2H/32: Khanga, 26 June 1879, Caïd ben Naceur to Capitaine Dubreuil; Constantine, 30 June 1879, Report—Général commandant la division; and Batna, 10 July 1879, Général commandant la subdivision, "Rapport résumant l'ensemble des faits / Insurrection—10 July 1879."

19. ANOM GGA 2H/32, Medina, 2 July and 5 August 1879, Report—Général commandant la subdivision; ANOM GGA 2H/33, Constantine, 22 June 1880, Minutes—Conseil de guerre.

20. ANOM GGA 2H/32, "État indiquant le montant de la contribution de guerre à imposer aux diverses fractions des Ouled Daoud d'après le dégré de culpabilité de chacun d'elles," and "État indiquant le montant de la contribution de guerre à imposer aux diverses fractions des Bou Sliman d'après le dégré de culpabilité de chacun d'elles."

21. ANOM GGA 2H/32, Batna, 10 July 1879, Général commandant la subdivision, "Rapport résumant l'ensemble des faits, Insurrection—10 July 1879."

22. ANOM GGA 2H/32, Tébessa, 16 July 1879, Rapport—Insurrection, Tébessa.

23. ANOM GGA 2H/32, "Depositions / Commission d'enquête sur les troubles de l'Aurès." For an example of the stance taken by the popular press, see "L'enquête sur l'Aurès," *La Nouvelliste d'Alger*, 23 September 1879.

24. Brower, *Desert Named Peace*, 5–7; Jennifer Sessions, "Making Settlers Muslim: Religion, Resistance, and Everyday Life in Nineteenth-Century French Algeria," *French History* 33 (2019): 260–261.

25. Sessions, "Making Settlers Muslim," 259–263.

26. ANOM Constantine B/2/1, Alger, 24 March 1876, GGA to Préfet.
27. ANOM Constantine B/2/1, Jemmapes, 17 March 1876, Préfet to GGA. On robberies, see various communiqués in the same carton.
28. ANOM Constantine B/2/1: Jemmapes, 9 March 1876, Administrateur de la Commune mixte to Sous-préfet; Guelma, 13 March 1876, Sous-préfet to Préfet; Constantine, 12 October 1876, Commissaires to Commissaire central; and Aïn-Régada, 18 September 1877, Administrateur de la Commune mixte to Préfet.
29. ANOM Constantine B/2/1, Alger, 28 March 1876, GGA to Préfet.
30. ANOM Constantine B/2/1: Alger, 20 October 1876, GGA to Préfet; El Arrouch, 22 August 1876, Officier de la Police judiciare to Préfet; and Philippeville, 28 August 1876, Massaoud and Ali Ben Slian to Préfet.
31. ANOM Constantine B/2/1: Jemmapes, 15 April 1876, Letter to Préfet; Constantine, 13 October 1876, Commissaire central to Préfet; El Arrouch, 28 October 1877, "Rapport rélatif à la capture du bandit Bougueraa"; Guelma, 12 November 1877, Sous-préfet to Préfet; 5 November 1877, Letter to Lieutenant Bresson; and Alger, 12 November 1877, GGA to Préfet. As early as March 1876, the Philippeville *procureur* complained angrily to the *préfet* that goums lazed around and refused to look for Bougerra unless forced to do so by European superiors. Philippeville, 14 March 1876, Procureur de la république to Préfet. Concerning GGA orders not to seize commonly held property, see Alger, 24 March 1876, GGA to Préfet.
32. ANOM Alger 1F/33, Tizi-Ouzou, January 1894, "Rapport sur la repression du banditisme," Sous-Préfet to GGA. The following account of the Arezki gang is taken from this official report.
33. As Michael Vann observes, the parading of captured rebels conveyed a message of colonial superiority while symbolically violating the person of the accused. Although in this case it did not end in a public execution of the type described by Vann, the message conveyed to the European population became enmeshed in a similarly humiliating spectacle. See Vann, "Of Pirates, Postcards, and Public Beheadings," 43–45.
34. On the brutal reality of colonial prisons, see Thénault, *Violence ordinaire*, chap. six.
35. Thénault, 51–54. On political antisemitism and attendant violence, see Roberts, *Citizenship and Anti-Semitism*, chap. 2; Lizabeth Zack, "French and Algerian Identity Formation in 1890s Algiers," *French Colonial History* 2 (2002): 115–143; and Geneviève Dermenjian, *La crise anti-juive oranaise (1895–1905): L'antisémitisme dans l'Algérie coloniale* (Paris, 1986).
36. On the Kabyle myth, see Lorcin, *Imperial Identities*.
37. Meynier, *L'Algérie révélée*, 85–88; Richard S. Fogarty, *Race and War in France: Colonial Subjects in the French Army, 1914–1918* (Baltimore, MD, 2008), 17–22, 31–35. The bonus payments also performed a more sinister function. As Algerians were subjects rather than citizens, for whom mandatory service went hand in hand with citizenship, the cash payoffs differentiated colonial "mercenaries" from their metropolitan counterparts.
38. Fogarty, *Race and War in France*, 2, 7–8, 25–27; Tyler Stovall, "The Colour Line behind the Lines: Racial Violence in France during the Great War," *American Historical Review* 103 (1998): 738–742.
39. Meynier, *L'Algérie révélée*, 97–103, 260, 395–407; Fogarty, *Race and War in France*, 23–27; Mahé, *Histoire de la Grande Kabylie*, 297–298. By 1918, the bounty of five francs

per head had increased to seven francs. Cash payments from families for replacement soldiers reached up to 500 francs. See ANOM Constantine 93, 2515, p. 93. In total, 172,019 Algerians served in the armed forces during the Great War, along with 109,000 workers. Those serving on the front lines tended to be younger, while factory workers were older men.

40. Forgarty, *Race and War in France*, 33.

41. Meynier, *L'Algérie révélée*, 395–407, 570; ANOM GGA 9H / 16: Mascara, 3 October 1914, "Sous-préfet to Préfet; Perrégaux, 6 October 1914, "Rapport du Maréchal du logis"; and Mascara, 10 October 1914, Sous-préfet to Préfet.

42. ANOM Constantine 93 / 5329, Bordj-Bou-Arréridj, 24 October and 13 November 1916, Administrateur de la Commune mixte to Sous-préfet.

43. Fogarty, *Race and War in France*, 25–27, 31–35; Fanny Colonna, *Le meunier, les moines, et le bandit: Des vies quotidiennes dans l'Aurès (Algérie) du XXe siècle* (Arles, 2010), 66; ANOM Constantine 93 / 2515, "Les Troubles insurrectionels de l'arrondissement de Batna en 1916." Although desertion rates fell to 605 in 1917, they mushroomed again to 948 in 1918. The latter figure undoubtedly corresponds to a huge increase in the number of Algerian dead and seriously wounded, from between 14,500 and 19,000 in 1914 to 1916 to 33,500 in 1917 and 55,500 in 1918. In total, 3,883 fled armed service throughout the war.

44. ANOM Constantine 93 / 5321, Alger, 20 December 1916, GGA to Préfet; ANOM Constantine 93 / 2515, "Les Troubles insurrectionels de l'arrondissement de Batna en 1916"; ANOM Constantine 93 / 20183, Sidi-Aïch, 8 February 1915, Administrateur de la Commune mixte de la Soummam to Sous-préfet (Bougie); ANOM Constantine 93 / 5326, 15 July 1915, Commissaire chef de la Sûreté générale to Préfet.

45. ANOM Alger 1F / 33, Azazga, 27 September 1915, Administrateur adjoint to Administrateur; ANOM Constantine 93 / 5320, Tébessa, 2 May 1915, Administrateur de la Commune mixte du Haut-Sebaou to Préfet, and Azazga, 30 September 1915, "État nominative des individus recherchés originaires des Communes mixtes de Port-Gueydon, Azazga, Sidi-Aïch et Akbou"; ANOM Constantine 93 / 5326, 5–11 December 1911, "Rapport hebdomadaire sur la situation politique, La Calle"; ANOM Constantine 93 / 5321: Oued Marsa, 9 January 1917, Administrateur de la Commune mixte to Sous-préfet (Bougie); Alger, 12 February 1917, Procureur générale to GGA; Akbou, 10 September 1918, Administrateur de la Commune mixte to Préfet; and Bougie, 24 October 1918, letter to GGA.

46. ANOM Alger 1F / 33, Tizi-Ouzou, 5 March 1919, Sous-préfet to Préfet; ANOM Constantine 93 / 5326, 5–11 December 1915, Administrateur de la Commune mixte, "Rapport hebdomadaire sur la situation politique et l'état d'esprit des indigènes de la Commune mixte de La Calle," and Constantine, 20 December 1915, Commissaire to Chef de la Sûreté générale. The situation was so dire for local authorities in certain areas that officers recommended that the *duwars* be locked down, allowing no one in or out without special authorization, and a ban on all weapons and provisions held outside of one's home village.

47. Attacks of all three types were frequent. See, for example, ANOM Constantine 93 / 20183: Sidi Aïch, 3 December 1914, Administrateur de la Commune mixte de la Soummam to Sous-préfet; Sidi-Aïch, 12 October 1915, Administrateur de la Commune mixte de Soummam to Sous-préfet (Bougie); and Administrateur de la Commune mixte du Haut Sebaou to Préfet (re crimes on the Constantine side of the departmental bor-

der); and ANOM Constantine 93/20066, Akbou, 28 August 1917, Administrateur de la Commune mixte to Préfet. For multiple attacks and concomitant official declarations, see ANOM Constantine 93/5321, Biskra, 26 December 1914, Maire to Préfet; ANOM Constantine 93/5326, Bône, 16 November 1915, Rapport du Capitaine Lizet, Commandant l'arrondissement de Bône; ANOM Constantine 93/20018, GGA to Sûreté générale de Constantine, "Rapport annuel 1916"; and ANOM Constantine 93/20066, Akbou, 17 September 1917, Administrateur de la Commune mixte to Préfet.

48. ANOM/Constantine 93/20183, Sidi-Aïch, 3 December 1914, Administrateur de la Commune mixte de la Soummam to Sous-préfet; ANOM Constantine 93/5326, La Calle, 12 November 1915, Administrateur de la Commune mixte to Sous-préfet; and ANOM Constantine 93/5329: Constantine, 23 August 1917, Directeur des postes et des télégraphes to Préfet; Alger, 31 August, 5 October, and 10 October 1917, GGA to Préfet; and Sétif, 6 October 1917, Sous-préfet to Préfet. As usual, Muslim victims went unnamed; the authors of police and administrative reports identified only Europeans, who alone were deemed valuable and worthy of attention.

49. Achille Robert, "Attaques de diligences," *Dépêche de Constantine*, 17 January 1918; ANOM Constantine 93/5329, Alger, 4 February 1918, GGA to Préfet.

50. ANOM Constantine 93/5329, Sidi-Aïch, 22 December 1914, Administrateur de la Commune Mixte de la Soummam to Sous-préfet; ANOM Constantine 93/5321, Biskra, 26 December 1914, Maire to Sous-préfet; ANOM/Constantine 93/20183, Sidi-Aïch, 12 October 1915, Administrateur de la Commune mixte de la Soummam to Sous-préfet, and Sidi-Aïch, 9 November 1915, Administrateur de la Commune mixte de la Soummam to Préfet; and ANOM/Constantine 93/5326, Bône, 4 February 1916, Administrateur de la Commune mixte d'Edough to Sous-préfet.

51. ANOM/Constantine 93/5322, Constantine, 6 November 1917, Sûreté générale, "Rapport spécial."

52. Didier Guignard, *L'abus de pouvoir dans l'Algérie coloniale* (Paris, 2010), 180, 183–188.

53. Guignard, pt. 1.

54. ANOM Constantine 93/20066, Constantine, 21 December 1914, Directeur des postes et des télégraphes to Général commandant la division, Constantine; ANOM/Constantine 93/5326, Alger, 3 November 1915, Directeur des Chemins de fer algériens to Préfet (Constantine), and Châteaudun-du-Rhumel, 6 April 1916, Administrateur de la Commune mixte to Préfet; ANOM/Constantine 93/5322, Meskiana, 1 May 1916, Administrateur de la Commune mixte to Préfet; ANOM/Constantine 93/5320, Châteaudun, 4 January 1917, Administrateur de la Commune mixte to Préfet; ANOM Constantine 93/20066, Akbou, 17 September 1917, Administrateur de la Commune mixte to Préfet.

55. Colonna, *Le meunier, les moines*, 68–70.

56. Thomas, *Empires of Intelligence*, 26. The phenomenon of "information panic" was common throughout the French Empire.

57. ANOM Constantine 93/20183: Constantine, 31 October 1916, Directeur des Postes et des télégraphes to Préfet; Sidi-Aïch, 5 March 1917, Administrateur de la Commune mixte de la Soummam to Sous-préfet (Bougie); Alger, 24 March 1917, GGA to Préfet; and Sidi-Aïch, 8 May 1917, Administrateur de la Commune mixte to Sous-préfet (Bougie).

58. ANOM Alger 1F/34, La Chiffia, 24 January 1907, Maire to Préfet.

59. ANOM Constantine 93/5327, Bône, 14 April 1918, "Rapport—Sûreté générale," and 22 June 1918, Administrateur de la Commune Mixte Edough to Sous-préfet.

60. ANOM Constantine 93/5329, Sétif, 25 August 1917, Sous-préfet to Préfet.

61. ANOM Constantine 93/5329, Aïn-Jinn, 16 August 1919, Adjoint maire to Préfet; "La question indigène," *La Voix des colons*, 29 February 1920; "L'Algérie est en danger," *Echo d'Alger*, 3 June 1920.

62. ANOM Constantine 93/5326, Alger, 22 October 1915, GGA to Préfet; ANOM Constantine 93/20183, Général commandant la division de Constantine, "Minute," n.d. (June 1916); ANOM Constantine 93/20066, Akbou, 27 July 1916, Adminstrateur de la Commune mixte to Sous-préfet, and Akbou, 19 September 1916, Administrateur de la Commune mixte to Préfet; ANOM Constantine 93/5322, Constantine, 11 November 1916, Commissaire de la Sûreté générale, "Rapport."

63. ANOM Constantine 93/20183, Sidi-Aïch, 3 November 1916, Administrateur de la Commune mixte de la Soummam to Sous-préfet (Bougie).

64. ANOM/Constantine 93/20066, Sidi-Aïch, 29 October 1915, Administrateur de la Commune mixte de la Soummam to Préfet; ANOM/Constantine 93/5321, Alger, 13 November 1918, GGA to Préfet.

65. Bat and Courtin, *Maintenir l'ordre colonial*, 13, 17, 39; Thomas, *Empires of Intelligence*, 5.

66. Thomas, *Empires of Intelligence*, 33–36. Worse still, the author notes, Muslims were perceived by officers to be religious fanatics and ignorant peasants, easily led into disorder by shrewd political manipulators.

67. ANOM Alger 1F/33, Alger, 22 December 1915, Sûreté Générale, "Rapport"; Constantine 93/5326, Souk-Ahras, 3 December 1915, Administrateur de la Commune mixte de Souk-Ahras to Sous-préfet (Guelma), and Guelma, 27 November 1915, Sous-préfet (Guelma) to Préfet; Constantine 93/5327, La Calle, 24 May 1917, Administrateur de Commune mixte to Sous-préfet (Bône).

68. ANOM Constantine 93/5329, Bordj-Bou-Arréridj, 29 May 1918, Administrateur de la Commune mixte to Sous-Préfet (Sétif).

69. ANOM Constantine 93/5320, Tébessa, 17 December 1914, Administrateur de la Commune mixte de Morsott to Préfet, and Constantine, 19 January 1915, Préfet to GGA; ANOM Constantine 93/5326, Constantine, 4 November 1915, Préfet to Sous-préfet (Bône); ANOM/Constantine 93/20066, Sidi-Aïch, 16 November 1915, Administrateur de la Commune mixte de la Soummam to Sous-préfet; "À travers Bône," *Dépêche de l'Est*, 22 and 30 April 1915. The authors of the cited newspaper column regularly published broadsides about insecurity, appending letters from angered Europeans.

70. ANOM/Constantine 93/20066, Alger, 5 November 1915, Préfet, Alger to Préfet, Constantine; ANOM Constantine 93/5326, Guelma, 27 November 1915, Sous-préfet to Préfet.

71. ANOM Constantine 93/20066, Michelet, 18 February 1916, Administrateur de la Commune mixte du Djudjura to Administrateur de la Commune mixte de Biban, and Alger, 24 February 1916, GGA to Préfet.

72. ANOM/Constantine 93/20066, Alger, 27 June 1915, GGA to Préfet (Constantine).

73. ANOM / Constantine 93 / 5326, La Calle, 4 September 1915, Administrateur de la Commune mixte de La Calle, "Rapport sur les operations de recherches"; ANOM Constantine 93 / 5322, Alger, 25 May 1916, GGA to Préfet; ANOM Constantine 93 / 20183, Constantine, 23 November 1916, Général Baschung, Commandant la division de Constantine to Préfet.

74. ANOM Constantine 93 / 20183, Sidi-Aïch, 30 January 1917, Administrateur de la Commune mixte to Sous-préfet (Bougie), and Bougie, 9 February 1917, Sous-préfet to Préfet.

75. ANOM Constantine 93 / 20066: Alger, 24 February 1916, GGA to Préfet; Akbou, 10 December 1915, Administrateur de la Commune mixte to Préfet; Constantine, 27 November 1915, GGA to Préfet; and Alger, 27 July 1915, GGA to Préfet (Constantine); ANOM Constantine 93 / 20183, Constantine, 15 May 1917, Général de Lartigue, Commandant la Division de Constantine to Préfet. Notables from various locales wrote to the prefect demanding an end to the practice of demanding payment for police operations.

76. ANOM Constantine 93 / 5320, Constantine, 2 February 1915, Commissaire chef, Sûreté Générale to Préfet.

77. ANOM Constantine 93 / 20183: Sidi-Aïch, 3 November 1916, Administrateur de la Commune mixte to Sous-préfet; Sidi-Aïch, 4 December 1916, "Rapport sur la situation politique des indigènes du 26 novembre au 3 décembre 1916"; Sidi-Aïch, 30 January 1917, Administrateur de la Commune mixte to Sous-préfet (Bougie); Bougie, 9 February 1917, Sous-préfet to Préfet; Constantine, 18 March 1917, Général de Lartigue to Préfet; and Constantine, 7 May 1917, Préfet to Général commandant la division-Constantine.

78. ANOM Constantine 93 / 20183, Sidi-Aïch, 19 January 1915, Rapport du Brigadier, Sidi-Aïch sur une bande de malfaiteurs; ANOM Constantine 93 / 5320, Constantine, 10 November 1915, Commissaire chef de la Sûrete générale to Préfet; ANOM Constantine 93 / 20066, Sidi-Aïch, 18 December 1915, Administrateur de la Commune mixte de la Soummam to Préfet; ANOM Constantine 93 / 5326, Laverdure, 4 February 1916, Administrateur de la Commune mixte de Séfia to Sous-préfet (Guelma); ANOM Constantine 93 / 20066, Akbou, 3 October 1916, Administrateur de la Commune mixte to Sous-préfet; ANOM Constantine 93 / 20183, Sidi-Aïch, 29 May 1917, Administrateur de la Commune mixte de la Soummam to Sous-préfet (Bougie); ANOM Constantine 93 / 5320: Tébessa, 9 June 1917, Administrateur de la Commune mixte to Préfet.

79. ANOM Constantine 93 / 5326, "Rapport sur les opérations de recherches de la bande de malfaiteurs occupant la region forestière de Bouhadjar / Souk-Ahras, Ouled-Bechia, Reguegma, et La Cheffia," 4 September 1915; ANOM Constantine 93 / 20066, Akbou, 10 December 1915, Administrateur de la Commune mixte to Préfet; ANOM Constantine 93 / 20018, GGA, "Rapport annuel de 1916."

80. ANOM Constantine 93 / 20066, Akbou, 28 September 1915, Administrateur de la Commune mixte to Préfet, and Constantine, 13 October 1916, Préfet to GGA; ANOM Constantine 93 / 20183, Sidi Aich, 7 March 1918, Administrateur de la Commune mixte de la Soummam to Préfet; ANOM Constantine 93 / 5321, Sidi-Aïch, 18 June 1918, Administrateur de la Commune mixte de la Soummam to Sous-préfet (Bougie).

81. Meynier, *L'Algérie révélée*, 85; ANOM Constantine 93/5326, La Calle, 4 September 1915, "Rapport sur les opérations de recherche"; ANOM Constantine 93/20183, Sidi-Aïch, 6 November 1915, Administrateur de la Commune mixte de la Soummam to Sous-préfet (Bougie).

82. ANOM Constantine 93/5326, Bône, 22 January 1916, Sous-préfet (Bône) to Préfet. Concerning Younes's death, see ANOM Constantine 93/5326, Laverdure, 18 December 1915, Préfet to Sous-préfet (Bône).

83. See, for example, ANOM Constantine 93/20183, Sidi-Aïch, 19 January 1915, Administrateur de la Commune mixte de la Soummam to Sous-préfet, and Sidi-Aïch, 1 February 1915, Administrateur de la Commune mixte de la Soummam to Sous-préfet; ANOM Constantine 93/5326: "Rapport sur la mort du bandit Abdellali Ammar abbatu le 17 janvier [1916]"; Bône, 14 March 1916, Sous-préfet to Préfet; and La Calle, 11 July 1916, Administrateur de la Commune mixte to Sous-préfet (Bône).

84. ANOM Constantine 92/20066, Constantine, 1 March 1916, Commissaire chef de la Sûreté générale to Préfet; ANOM Constantine 93/5326: Alger, 30 December 1915, GGA to Préfet; Bône, 29 May 1916, Administrateur de la Commune mixte to Sous-préfet (Bône); n.d. (May 1916), Général Baschung to Préfet; Constantine 93/5327, Bône, 7 July 1915, Sous-préfet to Préfet, and La Calle, 7 September 1915, Administrateur to Préfet.

85. ANOM Constantine 93/5326, Souk-Ahras, 23 November 1915, Administrateur de la Commune mixte to Sous-préfet; ANOM/Constantine 93/5321, Akbou, 22 January 1918, Administrateur de la Commune mixte d'Akbou to Sous-préfet.

86. ANOM Constantine 93/5320, Tébessa, 10 December 1914, Administrateur de la Commune mixte de Morsott to Préfet; ANOM Constantine 93/5326, Souk-Ahras, 23 November 1915, Administrateur de la Commune mixte to Sous-préfet (Guelma), and Lamy, 25 April 1916, Chef de Bataillon, "Rapport"; ANOM Constantine 93/5321, Oued-Marsa, 23 November 1916, Administrateur de la Commune mixte to Procureur de la République (Bougie), and Bougie, 9 February 1917, Sous-préfet to Préfet; ANOM Constantine 93/2515, "Les Troubles insurrectionels de l'arrondissement de Batna en 1916."

87. ANOM Constantine/5326: Constantine, 13 March 1916, Préfet to Sous-Préfet; La Calle, 27 March 1916 and 26 March–1 April 1916 ("rapport hebdomadaire"), Administrateur de la Commune mixte to Sous-préfet; and Alger, 15 April 1916, GGA to Préfet.

88. ANOM Alger 1F/33, Azazga, 10 July 1916, Administrateur de la Commune mixte du Haut-Sébaou to Préfet.

89. Meynier, *L'Algérie révélée*, 569–572; ANOM Constantine 93/2515, "Les Troubles insurrectionnels de l'arrondissment de Batna en 1916," 3–4, 12–14, 61–98, 181.

90. Meynier, *L'Algérie révélée*, 591; ANOM Constantine 93/2515, "Les Troubles insurrectionnels de l'arrondissement de Batna en 1916," 98–101, 108–110, 113.

91. ANOM Constantine 93/2515, "Les Troubles insurrectionnels de l'arrondissment de Batna en 1916," 14–40.

92. Meynier, *L'Algérie révélée*, 591.

93. ANOM Constantine 93/5321, Alger, 2 July, 3 September, and 28 December 1917, GGA to Préfet; Constantine 93/5329, Bordj-Bou-Arréridj, 21 December 1917, Administrateur de la Commune mixte to Sous-préfet. Unfortunately, precise and reliable crime statistics are unavailable for the period in question. However, the comparative number of cases and dossiers extant in the relevant archives supports the contention that crime rose dramatically during this time.

94. ANOM / Constantine 93 / 20066, Sidi-Aïch, 16 November 1915, Administrateur de la Commune mixte de la Soummam to Sous-préfet; ANOM Constantine 93 / 5326, Alger, 7 April 1916, GGA to Préfet; ANOM Constantine 93 / 5321: Akbou, 18 February 1917, Administrateur de la Commune mixte to Sous-préfet (Bougie); Constantine, June 1917, Préfet to GGA; Bougie, 29 March 1918, Sous-préfet to Préfet; and Akbou, 6 April 1918, Administrateur de la Commune mixte to Préfet. In his monthly report for January 1916, the Sous-préfet for Sétif claimed that *surveillance spéciale* was responsible for a substantial decrease in crime. Given its lack of success in other locations, it is likely that the executions and patrols played a far greater role in the declining crime rate. See ANOM Constantine, 93 / 20066, Rapport mensuel, January 1916.

95. ANOM Alger 1F / 33, Alger, 13 May 1918, GGA to Préfet.

96. Daniel Neep, *Occupying Syria under the French Mandate: Insurgency, Space, and State Formation* (Cambridge, UK, 2014), 72. Complaints were particularly numerous in Druze territory, where suspects were often forced into the so-called coal cellar, a cell five square meters in size and only 1.7 meters high. Many of those who were charged were not guilty but rather were victims of informants who had named them to receive a cash payment.

97. ANOM Constantine 93 / 5210, Sétif, 7 August 1917, Sous-préfet to Préfet.

98. ANOM Constantine 93 / 20066, Akbou, 9 January 1916, Administrateur de la Commune mixte to Préfet, and Alger, 7 February 1916, GGA to Préfet (Constantine); ANOM Constantine 93 / 5326: Alger, 14 March 1916, GGA to Préfet; La Calle, 27 March 1916 and 5 April 1916, Administrateur de la Commune mixte to Sous-préfet (Bône); and Bougie, 15 January 1917, Sous-préfet to Préfet.

99. Fogarty, *Race and War in France*, 252–260.

100. Meynier, *L'Algérie révélée*, 677–697.

101. ANOM Constantine 93 / 5329, Constantine, 21 June 1919, Commissaire chef, Sûreté général to Préfet. Illegal markets sprouted up throughout 1919 in Kroubs, Bizet, Conde-Smendou, Jemmapes, and Beni-Ouelbane.

102. ANOM Alger 1F / 34, Alger, 29 October 1920, General Deshayes de Bonnneval to Préfet.

103. McDougall, *History of Algeria*, 136–137; Rosenberg, *Policing Paris*; MacMaster, *Colonial Migrants and Racism*, 80.

104. ANOM Alger 1F / 33, Tigzirt, 11 April 1919, Garde champêtre to Sous-préfet.

105. ANOM Constantine 93 / 5329, Akbou, 6 May 1919, Administrateur de la Commune mixte to Préfet, and Bougie, 3 June 1919, Procureur de la République, Bougie to Sous-préfet.

106. ANOM Constantine 93 / 5329, Akbou, 7 June, 21 July, and 25 July 1919, Administrateur de la Commune mixte to Sous-préfet, Bougie.

107. ANOM Constantine 93 / 5329: Akbou, 13 August 1919, Administrateur de la Commune mixte to Préfet; Lafayette, 21 February 1920, Administrateur de la Commune mixte to Sous-préfet; and Alger, 4 March 1920, GGA to Préfet.

3. Unlawful Acts or Strategies of Resistance?

1. ANOM Constantine 93 / 1740, Bougie, 30 April 1935, Sous-préfet to Préfet.

2. See numerous reports in ANOM Constantine / 1740 detailing dozens of assaults and attempts to murder European and Algerian *gardes champêtres* throughout the interwar era.

3. Thomas, *Empires of Intelligence*, 202–204.

4. McDougall, *History of Algeria*, 131–133.

5. McDougall, 143–147; David Prochaska, *Making Algeria French: Colonialism in Bône, 1870–1920* (Cambridge, UK, 1990), 232–235; Omar Carlier, *Entre nation et jihad: Histoire sociale des radicalismes algériens* (Paris, 1995), 51–57.

6. McDougall, *History of Algeria*, 83–85, 143–145; Carlier, *Entre nation et jihad*, 111–121; Meuleman, *Le Constantinois entre les deux guerres mondiales*, 287–292.

7. Carlier, *Entre nation et jihad*, 36–38, 46–47; Kaddache, *Histoire du nationalisme algérien*, 471–475.

8. ANOM Oran 5I/101, 25 June 1938, "Le Parti du peuple algérien: Membres du groupement en France et en Algérie"; Kaddache, *Histoire du nationalisme algérien*, 444–445, 465.

9. Kaddache, 44–51; ANOM Alger 4I/6, Alger, 4 November 1937, Sûreté départementale d'Alger, "Rapport"; ANOM Oran 5I/102, Alger, 21 November 1937, Sûreté départementale d'Alger, "Rapport," and Alger, 25 February 1938, Police spéciale départementale, "Rapport."

10. ANOM Constantine B/3/567, Constantine, 15 July 1936, Sûreté départmentale de Constantine, "Meeting du Front populaire"; ANOM GGA 3CAB/89, Oran, 18 January 1937, Chef de la Sûreté départementale to Préfet; Allison Drew, *We Are No Longer French: Communists in Colonial Algeria* (Manchester, UK, 2014), chap. 4; Ahmed Koulaksiss, *Le Parti socialiste et l'Afrique du nord: De Jaurès à Blum* (Paris, 1991), 182, 247250, 266, 291; Thomas, *French Empire*, 247249; René Gallissot, *La République française et les indigènes: Algérie colonisée, Algérie algérienne (1870–1962)* (Paris, 2006), 105–114.

11. McDougall, *History of Algeria*, 155–161.

12. Isabelle Merle, "De la légalisation de la violence en contexte colonial," *Politix* 17 (2004): 139–147.

13. McDougall, *History of Algeria*, 152.

14. McDougall, 4.

15. Neil MacMaster, "The Roots of Insurrection: The Role of the Algerian Village Assembly (Djemâa) in Peasant Resistance, 1863–1902," *Comparative Studies in History and Society* 52 (2013): 419–422.

16. Kalyvas, *Logic of Violence*, 40–48.

17. Valentin Chémery, "Policing and the Problem of Crime within Local Communities in Colonial Algeria, ca. 1850–1890," in *Policing in Colonial Empires: Cases, Connections, Boundaries*, ed. Emmanuel Blanchard, Marieke Bloembergen, and Amandine Lauro (Brussels, 2017), 119, 127, 131.

18. For a discussion of the military defeat of rebels during colonization campaigns after 1830, see Gallois, *History of Violence*. On the failure of the Muqrani rebellion, see Ruedy, *Modern Algeria*, 77–79.

19. Samuel Kalman, "Criminalizing Dissent: Policing Banditry in the Constantinois, 1914–1918," in *Algeria Revisited: History, Culture, and Identity*, ed. Rabah Aissaoui and Claire Eldridge (London, 2017).

20. Thénault, *Violence ordinaire*, 40–62.

21. Amit Prakash, "Colonial Techniques in the Imperial Capital: The Prefecture of Police and the Surveillance of North Africans in Paris, 1925–circa 1970," *French Historical Studies* 36 (2013): 486; Thomas, *Empires of Intelligence*, 77–78; Richard Keller, *Co-*

lonial Madness: Psychiatry in French North Africa (Chicago, IL, 2007), 122–127, 138–152; Dominique Kalifa, Crime et culture au XIXe siècle (Paris, 2005), 257–262.

22. Stephen Legg, Spaces of Colonialism: Delhi's Urban Governmentalities (London, 2007), 213–215; Ranajit Guha, Dominance without Hegemony: History and Power in Colonial India (Cambridge, UK, 1997), 3–4, 24–28.

23. Peyroulou, Guelma, 1945, 66–68. The most notable widescale example of such actions was the Constantine riot of August 1934, which will be discussed in chapter 4.

24. Kamel Kateb, Européens, "indigènes," et juifs en Algérie (1830–1962) (Paris, 2001); Mahé, Histoire de la Grande Kabylie, chap. 1.

25. ANOM Constantine 93 / 5357, Jemmapes, 31 August 1934, Administrateur de la Commune mixte to Sous-Préfet, and Khenchela, 18 June 1935, Administrateur de la Commune mixte to Sous-Préfet.

26. Meuleman, Le Constantinois entre les deux guerres mondiales, 21, 38–48, 55–57, 100, 135, 142, 183–193. On the "economy of poverty" in the urban setting, see Prochaska, Making Algeria French, 124.

27. ANOM Constantine B / 3 / 360, Philippeville, 29 March 1924, Chef de la Brigade mobile, "Rapport spécial."

28. ANOM Constantine 93 / 20329: Sétif, 13 September 1920, "Police—rapport journalier"; Sétif, 18 September 1930, Sous-Préfet to Préfet; and Alger, 16 September 1930, GGA to Préfet; "Une grave affaire de trafic d'armes," Presse Libre, 31 June 1931.

29. ANOM Constantine 93 / 5379, Bougie, 9 December 1929, Brigade mobile de Batna, "Rapport spécial," and Constantine, 27 March 1930, "Rapport de l'inspecteur Defendin"; Constantine 93 / 5436, Aokas, 5 March 1932, Administrateur de la Commune mixte de l'Oued Marsa to Sous-Préfet (Bougie); ANOM Constantine 93 / 20329, Sétif, 11 June 1930, Commissaire chef de la Brigade mobile to Direcetur de la Sécurité générale.

30. ANOM Constantine 93 / 5347, Constantine, 30 September 1921, Commissaire chef de la Sûreté générale to Préfet; ANOM Constantine 93 / 20329, Sétif, 11 June 1930, Commissaire chef de la Brigade mobile to Directeur de la Sécurité générale; ANOM Constantine 93 / 5436, Bougie, 25 August 1938, Brigade mobile de Bougie, "Rapport spécial."

31. ANOM Constantine 93 / 5435, "Extrait du procès—verbal de la séance du 1 octobre 1925," Conseil général de Constantine, and Alger, 26 April 1929, GGA to Préfet; Constantine 93 / 20182, Constantine, 1 January 1929, "Rapport d'ensembles sur les travaux des Brigades mobiles, Constantine-1928"; Constantine 93 / 1733, Constantine, 1 January 1932, "Rapport d'ensembles sur les travaux des Brigades mobiles, 1931."

32. ANOM Constantine 93 / 5346, Alger, 29 January 1932, GGA to Préfet.

33. ANOM Constantine 93 / 5436, Alger, 1 February 1936, Procureur général to GGA.

34. ANOM Constantine 93 / 20072, Corneille, 17 October 1923, Administrateur de la Commune mixte de Bélezma to Préfet. See also ANOM Constantine 93 / 20073, Aïn-Beïda, 3 June 1924, Note du Commissaire chef de la Brigade mobile.

35. ANOM, Constantine 93 / 5334, Constantine, 12 July 1928, Sûreté générale de Constantine, "Rapport spécial."

36. ANOM Constantine 93 / 20074, Batna, 4 March 1924, "Rapport spécial," and Constantine, 29 March 1924, Commissaire chef de la Brigade mobile de Constantine

to Chef de la Sûreté générale; ANOM Constantine 93/20182, Constantine, 13 September 1929, "Rapport spécial"; ANOM Constantine 93/20163, Philippeville, 1 August 1934, "Rapport spécial"; ANOM Constantine 93/5436, Alger, 1 February 1936, Procureur général to GGA.

37. ANOM Constantine 93/20074: Constantine, 18 April 1923, "Rapport spécial"; Aïn-M'Sila, 15 January 1924, Administrateur de la Commune mixte to Préfet; and Constantine, 5 February 1924, Commissaire de la Sûreté générale to Chef de la Sûreté générale.

38. ANOM Constantine 93/5436, Batna, 23 December 1937, Chef de la Brigade mobile to Commissaire divisionnaire.

39. ANOM Constantine 93/20073, Constantine, 6 April 1924, "Rapport spécial"; ANOM Constantine 93/20182, Constantine, 6 February 1929, "Rapport spécial"; ANOM Constantine 93/20329, El-Milia, 4 April 1931, Administrateur de la Commune mixte to Préfet, and Constantine, 9 April 1931, "Rapport spécial de Commissaire chef de la Brigade mobile."

40. On the Beni-Falkai mine theft, see a series of reports in ANOM Constantine 93/20062, May–August 1922. Police concerns were justified, as thefts regularly occurred throughout Algeria during the interwar era. See, for example, ANOM Constantine 93/20074, Bône, 18 February 1924, "Rapport spécial"; ANOM Constantine 93/5379, Philippeville, 6 September 1929, Sûreté général, "Rapport special."

41. ANOM Constantine 93/5436, Constantine, 19 July 1937, Administrateur-Directeur, Sidi-Kember Mine to Administrateur de la Commune mixte de Collo.

42. ANOM Constantine 93/5436, Alger, 27 January 1938, GGA to Préfet. The administration took the danger so seriously that even the mere detonation of any device in a public place was classed in the criminal code as attempted murder. See Raymond Curat and André Knoertzer, *L'officier de police judiciaire en Algérie* (Alger, 1924), 335, 344345.

43. Keith Neilson and T. J. Otte, "Railpolitik: An Introduction," in *Railways and International Politics: Paths of Empire, 1848–1925*, ed. Keith Neilson and T. J. Otte (New York, 2006), 1–14; Lefeuvre, *Chère Algérie*, 25–30.

44. ANOM Constantine 93/20040, Morsott, December 1920, "Rapport mensuel"; ANOM Constantine 93/5397, Tébessa, 28 February 1930, Brigade mobile, Tébessa, "Rapport special." The Spahis and the Tirailleurs sénégalais were indigenous army units.

45. ANOM Constantine 93/5329, Constantine, 21 June 1919, Préfet to Général commandant la division; ANOM Constantine/20332, La Calle, 10 November 1925, Administrateur de la Commune mixte to Préfet.

46. ANOM Constantine 93/20043, Batna, 11 August 1921, "Rapport special"; ANOM Constantine 93/20072, Aïn-M'Sila, 31 March 1923, Administrateur de la Commune mixte to Préfet; Constantine 93/20074, Guelma, 21 June 1924, "Rapport special," and Bougie, 26 August 1926, "Rapport special"; ANOM Constantine 93/20074, Arrête, Commune mixte de Châteaudun, 4 September 1925; ANOM Constantine 93/20092, Aïn-Beida, 26 January 1928, "Rapport special."

47. J. A. Mangan, "Britain's Chief Export: Imperial Sport as Moral Metaphor, Political Symbol, and Cultural Bond," in *The Cultural Bond: Sport, Empire, Society*, ed. J. A. Mangan (New York, 1992), 1–9.

48. Philip Dine, "Shaping the Colonial Body: Sport and Society in Algeria, 1870–1962," in *Algeria and France, 1800–2000: Identity, Memory, Nostalgia*, ed. Patricia Lorcin (Syracuse, NY, 2006), 33–48.

49. Youcef Fates, *Sport et politique en Algérie* (Paris, 2009), 191–194, 257, 325; Youcef Fates, "Les marqueurs du nationalisme: Les clubs sportifs musulmans dans l'Algérie coloniale," *Quasimodo* 3–4 (1997), 121–129; Philip Dine, "France, Algeria, and Sport," in *Algeria and France, 1800–2000: Identity, Memory, Nostalgia*, ed. Patricia M. E. Lorcin (Syracuse, NY, 2006), 495–505.

50. ANOM Constantine 93 / 20189, Constantine, 24 November 1925, "Procès-Verbal."

51. ANOM GGA 9H / 39, Blida, 13 January 1937, Commissaire de police du 2e arrondissement to Commissaire chef, and "Audition de témoin (Celeste Morette)," 13 January 1937.

52. ANOM Constantine 93 / 5397, Constantine, 31 March 1930, Commissaire central to Préfet; ANOM Constantine 93 / 20082, Constantine, 28 May 1934, Commissaire central to Préfet; ANOM Constantine 93 / 20162, Bône, 25 March 1935, Commissaire central to Directeur de la Sûrete générale.

53. ANOM Constantine 93 / 20162, Constantine, 28 February 1935, Commissaire central to Préfet.

54. ANOM Constantine 93 / 20162, Bône, 25 March 1935, Commissaire central to Directeur de la Sécurité générale.

55. ANOM GGA 9H / 39, Constantine, 7 March 1938, Préfet to GGA.

56. ANOM GGA 9H / 39, "Rapport journalier / 9 mars 1941—Boufarik."

57. ANOM GGA 9H / 39, Alger, 20 January 1928, GGA to Préfets, Alger, Constantine, and Oran.

58. ANOM GGA 9H / 39, Alger, 11 January 1928 and 11 June 1931, letters to Préfets, and Oran, 28 March 1936, Conseil d'administration de l'Union sportive musulmane oranaise to GGA; ANOM Constantine 93 / 5378, Bône, 4 November 1934, mayoral decree.

59. ANOM GGA 9H / 39, Djidjelli, 18 January 1937 and 24 January 1938, Commissaire de police to Préfet, and Constantine, 14 April and 27 May 1938, Préfet to GGA. On the history of fan violence in Djidjelli, see ANOM GGA 9H / 39, Djidjelli, 15 May 1936, Maire to Sous-préfet, Bougie.

60. ANOM GGA 9H / 39, Oran, 1 April 1936 and 23 September 1936, Préfet to GGA, and Paris, 30 January 1937, Sous-secrétaire d'état to GGA.

61. ANOM GGA 9H / 39, Oran, 25 August 1938, Commissaire divisionnaire to Préfet; Hadj Salah, Conseiller municipal, Oran, "Le Cas des équipes musulmanes de football," *Oran Républicain*, 26 August 1938.

62. ANOM GGA 9H / 39: Constantine, 10 July 1933, "Rapport—Sûreté départementale de Constantine"; "Memo—mission du 26 au 28 mai 1935"; and Constantine, 21 November 1938, "Rapport, Police de Constantine."

63. ANOM GGA 9H / 39, Oran, 11 April 1938, Commissaire divisionnaire to Préfet.

64. Stoler, *Along the Archival Grain*, 181–198, 217. As Stoler asserts, the European role in causing criminal activity and unrest is often minimized or ignored, while the *indigène* is cast as barbaric and violent by nature rather than as responding to the colonial situation and their socioeconomic exploitation.

65. ANOM Constantine 93 / 20060, Lamy, 12 April 1921, Préfet to GGA; ANOM Constantine 93 / 20072, Bône, 12 September 1923, Report to Commissaire central; ANOM Constantine 93 / 20074, Bordj-Bou-Arréridj, 22 January 1926, Préfet to Sous-préfet (Sétif), and El-Milia, 30 August 1926, Administrateur de la Commune mixte to Préfet. The hijacking was not an isolated incident; this type of attack became a regular hazard throughout the 1920s.

66. ANOM Constantine 93 / 5327, Bône, 20 January 1920, GGA to Chef de la Sûreté générale; ANOM Constantine 93 / 5383, Bône, 26 November 1933, Les habitants de Duzerville to GGA.

67. Anne McClintock, *Imperial Leather: Race, Gender, and Sexuality in the Colonial Contest* (New York, 1995), 44; Ann Laura Stoler, *Race and the Education of Desire: Foucault's History of Sexuality and the Colonial Order of Things* (Durham, NC, 1995), 8; Jock McCulloch, *Black Peril, White Virtue: Sexual Crime in Southern Rhodesia, 1902–1935* (Bloomington, IN, 2000), 4–12, 26–32, 83; Angela Woollacott, *Gender and Empire* (Basingstoke, UK, 2006), 43–45. A key difference in the French case concerned the policing of female desire, which was less in evidence in official reports and correspondence. However, it is noteworthy that in both cases, white men were never charged with similar crimes against nonwhite women.

68. ANOM Constantine 93 / 5334, Philippeville, 16 May 1928, Commissaire de la Sûreté générale to Préfet; ANOM Constantine 93 / 20182, Batna, 11 June 1929, Inspecteur, Brigade mobile, "Rapport spécial." The demonization of European women in sexual relationships with Muslim men extended to murder cases, with conflicting results. In the case of a murdered brothel owner in Châteaudun, for example, police derisorily referred to the victim as the concubine of the Algerian murderer, and clearly did not take the case as seriously as other killings of Europeans. However, police referred to the killing of a French woman by a Muslim lover in Barika as a crime against the entire community, which essentially proved that Muslims represented a threat to Caucasian females throughout the colony. ANOM Constantine 93 / 20040, Châteaudun, November 1921, "Rapport Mensuel"; ANOM Constantine 93 / 5334, Barika, 3 April 1928, Administrateur de la Commune mixte de Barika to Sous-préfet.

69. McCulloch, *Black Peril, White Virtue*, 26–32.

70. ANOM Constantine 93 / 20207, Philippeville, 30 July 1936, Chef de la Brigade mobile, "Rapport spécial." There was a similar situation with regard to children, with only one reported case: in July 1936, a Guelma boy who joined an Algerian on a bird hunting excursion a few kilometers outside of town was sexually assaulted at knifepoint. See ANOM Constantine 93 / 20207, Guelma, 16 July 1936, "Rapport spécial."

71. ANOM Constantine 93 / 20162, Constantine, 11 June 1935, Commissaire central to Préfet; ANOM Constantine 93 / 20108, Bône, 29 July 1935, Commissaire central to Directeur de la Sécurité générale. In certain such cases, alcohol appeared to be a factor. In January 1935, a policeman and his brother were sitting down to dinner when a group of five young ladies burst into the apartment, claiming that a drunk Algerian had followed them for quite some distance. The man in question followed them into the apartment, demanded to see the women, and ended up in a brawl with the policeman and a colleague passing outside the building. See ANOM Constantine 93 / 1742, Bône, 9 January 1935, Commissaire central to Directeur de la Sécurité générale.

72. ANOM Constantine 93 / 20060, Bône, 12 September 1921, "Rapport de Chef de la Brigade mobile"

73. Ann Laura Stoler, *Carnal Knowledge and Imperial Power: Race and the Intimate in Colonial Rule* (Berkeley, CA, 2002), 58–59.

74. Kateb, *Européens, "indigènes," et juifs*, 176, 272; Mahé, *Histoire de la Grande Kabylie*, 288–290.

75. For example, see ANOM Constantine B / 3 / 360, Philippeville, 17 May 1926, Chef de la Brigade mobile, "Rapport spécial."

76. See, for example, ANOM Constantine 93 / 1745, Bougie, 16 January 1936, "Rapport spécial," and Batna, 21 April 1936, "Rapport spécial."

77. Confessions were often obtained after very lengthy (and fraudulent) interrogations of suspects. For a case where the fingerprints did not match, and neither witnesses nor murder weapon could be found, see ANOM Constantine 93 / 5397, Batna, 16 March 1930, "Rapport spécial."

78. ANOM Constantine 93 / 5379, "Rapport d'ensemble sur les travaux effectués et les résultats obtenus," Sûreté générale, 1929.

79. There are literally hundreds of police reports detailing Algerian murder cases in mundane terms, with the authors chalking matters up to yet another cheating spouse, angry sibling, etc. For the Sétif case file, see ANOM Constantine 93 / 20182, Sétif, 14 June 1929, Commissaire chef to Directeur de la Sécurité générale.

80. ANOM Constantine 93 / 5379, Sûreté générale de Constantine, "Rapport ensemble sur les travaux effectués et les résultats obtenus."

81. ANOM Constantine 93 / 20059, Sétif, 17–22 December 1921, "Rapport spécial," and Sétif, 15 December 1921, Commissaire de police to Sous-préfet; ANOM Constantine 93 / 5347, Guelma, 1 November 1922, Commissaire de la Sûreté générale, "Rapport special."

82. ANOM Constantine 93 / 20060, Bône, 14 May 1922, "Rapport sur l'assassinat de la veuve Dujau."

83. ANOM Constantine 93 / 20060, Bône, 26 April 1921, Administrateur de la Commune mixte d'Edough to Préfet; ANOM Constantine 93 / 20072, Batna, 3 January 1923, Commissaire chef de la Brigade mobile, Report.

84. Lefeuvre, *Chère Algérie*, 12–13, 36–38, 50–60, 76–81.

85. ANOM Constantine 93 / 5397, Constantine, 10 February 1930, Sûreté générale, "Rapport spécial"; ANOM Constantine 93 / 5327, Bône, 3 October 1930, Administration de la Commune mixte d'Edough to Sous-préfet, and Bône, 7 October 1930, Chef de la Brigade mobile to Préfet. On the penalties applied for trespassing and other infractions deemed illegal by Europeans, see Guignard, *L'abus de pouvoir*, 44–60.

86. ANOM Constantine 93 / 20040, Bône, 25 January 1921, GGA to Chef de la Sûreté générale.

87. ANOM Constantine 93 / 20043, Batna, 27 May 1921, Sous-préfet to Préfet, and MacMahon, 28 May 1921, Administrateur de la Commune mixte to Préfet.

88. ANOM Constantine 93 / 1744, Khenchela, 5 August 1937, Administrateur de la Commune mixte to Sous-préfet, Batna. For other examples, see Constantine 93 / 20063, Sétif, September 1921, "Service des communes mixtes", Rapport mensuel; ANOM Constantine 93 / 20074, Canrobert, 24 August 1926, Administrateur de la Commune mixte, Oum-el-Bouaghi to Préfet.

89. ANOM Constantine 93 / 20063, Service des Communes mixtes, Rapport mensuel, M'Sila, September 1921.

90. ANOM Constantine 93 / 5383, Jemmapes, 29 June 1934, Administrateur de la Commune mixte to Préfet, and Alger, 11 September 1934, GGA to Préfet.

91. Kaddache, *Histoire du nationalisme algérien*, 29–30.

92. ANOM Constantine 93 / 1744, Khenchela, 5 August 1937, Administrateur de la Commune mixte to Sous-préfet; Constantine 93 / 5321, Sidi-Aïch, 16 July 1918, Administrateur de la Commune mixte, Soummam to Sous-préfet, Bougie.

93. ANOM Constantine 93 / 20162, Collo, 1 April 1935, "Rapport de l'administrateur de la Commune mixte."

94. ANOM Constantine 93 / 20205, Bougie, 16 June 1936, "Rapport spécial."

95. As Richard Keller has noted, psychiatry frequently served as a convenient mask for colonial racism and violence, particularly in Algeria, where settlers and officials used it to suppress anticolonial sentiment. That the discipline could also assist in the emancipation of Arabs and Kabyles in practice rather than theory was never considered. Yet it was nonetheless regularly used to demonstrate the supposed primitiveness and criminality of Algerians. Keller, *Colonial Madness*, 1–18.

96. Chevandier, *Policiers dans la ville*; Roger Le Doussal, *Commissaire de police en Algérie (1952–1962): Une grenouille dans son puits ne voit qu'un coin de ciel* (Paris, 2011).

97. Partha Chatterjee, *The Nation and Its Fragments: Colonial and Postcolonial Histories* (Princeton, NJ, 1993), chap. 2.

98. See ANOM Constantine 93 / 20072, Alger, 24 March 1923, GGA to Préfet, and Aïn-Beida, 1 March 1923, Report to Commissaire chef, Brigade mobile; ANOM Constantine 93 / 20182, Constantine, 29 June 1929, "Rapport special."

99. ANOM Constantine 93 / 20332, Bordj-bou-Arréridj, 1 June 1925 and 16 June 1925, Administrateur de la Commune mixte, Maadid to Préfet, and Constantine, 5 June 1925, Général Odry, Commandant la division de Constantine to Préfet. On the Rif War, see Thomas, *French Empire*, 211–218.

100. ANOM Constantine 93 / 20332: Bordj-Bou-Arréridj, 1 June 1925, Administrateur de la Commune mixte, Maadid to Préfet; Constantine, 5 June 1925, General Odry, Commandant la division de Constantine to Préfet; and Bordj-Bou-Arréridj, 8 June 1925, Sous-préfet to Préfet.

101. ANOM Constantine 93 / 20074, Bône, 11 January 1928, Commissaire central to Directeur de la Sécurité générale.

102. ANOM Constantine 93 / 20074, Constantine, 7–16 January 1924, Commissaire chef de la Sûreté générale to Directeur de la Sécurité générale.

103. ANOM Constantine 93 / 5397: "Audition de témoin," 16 January 1930; Bône, 14 February 1930, Administrateur de la Commune mixte d'Edough to Sous-préfet; and Bône, 15 February 1930, Sous-préfet to Préfet.

104. ANOM Constantine 93 / 5398, Sétif, 3 May 1928, "Rapport du Capitaine Bellot, Commandant la section du Sétif."

105. ANOM Constantine 93 / 5397, Kerrata, 20 February 1930, Ali le Messaoud to Préfet, and Takitount, 6 March 1930, Administrateur de la Commune mixte to Préfet.

106. ANOM Constantine 93 / 5398, Sétif, 3 May 1928, "Rapport du Capitaine Bellot, commandant la section," and Akbou, 19 March 1928, Administrateur de la Commune mixte to Préfet; ANOM Constantine 93 / 20332, Sétif, 11 September 1925,

Sous-préfet to Préfet, and Bibans, August 1925, "Service des Communes mixtes—Rapport mensuel."

107. ANOM Constantine 93 / 20074, Sétif, 11 December 1924, "Rapport special," and Philippeville, 7 January 1925, Commissaire de la Sûreté générale to Chef de la Sûreté générale; ANOM Constantine 93 / 1345, Collo, 6 April 1929, Maire de la commune to Préfet; ANOM Constantine 93 / 5357, Biskra, 9 April 1935, Secrétaire-inspecteur Reitz to Maire; ANOM Constantine 93 / 20205, Bône, 18 May 1936, Commissaire central to Directeur de la Sécurité générale; ANOM Constantine 93 / 1740, Oued Meriel, 4 April 1939, "Rapport du Caïd."

108. ANOM Constantine 93 / 20043, Batna, 30 July, 6 September, and 1 October 1921, Sous-préfet to Préfet.

109. Berlière and Levy, *Histoire des polices en France*, 562–567; ANOM Constantine 93 / 20040, Constantine, 27 June 1916, Préfet to Commissaire central; ANOM Constantine 93 / 1740, Oued Meriel, 4 April 1939, Caïd to Administrateur.

110. ANOM Constantine 93 / 20072: Bordj-Bou-Arréridj, 10 April 1923, Administrateur de la Commune mixte to Sous-Préfet; Bône, 17 April 1923, Adminstrateur de la Commune mixte to Préfet; and Tebessa, 18 May 1923, Administrateur de la Commune mixte to Préfet; ANOM Constantine 93 / 5332, Constantine, 4 October 1923, Commissaire chef de la Sûreté générale to Directeur de la Sécurité générale; ANOM Constantine 93 / 5379, Constantine, 24 October 1929, Chef de la Brigade mobile to Directeur de la Sécurité générale; ANOM Constantine 93 / 20162, Constantine, 23 May 1935, Commissaire central to Préfet; ANOM Constantine 93 / 5379, Sûreté générale, 1929, "Rapport d'ensemble sur les travaux effectués et les resultats obtenus."

111. See, for example, ANOM Constantine 93 / 5332, Constantine, 28 July 1922, Commissaire chef de la Sûreté générale to Directeur de la Sécurité générale.

112. ANOM Constantine 93 / 5332, Constantine, 5 October 1923, Commissaire de la Sûreté générale to Chef de la Sécurité générale; ANOM Constantine 93 / 1742, Alger, 15 October 1935, Procureur général to Préfet. The sentences were carried out shortly after dawn, prior to the beginning of the workday, when crowds began to gather in the streets.

113. ANOM Constantine 93 / 20074, El-Milia, 9 August 1926, Administrateur de la Commune mixte to Préfet.

114. ANOM Constantine 93 / 5334, Barika, 26 March 1928, Administrateur de la Commune mixte to Préfet; ANOM Constantine 93 / 5357, Constantine, 5 April 1935, Préfet to Maire, Biskra.

115. ANOM Constantine 93 / 20060, "Procès verbal," 24 July 1921, and Alger, 7 September 1921, GGA to Préfet; ANOM Constantine 93 / 20043, Khenchela, 4 November 1922, Commissaire de police to Préfet; ANOM Constantine 93 / 20072, Akbou, 28 February 1923, Administrateur de la Commune mixte to Préfet; ANOM Constantine 93 / 5383, Bône, 26 November 1933, Les habitants de Duzerville to GGA.

116. Sherman, *State Violence and Punishment in India*, 5–8, 36–40.

4. Colonial Policing during Wartime

1. Jacques Cantier, *L'Algérie sous le regime de Vichy* (Paris, 2002), 54.
2. Cantier, 40–41, 52–53.

3. Cantier, 82–92; Kalman, *French Colonial Fascism*, 85, 100–104. The exception to the mayoral rule was the Oran chief *abbé* Gabriel Lambert, whose immoral and corrupt conduct led to his outright dismissal.

4. On the prevalence of the Extreme Right in Algeria, see Kalman, *French Colonial Fascism*.

5. Cantier, *L'Algérie sous le regime*, 141–146.

6. Cantier, 59–60, 65–81.

7. Cantier, 67–81; Roberts, *Citizenship and Antisemitism*, 272, 283–284.

8. Lefeuvre, *Chère Algérie*, 209–211.

9. Cantier, *L'Algérie sous le regime*, 55, 111–118, 169–176.

10. Alfred Salinas, *Pétain, Algérie et la revanche* (Paris, 2018), 266–267; Pierre Darmon, *L'Algérie de Pétain: Les populations algériennes ont la parole, septembre 1939–novembre 1942* (Paris, 2014), 196.

11. Berlière, *Le monde des polices*, 169–173.

12. Kalman, "Avec une brutalité," 49–51.

13. Kalman, 52–59.

14. Cantier, *L'Algérie sous le regime*, 33; Julian Jackson, *France: The Dark Years, 1940–1944* (Oxford, 2001), 169, 179, 220–223. For examples of concerns about police and gendarme POWs, see ANOM Constantine 93 / 6791, notes of 27 and 29 November 1940. Unfortunately, there is no information about the number of settler and Algerian prisoners, in these or other documents.

15. Jackson, *Dark Years*, 161–163.

16. Berlière, *Le monde des polices*, 175, 192–193.

17. Salinas, *Pétain, Algérie et la revanche*, 248, 257–261.

18. Salinas, 252–253.

19. ANOM Alger 1F / 422, GGA, "Arrête," 20 April 1940, and Alger, 19 March 1941, Commissaire central to Préfet. The ultimate failure of the plan to hire trainees to replace missing officers led to a desperate November 1942 announcement that the newly hired would be paid the same wages and benefits as those they replaced. See ANOM Alger 1F / 439, GGA, "Arrête," 23 November 1942.

20. ANOM Constantine 93 / 6786, Souk-Ahras, 16 July 1941, Maire to Préfet.

21. ANOM Constantine 93 / 6786, Alger, 7 July 1941, Colonel Gross, Chef de la delegation de la Direction des services de l'armistice to GGA, and "Note memorandum," n.d. (November 1941).

22. ANOM Constantine 93 / 6885, Constantine, 23 June 1942, Préfet to Commissaire central. In addition to rival services poaching members, the Italian delegation of the Contrôle de l'armée made numerous attempts to commandeer goums and / or *douairs*, but was soundly rebuffed by the French authorities. See ANOM GGA 9H / 26, Alger, 10 May 1941, Colonel Gross, Chef de la délégation de la Direction des services de l'armistice de l'Afrique du nord to GGA.

23. ANOM Oran / 167, Oran, 24 August 1943, Commissaire principal, RG to Préfet.

24. ANOM Alger 1F / 439, Alger, 18 January 1943, GGA to Préfet; ANOM Constantine 93 / 6884, Constantine, 14 June 1943, Lieutenant-Colonel Commandant la gendarmerie du département to Préfet, and Constantine, 10 June 1943, "Rapport du Chef d'escadron Ducay."

25. Darmon, *L'Algérie de Pétain*, 203–206.

26. ANOM Alger 91303 / 67, Alger, 22 August 1941, Préfet to Sous-préfet, Miliana.
27. Jackson, *Dark Years*, 128–129.
28. On fears of pro-British sentiment, see ANOM Alger 91303 / 67, Alger, 8 July 1940, Préfet to Sous-préfet. For an actual rare sighting of Gaullist propaganda, see ANOM Alger 91303 / 67, Miliana, 9 May 1941, Sous-préfet to Administrateurs and Commissaires de police.
29. ANOM Constantine 93 / 7131, Constantine, 17 October 1941, Police d'état, "Rapport."
30. Jackson, *Dark Years*, 228, 433–436.
31. ANOM Constantine 93 / 7133, Constantine, 20 October 1941, Commissaire central to Préfet.
32. ANOM Constantine 93 / 7133, Aïn-M'lila, 13 October 1941, "Procès-verbal."
33. Cantier, *L'Algérie sous le regime*, 33–34.
34. ANOM Alger 91303 / 67, Alger, 20 May 1940, anonymous letter to the Inspecteur-général. The archives are full of similar accusations.
35. ANOM Alger 91303 / 67, Vialar, 19 August 1940, Administrateur de la Commune mixte, Sersou to Chef de la brigade, and Alger, 13 August 1940, Préfet to Sous-préfet, Miliana.
36. ANOM Alger 91303 / 67, Vialar, 27 September 1940 and 19 December 1940, Administrateur de la Commune Mixte to Sous-préfet. Once again, dozens of anonymous letters denouncing Communists, and official reports evincing concerns about them, can be found in the archives.
37. Cantier, *L'Algérie sous le regime*, 337–340.
38. See, for example, ANOM Alger 91303 / 67, Alger, 1 August 1940, "Renseignement."
39. ANOM Constantine 93 / 6782, Constantine, 30 July 1940, Commissaire principal, RG to Préfet; Cantier, *L'Algérie sous le regime*, 160–161.
40. ANOM Alger 91303 / 67, Alger, 28 January, 15 April, 2 July, and 21 August 1941, prefectorial circulars.
41. NAGB / FO / 371 / 49275, Alger, 9 February 1945, Consul-General Carvell to Duff Cooper.
42. For a discussion of antisemitism and the Algerian Extreme Right, see Kalman, *French Colonial Fascism*. Census data are from Colette Zytnicki, "La politique antisémite du régime de Vichy dans les colonies," in *L'empire colonial sous Vichy*, ed. Jacques Cantier and Eric Jennings (Paris, 2004), 155.
43. Jackson, *Dark Years*, 355–358; Darmon, *L'Algérie de Pétain*, 342–345; Daniel J. Schroeter, "Between Metropole and French North Africa: Vichy's Anti-Semitic Legislation and Colonialism's Racial Hierarchies," in *The Holocaust and North Africa*, ed. Aomar Boum and Sarah Abrevaya Stein (Stanford, CA, 2019), 43.
44. Darmon, *L'Algérie de Pétain*, 387–388; Susan Slymovics, "'Other Places of Confinement': Bedeau Internment Camp for Algerian Jewish Soldiers," in Boum and Stein, 99.
45. Roberts, *Citizenship and Antisemitism*, chap. 1–2.
46. Kalman, *French Colonial Fascism*.
47. For an excellent and detailed account of the Constantine riot, including the context, European provocations, and the events and aftermath, see Joshua Cole, *Lethal Provocation: The Constantine Murders and the Politics of French Algeria* (Ithaca, NY, 2019).

48. Roberts, *Citizenship and Antisemitism*, 251–253, 288–289.

49. ANOM Constantine 93 / 7131, Constantine, 13 May 1942, Commissaire central to Préfet, and Constantine, 10 August 1942, Police d'état, "Rapport."

50. Darmon, *L'Algérie de Pétain*, 385; ANOM Constantine 93 / 7131, Constantine, 22 December 1942, Police d'état, "Rapport."

51. ANOM Oran / 69, Oran, 30 September 1944, Police d'état, "Rapport."

52. Kalman, "Avec une brutalité," 54–57.

53. ANOM Constantine 93 / 6782, Constantine, 24 November 1942, Salomon Albuche to Préfet; ANOM Constantine 93 / 1584, Constantine, 23 October 1944, Commissaire central to Préfet.

54. Schroeter, "Between Metropole and French North Africa," 19–21, 147–148.

55. On Jewish-Muslim relations in Algeria, both collaborative and belligerent, see Ethan Katz, *The Burdens of Brotherhood: Jews and Muslims from North Africa to France* (Cambridge, UK, 2015), chap. 2. Comprehensive accounts of the Constantine riots can be found in Cole, *Lethal Provocation*, and Roberts, *Citizenship and Anti-Semitism*, chap. 4. On attempts to exploit Muslim anger at the Crémieux Decree, see Cole, *Lethal Provocation*, chap. 6.

56. ANOM Constantine 93 / 6786, Batna, 2 August 1943, Inspecteur de la police, RG, Batna to Commissaire chef, RG, Constantine.

57. ANOM Oran / 69, Oran, 30 August 1944, Police d'état, "Rapport."

58. Cole, *Lethal Provocation*, 87.

59. Cantier, *L'Algérie sous le regime*, 142–146; ANOM Oran 5I / 164, Alger, 6 June 1942, Directeur de la Sécurité générale to Directeur des affaires musulmans.

60. ANOM Constantine 93 / 7023, "Rapport mensuel-mars 1943"; ANOM Constantine 93 / 6783, Sétif, 20 February 1943, "Rapport du Chef d'escadron Morin."

61. Cantier, *L'Algérie sous le regime*, 185–190. The Zeralda mayor and his accomplices were charged, tried, and jailed for their roles in the jailhouse murders in 1944, well after the Free French had taken the reins in Algeria.

62. ANOM Constantine 93 / 6887, Bou-Saada, 27 December 1941, Commissaire de police to Préfet; ANOM Alger 1F / 422, Blida, 21 June 1944, RG, "Rapport"; Constantine 93 / 1584, Saint-Arnaud, 26 July 1944, Commissaire de police to Préfet.

63. Cantier, *L'Algérie sous le regime*, 111–114.

64. Cantier, 173–180.

65. ANOM Constantine 93 / 6885, Bône, 23 June 1942, Memo, Brigade économique.

66. ANOM Constantine 93 / 6885, Constantine, 27 January 1942, Commissaire central to Chef de la Brigade de surveillance des prix; "Reorganisation des services de la Brigade économique de la Police d'État de Bône."

67. ANOM Constantine 93 / 6884, Constantine, 23 June 1942, Commissaire de Police Jean Besse to Commissaire central.

68. ANOM Oran / 3, Oran, 23 November–22 December 1942, "État d'affaires instruites, Service de la répression des fraudes et de la surveillance des prix." Interestingly, the only cases referred to trial involved Europeans, perhaps due to the fear of inciting rebellion.

69. ANOM Oran / 3, Oran, 23 December 1942, Police d'Oran, "Rapport."

70. ANOM GGA 9H / 26, Tébessa, 12 August 1940, Brigade mobile to GGA; ANOM Constantine 93 / 7131, Sidi-Aïch, 7 September 1942, Administrateur de la Commune mixte, Soummam to Préfet.

NOTES TO PAGES 137–141   225

71. ANOM Constantine 93 / 7133, Philippeville, 25 March 1942, "Rapport spécial."
72. Literally dozens of monthly reports can be found in the wartime archives of all three departments. On these trends, see, for example, ANOM Oran / 3, Oran, 24 June 1943, Commissaire divisionnaire to Préfet, and Oran, 21 November–22 December 1942, 21 May–20 June 1944, 21 October–22 November 1944, "État d'affaires instruites / Service de la répression des fraudes et de la surveillance des prix"; ANOM Oran 1F / 90, 1 January–31 December 1943, "État des infractions / marché noir."
73. ANOM Constantine 93 / 7133, Constantine, 23 March 1942, Commissaire central to Préfet, and Constantine, 7 October 1942, Police d'état, "Rapport."
74. ANOM Constantine 93 / 7131, Constantine, 4 September and 10 October 1942, Commissaire chef de la Brigade économique, "Rapport," and Constantine, 7 October 1942, Police d'état, "Rapport."
75. ANOM Constantine 93 / 1576, Le Khroub, 1 April 1943, Commissaire de police to Sous-préfet.
76. ANOM Alger 1F / 439: Alger, 11 September 1944, Commissaire principal to Commissaire divisionnaire; Alger, n.d. (September 1944), GGA to Préfet; Alger, 23 November 1944, Préfet to GGA; and Alger, 20 October 1944, Chargé de mission, Office régional de travail to Préfet.
77. ANOM Oran / 69, Oran, 18 September 1944, Commandant des Gardiens de la paix to Commissaire divisionnaire.
78. ANOM Constantine 93 / 1576, Le Khroub, 23 June 1943, Commissaire de police to Préfet; ANOM Oran 1F / 90, Oran, 10 November 1953, Préfet, "Communiqué de presse."
79. ANOM Oran 1F / 90, Oran, 23 December 1943, Commissaire central adjoint to Commissaire divisionnaire.
80. ANOM Constantine 93 / 1583, Constantine, 20 March 1944, Commissaire central, "Rapport."
81. AOM Constantine 93 / 6885, Philippeville, 29 June 1942, Commissaire central, "Memento des consignes permanentes relatives à la police des marchés." For an example of sentencing under Vichy, see Constantine, 31 March 1942, Commissaire chef de 1er Brigade mobile to Commissaire divisionnaire.
82. ANOM GGA 9H / 26, Alger, 14 August 1944, Commissaire chef, Brigade économique to Directeur de la sécurité générale; Oran / 25, Oran, 10 November 1943 and 25 April 1944, Préfet, "Circulaires," and Alger, 7 April 1944, GGA to Préfet, Oran; Alger 1F / 439, Alger, 30 October 1944, Préfet to GGA.
83. ANOM Alger 1F / 422: Alger, n.d. (August 1942), Préfet to GGA; Tii-Ouzou, 20 August 1942; Alger, 24 August 1942, Préfet to Controleur chef; Alger, 26 August 1942, Controleur-chef to Préfet.
84. ANOM Oran / 69, Oran, 8 November 1940, Préfet to Général commandant la service.
85. ANOM Constantine 93 / 6783, Constantine, 17 September 1943, Préfet to Commissaire central.
86. ANOM Constantine 93 / 7133, Constantine, 15 December 1941, ketter to the Chef de la division.
87. ANOM Constantine 93 / 6783, Constantine, 31 August 1942, Commissaire central to Préfet; Constantine 93 / 7023, Oued Zenati, 27 May 1943, Maire to Préfet.

88. ANOM Constantine 93 / 6786, Bône, 13 October 1943, Commissaire chef de la Brigade économique to Commissaire central.
89. ANOM Constantine 93 / 1576, Tébessa, 30 January 1943, Commissaire de police, "Rapport spécial."
90. ANOM Constantine 93 / 1576, Tébessa, 2 June 1943, Commissaire de police, "Rapport spécial."
91. Numerous reports of this type can be found in the relevant archives. For examples, see ANOM Oran / 69, 2 and 5 September 1944, Police d'état, "Rapport."
92. ANOM Constantine 93 / 1576, Le Khroub, 1 April 1943, Commissaire de police to Sous-préfet, Constantine.
93. ANOM Constantine 93 / 1576, Khenchela, 23 April 1943, Commissaire de police to Sous-préfet, Batna.
94. ANOM Oran / 69, Oran, 6 February 1944, Renseignements généraux, "Rapport."
95. ANOM Constantine 93 / 1576, Bône, 28 April 1943, "Rapport du Capitaine Campan," and Constantine, 20 May 1943, Police d'état, "Rapport."
96. ANOM Constantine 93 / 6889, Constantine, 3 March 1944, Commissaire de police, RG to Préfet.
97. ANOM GGA 9H / 26, Alger, 1 September 1944, Commissaire central, "Rapport."
98. ANOM Constantine 93 / 1576, Constantine, 21 April 1943, Police d'état, "Rapport."
99. ANOM Constantine 93 / 1576, Aïn-Beïda, 1 June 1943, Commissaire de police, "Rapport," and Constantine, 28 June 1943, Commissaire principal, "Rapport."
100. ANOM Constantine 93 / 1576, Constantine, 5 June 1943, Commissaire central, "Rapport" and Préfet to Général commandant la division.
101. ANOM Oran 1F / 71, "Notice concernant M. Albert Dominici," January 1944.
102. ANOM Alger 9301 / 106, Alger, 17 October 1941, Préfet to Sous-préfets, Maires, and Administrateurs, and Alger, 2 June 1942, Préfet, "Circulaire"; Oran / 67, Oran, 18 September 1943, letter from Noel Liedo. The prefect's position was so severe that even the Vichy minister of the interior, Pierre Pucheu, asked that it be modified. See ANOM Alger 9301 / 106, Vichy, 15 April 1942, Minister of the Interior to Préfets.
103. Berlière, *Le monde des polices*, 203–208.
104. ANOM Oran / 67, Oran, 28 December 1943, Préfet to GGA.
105. ANOM Constantine 93 / 6826, Tlemcen, 21 June 1943, Sous-préfet to Préfet and Commissaire de police, "Affaire Fusero," and Alger, 30 October 1943, GGA, "Arrête."
106. ANOM Oran / 69, Oran, 12 January 1944, Commissaire principal to Préfet.
107. ANOM Constantine 93 / 6826, Oran, 1 February 1943, Préfet to GGA, and Alger, 8 June 1944, GGA, "Arrête." Susini's service record is attached to these documents.
108. ANOM Constantine 93 / 6783, "Liste des SOL de Bougie," n.d. (1943).
109. ANOM Oran / 69, Alger, 27 December 1943, "Commission rogatoire"; ANOM Constantine 93 / 6887, Tiaret, 31 December 1945, Chef de poste des RG to Commissaire principal. The PPF leader, Marcel Urban, had also worked as a recruiter for the Légion anti-bolchevique.
110. ANOM GGA 9H / 26, Alger, 18 March 1944, Commissaire central, "Rapport"; Constantine 93 / 1584, Constantine, 18 September 1944, Commissaire central to Préfet.

111. ANOM Constantine 93 / 6829, Constantine, 30 July 1943, Préfet, "Circulaire" and "Extrait du Journal official du 10 juillet 1943"; ANOM Alger 1F / 439, Alger, 30 October 1943, GGA, "Arrête," and Préfet to GGA, Memo (n.d.); Constantine 93 / 6885, Alger, 18 November 1943, GGA to Préfet; ANOM Alger 1F / 422, Alger, 22 March 1944, GGA to Préfet.

112. As Henry Rousso has noted, the Gaullists performed an abrupt volte-face at war's end, putting the brakes on purging and resistance claims to legitimacy and instead attempting to sweep collaboration and occupation under the rug. See Rousso, *The Vichy Syndrome: History and Memory in France since 1944* (Cambridge, UK, 1991).

5. Policing Colonial Politics

1. "Féroce pression administrative," *La Liberté*, 8 November 1945; AN BB / 18 / 3608, Alger, 26 July 1946, Procureur générale, Alger to Garde des Sceaux.
2. McDougall, *History of Algeria*, 185–187.
3. McDougall, 182–185, 189–190.
4. Martin Evans, *Algeria: France's Undeclared War* (Oxford, 2012), 85–91, Malik Rahal, *L'UDMA et les Udmistes: Contribution à l'histoire du nationalisme algérien* (Alger, 2017), 19.
5. McDougall, *History of Algeria*, 182–185.
6. McDougall, 188; Evans, *France's Undeclared War*, 105–106; Gilbert Meynier, *Histoire intérieure du FLN, 1954–1962* (Paris, 2002), 70–72, 76–78.
7. Kaddache, *Histoire du nationalisme algérien*, 784.
8. Kaddache, 785, McDougall, *History of Algeria*, 189–191.
9. Kaddache, *Histoire du nationalisme algérien*, 786–792; McDougall, *History of Algeria*, 188; Meynier, *Histoire intérieure du FLN*, 89–91. The PPA newspaper *El Maghreb El Arabi* chided Abbas as "M. La France, c'est moi," while the UDMA consistently referred to their competitors as "extremists."
10. Berlière and Levy, *Histoire des polices en France*, 302–309, 312–313.
11. Clive Emsley, "Introduction: Political Police and the European Nation-State in the Nineteenth Century," in *The Politics of Policing in the Twentieth Century*, ed. Mark Mazower (Providence, RI, 1997), 1.
12. Berlière and Lévy, *Histoire des polices en France*, 351; Jean-Emile Vié, *Mémoires d'un directeur des Renseignements généraux* (Paris, 1988); Rosenberg, *Policing Paris*, 106.
13. Thomas, *Empires of Intelligence*, 223–224, 264–265, 293–295, 299–301.
14. For a comprehensive treatment of the issue, see Emmanuel Blanchard, *La police parisienne et les Algériens (1944–1962)* (Paris, 2011).
15. For the view that officials and police did not fully engage with nationalism until the outbreak of the War of Algerian Independence in 1954, see, for example, Vié, *Mémoires d'un directeur*, 23–26; and Peyroulou, "Rétablir et maintenir." Vié was a retired director of the RG, and his view is representative of various official memoirs in which ex-police and officials attempt to justify their perceived inaction in the face of subsequent events. However, blaming a lack of resources and personnel runs counter to the quite apparent antinationalist campaign in Algeria well before 1954, as detailed throughout this chapter.
16. Mohamed Harbi, *Aux origins du FLN: Le populisme révolutionnaire en Algérie* (Paris, 1975), 165.

17. On the Indigénat, see McDougall, *History of Algeria*, 123–128. For a discussion of the precarious state of the Algerian economy prior to 1939, see Jacques Marseille, *Empire colonial et capitalisme français: Histoire d'un divorce* (Paris, 1984), and Meuleman, *Le Constantinois entre les deux guerres mondiales*.

18. MacMaster, *Colonial Migrants and Racism*, 76–94.

19. Jacques Simon, *L'Étoile nord-africaine (1926–1937)* (Paris, 2003), 80–81, 92, 101–115.

20. Simon, 145–149, 156–157, 162–164, 170, 190–191, 202–209.

21. Carlier, *Entre nation et jihad*, 36–38, 46–47; Kaddache, *Histoire du nationalisme algérien*, 471–475.

22. ANOM Oran 5I/101, 25 June 1938, "Le Parti du peuple algérien: Membres du groupement en France et en Algérie"; Kaddache, *Histoire du nationalisme algérien*, 444–445, 465.

23. Hachemi Baghriche, *Militant à 15 ans au Parti populaire algérien (PPA): Le pont de la liberté* (Paris, 2005), 13–17, 32–33, 54–55.

24. Baghriche, 44–51; ANOM Alger 4I/6, Alger, 4 November 1937, Sûreté departementale d'Alger, "Rapport"; ANOM Oran 5I/102, Alger, 21 November 1937, Sûreté departementale d'Alger, "Rapport," and Alger, 25 February 1938, Police spéciale departementale, "Rapport."

25. ANOM Oran 5I/101, Oran, 14 November 1937, Governor General, memorandum; Kaddache, *Histoire du nationalisme algérien*, 501–502.

26. Kaddache, *Histoire du nationalisme algérien*, 575–576; Simon, *Le PPA*, 90–97; Jacques Simon, *L'Algérie dans la deuxième guerre mondiale* (Paris, 2015), 153–154.

27. Harbi, *Aux origines du FLN*, 110–126; Simon, *L'Algérie*, 177–182; Rey-Goldzeiguer, *Aux origines de la guerre*, 193–198.

28. ANOM Oran 5I/104: Mascara, 13 June 1944 and 26 September 1944, Inspecteur Carlotti, PRG to Commissaire principal; Oran, 11 September 1944, Chef de poste, "Rapport"; and 4 October 1944, "Renseignements"; Oran, 19 October 1944, Préfet to GGA.

29. Simon, *Le PPA*, 110–115, 126–133, 143–155; Simon, *L'Algérie*, 184–192; Benjamin Stora, *Messali Hadj, 1898–1974* (Paris, 2004), 189–191.

30. AN BB/18/3608, Alger, 26 February 1945 and Alger, 1 May 1945, Procureur général, Alger to Garde des sceaux; Simon, *L'Algérie*, 193–195; Meynier, *Histoire intérieure du FLN*, 64–65.

31. Simon, *Le PPA*, 179–185; Rey-Goldzeiguer, *Aux origines de la guerre*, 228–245; Kaddache, *Histoire du nationalisme algérien*, 625–675. Messali Hadj's house arrest was moved from the Sahara to Reibell to Brazzaville and finally back to Algeria, where he remained until June 1946.

32. See, for example, AN BB/18/3608, Centre d'information et d'études, *Bulletin mensuel d'information*, April 1945; ANOM Oran 5I/104: Mascara, 13 June, 11 September, and 26 September 1944, Inspecteur Carlotti, Chef de poste, PRG to Commissaire principal; Oran, 4 October 1944, "Renseignements"; Oran, 19 October 1944, Préfet to GGA. On the 16 April riot, see AN BB/18/3608, Alger, 1 May 1945, Procureur général, Alger to Garde des Sceaux. Of the seven arrested, none were PPA members.

33. AN BB/18/3608, Centre d'information et d'études, *Bulletin mensuel d'information*, April 1945; Stora, *Messali Hadj*, 191–197; Rey-Goldzeiguer, *Aux origines de la guerre*,

205–206, 222–223; Kaddache, *Histoire du nationalisme algérien*, 625–635; André Nouschi, *La naissance du nationalism algérien* (Paris, 1962), chap. 5.

34. AN BB/18/3608, Batna, 10 May 1945, Chef de la circonscription de police to Sous-préfet; AN BB/18/3610, Alger, 2 May 1945, Commissaire divisionnaire, "Rapport," and Alger, 8 May 1945, Procureur général to Garde des Sceaux; Simon, *Le PPA*, 179–185; Rey-Goldzeiguer, *Aux origines de la guerre*, 228–245; Kaddache, *Histoire du nationalisme algérien*, 625–675.

35. AN BB/18/3610, Alger, 18 May 1945, Procureur général to Garde des Sceaux; Kaddache, *Histoire du nationalisme algérien*, 653. In Alger, for example, police attacked one thousand Muslim protesters crying "Liberez Messali!," leading to a riot in which thirty Europeans and twenty-five Algerians were injured and one Arab killed. However, dozens of protesters were arrested and order quickly was restored.

36. AN BB/18/3610, Alger, 12 and 23 May 1945, Procureur général to Garde des Sceaux; Simon, *Le PPA*, 179–198, and *L'Algérie*, 199–202; Rey-Goldzeiguer, *Aux origines de la guerre*, 271–289; Kaddache, *Histoire du nationalisme algérien*, 657–661. Those arrested included moderates like Ferhat Abbas and the 'ulama, along with PPA members. On military tribunals and their role, see Peyroulou, *Guelma, 1945*, 255–269.

37. Naegelen, *Mission en Algérie*, 14.

38. Jacques Simon notes that "la direction du PPA s'est trouvée placée devant un mouvement insurrectionnel, qu'elle avait initié et impulsé, sans toutefois en comprendre la nature et la logique interne [the PPA leadership found itself lumped in with the insurrectionary movement that it had founded and encouraged, yet without a clue about its character and internal logic]." Simon correctly asserts that the PPA's heart was willing, but its hands were too weak to contemplate open revolt. The wave of arrests left the group impotent, and it is telling that local PPA members tried to calm crowds in Kabylia, only to be resolutely ignored, as their leadership was in hiding and even the ultra-committed young militants were neutralized. See Simon, *Le PPA*, 171; Kaddache, *Histoire du nationalisme algérien*, 625–675; Rey-Goldzeiguer, *Aux origines de la guerre*, 193–198; Stora, *Messali Hadj*, 191–197.

39. Simon, *L'Algérie*, 203–208, 221–223; Meynier, *Histoire intérieure du FLN*, 66–69.

40. AN BB/18/3609, Centre d'informations et d'études, *Bulletin mensuel d'information*, May 1945 and 20 April–20 May 1947; AN BB/18/3610, Alger, 19 May 1945, Procureur général to Garde des Sceaux, and Sétif, 27 May 1945, Rapport du Chef d'escadron Babillon, Commandant la Compagnie de gendarmerie à Sétif. In his monthly report, the general in command consistently portrayed the PPA as a clandestine threat merely biding its time before whipping the population into a frenzy of armed rebellion; Europeans were right to be wary, and the government had a duty to forcefully terminate the organization. See AN BB/18/3608, Alger, 1 June–1 October 1945, "Gendarmerie en AFN, Synthèse mensuelle."

41. "La tragique bilan des émeutes de la region de Sétif," *Echo d'Alger*, 19 May 1945; AN BB/18/3608: Alger, 1 July 1945, Commandant général de la gendarmerie, Synthèse mensuelle, June 1945; Paris, 2 January 1946, letter from Pierre Kador, Sécretaire-générale of Secours populaire français; Alger, 9 February 1946, Procureur général to Garde des Sceaux; BB/18/3610, Alger, 29 August 1945, Procureur général to Garde des Sceaux.

42. ANOM Oran 5I/102, Oran, 10, 17, 23 July 1945, Reports of Commissaires principaux and PRG; AN BB/18/3608, Mascara, 20 May and 11 June 1945, Rapport du Capitaine Espagnet. In total, Oran police and gendarmes arrested 569 PPA members.

43. ANOM Constantine 93/7137, Bougie, 26 June 1945, Rapport du Capitaine Escande; AN BB/18/3609, Alger, 1 July 1945, Commandant général de la gendarmerie en AFN, Synthèse mensuelle, June 1945.

44. ANOM Constantine 93/7137, Constantine, 21 September 1945, Commandant de justice militaire to Général commandant la division and Constantine, 18 October 1945, Commissaire divisionnaire to Directeur de la Sécurité générale; Oran 5I/102, Oran, 9 January 19 1946, PRG, "Rapport"; BB/18/3608, Centre d'informations et des études, *Bulletin mensuel d'information*, May, August, September 1945, and Oran, 28 January 1946, Lieutenant-Colonel Camadou, Commissaire du gouvernement près de tribunal militaire to ministère des armées. All criminal cases arising from the May "events" were referred to the military tribunal, due to their authority during wartime, unless that body declined to press charges, opening the door to civil courts. Soldiers also received punishments of *degradation militaire* (loss of military status). On the general amnesty, see Simon, 234.

45. Simon, *Le PPA*, 208–229; Rey-Goldzeiguer, *Aux origines de la guerre*, 326–356.

46. AN BB/18/3613, "Statuts du MTLD"; Oran 5I/106, Alger, 3 April 1951, Préfet to GGA.

47. ANOM Oran 92/102, Oran, 24 January 1948, Préfet to GGA. Naegelen was a socialist and a former AN minister of education.

48. AN BB 18/3608, Alger, 16 May 1945, Procureur général to Garde des Sceaux, and Mostaganem, 24 September 1945, Commissaire général to Governor General; AN BB/18/3610, Alger, 16–18 May and 7 June 1945, Procureur général to Garde des Sceaux.

49. AN BB/18/3608, Alger, 25 April 1946, Procureur général, Alger to Garde des Sceaux; AN BB/18/3610, Alger, 16 May 1945, Procureur général, Alger to Garde des Sceaux; ANOM Oran 5I/101, Oran, 16 January 1946, PRG, "Rapport." *Frères Algériens* was so successful that it ran for several years. See AN BB/18/3611, Bougie, 7 April 1946, Rapport du Capitaine Escande, commandant la section.

50. Kaddache, *Histoire du nationalisme algérien*, 765–766; Simon, *Le MTLD*, 48.

51. Evans, *France's Undeclared War*, 92–94, 107–108.

52. Sylvie Thénault, *Une drôle de justice: Les magistrats dans la guerre d'Algérie* (Paris, 2004), 24–25.

53. AN BB/18/3608, Alger, 8 July and 30 November 1946, 30 October 1947, Procureur général to Garde des Sceaux; BB/18/3614, Alger, 3–4 March 1949, Procureur général to Garde des Sceaux. It is worth noting the prioritization of propaganda well after the establishment of the OS and police suspicions that the MTLD was a front for revolutionary militancy. See AN BB/18/3610, Tlemcen, 1 May 1945, "Rapport spéciale," Commissaire central; AN BB/18/3615, Alger, 15–17 March 1950, Procureur général to Garde des Sceaux.

54. ANOM Oran 5I/104, Tlemcen, 13 April 1948, Commissaire principal to Sous-préfet.

55. ANOM Alger 1F/223, Alger, 3 September 1947, "Arrête"; Constantine 93/1297, Philippeville, 9 July 1947, Inspecteur de la PRG to Sous-préfet; ANOM Oran 5I/106, Mascara, 5 December 1952, Chef de police de la PRG to Commissaire divisionnaire;

AN BB/18/3608, Alger, 25 April–2 September 1946, Procureur général to Garde des Sceaux; Batna, 23 August 1946, "Rapport du capitaine commandant la section"; AN BB/18/3613, Alger, 24 June 1949, Procureur général to Garde des Sceaux.

56. For a case of arrest and subsequent release on promise to leave town, see ANOM Oran 5I/104, Oran, 27 May 1938, Commissaire divisionnaire to Préfet.

57. ANOM Constantine 93/1299, Sidi-Aïch, 13 January 1948, Administrateur de la Commune mixte Soummam to Sous-Préfet, and Constantine, 3 April 1948, Gendarmerie nationale, "Procès-verbal"; ANOM Alger 1F/216, Medea, 30 March 1948, Rapport du Lieutenant Dubouin, Commandant la section de gendarmerie; ANOM Alger 4I/224, Tizi-Ouzou, 5 January 1950, Sous-préfet, "Circulaire."

58. ANOM Constantine 93/1299, Bône, 29 January 1948, Report to Commissaire principale, Constantine. Baki was also charged with "atteinte à la souveraineté française" for a May speech in which he proclaimed it a Muslim duty to join the MTLD, stated that the party's orders came from Egypt and not Alger, and that Hadj had been imprisoned and tortured. See AN BB/18/3612: Alger, 3 May 1948, Procureur générale to Garde des Sceaux.

59. ANOM Constantine 93/1299, Bougie, 20 July 1948, Inspecteur de la PRG, Bougie to Commissaire principal, Constantine; ANOM Alger 1F/150, Port-Gueydon, 15 April 1950, Rapport du Gendarme; AN BB/18/3616, Alger, 22 August 1950, Procureur général to Garde des Sceaux.

60. AN BB/18/3608: Alger, 26 September 1945, Procureur général to Garde des Sceaux; AN BB/18/3609, Tizi-Ouzou, 18 March 1947, "Rapport du Capitaine Rinsant, commandant la section de gendarmerie"; AN BB/18/3612, Alger, 22 June 1948, 14 June 1949, Procureur général to Garde des Sceaux. Hadj's public appearances were consistently subject to prefectorial bans due to heavy police surveillance of his every move.

61. ANOM Constantine 93/1299, Sidi-Aïch, 13 January 1948, Administrateur de la Commune mixte, Soummam to Procureur de la République, Bougie. The MTLD did nevertheless manage to land nine seats in April 1946 regional elections. See Rabah Aissaoui, *Immigration and National Identity: North African Political Movements in Colonial and Postcolonial France* (London, 2009), 129–137.

62. Simon, *Le MTLD*, 39–42; Kaddache, *Histoire du nationalisme algérien*, 744–746. In the town of Champlain alone, police violence killed four, wounded forty, and arrested two hundred Algerian voters.

63. ANOM Constantine 93/1297, Philippeville, 20 April 1948, Commissaire de la Police judiciaire to Procureur de la république; ANOM Constantine 93/1299, Philippeville, 2 April 1948, Sous-préfet to Préfet, and Oued-Marsa, 8 April 1948, Administrateur to GGA, Préfet, and Sous-préfet.

64. AN BB/18/3611, Alger, 12 April 1948, Procureur général to Garde des Sceaux; AN BB/18/3612, Alger, 22 December 1948, Procureur général to Garde des Sceaux; AN BB/18/3613, Alger, 20 August 1948, Procureur général to Garde des Sceaux. Police noted that the directives to militants concerning elections were followed in numerous instances, most notably in Blida in the department of Alger.

65. Kaddache writes that *"L'Action algérienne* fut le premier journal clandestin algérien. Son caractère secret, la violence de ses articles . . . contrastaient avec la modération d'*Egalité* [*L'Action algérienne* was the first clandestine newspaper in Algeria. Its secretive nature, the violence of its articles . . . provided a stark contrast to the

moderation of *Egalité*]." Despite tremendous efforts, officers could not locate either the editors or the printshop, and the illicit nature of the publication only increased its allure. In Kaddache, *Histoire du nationalisme algérien*, 621–622, 765–766.

66. ANOM Constantine 93/1293, Alger, 3 March 1948, GGA to Préfet; AN BB/18/3613, Alger, 21 January 1948, Procureur général to Garde des Sceaux, and Paris, 3 February 1950, Vice-Président du Conseil to Garde des Sceaux; AN BB/18/3614: Alger, 28 May 1949, Procureur général to Garde des Sceaux; AN BB/18/3615, Paris, 9 December 1948, Vice-Président du Conseil to Garde des Sceaux. On police searches and seizures, see numerous cases in Alger 4I/226 and Constantine 93/1293-94–99.

67. ANOM Oran 5I/102, Mascara, 21 December 1945 Commissaire de police to Sous-préfet; ANOM Oran 5I/104, Tlemcen, 4 September 1947, Commissaire principal to Sous-préfet, and 20 September 1947, Police d'état, Mostaganem, "Procès verbal"; ANOM Oran 5I/105, Oran, 16 September 1950, SLNA Report.

68. Thénault, *Une drôle de justice*, 21, 26; AN BB/18/3609: Alger, 30 June 1947, Procureur général to Garde des Sceaux; Alger, 15 July 1947, GGA to Préfet, Alger; Minister of Justice, memorandum, 24 July 1947; Alger, 24 July 1947 and 7 February 1949, Procureur général to Garde des Sceaux; BB/18/3613, Berroughia, June 1948, "Rapport mensuel," and Paris, 29 August 1950, GGA to Minister of the Interior.

69. ANOM Oran 5I/107, "Implantation et effectifs du PPA clandestin." In the department of Alger, the PPA boasted 12,777 members, Constantine 7,121, Oran 1,820, and the Sahara 2,152.

70. ANOM Oran 5I/101, Oran, 19 September 1946, PRG, "Rapport; ANOM Alger 1F/148, Médéa, 4 February 1948, Inspecteur de la PRG to Commissaire divisionnaire, and Alger, 8 March 1948, Commissaire divisionnaire to Directeur général de la sécurité générale.

71. AN BB/3609: "Voyage de Messali en Kabylie," 26 March 1947; Paris, 24 May–2 June 1947, Minister of Interior to Garde des Sceaux; and Rapport, PG, Alger, 5 July 1947. In Mizrana, the intimidation of nonmembers resulted in the stabbing of a local who refused to attend a PPA meeting.

72. AN BB/18/3609: Bougie, 9 November 1946, Rapport du Capitaine Escande, Commandant le section; Taher, December 1946, Juge de paix to Procureur, Bougie; Bougie, 7 December 1946, Rapport à Procureur de la République, Bougie; Alger, 5 July 1947, Rapport, Procureur général, Alger; Alger, 31 October 1947 and 22 June 1948, Procureur général to Garde des Sceaux. Detailed reports on court activities from March to July 1948 in Jemmapes, Bougie, Batna, Taher, and El-Arrouch can be found in Constantine 93/1297.

73. AN BB/8/3609: "Résumé du rapport du Capitaine Rinsant, commandant la gendarmerie de Tizi-Ouzou," 1947; Alger, 22 April and 29 July 1947, Procureur général to Garde des Sceaux; Tizi-Ouzou, 25 April 1947, Chef de Poste, PRG to Commissaire divisionnaire, Alger; and Alger, 29 July 1947.

74. ANOM Alger 4I/225, Tizi-Ouzou, 26 November 1947, Sous-préfet to Préfet; "Comment les hommes de main du PPA terrorisent la Kabylie," *La Bataille*, 6 December 1947; AN BB/18/3609, 22 August and 29 December 1947, Procureur général to Garde des Sceaux; AN BB/18/3608, Alger, 16 January 1948, Procureur général to Garde des Sceaux. The latter reports list dozens of incidents involving PPA sections in Kabylia and armed violence.

75. AN BB/18/3609, Alger, 21 May and 1 September 1948, Procureur général to Garde des Sceaux.

76. AN BB/18/3609, Alger, 1 September 1948, Procureur général to Garde des Sceaux. Despite the realization that the primary motive was political, the prosecutor continued to parrot stereotypes about Berbers. They were called litigious, mercenary, quarrelsome, stingy, scheming, and lying, and they supposedly engaged in hatred, vendettas, and murder. That they went largely unpunished was due solely o their expertise in the "science de mensonge" (science of lies).

77. ANOM Alger 4I/225, Tizi Ouzou, 8 October 1945, "Rapport du Lieutenant Risant."

78. ANOM Alger 1F/216, "Rapport sur la situation du département au point de vue de la sécurité et de l'ordre public," September 1948; ANOM Alger 4I/225, Alger, 31 July 1948, SLNA, "Rapport"; ANOM Constantine 93/1117, Alger, 20 April 1949, "Note de recherches."

79. Carlier, *Entre nation et jihad*, 271–292; Meynier, *Histoire intérieure du FLN*, 83–88.

80. Hocine Ait Ahmed, *Mémoires d'un combattant, 1942–1952* (Paris, 1983), 133–135.

81. Simon, *Le MTLD*, 43–47, 58–60; AN BB/18/3613, Paris, 29 August 1950, GGA to Minister of the Interior.

82. ANOM Alger 4I/224, "Les Origines du PPA"; ANOM Alger 1F/213, "Procès-verbal," 9 March 1950 and 12–13 April 1950; AN BB/18/3613, Minister of Justice, "Notes sur les affaires d'Algérie," 25 September 1950.

83. Ait Ahmed, *Mémoires d'un combattant*, 140–141; ANOM Alger 1F/213, "Procès-verbal," 9 April 1950, and Médéa, 14 August 1950, Inspecteur de la PRG to Commissaire divisionnaire, Alger.

84. ANOM Oran 5I/107, "L'organisation secrete du PPA en Algérie," 18 September 1952.

85. ANOM Alger 1F/213, "Procès-verbal," 23 April 1950; ANOM Alger 4I/225, SLNA, May 1950, "L'Organisation spéciale."

86. ANOM Alger 4I/225, SLNA, May 1950, "L'Organisation spéciale; ANOM Alger 1F/213, Alger, 9 May 1950, Commissaire divisionnaire, PRG to Préfet.

87. ANOM Alger 4I/225, SLNA, May 1950, "L'Organisation spéciale.

88. ANOM Alger 1F/213, "Procès-verbal," 10 May 1950.

89. ANOM Alger 1F/213, "Procès-verbal," 25 April 1950.

90. ANOM Alger 1F/213, "Procès-verbal," 15 April 1950.

91. ANOM Alger 1F/213, "Procès-verbal," 10 April 1950.

92. AN BB/18/3615, *Bulletin politique de quinzaine*, 16–31 March 1950, and Alger, 14 October 1950, Procureur général to Garde des Sceaux; ANOM Oran 5I/107, "Au nom d'Allah" (OS instruction manual).

93. Aissaoui, *Immigration and National Identity*, 129–137.

94. AN BB/18/3615, Alger, 21 July 1949, GGA to Minister of the Interior. The memo refers to an improbable alliance of backers for the secret terrorist units, including the Arab League, Morocco's Istliqlal, and the Tunisian Néo Destour group.

95. AN BB/18/3615, *Bulletin politique de quinzaine*, 16–31 March 1950. Departments were organized into districts, which were then subdivided into *kasmas* (subdistricts), groups, and subgroups. Each group was composed of a leader, a *sous-chef*, and members ranging from four (in a small village) to twenty-four (for a large town). In a move

that presaged FLN tactics during the Algerian war, to avoid police detection, members of subgroups knew only each other and one masked outside contact, and involvement in politics was strictly forbidden to avoid suspicion.

96. On the initial arrests, see Kaddache, *Histoire du nationalisme algérien*, 793; ANOM Constantine 93 / 1117, Oued-Zenati, 10 April 1950, "Rapport spécial." For (often lurid) press accounts, see "Le Vaste complot PPA découvert à Bône," *Dépêche algérienne*, 28 March 1950; "Vingt-huit conspirateurs écroués à Bône," *Echo d'Alger*, 28 March 1950; "Trente-cinq conspirateurs sous les verrous," *Journal d'Alger*, 29 March 1950.

97. AN BB / 18 / 3615, Bône, 23 March 1950, Commissaire de la Police judiciaire to Procureur, Bône; AN BB / 18 / 3616, Alger, 30 March 1950, Procureur général to Garde des Sceaux.

98. Dozens of reports on police raids against the OS can be found in several cartons: ANOM Alger 1F / 213 and 4I / 224–225, Constantine 93 / 1117, and BB / 18 / 3615–3616. Police and prosecutors consistently demanded that Khider's parliamentary immunity be lifted due to his purported participation in the leadership of the OS and the Oran post office robbery. For a prototypical example, see AN BB / 18 / 3613, Alger, 13 December 1950, Procureur général to Garde des Sceaux.

99. On the torture and murder of Algerians during the War of Independence, see Raphaëlle Branche, *La torture et l'armée pendant la Guerre d'Algérie* (Paris, 2001).

100. "Tribunel militaire," *Dépêche algérienne*, 27 February 1946; "Deuxième journée de la procès des 21," *Alger républicain*, 27 February 1946. On the "hernia" claim, see ANOM Alger 4I / 6, Alger, 20 September 1945, PRG, "Rapport spécial." The accounts of torture did not prevent the tribunal from finding the accused guilty and sentencing him to hard labor and deprivation of rights. ANOM Alger 4I / 6, Alger, 5 September 1946, PRG, "Rapport spécial."

101. Gaston Mesguiche, Secrétaire du Secours populaire algérien, "22 Accusés comparaissent," *Alger républicain*, 23 January 1946.

102. See, for example, ANOM Constantine 93 / 1299, Philippeville, 20 October 1947, Sous-préfet to Préfet.

103. For accounts of torture, see "Arrestations, tortures, expeditions punitives se multiplient dans l'Algérois et en Oranie," *Franc-tireur*, 9 May 1950; "Une delegation d'élus MTLD chez le Procureur général," *Alger républicain*, 15 April 1950; "La Machination policière s'éffondre dès la 1ere audience," *Alger républicain*, 17 August 1951. Regarding forced confessions and police denials, see ANOM Oran 5I / 106, Oran, 20 February 1951, PRG, "Rapport." On European newspapers' suspicions, see "À propos du procès des PPA de Bône," *Echo d'Alger*, 14 August 1951.

104. "Verdict au procès de la posse d'Oran," *Alger républicain*, 23 June 1952; ANOM Oran / 132, Oran, 21 July 1952, PRG, "Rapport."

105. AN BB / 18 / 3613, Paris, 29 August 1950, GGA to Minister of the Interior.

106. ANOM Oran 5I / 106, Oran, 20 February 1951, PRG, "Rapport"

107. ANOM Oran 5I / 101, Tlemcen, 10 May 1950, Police judiciare, "Rapport spécial."

108. ANOM Oran 5I / 107, Oran, 22 May 1950, Police judiciaire, "Rapport spécial"; ANOM Oran 5I / 106, Oran, 20 February 1951, PRG, "Rapport."

109. ANOM Constantine 93 / 1117, "État des poursuites / 1950," and Constantine, 19 June 1950, Commissaire principal, PRG to Préfet; ANOM Oran 5I / 106, "Condem-

nations prononcés par le Tribunel correctionnel d'Oran à l'audience du 6 mars 1951"; "Affaire dite complot PPA," *Oran républicain*, 11 March 1951.

110. AN BB/18/3615, Bône, 30 June 1951, Substitut, Procureur de Bône to Procureur général; ANOM Alger 4I/224, Alger, 23 August 1951, Commissaire de police to Commissaire divisionnaire; "Prémiere victoire contre la repression," *Alger républicain*, 29 August 1951.

111. ANOM Alger 4I/224, Blida, 11 March 1952, Inspecteur de la PRG to Commissaire divisionnaire, and Blida, 18 March 1952, Commissaire principal to Sous-préfet; AN BB/18/3616, Alger, 13 May 1952, Procureur général to Garde des Sceaux; "De partout des voix s'élèvent: acquittez les 56 de Blida," *Algérie libre*, 8 November 1951.

112. Thénault, *Une drôle de justice*, 32–34, 40–50, 68–71.

113. AN BB/18/3608, Alger, 9 June 1951, GGA to Garde des Sceaux.

114. Kaddache, *Histoire du nationalisme algérien*, 795–796.

115. ANOM Oran/132, Tract—"Education pratique d'un militant."

116. ANOM Alger 5I/224, Tizi-Ouzou, 3 January 1950, Sous-préfet to Préfet.

117. ANOM Alger 1F/150–151: Aïn-Bessam, 18 March 1940, Administrateur des services civils to Sous-préfet; Alger 4I/224, Aumale, 23 March 1950, Sous-préfet to Préfet; and Lavigerie, 7 March 1950, Administrateur, Djendel to Sous-préfet, Miliana.

118. ANOM Oran 5I/101, Tiaret, 29 June 1950, "Rapport du Commandant."

119. ANOM Oran 5I/106, "Rélizane: Rafle ou intimidation de la police d'état," *Alger républicain*, 26 April 1951; "1200 manifestants défilent dans les rues de Souma," *Dépêche quotidienne*, 13 May 1951; "À Souma, 1200 individus du MTLD insultent la France," *Journal d'Alger*, 15 May 1951.

120. "Rélizane: Rafle ou intimidation de la police d'état," *Alger républicain*, 26 April 1951.

121. ANOM Alger 1F/216: Alger, 18 May 1951, MTLD/PCA élus to Préfet; Affreville, 24 May 1951, "Rapport de Lt. Tibère-Inglesse"; "Deploiement de force à Souma," *Alger républicain*, 2 June 1951; and Blida, 4 June 1951, PRG, "Rapport."

122. ANOM Oran 5I/106, Aïn-Témouchent, 17 January 1952, Commissaire chef to Sous-préfet; "Descentes de police," *Alger républicain*, 18 January 1952.

123. ANOM Alger 1F/223, Alger, 5 May 1952, PRG, "Renseignement"; ANOM Oran/132, Alger, 9–10 January 1953, MTLD press release, and Oran/9, 13, 15 January 1953, PRG, "Rapport."

124. ANOM Constantine 93/1117, Alger, 13 June 1950, RG, "Notes de recherches."

125. See, for example, the Oran figures in ANOM Oran 5I/107: Oran, 23 September 1950, PRG, "Rapport"; "Le MTLD-PPA: Implantation dans le département d'Oran," n.d. (1953); GGA, "Note sur l'organisation secrète du PPA dans le région de Bougie-Sétif," n.d. (1953); Oran, 26 February 1953, PRG, "Rapport"; Tlemcen, 29 December 1953, "Rapport du Capitaine Joulie"; El Mina, 24 December 1953, Caïd to Administrateur de la Commune Mixte; and Tlemcen, 3 March 1954, Sous-préfet to Préfet.

126. McDougall, *History of Algeria*, 193–194.

127. ANOM Oran/132, Sidi-Bel-Abbès, 14 December 1953, Inspecteur Principal, PRG to Commissaire divisionnaire; ANOM Oran 5I/107, Tlemcen, 26 February 1954, Sous-préfet to Préfet; "Cinq arrestations pour détentions d'armes ou recel," *Echo d'Oran*, 14 May 1954.

128. McDougall, *History of Algeria*, 194–195.

Conclusion

1. On the origins and development of the FLN and the War of Independence, see Evans, *France's Undeclared War*, chap. 5; McDougall, *History of Algeria*, chap. 5.
2. Le Doussal, *Commissaire de police en Algérie*, 247–251; Paul Villatoux and Marie-Catherine Villatoux, *La république et son armée face au 'péril subversif': Guerre et actions psychologiques en France (1945–1960)* (Paris, 2005), 341–345, 382–385; Vié, *Mémoires d'un directeur*, 130–143.
3. Jean-Louis Courtois and Michel Lejeune, *Les CRS en Algérie* (Paris, 2010), 13–27, 33, 44, 53–54, 68–76.
4. Berlière and Lévy, *Histoire des polices en France*, 363; Blanchard, *La police parisienne*, 278.
5. Peyroulou, "Rétablir et maintenir," 121.
6. Evans, *France's Undeclared War*, 226–248.
7. Le Doussal, *Commissaire de police en Algérie*, 673–675.
8. Courtois and Lejeune, *Les CRS en Algérie*, 147, 196, 219–220, 271–275. Thousands more CRS agents arrived in 1960 as the fight became a two-front struggle. Others were hired from European communities in Algeria itself, although this proved highly problematic. In November 1961, twelve officers in Tizi-Ouzou defected to the OAS with a large cache of weapons. Worries about similar incidents in other units led to a wholesale purge.
9. Berlière and Lévy, *Histoire des polices en France*, 241–243.
10. Peyroulou, "Rétablir et maintenir," 122–124; Prakash, "Colonial Techniques," 503–504.
11. Blanchard, *La police parisienne*, 352.
12. Meynier, *Histoire intérieure du FLN*, 280–287.
13. Peyroulou, "Rétablir et maintenir," 119–121.
14. Meynier, *Histoire intérieure du FLN*, 280–285.
15. Meynier, 327–328; Raphaëlle Branche, "La torture pendant la guerre d'Algérie," in Harbi and Stora, *La guerre d'Algérie*, 381–382.
16. Branche, "La torture pendant la guerre," 383–384; Blanchard, *La police parisienne*, 336–337, 344.
17. For a detailed description of such practices, see Branche, *La torture et l'armée*, chap. 16.
18. Branche, 28–34.
19. Arnold, *Police Power and Colonial Rule*, 2–4.
20. Thomas, *Violence and Colonial Order*, 6–7.
21. On the notion of structural violence, see Étienne Balibar, *Politics and the Other Scene* (London, 2002). For a discussion of cultural violence, see Pierre Bourdieu, *Langage et pouvoir symbolique* (Paris, 2001).
22. Frédéric Bobin and Olivier Faye, "Emmanuel Macron 'reconnaît' la responsabilité de France dans l'assassinat d'Ali Boumendjel en Algérie," *Le Monde*, 3 March 2021, https://www.lemonde.fr/afrique/article/2021/03/03/france-algerie-emmanuel-macron-reconnait-la-responsabilite-de-la-france-dans-l-assassinat-d-ali-boumendjel_6071806_3212.html.
23. The entire report can be found at Benjamin Stora, *Les questions mémorielles portant sur la colonisation et la guerre d'Algérie*, January 2021, https://www.vie-publique.fr/sites/default/files/rapport/pdf/278186.pdf.

Bibliography

Archives

Archives nationales (Paris)

BB 18 / 3608, 3609, 3610, 3611, 3612, 3613, 3614, 3615, 3616, 4103, 7079
F7 / 13412, 13170, 13171, 13178, 13412

Archives nationales d'Alger (Algérie)

16E1 / 03 / 02

Archives nationales d'Outre-mer (Aix-en-Provence)

Alger 9301 / 106, 107
Alger 91303 / 67
Alger 1F / 15, 33, 34, 36, 37, 53, 147, 148, 149, 150, 151, 154, 155, 213, 215, 216, 217, 218, 223, 413, 422, 439, 499, 500
Alger 91 / F / 9, 10, 13
Alger 1K / 37
Alger 4I / 3, 4, 5, 6, 174, 222, 224, 225, 226, 228
Constantine 93 / 1097, 1100, 1101, 1111, 1112, 1117, 1118, 1130, 1288, 1293, 1294, 1295, 1297, 1298, 1299, 1308, 1313, 1345, 1346, 1378, 1381, 1572, 1573, 1576, 1577, 1578, 1579, 1580, 1582, 1583, 1584, 1733, 1740, 1742, 1744, 1745, 1750, 1757, 2515, 5301, 5302, 5310, 5319, 5320, 5321, 5322, 5323, 5326, 5327, 5329, 5332, 5334, 5337, 5338, 5344, 5345, 5346, 5347, 5348, 5353, 5357, 5371, 5378, 5379, 5382, 5383, 5384, 5392, 5394, 5397, 5398, 5399, 5400, 5434, 5435, 5436, 5779, 5931, 6759, 6782, 6783, 6786, 6789, 6790, 6791, 6823, 6824, 6825, 6826, 6829, 6830, 6863, 6864, 6875, 6878, 6879, 6880, 6884, 6885, 6886, 6887, 6888, 6889, 6891, 6919, 6972, 6973, 6974, 6975, 7023, 7131, 7133, 7137, 7146, 7392, 7440, 7445, 7446, 7447, 7448, 7470, 7471, 7653, 7654, 7665, 20001, 20002, 20003, 20010, 20011, 20015, 20016, 20017, 20018, 20024, 20025, 20040, 20042, 20043, 20044, 20059, 20060, 20062, 20063, 20066, 20067, 20071, 20072, 20073, 20074, 20092, 20093, 20108, 20109, 20147, 20148, 20162, 20163, 20182, 20183, 20189, 20190, 20205, 20206, 20207, 20322, 20329, 20330, 20331, 20332, 20334, 20335
Constantine B / 2 / 1, 8
Constantine B / 3 / 360, 567
GGA 1H / 86
GGA 2H / 32, 33, 34, 35, 36, 37, 86, 87, 88, 89, 90, 122

238 BIBLIOGRAPHY

GGA 8H / 10, 29
GGA 9H / 1, 2, 16, 26, 29, 32, 39, 44, 48
GGA 11H / 55
GGA 2R / 122
GGA 3R / 7, 12, 18, 19, 22, 23, 44, 201, 212, 214, 215, 218, 219, 244, 262, 263, 264, 265, 270, 272, 274, 303, 304, 305
GGA 3CAB / 89, 99
Oran 92 / 3, 31, 67, 69, 99, 102, 111, 132, 133, 134, 167, 357, 358, 359, 360, 443, 452, 463, 484, 568, 576, 2386, 2406, 2421, 2422, 2423, 2432, 2438, 2468, 2469, 2529, 2577, 3268
Oran 1F / 70, 71, 72, 73, 74, 75, 76, 77, 78, 79, 80, 81, 82, 83, 84, 90, 92, 95, 96, 107, 108, 111
Oran 2F / 69
Oran 5I / 101, 102, 104, 105, 106, 107, 163, 164
Oasis 50, 52, 53, 61, 66, 73, 81

National Archives of Great Britain
FO / 141 / 1052
FO / 371 / 49275, 49276, 97086, 102936, 102940, 108591
FO / 881 / 8600X

Service historique de la défense (Vincennes)
1H / 216, 375, 2845, 2849, 2850, 2851, 2854, 2859, 2862, 2864, 3197
5N / 22

Newspapers

Action algérienne
Alger républicain
Algérie libre
Bulletin de la police criminelle
Dépêche algérienne
Dépêche de Constantine
Dépêche de l'Est
Dépêche quotidienne
Echo d'Alger
Echo d'Oran
Echo du soir
El Mograbi el arabi
El Ouma
Franc-tireur
Journal d'Alger
La Liberté
La Nouvelliste d'Alger
La Voix des colons
Le Morbacher

Nation algérienne
Nouvelle Oranie
Oran matin
Oran républicain
Presse libre

Primary and Secondary Sources

Abbas, Ferhat. *Le manifeste du peuple algérien: Suivi du Rappel du peuple algérien.* Paris: Orients Éditions, 2013.
Abitbol, Michel. *The Jews of North Africa during the Second World War.* Detroit, MI: Wayne State University Press, 1989.
Agéron, Charles-Robert. *Histoire de l'Algérie contemporaine*, vol. 2, *1871–1954.* Paris: Presses universitaires de France, 1979.
Aissaoui, Rabah. *Immigration and National Identity: North African Political Movements in Colonial and Postcolonial France.* London: I. B. Tauris, 2009.
Aissaoui, Rabah. "'Nous voulons dechirer le baillon et briser nos chaines': Racism, Colonialism, and Universalism in the Discourse of Algerian Nationalists in France between the Wars." *French History* 17 (2003): 186–209.
Aissaoui, Rabah, and Claire Eldridge, eds. *Algeria Revisited: History, Culture, and Identity.* London: Bloomsbury, 2017.
Aït Ahmed, Hocine. *Mémoires d'un combatant: L'esprit de l'indépendance, 1942–1952.* Paris: Éditions Sylvie Messinger, 1983.
Anderson, David. *Histories of the Hanged: Britain's Dirty War in Kenya and the End of Empire.* London: Phoenix, 2005.
Anderson, David, and David Killingray, eds. *Policing the Empire: Government, Authority, and Control, 1830–1940.* Manchester, UK: Manchester University Press, 1991.
Arnold, David. *Police Power and Colonial Rule: Madras, 1859–1947.* Oxford: Oxford University Press, 1987.
Asseraf, Arthur. *Electric News in Colonial Algeria.* Oxford: Oxford University Press, 2019.
Baghriche, Hachemi. *Militant à 15 ans au Parti populaire algérien (PPA): Le pont de la liberté.* Paris: L'Harmattan, 2005.
Balibar, Étienne. *Politics and the Other Scene.* London: Verso, 2002.
Barthes, Roland. *Camera Lucida: Reflections on Photography.* London: Hill and Wang, 1981.
Bat, Jean-Pierre, and Nicolas Courtin, eds. *Maintenir l'ordre colonial: Afrique et Madagascar, XIXe–XXe siècles.* Rennes: Presses universitaires de Rennes, 2012.
Belkin, Jordanna. "The Boot and the Spleen: When Was Murder Possible in British India?" *Comparative Studies in Society and History* 48 (2006): 462–493.
Berlière, Jean-Marc. *Le monde des policiers en France.* Paris: Éditions complexe, 1996.
Berlière, Jean-Marc. *Naissance de la police moderne.* Paris: Perrin, 2012.
Berlière, Jean-Marc, Catherine Denys, Dominique Kalifa, and Vincent Millot, eds. *Métiers de police: Être policier en Europe, XVIIIe–XXe siècles.* Rennes: Presses universitaires de Rennes, 2008.
Berlière, Jean-Marc, and René Levy. *Histoire des polices en France: De l'ancien régime à nos jours.* Paris: Nouveau Monde, 2013.

BIBLIOGRAPHY

Bernault, Florence. *Enfermement, prisons, et châtiments en Afrique: Du XIXe siècle à nos jours*. Paris: Karthala, 1999.
Blanchard, Emmanuel. *La police parisienne et les algériens (1944–1962)*. Paris: Nouveau Monde, 2011.
Blanchard, Emmanuel, Marieke Bloembergen, and Amandine Lauro, eds. *Policing in Colonial Empires: Cases, Connections, Boundaries*. Brussels: Peter Lang, 2017.
Blanchard, Emmanuel, and Joël Glasman. "Le maintien de l'ordre dans l'empire français: Une historiographie emergente." In *Maintenir l'ordre colonial: Afrique et Madagascar, XIXe–XXe siècles*, edited by Jean-Pierre Bat and Nicolas Courtin, 11–41. Rennes: Presses universitaires de Rennes, 2012.
Boum, Aomar, and Sarah Abrevaya Stein, eds. *The Holocaust and North Africa*. Stanford, CA: Stanford University Press, 2019.
Bourdieu, Pierre. *Langage et pouvoir symbolique*. Paris: Fayard, 2001.
Bouvaresse, Jacques. *Les délégations financières algériennes, 1898–1945*. Mont-Saint-Aignan: Publications des universités de Rouen et du Havre, 2008.
Branch, Daniel. *Defeating Mau Mau, Creating Kenya: Counterinsurgency, Civil War, and Decolonization*. Cambridge: Cambridge University Press, 2009.
Branche, Raphaëlle. "'Au temps de la France': Identités collectives et situation coloniale en Algérie." *Vingtième siècle* 117 (2013): 199–213.
Branche, Raphaëlle. *La torture et l'armée pendant la guerre d'Algérie*. Paris: Gallimard, 2001.
Branche, Raphaëlle. "La torture pendant la guerre d'Algérie." In *La guerre d'Algérie (1954–2004): Fin de l'amnésie*, edited by Mohammed Harbu and Benjamin Stora, eds. Paris: Robert Laffont, 2004.
Brower, Benjamin Claude. *A Desert Named Peace: The Violence of France's Empire in the Algerian Sahara, 1844–1902*. New York: Columbia University Press, 2009.
Brubaker, Rogers. *Citizenship and Nationhood in France and Germany*. Cambridge, MA: Harvard University Press, 1992.
Burton, Antoinette. *Dwelling in the Archive: Women Writing House, Home, and History in Late Colonial India*. Oxford: Oxford University Press, 2003.
Cabral, Amilcar. *Resistance and Decolonization*. London: Rowman and Littlefield, 2016.
Campbell, Caroline. *Political Belief in France, 1927–1945: Gender, Empire, and Fascism in the Croix de Feu and Parti social français*. Baton Rouge: Louisiana State University Press, 2015.
Cantier, Jacques. *L'Algérie sous le regime de Vichy*. Paris: Odile Jacob, 2002.
Cantier, Jacques. "Les gouverneurs Viollette et Bordès et la politique algérienne de la France à la fin des années vingt." *Révue française de l'histoire d'Outre-mer* 84 (1997): 25–49.
Cantier, Jacques, and Eric Jennings, eds. *L'empire colonial sous Vichy*. Paris: Odile Jacob, 2004.
Carlier, Omar. *Entre nation et jihad: Histoire sociale des radicalismes algériens*. Paris: Presses de Sciences Po, 1995.
Çelik, Zeynep. *Urban Forms and Colonial Confrontations: Algiers under French Rule*. Berkeley: University of California Press, 1997.
Chatterjee, Partha. *The Nation and Its Fragments: Colonial and Postcolonial Histories*. Princeton, NJ: Princeton University Press, 1993.

Chémery, Valentin. "Policing and the Problem of Crime within Local Communities in Colonial Algeria, ca. 1850–1890." In *Policing in Colonial Empires: Cases, Connections, Boundaries*, edited by Emmanuel Blanchard, Marieke Bloembergen, and Amandine Lauro, 119–136.Brussels: Peter Lang, 2017.

Chevandier, Christian. *Policiers dans la ville: Une histoire des gardiens de la paix*. Paris: Gallimard, 2012.

Clancy-Smith, Julia A. *Rebel and Saint: Muslim Notables, Populist Protest, Colonial Encounters (Algeria and Tunisia, 1800–1904)*. Berkeley: University of California Press, 1994.

Cole, Joshua. *Lethal Provocation: The Constantine Murders and the Politics of French Algeria*. Ithaca, NY: Cornell University Press, 2019.

Cole, Simon A. *Suspect Identities: A History of Fingerprinting and Criminal Identification*. Cambridge, MA: Harvard University Press, 2001.

Collot, Claude. *Les institutions de l'Algérie durant la période coloniale (1830–1962)*. Paris: CNRS, 1987.

Colonna, Fanny. *Le meunier, les moines, et le bandit: Des vies quotidiennes dans l'Aurès (Algérie) du XXe siècle*. Arles: Actes Sud, 2010.

Cooper, Frederick, and Ann Laura Stoler, eds. *Tensions of Empire: Colonial Cultures in a Bourgeois World*. Berkeley: University of California Press, 1997.

Correale, Francesco. *La grande guerre des trafiquants: Le front colonial de l'Occident maghrébin*. Paris: L'Harmattan, 2014.

Courriou, Morgan, and M'hamed Oualdi, eds. *Une histoire sociale et culturelle du politique en Algérie et au Maghreb*. Paris: Éditions de la Sorbonne, 2018.

Courtois, Jean-Louis, and Michel Lejeune. *Les CRS en Algérie*. Paris: Marine, 2010.

Curat, Raymond, and André Knoertzer. *L'officier de police judiciaire en Algérie*. Alger: n.p., 1924.

Darmon, Pierre. *L'Algérie de Pétain: Les populations algériennes ont la parole, septembre 1939–novembre 1942*. Paris: Perrin, 2014.

Davidson, Naomi. *Only Muslim: Embodying Islam in Twentieth-Century France*. Ithaca, NY: Cornell University Press, 2012.

Davis, Bradley Camp. *Imperial Bandits: Outlaws and Rebels in the China-Vietnam Borderlands*. Seattle: University of Washington Press, 2017.

Déjeux, Jean. "Un bandit dans l'Aurès, de 1917 à 1921." *Revue de l'Occident musulman et de la Médeterranée* 26 (1978): 35–54.

Denis, Vincent, and Catherine Denys, eds. *Police d'empires, XVIIIe–XIXe siècles*. Rennes: Presses universitaires de Rennes, 2012.

Dermenjian, Geneviève. *La crise anti-juive oranaise (1895–1905): L'antisémitisme dans l'Algérie coloniale*. Paris: L'Harmattan, 1986.

Dine, Philip. "Shaping the Colonial Body: Sport and Society in Algeria, 1870–1962." In *Algeria and France, 1800–2000: Identity, Memory, Nostalgia*, edited by Patricia Lorcin, 33–48. Syracuse, NY: Syracuse University Press, 2006.

Djeghloul, Abdelkader. "Hors-la-loi, violence arabe et pouvoir colonial en Algérie au début du XXe siècle: Les frères Boutouizerat." *Revue de l'Occident musulman et de la Méditerranée* 38 (1984): 55–63.

Drew, Allison. *We Are No Longer French: Communists in Colonial Algeria*. Manchester, UK: Manchester University Press, 2014.

Ebel, Edouard. "Gendarmerie et contre-insurrection, 1791–1962." *Revue historique des armées* 268 (2012): 3–11.
Elkins, Caroline, and Susan Pederson. *Settler Colonialism in the Twentieth Century*. New York: Routledge, 2005.
Emsley, Clive. "Introduction: Political Police and the European Nation-State in the Nineteenth Century." In *The Politics of Policing in the Twentieth Century*, edited by Mark Mazower, 1–26. Providence, RI: Berghahn, 1997.
Emsley, Clive, and Barbara Weinberger. *Policing Western Europe: Politics, Professionalism, and Public Order, 1850–1940*. Westport, CT: Greenwood Press, 1991.
Evans, Martin. *Algeria: France's Undeclared War*. Oxford: Oxford University Press, 2012.
Evans, Martin. "Towards an Emotional History of Settler Decolonization: De Gaulle, Political Masculinity, and the End of French Algeria." *Settler Colonial Studies* 8 (2018): 213–243.
Fanon, Frantz. *Les damnés de la terre*. Paris: Éditions Maspero, 1968.
Fates, Youcef. "Les marqueurs du nationalisme: Les clubs sportifs musulmans dans l'Algérie colonial." *Quasimodo* 3–4 (1997): 121–129.
Fates, Youcef. *Sport et politique en Algérie*. Paris: L'Harmattan, 2009.
Fogarty, Richard S. *Race and War in France: Colonial Subjects in the French Army, 1914–1918*. Baltimore, MD: Johns Hopkins University Press, 2008.
Gallissot, René. *La république française et les indigènes: Algérie colonisée, Algérie algérienne (1870–1962)*. Paris: Éditions de l'Atelier, 2006.
Gallois, William. *A History of Violence in the Algerian Colony*. New York: Palgrave, 2013.
Genty, Jean-René. *Le mouvement nationaliste algérien dans le nord (1947–1957)*. Paris: L'Harmattan, 2008.
Gershovich, Moshe. *French Military Rule in Morocco: Colonialism and Its Consequences*. New York: Frank Cass, 2000.
Gibson, Nigel C. *Fanon: The Postcolonial Imagination*. Cambridge: Polity, 2003.
Gildea, Robert. *Fighters in the Shadows: A New History of the French Resistance*. London: Faber & Faber, 2015.
Giraud, Georges. *Notice sur l'organisation et le fonctionnement de la Police scientifique en Algérie*. Alger: n.p., 1928.
Gosnell, Jonathan K. *The Politics of French Algeria, 1930–1954*. Rochester, NY: University of Rochester Press, 2002.
Guha, Ranajit. *Dominance without Hegemony: History and Power in Colonial India*. Cambridge: Cambridge University Press, 1997.
Guha, Ranajit, ed. *Subaltern Studies: Writings on South Asian History and Society*. Vol. 1. Oxford: Oxford University Press, 1982.
Guignard, Didier. *L'abus de pouvoir dans l'Algérie coloniale*. Paris: Presses universitaires de Paris Ouest, 2010.
Hannoum, Abdelmajid. *Violent Modernity: France in Algeria*. Cambridge, MA: Harvard University Press, 2010.
Harbi, Mohammed. *Aux origins du FLN: Le populisme révolutionnaire en Algérie*. Paris: Éditions Complexe, 1975.
Harbi, Mohammed. *La guerre commence en Algérie*. Paris: Éditions Complexe, 1989.

Harbi, Mohammed, and Benjamin Stora, eds. *La guerre d'Algérie (1954–2004): Fin de l'amnésie*. Paris: Robert Laffont, 2004.
Haroun, Ali. *La 7e Wilaya: La guerre du FLN en France, 1954–1962*. Paris: Éditions du Seuil, 1986.
Hassett, Dónal. *Mobilizing Memory: The Great War and the Language of Politics in Colonial Algeria, 1918–1939*. Oxford: Oxford University Press, 2019.
Henni, Ahmed. *Économie de l'Algérie coloniale, 1830–1954*. Alger: Chihab Éditions, 2018.
Hobsbawm, Eric. *Bandits*. London: New Press, 2000.
House, Jim, and Neil MacMaster. *Paris 1961: Algerians, State Terror, and Memory*. Oxford: Oxford University Press, 2009.
Jackson, Julian. *A Certain Idea of France: The Life of Charles de Gaulle*. London: Allen Lane, 2018.
Jackson, Julian. *France: The Dark Years, 1940–1944*. New York: Oxford University Press, 2003.
Kaddache, Mahfoud. *Histoire du nationalisme algérien*. Paris: EDIF, 2000.
Kalifa, Dominique. *Crime et culture au XIXe siècle*. Paris: Éditions Perrin, 2005.
Kalifa, Dominique. *Vice, Crime, and Poverty: How the Western Imagination Invented the Underworld*. New York: Columbia University Press, 2019.
Kalifa, Dominique, and Pierre Karila-Cohen, eds. *La commissaire de police au XIXe siècle*. Paris: Publications de la Sorbonne, 2008.
Kalman, Samuel. "Criminalizing Dissent: Policing Banditry in the Constantinois, 1914–1918." In *Algeria Revisited: History, Culture, and Identity*, edited by Rabah Aissaoui and Claire Eldridge, 19–38. London: Bloomsbury, 2017.
Kalman, Samuel. *French Colonial Fascism: The Extreme Right in Algeria, 1919–1939*. New York: Palgrave, 2013.
Kalman, Samuel, and Sean Kennedy, eds. *The French Right between the Wars: Political Movements and Intellectual Trends from Conservatism to Fascism*. New York: Berghahn, 2014.
Kalyvas, Stathis R. *The Logic of Violence in Civil War*. Cambridge: Cambridge University Press, 2006.
Kateb, Kamel. *Européens, "indigènes," et juifs en Algérie (1830–1962)*. Paris: Presses universitaires de France, 2001.
Katz, Ethan. *The Burdens of Brotherhood: Jews and Muslims from North Africa to France*. Cambridge: Cambridge University Press, 2015.
Katz, Jonathan G. *Murder in Marrakesh: Émile Beauchamp and the French Colonial Adventure*. Bloomington: Indiana University Press, 2006.
Keller, Kathleen. *Colonial Suspects: Suspicion, Imperial Rule, and Colonial Society in Interwar West Africa*. Lincoln: University of Nebraska Press, 2018.
Keller, Richard C. *Colonial Madness: Psychiatry in French North Africa*. Chicago: University of Chicago Press, 2007.
Koulaksiss, Ahmed. *Le Parti socialiste et l'Afrique du nord: De Jaurès à Blum*. Paris: Armand Colin, 1991.
Le Cour Grandmaison, Olivier. *De l'indigénat. Anatomie d'un "monstre" juridique: Le droit colonial français en Algérie et dans l'empire français*. Paris: La Découverte, 2010.

Le Doussal, Roger. *Commissaire de police en Algérie (1952–1962): Une grenouille dans son puits ne voit qu'un coin de ciel.* Paris: Riveneuve, 2011.
Laskier, Michael. "The Jews of the Maghrib during the Second World War." *Africana* 16 (1994): 365–390.
Laskier, Michael. "Between Vichy Antisemitism and German Harassment: The Jews of North Africa during the Early 1940s." *Modern Judaism* 11 (1991): 343–369.
Lazreg, Marnia. *The Eloquence of Silence: Algerian Women in Question.* New York: Routledge, 1994.
Leconte, Daniel. *Les pied-noirs: Histoire et portrait d'un communauté.* Paris: Seuil, 1980.
Lefeuvre, Daniel. *Chère Algérie: La France et sa colonie, 1930–1962.* Paris: Flammarion, 2005.
Legg, Stephen. *Spaces of Colonialism: Delhi's Urban Governmentalities.* London: Blackwell, 2007.
Levine, Philippa, ed. *Gender and Empire.* Oxford: Oxford University Press, 2009.
Lorcin, Patricia M. E., ed. *Algeria and France, 1800–2000: Identity, Memory, Nostalgia.* Syracuse, NY: Syracuse University Press, 2006.
Lorcin, Patricia M. E. *Imperial Identities: Stereotyping, Prejudice, and Race in Colonial Algeria.* London: I. B. Tauris, 1995.
Lorcin, Patricia M. E. "Women, Gender, and Nation in Colonial Novels in Interwar Algeria." *Historical Reflections / Réflexions historiques* 28 (2002): 163–184.
Lorcy, Damien. *Sous le régime du sabre: La gendarmerie en Algérie, 1830–1870.* Rennes: Presses universitaires de Rennes, 2011.
Loubet del Bayle, Jean-Louis. *Police et Politique: Une approche sociologique.* Paris: L'Harmattan, 2012.
Luc, Jean-Noël, ed. *Gendarmerie, État, et société au XIXe siècle.* Paris: Publications de la Sorbonne, 2002.
MacMaster, Neil. *Colonial Migrants and Racism: Algerians in France, 1900–62.* New York: Palgrave, 1997.
MacMaster, Neil. "The Roots of Insurrection: The Role of the Algerian Village Assembly (Djemâa) in Peasant Resistance, 1863–1902." *Comparative Studies in History and Society* 52 (2013): 419–447.
Mahé, Alain. *Histoire de la Grande Kabylie, XIXe–XXe siècles: Anthropologie historique du lien social dans les communautés villageoises.* Paris: Éditions Bouchêne, 2000.
Manchon, Michaël. *lLe Racing universitaire d'Ager, 1927–1962: Un club sportif universitaire en milieu colonial.* Nice: Éditions Jacques Gandini, 2005.
Mann, Gregory. "What Was the Indigénat? The 'Empire of Law' in French West Africa." *Journal of African History* 50 (2009): 331–353.
Mangan, J. A. "Britain's Chief Export: Imperial Sport as Moral Metaphor, Political Symbol, and Cultural Bond." In *The Cultural Bond: Sport, Empire, Society*, edited by J. A. Mangan, 1–9. New York: Routledge, 1992.
Mangan, J. A., ed. *The Cultural Bond: Sport, Empire, Society.* New York: Routledge, 1992.
Marseille, Jacques. *Empire colonial et capitalisme français: Histoire d'un divorce.* Paris: Albin Michel, 1984.
Marynower, Claire. *L'Algérie à gauche, 1900–1962.* Paris: Presses universitaires de France, 2018.

Mazower, Mark, ed. *The Policing of Politics in the Twentieth Century.* Providence, RI: Berghahn Books, 1997.
McClintock, Anne. *Imperial Leather: Race, Gender, and Sexuality in the Colonial Contest.* New York: Routledge, 1995.
McCulloch, Jock. *Black Peril, White Virtue: Sexual Crime in Southern Rhodesia, 1902–1935.* Bloomington: Indiana University Press, 2000.
McDevitt, Patrick. *May the Best Man Win: Sport, Masculinity, and Nationalism in Great Britain and the Empire, 1880–1935.* New York: Palgrave, 2008.
McDougall, James. *A History of Algeria.* Cambridge: Cambridge University Press, 2017.
Meuleman, Johan Hendrick. *Le Constantinois entre les deux guerres mondiales: L'évolution économique et sociale de la population rurale.* Amsterdam: Van Gorcum, 1984.
Merle, Isabelle. "De la légalisation de la violence en contexte colonial." *Politix* 17 (2004): 137–162
Merriman, John. *Police Stories: Building the French State, 1815–1851.* Oxford: Oxford University Press, 2006.
Meynier, Gilbert. *Histoire intérieure du FLN, 1954–1962.* Paris: Fayard, 2004.
Meynier, Gilbert. *L'Algérie révélée: La guerre de 1914–1918 et le premier quart du XXe siècle.* Paris: Librarie Droz, 1981.
Monjardet, Dominique. *Ce que fait la police: Une sociologie de la force publique.* Paris: Éditions La Découverte, 1994.
Morlat, Patrice. *La répression coloniale au Vietnam (1908–1940).* Paris: L'Harmattan, 1990.
Muschalek, Marie. *Violence as Usual: Policing and the Colonial State in German Southwest Africa.* Ithaca, NY: Cornell University Press, 2019.
Naegelen, Marcel-Edmond. *Mission en Algérie.* Paris: Flammarion, 1962.
Nart, Raymond. *Histoire intérieure de la rébellion dans les Aurès.* Paris: L'Harmattan, 2015.
Neep, Daniel. *Occupying Syria under the French Mandate: Insurgency, Space, and State Formation.* Cambridge: Cambridge University Press, 2014.
Neilson, Keith, and T. J. Otte, eds. *Railways and International Politics: Paths of Empire, 1848–1925.* New York: Routledge, 2006.
Nouschi, André. *La naissance du nationalism algérien.* Paris: Éditions de Minuit, 1962.
Padwa, Howard. *Social Poison: The Culture and Politics of Opiate Control in Britain and France, 1821–1926.* Baltimore, MD: Johns Hopkins University Press, 2012.
Peyroulou, Jean-Pierre. *Guelma, 1945: Une subversion française dans l'Algérie coloniale.* Paris: La Découverte, 2009.
Planche, Jean-Louis. *Sétif 1945: Histoire d'un massacre annoncé.* Paris: Perrin, 2006.
Prakash, Amit. "Colonial Techniques in the Imperial Capital: The Prefecture of Police and the Surveillance of North Africans in Paris, 1925–circa 1970." *French Historical Studies* 36 (2013): 479–510.
Prochaska, David. *Making Algeria French: Colonialism in Bône, 1870–1920.* Cambridge: Cambridge University Press, 1990.
Rahal, Malika. *L'UDMA et les Udmistes: Contribution à l'histoire du nationalisme algérien.* Alger: Éditions Harzakh, 2017.

Recham, Belkacem. *Les musulmans algériens dans l'armée française (1919–1945)*. Paris: L'Harmattan, 1996.
Reiner, Robert. *The Politics of the Police*. Oxford: Oxford University Press, 2010.
Rey-Goldzeiguer, Annie. *Aux origines de la guerre d'Algérie, 1940–1945*. Paris: La Découverte, 2002.
Rid, Thomas. "Razzia: A Turning Point in Modern Strategy." *Terrorism and Political Violence* 21 (2009): 617–635.
Roberts, Sophie B. *Citizenship and Anti-Semitism in French Colonial Algeria, 1870–1962*. Cambridge: Cambridge University Press, 2017.
Rosenberg, Clifford. *Policing Paris: The Origins of Modern Immigration Control between the Wars*. Ithaca, NY: Cornell University Press, 2006.
Rousso, Henry. *The Vichy Syndrome: History and Memory in France since 1944*. Cambridge: Cambridge University Press, 1991.
Ruedy, John. *Modern Algeria: The Origins and Development of a Nation*. Bloomington: University of Indiana Press, 1992.
Saaida, Oissila. *Algérie coloniale: Musulmans et chrétiens—le contrôle de l'État (1830–1914)*. Paris: CNRS Éditions, 2015.
Said, Edward. *Orientalism*. New York: Vintage, 1979.
Salinas, Alfred. *Pétain, Algérie et la revanche*. Paris: L'Harmattan, 2018.
Schroeter, Daniel J. "Between Metropole and French North Africa: Vichy's Anti-Semitic Legislation and Colonialism's Racial Hierarchies." In *The Holocaust and North Africa*, edited by Aomar Boum and Sarah Abrevaya Stein, 19–49. Stanford, CA: Stanford University Press, 2019.
Scott, James C. *Domination and the Arts of Resistance: Hidden Transcripts*. New Haven, CT: Yale University Press, 1990.
Scott, James C. *Weapons of the Weak: Everyday Forms of Peasant Resistance*. New Haven, CT: Yale University Press, 1987.
Sessions, Jennifer. *By Sword and Plow: France and the Conquest of Algeria*. Ithaca, NY: Cornell University Press, 2011.
Sessions, Jennifer. "Making Settlers Muslim: Religion, Resistance, and Everyday Life in Nineteenth-Century French Algeria." *French History* 33 (2019): 259–277.
Sherman, Taylor. *State Violence and Punishment in India*. New York: Routledge, 2010.
Simon, Jacques. *L'Algérie dans la deuxième guerre mondiale*. Paris: L'Harmattan, 2015.
Simon, Jacques. *Le MTLD (Le Mouvement pour le triomphe des libertés démocratiques), 1947–1954*. Paris: L'Harmattan, 2003.
Simon, Jacques. *Le PPA (Le Parti du peuple algérien) (1937–1947)*. Paris: L'Harmattan, 2005.
Simon, Jacques. *L'Étoile nord-africaine (1926–1937)*. Paris: L'Harmattan, 2003.
Simon, Jacques. *Messali Hadj, 1898–1974: La passion de l'Algérie libre*. Paris: Tirésias, 1998.
Sinclair, Georgina. *At the End of the Line: Colonial Policing and the Imperial Endgame*. Manchester, UK: University of Manchester Press, 2006.
Slymovics, Susan. "'Other Places of Confinement': Bedeau Internment Camp for Algerian Jewish Soldiers." In *The Holocaust and North Africa*, edited by Aomar Boum and Sarah Abrevaya Stein, 95–112. Stanford, CA: Stanford University Press, 2019
Stoler, Ann Laura. *Along the Archival Grain: Epistemic Anxieties and Colonial Common Sense*. Princeton, NJ: Princeton University Press, 2009.

Stoler, Ann Laura. *Carnal Knowledge and Imperial Power: Race and the Intimate in Colonial Rule.* Berkeley: University of California Press, 2002.
Stoler, Ann Laura. *Race and the Education of Desire: Foucault's History of Sexuality and the Colonial Order of Things.* Durham, NC: Duke University Press, 1995.
Stora, Benjamin. *La gangrène et l'oubli: La mémoire de la guerre d'Algérie.* Paris: La Découverte, 1998.
Stora, Benjamin. *Messali Hadj, 1898–1974.* Paris: L'Harmattan, 2004.
Stovall, Tyler. "The Colour Line behind the Lines: Racial Violence in France during the Great War." *American Historical Review* 103 (1998): 737–769.
Surkis, Judith. *Sex, Law, and Sovereignty in French Algeria, 1830–1930.* Ithaca, NY: Cornell University Press, 2019.
Temlali, Yassine. *La genèse de la Kabylie: Aux origins de l'affirmation berbère en Algérie (1830–1962).* Alger: Éditions Harzakh, 2015.
Thénault, Sylvie. "Baya Hocine's Papers: A Source for the History of Algerian Prisons during the War of Independence." *Historical Reflections / Réflexions historiques* 46 (2020): 110–127.
Thénault, Sylvie. *Une drôle de justice: Les magistrats dans la guerre d'Algérie.* Paris: La Découverte, 2004.
Thénault, Sylvie. *Violence ordinaire dans l'Algérie coloniale.* Paris: Odile Jacob, 2012.
Thomas, Martin. *Empires of Intelligence: Security Services and Colonial Disorder after 1914.* Berkeley: University of California Press, 2008.
Thomas, Martin. *The French Empire between the Wars: Imperialism, Politics, and Society.* Manchester, UK: University of Manchester Press, 2005.
Thomas, Martin. *Violence and Colonial Order: Police, Workers, and Protest in European Colonial Empires, 1918–1940.* Cambridge: Cambridge University Press, 2012.
Tilly, Charles. *The Politics of Collective Violence.* Cambridge: Cambridge University Press, 2003.
Trumbull, George R., IV. *An Empire of Facts: Colonial Power, Cultural Knowledge, and Islam in Algeria, 1870–1914.* Cambridge: Cambridge University Press, 2009.
Urban, Yerri. *L'indigène dans le droit colonial français, 1865–1955.* Paris: Fondation Varenne, 2010.
Vann, Michael G. "Of Pirates, Postcards, and Public Beheadings: The Pedagogic Execution in French Colonial Indochina." *Historical Reflections / Réflexions historiques* 36 (2010): 39–58.
Vann, Michael G. "Sex and the Colonial City: Mapping Masculinity, Whiteness, and Desire in French Occupied Hanoi." *Journal of World History* 28 (2017): 395–435.
Verdès-Leroux. Jeannine. *Les français d'Algérie, de 1830 à nos jours.* Paris: Fayard, 2001.
Vié, Jean-Emile. *Mémoires d'un directeur des Renseignements généraux.* Paris: Albin Michel, 1988.
Villatoux, Paul, and Marie-Catherine Villatoux. *La république et son armée face au "péril subversif": Guerre et actions psychologiques en France (1945–1960).* Paris: Indes savantes, 2005.
Weiner, Martin. *An Empire on Trial, Race, Murder, and Justice under British Rule, 1870–1935.* Cambridge: Cambridge University Press, 2009.
Wilder, Gary. *The French Imperial Nation-State: Negritude and Colonial Humanism between the Two World Wars.* Chicago: University of Chicago Press, 2005.

Woollacott, Angela. *Gender and Empire*. Basingstoke, UK: Palgrave, 2006.
Zack, Lizabeth. "French and Algerian Identity Formation in 1890s Algiers." *French Colonial History* 2 (2002): 115–143.
Zytnicki, Colette. "La politique antisémite du régime de Vichy dans les colonies." In *L'empire colonial sous Vichy*, edited by Jacques Cantier and Eric Jennings, 153–176. Paris: Jacob, 2004.

INDEX

Abbas, Ferhat, 14, 86, 142, 152, 184, 227n9, 229n36; and the AML, 43; elections, 149, 165; and nationalism, 133–134, 149; and the police/gendarmerie, 45; and the PPA-MTLD, 156; and the UDMA, 166

Administrators (communes), 8, 11, 55, 59, 69–70, 79, 82, 94, 122; authority and responsibilities, 73, 108; and banditry, 54, 60, 72–74, 77, 187; and conscription riots, 65; enforcement of legal code, 86, 89; and informants, 72; and local populations, 73–74, 77; murder of, 78; police/gendarmerie oversight, 25–26, 73, 112; and police recruitment, 39–40, 46; and the PPA-MTLD, 159, 163, 179; racial stereotyping, 109, 115; security concerns, 93, 99; and surveillance spéciale, 114; under the Vichy regime, 133

Ait Ahmed, Hocine, 18, 155, 171, 178, 181

Alger (city), 5, 39, 51, 152, 166, 191; Algerian War of Independence in, 183; banditry in, 72; black markets, 135; conscription riots in, 65; crime in, 137–138; policing in, 5, 24, 138, 157, 162; population, 89, 107; PPA-MTLD in, 162; protests in, 157–158; racism in, 134; under the Vichy regime, 118, 129, 135

Alger (Department), 6, 59; Algerian War of Independence in, 185; anti-nationalism in, 160, 165; arms dealing in, 172; banditry in, 73, 80; crime in, 134; elections in, 165; FLN-ALN in, 185; policing in, 38, 160, 180; population, 89, 105; PPA-MTLD in, 168, 180; under the Vichy regime, 117, 127

Algerians, 4, 10, 20, 93, 128, 131, 157, 164; and anti-colonialism, 78, 101, 109, 134, 159, 165, 167; antisemitism, 129–133; and banditry, 62, 78; and crime, 95, 103–108, 138, 165; emigration, 180–181; European perceptions of, 103–104, 138, 157, 182; legal status, 108; murder of, 78, 105–106,

134; and nationalism, 109, 127, 134–135, 165, 167; and police brutality, 158, 167; in the police/gendarmerie, 20, 23–24, 40–51, 120, 123, 132–133; population, 10; poverty, 119, 135, 164; press, 154; public opinion, 133, 167; and racial boundaries, 4, 68, 103–104, 134, 167; segregation, 90, 96; during World War II, 118–119, 124–125, 127, 133–137, 141

Algerian War of Independence (1954–1962), 2, 10, 13–15, 17–18, 26, 32, 116, 147, 191; Barricades Week, 186; Battle of Algiers, 185–187, 189; Constantine uprising, 188; executions, 188; FLN, 181, 183–189; judicial repression, 178; massacres, 184, 188; military, 176; OAS, 186; paratroopers, 178, 183–189; policing, 115, 176, 183–188; security zones, 185; state of emergency, 185; suspension of civil liberties, 187; torture, 178, 183–189; troop complement, 33

Algérie française, 2, 4, 20, 37, 120, 147, 150–152, 160, 177, 179, 186

Amis du manifeste et de la liberté (AML), 43, 156–159

anti-colonialism, 4, 6, 10–12, 15–16; anti-colonial violence, 2, 10–11, 16, 68, 70, 83–90, 95, 97, 102–111, 114, 154, 156, 160, 167, 169–171; banditry and, 54, 68, 70–71, 76, 81; and communism, 85, 126; crime and, 16, 88–89, 93–94, 103–104, 108–114, 171; and elections, 148–151; against European hegemony, 16, 83, 169, 176; and food shortages, 157; and insurrection, 12, 77–78, 82, 115; and murder, 105–109; and nationalism, 84, 99, 116, 149, 151, 160–164, 167, 169–171, 176; against officials, 108–109; against police/gendarmes, 40, 77, 83–84, 112–113, 116; propaganda, 110; resistance, 115–116, 125–126, 169; and sport, 96–101; trail derailments and, 94–95

249

INDEX

antisemitism, 62; colonial fascism and, 128–129; in the Constantine riots (1934), 84, 130, 133; murder of Jews, 109, 129; Muslim, 132–133; in police, 120, 130–131; politicians, 129–131; propaganda, 129; settler, 146; under the Vichy regime, 118–120, 127–129, 140; violence, 129–132
Arabs, 2, 5, 7–9, 12–13, 15–18, 70, 81, 110; during the Algerian War of Independence, 178, 184, 186–187; anti-colonial violence, 96–99, 101, 155; anti-colonialism, 4, 16–17, 82, 84–86, 111, 155–158, 164, 182, 188, 191; antisemitism, 130, 132; armed resistance, 77, 87, 134; arms sales, 91–93; assault victims, 109, 141–142, 181; and the black market, 138; and crime, 88, 108, 190; economy, 88–89, 107, 119, 127; European perceptions of, 12, 65, 88, 92–93, 95, 107, 109, 112, 115, 118, 121, 127, 155, 180; factory labor, 31, 125, 152; as informants, 72, 187; massacre of, 158, 184, 187, 191; murder of, 105–109, 149, 158, 184, 187; and the murder of Europeans, 101, 106, 108–109; and nationalism, 37, 86–87, 149; non-cooperation with authorities, 29–30, 71–72; police brutality towards, 111–115, 121, 134, 181, 184, 186–187; policing of, 20, 22, 24, 27–29, 37, 79, 180, 190; poverty/unemployment, 31, 89–90, 107, 109, 134–135, 152; and the PPA-MTLD, 163, 168; rebellion, 25, 59, 191; in sports, 96–100; subject status, 7, 57, 68, 86, 101, 127, 130, 150, 153; torture of, 186, 191; under the Vichy regime, 125, 127
archives, 11–14, 54–55, 71, 104, 135, 205n3
armaments, 170; ammunition, 90–92, 173; armories, 92–93; arrests, 111, 115, 180–181; blasting powder, 60, 92–93; explosives, 68, 93–95, 173; firearms, 90–92, 109–110, 170–173; grenades, 171–172; illegal possession, 180–181; mines, 93–94; prohibition, 92–93, 185, 188; seizures by police, 31, 90–93, 112–113, 160, 164, 170, 175, 186; submachine guns, 169–173; trafficking, 31, 90–94, 116, 170; transport, 91
Armée de liberation nationale (ALN), 184–185, 189, 191
assault, 88, 163; of Algerians, 88–89, 143; by allied soldiers, 141–143; and armed robbery, 102; and banditry, 54, 68, 74, 81; of business owners/managers, 102; of children, 112, 147; of Europeans, 84, 102–103, 115, 143, 190; at football grounds, 96–97; by law enforcement, 111–115, 165, 186–187; of officials, 84, 107–109, 143; of police/gendarmes, 83–84, 102, 108–110, 114, 170; by PPA members, 160, 169; prosecution of, 102, 115; and riots, 78; and tax collection, 108–109; of women, 112, 143
Assemblée algérienne, 149–150, 164, 176–177, 180
Aurès, 35, 38, 53–54, 60, 62, 66, 68, 77, 149, 188

banditry, 11–12, 16–18, 87, 89, 169, 174–175, 185–186, 190–191; anti-conscription, 63; and anti-imperialism, 63, 68, 77, 81–82, 170; and armed robbery, 60–61, 170; and arms dealing, 170; bandits d'honneur, 55; capture/execution of, 75–76; and crime, 67–68, 70, 72–74; deserters and, 11, 65–66, 71; family members, 76, 78–79, 82; gangs, 60–62, 66–68, 70, 73–81, 170; killing of, 61, 187; and murder, 68–70, 77–79; and nationalism, 68–69, 71–73, 160, 170; OS and, 171; policing of, 25, 53–55, 62, 71, 73, 76–77, 185–186; post-1918, 80–82; PPA-MTLD and, 168–170, 175, 182; public assistance, 55, 61, 71–82; trials of, 75
Batna, 24, 35–36, 44, 77–78, 91, 109, 113, 132, 145, 159, 163
Battle of Algiers, 183, 185–197, 189
Bechara (cattle theft), 4, 24–25, 62, 73, 80, 88
Belouizdad, Mohamed, 155, 171
Ben Bella, Mohamed, 18, 172, 178, 181
Bendjelloul, Mohamed, 86, 100, 152
Biskra, 32–34, 44, 56–57, 67, 101, 115
black market, 25, 80; clandestine abattoirs, 136–137; clothing, 135–138; food, 136–140; fuel, 137–139; identity papers, 137; Jews and, 129; Muslims and, 136–138; police involvement in, 140–141; price gouging, 135–141; press-public and, 139; ration cards, 135–136; restaurants and, 136; smuggling and, 136–137; soap, 139; soldiers and, 138–139; wool, 137; during World War II, 119, 121–123, 127, 129, 133–141
Blida, 97, 100, 158, 178, 231n64
Blum, Léon, 120–121
Blum-Viollette bill (1936), 85, 132
Bône, 5, 95, 104; banditry in, 67, 74–76; crime in, 72, 102, 104–107; football violence in,

INDEX

98; insurrections in, 149; OS in, 174–175, 178; police brutality, 113; policing in, 34–35, 41, 44, 48, 56, 111, 122, 136, 141; population, 34, 89; PPA-MTLD in, 164; during World War II, 122, 135–136, 142
Bordj-Bou-Arreridj, 32, 65, 72, 110–111
Bougie, 44, 46, 78–79, 90–92, 95, 109, 160, 168, 175
brawls, 113, 131, 142–143, 146
brigade économique, 122–123, 136–141
brigades mobiles, 21–22, 26, 31, 73–74, 91, 93, 170
brigades rurales, 23–25
budgets, 30, 35, 37, 68, 139, 168
Bugeaud, Thomas, 4, 6–7, 189–190

cafés maures, 19, 25, 27, 73, 79, 115, 152, 161, 168, 180, 185, 188
caids, 8, 57–58, 64, 108, 142, 162, 165, 197n12; assassination of, 66, 70, 73–74, 170; assaults on, 70, 78, 108, 169–170; and bandits, 76, 108; and crime, 108, 114, 137; death threats against, 169; enforcement of laws, 86; and insurrection, 57–58, 60, 77; and nationalism, 148, 156; obstruction of justice, 93, 115; and the OS, 174; relations with police/gendarmes, 23, 25, 105, 112–114
casbah (Alger), 10, 62, 72, 84, 178, 180, 187
cavaliers, 19, 25, 30, 36, 40, 58, 60, 66, 68, 72, 109, 165, 169
chantiers de la jeunesse, 118, 143
chasseurs d'Afrique, 60, 63, 65
Châteaudun-du-Rhumel, 49, 68, 110
Chatigneau, Yves (governor general), 149–150, 156–157, 162, 182
Collo, 48–49, 92–93, 113
colonial violence, 4, 6, 181, 191; during the Algerian War of Independence, 184–189; allied soldiers and, 141–142; French army and, 56, 142, 185, 191; and French hegemony, 88, 111–116, 120–121, 147, 149, 151, 162, 167–170, 180, 182, 184–191; massacres, 149, 158, 167, 182–183, 187–189; and murder, 105; officials and, 134, 151, 182; police/gendarmerie and, 4, 40, 47, 62, 86, 110–115, 134, 147, 151, 157–158, 167, 170, 175–177, 180, 184–191; against the PPA/MTLD, 151, 157–158, 169–170, 175–177, 182; torture, 186, 191; Vichy regime and, 134, 147
Comité nationale française de l'épuration, 127, 132

Comité révolutionnaire d'unité et d'action, 171, 181
Commisariat général aux Questions juives, 128
communes de pleine exercice, 7–8, 24–25, 33, 40
communes mixtes, 7–8, 68, 83, 107; administrators, 108, 115; arms traffic in, 93; banditry in, 53, 60–61, 72–73, 170; crime in, 78, 190; elections in, 165; nationalism in, 148; policing in, 8, 25, 33, 40–41, 79; PPA-MTLD in, 161, 165, 168, 170; riots in, 77
communism, 199n49; and Algerian nationalism, 126, 151, 153; anti-communism, 42, 118–120, 125–126, 144; internment, 126–127; mass arrests, 126–127; membership/organization, 126; Parti communiste français, 85, 152; police inquiries, 22, 125; propaganda, 126; riots, 23; settlers and, 151; Vichy regime and, 118–126, 144
Compagnies républicaines de sécurité (CRS), 23, 121, 180, 185–186, 236n8
Compagnons de France, 125–126
Constantinois, 11, 15, 18, 64; 8 May 1945 in, 37, 157–159; anti-colonialism in, 81, 87, 111; arms traffic in, 93; banditry in, 54–55, 66, 72, 76, 80–82, 87, 170, 191; desertion in, 78; murder in, 105; population, 105; rebellion in, 77–78, 87, 102, 158; security concerns, 33; topography, 64, 169; train derailments in, 94
Constantine (city), 36, 60, 70, 77, 94–95, 107, 133, 140, 156, 168; antisemitism in, 129–130; arms dealing in, 91, 93; football violence, 97, 100; murder in, 107; nationalism in, 133, 154, 158; policing in, 24, 35–36, 41–44, 46, 48, 122, 125, 143, 154; population, 89; PPA-MTLD in, 163; riot (5 August 1934), 35, 84, 130, 133, 158; during World War II, 123, 125, 137–140
Constantine (department), 2, 6, 16, 28–29, 80, 89, 110–111, 134, 143; 8 May 1945 in, 149, 158; Algerian War of Independence in, 188; anti-colonialism, 89; arms traffic in, 92; banditry in, 53, 73, 80–81; electoral fraud, 165; football violence in, 97–98; gendarmerie, 34–36, 92, 110; and nationalism, 160; OS in, 175; policing in, 34, 36, 38, 44, 92, 105, 145, 160, 165; population, 89, 105; PPA-MTLD in, 168, 178, 181; rebellion in, 56–58; during World War II, 117–123, 134, 136, 145

INDEX

Corps civil de douairs, 17, 25–26, 122–123, 139–140
crime, 2–4, 6, 10–12; anti-colonial, 6, 10–11, 84–90, 93–99, 101–109, 114–115, 134, 169–170; banditry and, 54–55, 67, 81, 170; crime rate, 19, 24, 88; crime scenes, 27–28; criminal investigations, 71, 90–91, 105–107; criminalization of nationalist politics, 151, 176–177; economy and, 80, 105; football violence, 96–99; gangs, 66–68, 91, 102, 170, 177; in Kabylia, 59, 105–106, 169–170; murder, 105–108, 164–170; Muslim victims, 88, 105–106, 190; officials and, 99, 108–109; policing and, 40, 88, 105–106, 110–113, 122; poverty and, 59; prioritization of European victims, 4, 190; race and, 104–109, 115; and security, 6, 108; sexual assault, 103–104; violent, 11–12, 75, 78, 102–115, 169–171; during World War II, 122, 135–143, 144
criminal justice system, 3, 40, 81; court proceedings, 102; criminal code, 44, 75, 88; defense attorneys, 28, 178; evidence, 105; penal law, 41; practices, 115; prosecutions, 114; prosecutors, 28, 81, 160, 166, 170, 177–178; racial bias, 114–115
Croix de Feu/Parti social français, 14, 100, 118, 120, 128–129, 144

Debaghine, Lamine, 149, 155, 161, 171
De Gaulle, Charles, 43, 122, 124, 132, 186
Délégations financières, 7, 23, 68, 117, 149, 153
deputy prefects, 113, 159, 163; and banditry, 53, 62, 74, 76, 79; and crime, 99, 108, 111; during the Great War, 65; meeting bans, 164; and police recruitment/discipline, 40, 48, 50; and policing, 179; under the Vichy regime, 134
deserters, 11, 70, 205n5, 208n43; and bandit gangs, 66, 68, 74, 81; capture of, 73, 77; in the Constantinois, 11, 54–55, 63–64, 78; during the Great War, 65–66, 71, 73, 81; post-1918, 81; and the PPA/MTLD, 170; trials, 75; during World War II, 138
Direction de la sécurité générale, 20, 43, 122, 126
Direction de la surveillance du territoire (DST), 22–23, 176, 185
djemâas, 8, 76, 109, 134, 148, 165, 168–170, 182, 185
droit de séjour, 75, 114, 160

Duval, Raymond, 149, 159
duwars, 1, 8, 19, 198n46; anti-colonialism in, 72, 78, 160; arms seizures in, 92; banditry in, 55, 60–61, 67–68; crime in, 190; dwelling searches, 92, 106; murder in, 108; OS in, 174; policing in, 24–25, 30–31, 70; PPA-MTLD in, 160–161, 168–169, 180; rebellion in, 77, 82

economy, 10, 35, 68, 84, 89–90, 94, 119, 157; agricultural, 35, 54–58, 70, 89, 95, 106–107, 119–120, 135, 157, 159; Algerian businesses/shops, 32, 56, 70, 80, 89, 95, 127, 168; Algerian wages, 31, 89–90, 106; and banditry, 56, 68; black market, 135–141; boycotts, 168; customs/duties, 35, 89, 122, 140; during the Great War, 80, 125, 127, 134–135; European trade, 10, 56, 90, 95, 119–120, 168; and French hegemony, 109–110; Great Depression, 35, 80, 89, 159; harvests, 55–59, 62, 107; import-export trade, 135, 157; industrial, 95, 157; inflation, 80; livestock, 89, 157, 159; market closures, 78, 140; prices, 80, 107, 157; shopkeepers, 85, 135; taxation, 35, 89; unemployment, 80, 95, 152–153; urban, 89–90, 119–120, 135, 153, 157; wages, 152–153; during World War II, 119–120, 127, 129, 134–135
Edough, 68, 74–76, 112
education, 9, 41, 44, 85–86, 119, 154, 161–162, 171, 173, 181
elections, 150, 154, 157, 165; boycotts, 150; electoral reform, 157; European candidates, 150; fraud, 164–167, 182–183; killing of voters, 148; municipal, 154, 156, 165, 171; Muslim electoral college, 80, 86; nationalism and, 148, 150, 154, 156; official vote rigging, 150, 162, 164–165, 187; police/gendarmerie and, 164–165, 180; PPA-MTLD in, 150, 154, 156, 161, 164–168, 171, 180–183; regional, 156, 164–165, 171; voter intimidation, 150, 165
El Maghreb el arabi, 161, 166, 227n9
Étoile nord-africaine (ENA), 85, 87, 99–101, 148–149, 152–154, 176
évolués, 9, 41, 80, 85–87, 100, 118, 152, 155

fascism, 14, 30, 51, 100–101, 117–121, 124, 128–132, 140, 143–147, 151
Fédération des élus musulmans, 9, 85–86, 100, 152, 154–155
football violence, 84, 95–101, 155

INDEX

France, 3, 6, 11, 20, 27, 37, 59, 63–64, 108, 117–120, 132, 149–150, 164, 190; Algerians in, 151–152, 157, 170, 173; and the Algerian War of Independence, 184–185, 189; anti-communism in, 126; antisemitism in, 120; and arms dealing, 91–92, 172; colonial police recruitment in, 39; criminal justice in, 182; emigration to, 80, 90, 119, 153; gendarmerie in, 22; the Holocaust in, 128; police violence in, 113; policing in, 30, 54, 71, 113, 120–121, 151–152, 185, 190; during World War II, 117–118, 120–121, 124–126, 144–146
fraud, 62, 94, 122, 129, 137–138, 148, 164–166, 180–183
freemasons, 17, 42, 118–121, 146–147
Front de liberation nationale (FLN), 37, 178, 181, 183–191

gardes champêtres, 4, 19, 21–22, 25, 83–84, 169, 180
gardes forestières, 21–22, 45, 71, 76–78, 83–84, 113–114
gardes républicaines mobiles, 15, 22, 34, 38, 121, 199n60
gardiens de la paix, 43–44, 50
Gaullism/Free French, 17, 43, 118, 121–127, 132–136, 139–147, 227n112
gendarmerie, 3–5, 8, 10–12, 15–17, 21, 40, 55, 92, 105, 115; and 8 May 1945, 37, 47; during the Algerian War of Independence, 178, 184–189; Algerians in, 20, 23–26, 40–51, 71, 105, 108, 120, 133, 159, 202n101; anti-communism in, 121; antisemitism in, 120, 131; Arabic literacy, 5, 13, 15, 42, 72, 105, 127; arrests, 41, 93, 110–115, 121, 125, 138, 157, 162, 165, 168, 170, 175, 185, 190; assaults on gendarmes, 70, 74, 77, 102, 108–111, 115, 158; and banditry, 16, 53–55, 59–60, 66–68, 70–79, 170; barracks/housing, 33, 35–40; brigades, 5, 33, 36, 89, 113, 120, 125; brigadiers, 112–113, 125; brutality, 62, 72, 76–77, 81–82, 86, 111–113, 120–121, 131, 147, 170, 175–176; budgets, 33, 35–37, 40; commanders, 74, 110–111, 159, 180; corruption in, 113; defense of racial hegemony/imperial rule, 10, 15, 40–41, 54, 71–72, 83–89, 109–111, 120, 148, 190–191; destruction of property, 77, 86; diet, 38–39; discipline, 47–51, 122, 162; education/literacy, 34, 42, 201n87; and fascism, 120–121, 145; and football violence, 97–99; house searches, 60, 76, 78, 92, 110–112, 175, 180; illness/disease, 38–39; informants, 31, 60–61, 72, 75, 79, 81, 137, 169; intelligence gathering, 3, 22, 73, 137, 190; interrogations, 113, 175–176; investigative techniques, 29; in Kabylia, 105; killing of suspects, 75–76, 111, 169–170, 175; manhunts, 73, 75, 106; and massacres, 159, 184; moral standards, 39, 42; murder cases, 105–106, 109; and nationalism, 126, 152, 157; and the OS, 174–175; patrols, 3–4, 22, 33, 36, 72–73, 75, 78, 110–111, 136, 180; pensions, 42; physical fitness requirements, 39, 42, 201n87; and the PPA-MTLD, 157, 160–165, 168–170, 180–182; prisoners of war, 121–122; procedural regulations, 112; promotions, 39, 42, 47; race and, 41–42, 50–51, 112–113, 120, 128, 147; racial policing, 3, 10–11, 15, 27–29, 39–40, 54, 71, 83–84, 89, 105–106, 121, 125, 131, 147, 190–191; raids, 31, 138, 169, 175; recruitment, 24, 31–33, 38–40, 42; reports, 121, 179; and riots, 65, 120; roundups, 111–112; salaries, 33, 38–39, 43; search warrants, 166; shootings, 111, 115, 148, 169; staffing shortages, 5, 12, 19, 22, 31, 38, 78, 122–124, 139–140, 170, 185, 199nn60–61; surveillance, 3, 22, 53, 55, 60–62, 73, 88, 92, 121–122, 125–126, 168, 190–191; and torture, 176, 189; training, 39, 120, 122; uniforms, 109–110; vacations/leaves, 32–33, 38; vehicles, 22, 38, 89, 180, 196n12; working conditions, 24, 32, 36, 38–39; during World War II, 17, 43, 117, 120–122, 126–127, 136–137, 144–145
Gestapo, 161–162, 189
Giraud, Henri, 43, 131–132
goums, 25, 40, 58, 63, 66, 73, 76, 108–113, 185–186, 207n31
Governor General of Algeria, 5–6, 9, 11, 18, 64, 91, 115; and 8 May 1945, 159; administrative detention, 9, 79, 127, 138; during the Algerian War of Independence, 178, 184–185, 188–189; anti-communism, 127, 144; and arms traffic, 92, 94; and banditry, 60, 67, 72–73, 187; budgets, 24, 30, 35–37; and crime, 107, 139, 142; and nationalism, 156, 162, 187; and the OS, 174, 177; and police/gendarmerie recruitment/staffing, 39, 41, 43, 49, 122–123; and police oversight,

Governor General of Algeria (*continued*)
20–26, 34–36, 71, 73, 77–80, 99, 114, 120, 145–146, 168, 185; and the PPA-MTLD, 159, 162, 166–167; security concerns, 102; and sport, 100; during World War II, 117–118, 127
Great War, 11, 15, 17–18, 35, 52–55, 63–65, 71–72, 80–82, 88–90, 152, 185–186
Guelma, 18, 29, 37, 43, 53, 98, 124, 149, 158, 163, 175, 180–182

Hadj, Messali, 14, 18, 37, 85, 87, 133–134, 154–155, 160, 164–166, 168, 171, 184; anti-colonialism, 99, 164, 167; arrest, 149, 155, 164, 182, 228n31; and clandestine courts/djemâas, 168; deportation/exile, 151, 167; and elections, 148; and the ENA, 153; imprisonment, 85, 149, 154–157, 182; Messalism, 155–156, 171, 181–182; militant challenges to, 181–182; and the PPA-MTLD, 154, 161; and reformism, 156, 171; surveillance of, 22
home invasions, 67–70, 106, 142

Ibáñez, Thomas, 126
impôts arabes, 7, 35, 109, 125
indigénat, 8, 10, 68, 86–87, 107–108, 114, 153, 162, 187, 190
insoumis, 54–55, 66, 70–73, 75, 77, 81–82, 138, 170, 205n5
Inspecteur general de l'administration en mission extraordinaire (IGAME), 178
insurrections, 56–59, 62, 77–78, 84–87, 93, 99, 108–110, 115, 119, 122, 142, 155, 170–171, 176, 188
intelligence, 3–4, 6; and the Algerian War of Independence, 186; and anti-colonialism, 4; and arms traffic, 92; and banditry, 61–62, 68; Bureaux arabes and, 4; failures of, 68; intelligence bureaus, 134; intelligence state, 13; police/gendarmerie and, 123, 137; and the PPA-MTLD, 179; and racial hegemony/imperial order, 4, 190; the Renseignements généraux and, 179; rumours and, 105, 140, 156–157, 159; the Service de liaisons Nord-africaines and, 179; threat assessments, 190; and the Vichy regime, 121–123, 134, 137
Islam, 9, 25, 54–59, 62–63, 84, 88, 100, 109, 152, 160, 173; and banditry, 54, 62; European portrayals of, 56–59, 84, 88; murder and, 109; and the police/gendarmerie, 25; PPA-MTLD and, 160, 168, 171; Qur'anic law, 9, 86, 130, 168; religious rebellions, 55–61; and security concerns, 34, 84; and sport, 96

Jemmapes, 35–36, 60–61, 175
Jews, 17, 68, 118–119, 128–130; and antifascism, 146; arrest and imprisonment, 128, 130; assaults on, 129–130; attacks against antisemites, 129–131; Crémieux decree, 7, 26, 119, 127–128, 130–132, 190; demonization of, 118, 127–129; Jewish statute, 119, 128; and Muslims, 109, 132–133; persecution/harassment, 129, 134; in the police/gendarmerie, 140, 146–147; policing of, 121, 128–129; political antisemitism, 62, 128–129; during World War II, 17, 42, 118–121, 124, 127–130, 134
Jonnart Law, 80, 86, 132
judiciary, 2, 8–9, 27, 94, 151; and the Algerian War of Independence, 178; assaults on judges, 143; clandestine courts, 168–169; clemency, 114; courthouses, 177; and crime scenes, 27–28; defense of colonial hegemony, 111; European courts, 8–9, 113, 139, 166; European judges, 168, 177–178, 182; exclusion of Algerians, 8; magistrates, 70, 111, 168, 178; military tribunals, 137, 159–160, 167, 176, 178, 183; Muslim courts/judges, 8, 167; and police discipline/corruption, 48; PPA-MTLD and, 163, 168, 178; racial bias, 113–115; sentencing, 114; suspended sentences, 139; *tribunals répressifs*, 8
juries, 27–28, 113, 115, 168

Kabyles, 2, 4, 7–9, 12–13, 15–20, 68, 70, 81, 85, 105–108, 149–152; in the Algerian War of Independence, 178, 184, 186–187, 189; anti-colonialism, 4, 16–17, 53, 61, 68, 82, 84, 86, 111, 127, 155, 164, 168, 182, 188, 191; anti-colonial violence, 99, 101, 155; antisemitism, 130, 132; armed resistance, 77, 87, 134; arms traffic, 91–93; arrest and imprisonment of, 29, 37, 79, 90–92, 178, 190; assault on, 109, 141–142, 181, 184, 187; and banditry, 55, 59, 73, 75; citizenship/status, 7, 57, 86, 101, 127, 130, 150, 153; conscription of, 63; and crime, 59, 88, 101, 108; demographics, 89; economy, 88–89, 107, 119, 127; elections, 149; in the ENA, 153; European perceptions of, 12, 60, 65, 79, 92, 107–112,

115, 121, 127, 155, 170, 180, 233n76; factory labor, 31, 68, 107, 125, 152; and the FLN, 189; in goums, 63; as informants, 72, 187; Kabyle myth, 9, 63; massacre of, 158, 184, 187, 191; murder of, 105–109, 158, 184, 187; and the murder of Europeans, 101, 106–109, 149; and nationalism, 37, 86–87, 149, 153, 155; police brutality against, 111–115, 121, 134, 181, 184, 186–187; in the police/gendarmerie, 25, 40–51, 71; policing of, 20, 22, 28, 79, 163; poverty and unemployment, 31, 59, 89–90, 107, 109, 152; and the PPA-MTLD, 163, 169–170; rebellions, 35, 170–191; and sport, 96, 99–100; torture of, 186, 191
Kabylia, 89; during the Algerian War of Independence, 185; anti-colonialism in, 168–169; arms traffic/seizures in, 160, 172; banditry in, 32, 53–54, 59–61, 73, 169–171, 175; bechara in, 32; clandestine courts in, 168–169; crime in, 59–60, 89, 105; deserters in, 63; economy, 127, 135; elections, in, 150; European perceptions of, 38, 59, 62, 105, 169–170; FLN-ALN in, 185; military recruitment in, 63; OS, 171, 174; paramilitarism in, 169; policing in, 32, 38, 58, 60, 160, 164, 170; population, 105; PPA-MTLD in, 164, 168, 171, 174; rebellion in, 56–59; smuggling in, 137; terrain, 59, 61, 73–74, 80, 89, 170–171; during World War II, 133, 135, 137
Kaddache, Mahfoud, 150, 158, 231n65
Khenchela, 57–58, 77, 142
Khider, Mohamed, 161, 172, 175, 178, 181, 234n8
kidnapping, 61, 77, 103, 143, 175
Krim, Mohamed (Belkacem), 173, 180, 185

labor, 13, 84–86, 89–95, 102, 106, 112, 125, 139, 152–156, 159, 173, 184; Algerian, 152–154; in factories, 31, 64, 85, 90, 93, 152–155; firings, 102; during the Great War, 64; Kabyle, 153; and the left, 127; murder by, 106–107; and nationalism, 154–155; protest by, 6, 127, 156; and racism, 153; strikes, 32, 127; surveillance of, 152; unions, 31; wages, 107, 152–153; working conditions, 107, 153; during World War II, 119, 121, 125, 127
La Calle, 65–66, 72–79, 122
Lahouel, Hocine, 85, 154, 171, 180–181
Laval, Pierre, 117, 126, 144, 146

law enforcement, 4, 8, 10, 15, 39–40, 68, 120; and anti-nationalism, 151, 162, 169, 179, 181–182; and banditry, 78, 81; in communes mixtes/pleine exercice, 8; and fascism, 120–121; hatred of, 111–112; and the intelligence state, 4; masculinity and, 15; Muslim, 108; and the OS, 175; and the PPA-MTLD, 168, 170, 177, 179, 182; procedures, 29; race and, 10, 105, 131; rural, 21–22; and torture, 177; use of violence, 162; during World War II, 120–121, 128, 130
legal code, 86; and arms sales, 92; atteinte à la souveraineté française, 154, 164–165, 167, 177; and the civilizing mission, 162; collective punishment, 115; and colonial hegemony, 88, 190; and electoral fraud, 164; enforcement of, 108; indigénat, 8, 10, 68, 86–87, 107–108, 114, 153, 162, 187, 190; and nationalism, 134; penal law, 86, 138, 167; in police entrance exams, 4, 44; and policing, 151; PPA/clandestine courts, 168; precedents, 114; the press and, 166; racial bias in, 108, 114; reconstitution de ligue dissoute, 154, 165; under the Vichy regime, 138
looting, 54, 93, 132, 138

MacMahon, 33, 36, 65, 77–78
Manifeste du peuple algérien, 149, 155
Margueritte Affair, 59
Martin, Henry, 157
Mascara, 21, 31, 57, 65, 160
Massu, Jacques (colonel), 187–188
mayors, 7, 55, 159–160; adjoints, 164–165; and banditry, 71, 73; and crime, 99; and fascism, 118, 120; murder of, 109; and police oversight, 21, 25, 39–40, 46–49, 73, 122, 145; and the PPA-MTLD, 179; under the Vichy regime, 118, 123
mechtas, 83, 102, 142; during the Algerian War of Independence, 188; arms seizures in, 79, 92; and banditry, 53, 55, 60, 67, 72, 74, 76, 82; crime in, 190; murder in, 108; nationalism in, 74; occupation of, 78; the OS in, 174; policing in, 30, 70, 74, 92, 106, 110–111, 190; the PPA-MTLD in, 169, 181; racial tensions and, 81; rebellions in, 78, 111
military (French), 4, 6; Algerians in, 42–43, 63, 133, 173; in the Algerian War of Independence, 176, 184–189; antisemitism in, 131; and banditry, 61, 72–73,

military (French) (*continued*)
76–77, 79–82, 170; and Barricades Week, 186; brutality, 6, 56, 59, 62, 73–74, 78–79; cavalry, 65, 80; the Challe offensive, 186; commanders/officers, 33, 64, 74, 78; conscription, 31, 53–54, 63–66, 76–78; Conseil de guerre, 57–58, 66; and deserters, 54–55; garrisons, 89; gendarmerie oversight, 22; intelligence services, 61, 71; Jews in, 132–133; and massacres, 149, 158, 167, 182–183, 187–189; military police, 138, 141; military rule/Algeria (1830–1870), 6–7; and the Muqrani rebellion, 56; and nationalism, 157, 160, 164, 182; paratroopers, 176, 178, 185–188; prisoners of war, 122; and property destruction, 77–78; recruitment, 63–65, 70; suppression of insurrections, 57–58, 87, 109; and torture, 185–189; tribunals, 137, 159, 167, 176, 178, 183; troops, 6, 58, 78; during World War II, 119, 122, 125, 138–142

Moch, Jules, 40, 166
Mollet, Guy, 178, 187
Morocco, 23, 37–39, 64, 110, 187, 233n94
Moutet, Marius, 85
Mouvement pour le triomphe des libertés démocratiques (MTLD), 18, 162; and Algerian independence, 161; anti-colonialism, 164, 167, 171, 176; arrest of candidates, 150, 165, 179; banning of, 161, 167, 173, 187, 191; criminalization of, 152, 165, 167, 171; in elections, 43, 149–150, 160–161, 164–167, 171; electoral boycott, 150, 161; electoral campaigns, 161, 163; electoral fraud against, 37, 150, 165–166, 180, 182; in Kabylia, 170; leadership, 170, 176; meetings, 179; membership, 18, 167, 173, 179; militants, 150; municipal councillors, 164–166; and paramilitarism, 171; police informants in, 31, 50; policing of, 161, 165; propaganda, 161, 167; rallies, 164; and the UDMA, 151

M'Sila, 25, 29–30, 46, 79, 108, 111
municipal councils, 7, 36; councillors, 102, 115, 145, 164; and fascism, 120; police oversight, 36, 48; PPA-MTLD and, 164–166, 173, 180; settlers and, 126; during World War II, 126, 134–135

murder, 62, 78, 84, 87–88, 116; of Algerians, 88–89, 105–108, 142, 186–187, 219n79; anti-colonial, 105–109; assassinations, 81, 108, 169, 172–175; attempted murder, 91; banditry and, 54, 60–61, 66–70, 77, 81; cases, 27–28, 73; of children, 106, 134, 189; crimes of passion, 105; of Europeans, 28, 68–69, 78, 81, 87, 103, 106, 109, 134, 159, 190; executions, 70, 114; of guards, 78, 110; hitmen, 81, 174–175; manslaughter, 113; massacres (settler-military), 149, 158–161, 167, 182–183, 187–189; nationalism and, 134, 169; of officials, 78, 108–109; by police, 113, 134, 158–161, 186–189; of police/gendarmes, 73–74, 180; policing of, 71; PPA-MTLD and, 169, 174–175; revenge, 106, 108; by soldiers, 142, 187, 189; state-sanctioned, 72; suspects, 170, 189; trials/sentencing, 114; and tribal/family disputes, 105; witnesses to, 29, 103; of women, 103, 106–107, 134, 189

Naegelen, Marcel-Edmond (governor general), 37, 150, 161–163, 165, 182
nationalism, 6, 11, 14, 16–18, 82, 84–85, 109, 152, 159, 186–187; and 8 May 1945, 37, 43, 149, 158–159; anti-colonialism, 16, 88–89, 111; banditry and, 53, 68, 70, 76, 169; clandestine, 155; and communism, 151; and crime, 109–111, 114, 138; criminalization of nationalist politics, 18, 34, 148, 151, 155, 163, 166–167, 171, 177, 182–183; and economic conditions, 31, 85, 159; and elections, 148, 150, 168, 180; during the Great War, 65, 74; and independence, 11, 55, 78, 99, 148–149, 157, 176; and Islam, 160; and labor migration, 81, 85; movements, 93, 99, 116, 147, 149, 154–155; official persecution of, 118–119, 159–161, 180; paramilitarism, 169; in the police and gendarmerie, 25, 50, 120; policing of, 40, 43, 47, 120, 152–160, 167; popularity of, 37, 51, 88, 147, 155, 179; press, 168; propaganda, 110–111, 135, 163–168; radicalization of, 149–150; rebellion, 23, 49, 84, 88, 115, 153–157; rural/peasant, 149, 184; scouts and, 160; and security concerns, 34, 37, 85, 127, 135; and sport, 96–101; students and, 85; subaltern, 86–87; surveillance of nationalist movements, 38, 133; and violence, 89, 110–111, 116, 155, 160; women and, 14, 159; during World War II, 115, 118–119, 125–126, 133–135

officials, 4–6, 11–12, 81, 86, 170; abuse of power/corruption, 6, 79, 109, 182; administrative crackdowns, 160, 166–167;

INDEX 257

Algerian, 23, 79, 108–109, 168–169; during the Algerian War of Independence, 183; antisemitism of, 129–134; assaults on, 68, 84, 88–89, 93–95, 101, 107–109, 169–170, 180; and banditry, 63, 81–82, 170; and colonial violence, 134, 151; and communism, 127, 199n49; and crime, 88, 190; criticism of, 72, 88, 135; and electoral fraud, 37, 164–165; inquests, 159; and insurrections, 57, 109, 158; murder of, 78, 106, 108–109; and nationalism, 11–12, 30, 111, 134, 148, 151, 167, 182, 186; and police/gendarmerie recruitment, 42, 46; and police oversight, 79, 112, 145; and the PPA-MTLD, 154, 157–160, 164, 166–168, 170, 176–177, 180, 182; security concerns, 36, 95–96, 99, 102, 108, 111, 157–158; and sport, 100; and surveillance spéciale, 78–79; and torture, 176–177; during World War II, 118, 129

Oran (department), 6, 21, 29, 123, 144, 199n49; during the Algerian War of Independence, 185; colonial violence in, 121, 176; fascism in, 120, 144–145; nationalism in, 148, 160; OS in, 178; police brutality in, 121, 176; policing in, 32, 122, 140, 160, 180; population, 88–89, 105, 168; PPA-MTLD in, 168, 180; during World War II, 126, 130, 135–139, 145

Oran (town), 5, 36, 138, 146; antisemitism in, 131; colonial violence in, 121, 176; communism in, 126; crime in, 171; fascism in, 120, 145; informants in, 31; nationalism, 158; police brutality in, 121, 176; policing in, 21, 23–24, 32, 36, 38, 43–44, 101, 121, 138, 141, 145, 156, 176, 180; population, 89; PPA-MTLD in, 156, 176, 180; racial tensions in, 132–133; riots in, 65; sport in, 100–101; trials in, 160; during World War II, 126, 130, 135, 142

Organisation secrète, 18, 37, 170–186, 188

paramilitarism, 168–170, 186
Paris, 6, 26, 128, 152, 166, 191; Algerian nationalism in, 85, 107, 152–154; during the Algerian War of Independence, 183, 189; Algerian workers in, 80, 90, 153; German occupation of, 117, 128; police strike, 144; policing in, 20, 152, 189; slums, 90, 153
parliamentary commissions, 5–6, 166
Parti communiste algérien, 22, 31, 38, 85, 125–127, 149–151, 166, 180

Parti du peuple algérien, 11–12, 17–18, 22, 87, 101, 157, 187, 191, 204n33, 227n9, 229nn36–37; and 8 May 1945, 158–159; during the Algerian War of Independence, 154–155, 161, 164; anti-colonialism, 99, 153, 155, 162, 164, 166, 169, 171, 176–177; arms possession, 164, 169, 180–181; arrest and imprisonment, 151–160, 162–165, 168–169, 173–174, 178, 180–181; assassination campaigns, 170; and banditry, 168–170, 175; banning of, 149, 159–165, 167, 182; Berberist crisis, 171; boycotts, 168–169; cells, 155, 160, 181–182; central committee, 156, 172; clandestine, 168–169, 171; and communism, 85, 155; congresses, 171; criminalization of, 148, 152–153, 165–167, 171, 177, 182–183; in djemâas, 165; elections, 18, 43, 85, 148–149, 154, 156, 161, 164–166, 168, 181; factionalization, 151, 155–156, 160–161, 168, 171, 181–182; fundraising, 179, 181; and insurrection, 155, 157, 171; and Islam, 156, 160; in Kabylia, 169–170; leadership, 154–160, 164, 168–170, 176–180; mass meetings, 159, 163–165, 167, 169, 177, 179; membership, 18, 37, 85, 153–156, 163, 167–168, 170, 179–182, 222n69; militants, 150, 155, 158–161, 164–165, 168–169, 174, 180–181; and money laundering, 173; municipal councillors, 164–165; newsvendors, 166, 177; officials and, 159–160; origins of, 152–155; paramilitarism in, 168–175, 177; police informants in, 31, 50, 164, 169; policing of, 37–38, 47, 121, 151, 154, 164, 170, 176, 181; popularity of, 153–157, 159, 167, 169, 179; posters and tracts, 161–163, 166–167, 178–179; press, 150, 155–157, 162–168, 178, 182–183; printshops, 160, 162, 166; propaganda, 156, 161–162, 164–168, 177, 179, 181; protests/demonstrations, 156–159, 164, 179, 227n35; recruitment, 156–159; and reformism, 151; schools, 181; scouts in, 160, 175; sections, 154–155, 164; and sport, 101; students in, 154–155, 181; surveillance of, 22, 32, 158, 162; sympathizers, 169–170; and violence, 95, 169; during World War II, 155; youth and, 154–156, 170–171, 173, 175, 179, 181
Parti populaire français, 14, 118, 120, 124, 128–129, 144–146, 226n109
peasants, 84, 86–87, 106–107, 119, 135, 149, 152–156, 184

INDEX

Pétain, Philippe, 117–120, 124–127, 130, 140, 144–147
Philippeville, 14, 29, 41, 50–51, 90, 95, 103–104, 137, 139, 175, 207n31
police, 2–5, 10–12, 15–17, 39–40, 55, 62, 66, 68, 94, 167, 172; abuse of women, 77, 79, 112, 121, 176; during the Algerian War of Independence, 176, 184–189; Algerians in, 4, 20, 23–26, 30, 40–41, 46–51, 71, 74, 105, 108, 120, 123, 132, 168, 204nn133–134; anti-communism in, 42, 120–121, 125–127, 151, 219n80; antisemitism in, 42, 119–120, 128–130, 140, 145; Arabic/literacy, 11–12, 15, 41–44, 71–72, 105, 123, 145, 203n107; arms seizures, 31, 90–93, 112–113, 160, 164, 175, 186; arrests, 41, 83, 90–93, 97, 111–115, 121, 124–126, 132, 137–140, 143, 151, 154–155, 158, 160–170, 175–182, 185–190; assaulting an officer, 68, 70, 73, 83, 105–109, 115, 140–141, 143, 158, 162, 188; autopsies, 27; and banditry, 16, 53–55, 59–60, 71, 73, 78, 81–82; and the black market, 121–122, 136–137; border patrols, 122; bribes, 140–141, 162; brigadiers, 44–48, 120; budget, 20–21, 31, 34–38, 40, 139; checkpoints, 92; commissaires, 3, 21, 30, 34, 39, 41, 45, 47, 50, 101, 106, 122, 125–127, 137–141, 145, 151, 176, 180; corruption, 21; as counterinsurgency forces, 5, 51, 87, 109, 122, 148, 151, 164–166; criminal activity by, 48, 111–112, 134; and the criminalization of politics, 72, 151, 155; defense of racial hegemony/ imperial rule, 2, 10, 15, 39–41, 49, 54, 71, 83–89, 110–111, 120, 151–154, 166, 186–190; at demonstrations, 157–158, 164; discipline, 40, 47–51, 122, 162, 204n126; education/literacy in, 34, 41, 44, 46, 123; evidence, 114–115; false arrests, 105, 111–112, 186–187; and fascism, 120–121, 143–145; fingerprinting, 21, 27–29, 111, 154, 163; and football violence, 97–99; footprint analysis, 28; forced confessions, 176–178, 219n77; forensics, 140; freemasons in, 146; and Gaullism, 145–146; handwriting analysis, 27; house searches, 78, 90, 92, 95, 111–114, 126–127, 137, 154, 160, 162, 175–176, 180, 186, 188; identification lineups, 29; illegal search and seizure, 178; informants, 21, 30–31, 60, 71–72, 79, 81, 90, 100, 133, 137, 151–152, 163–164, 169, 174, 179, 185, 187, 199n49; inspectors, 39, 46; intelligence gathering, 3–4, 47, 73, 123, 126–127, 137, 190; interagency relations, 26, 122, 180, 185; interrogations, 92, 112–113, 126–127, 140, 160, 175–179, 186–187; Jews in, 140, 146; killing of suspects, 75–76, 111, 113, 134, 170, 175–177, 184–186; laboratories, 21, 27, 29; manhunts, 73, 95; and massacres, 158–159, 184; morgues, 27; municipal, 20–21, 41, 45–48, 71, 81, 122, 179; murder cases, 105–109; and the OS, 175, 183; passport/visa/identification control, 32, 152, 162; patrols, 3, 78, 110–111, 122, 132, 136, 139, 141; performance reviews, 46; photography, 21, 27, 111; physical fitness, 39, 41, 44, 140; police brutality, 72, 76–77, 79, 82, 86, 111–116, 120–121, 126–127, 131, 144, 147–151, 154, 157, 160, 170, 175–176, 186; police harassment, 111–113, 115, 126, 128, 151, 153; police stations, 34, 40, 125; and the PPA-MTLD, 153–168, 179–182; procedural regulations, 112; promotion, 39–40, 46–47; property destruction, 79, 112, 189; public complaints, 140–141, 176–177; race and, 41, 48–49, 112–113, 120–121, 124, 147; racial policing, 2–3, 10–11, 15, 29, 47, 51, 54, 83–84, 88–89, 95, 105–106, 110, 120, 125, 131, 138, 145, 147, 152, 187–191, 219n79; raids, 90–91, 112, 138–140, 155, 160, 162, 164, 175, 179; recruitment, 32–33, 38–44, 47; reports, 28, 91, 98–100, 102, 105–106, 122, 134, 151, 179, 190, 219n79; riot squads, 13, 120; roundups, 11–112, 134, 138, 159, 188; rural, 81, 111; salaries, 38, 44–45, 68, 123; search warrants, 166, 176; seizures, 86, 136, 139; and settlers, 147, 151; sexual assault cases, 103–104; shootings, 111, 113–115, 157, 188; staffing shortages, 12, 21, 26, 32, 36–38, 122–124, 139–140, 152; sting operations, 137; surveillance, 21, 38, 53, 55, 68, 73, 88, 90–92, 100, 121–122, 125–127, 132–133, 136–140, 144, 151–154, 158, 179, 185, 190–191; suspensions, 48, 145; telephones, 29, 121–122; and torture, 144, 165, 175–177, 186–188; training, 29, 39, 120–122, 141; undercover work, 126; unions, 46; vacations/leaves, 32, 48, 122; vehicles, 21, 180; under the Vichy regime, 17, 39, 117, 121–122, 125–127, 136, 143–146; wiretaps, 152, 185
Police administrative, 20, 123
Police d'état, 23, 36, 41, 44, 120, 140–141

INDEX

Police judiciaire (PJ), 5, 8, 15, 20–22, 26, 31, 39, 41, 44–47, 60, 122, 126–127, 139, 174–177, 185–189
Popular Front, 85, 120–121, 125, 153–154
population, 7, 10; citizenship, 7; density, 35; disease and, 78, 80, 90; European, 88–89, 102, 105, 190; famine and, 78, 80, 89–90; mortality rates, 90; in Oran, 32; population growth/Algerian, 7, 10, 21, 32, 89, 102, 105, 107; rural depopulation, 35; statistics, 88, 105; urbanization, 84, 87, 89–90
postes, télégraphes, et téléphones (PTT), 115, 122, 153, 160, 171, 173, 185, 234n98
poverty, 6, 84, 89, 107, 109, 152; Algerian, 164, 182; and banditry, 54–55, 80; and crime, 30, 94, 110, 120; and disease, 159; European, 135; food shortages, 133–135, 141, 149, 156–157, 159; and informants, 31; and nationalism, 127, 134, 164; officials and, 162; press coverage, 161; and starvation, 31, 80, 119–120, 133–135, 156, 159; during World War II, 119–120, 126–127, 135
prefects, 92, 161; Alger, 24, 41, 49, 73, 127, 139, 144; authority/responsibilities of, 73, 118; and banditry, 60–61, 71, 73–74, 78–80, 187; budgets/resources, 32, 34, 38, 139–140; Constantine, 34, 38, 73, 78, 95, 140, 143; and crime, 62, 100, 139; Oran, 24, 32, 100, 139, 144–145; and police oversight, 21, 26, 46, 71, 114, 144, 185; and police recruitment/promotions/discipline, 39–48, 140; prefectorial bans, 162; security concerns, 80, 143; during World War II, 117, 123, 127
press, 13, 85; and 8 May 1945, 159; 1881 statute, 166; Algerian, 13, 154–155, 165–166, 176; anti-nationalism in, 154, 169, 179; antisemitism in, 128–129; Arab language, 55, 84; banning of, 150, 154, 166, 182; censorship, 125, 153, 165–166; communist, 127, 166; European, 56, 67, 70, 91, 158–159, 166, 169, 175–179; Gaullist, 127; on the left, 85, 125, 176; nationalist, 37, 84, 150, 153–156, 161, 168, 182; newspaper vendors, 155, 166, 177; PPA-MTLD, 150, 157, 161–163, 166–168, 178, 182–183, 227n9; racial bias in, 37, 158, 169; reformist, 166; reporters, 177; revelations of torture, 176–177; seizures of, 153, 162–163, 166; during World War II, 119, 125, 127, 139

prisons, 2, 87–88, 168, 184; Alger, 178; during the Algerian War of Independence, 178, 186–187; arbitrary detention, 115, 127, 130, 186; bandits in, 62, 73, 75; cells, 154; concentration camps, 77, 119, 128; Coudiat, 154; death sentences, 75, 114, 127, 134, 144; deaths in, 78, 134; deserters in, 63; escapes, 59, 62, 66, 74–75; hard labor, 75, 114, 127, 160; house arrest, 81, 86, 134, 144, 156–157; internment camps, 122, 138, 144, 165, 173; interrogation and torture in, 186, 189; Jews in, 129–130; Lambèse, 60; life sentences, 75, 114, 127, 144; municipal, 79; nationalists in, 85, 160; Orléansville, 173; political prisoners, 126–127; PPA-MTLD in, 160–163, 166–167, 177–179, 182; preventative detention, 167; prison farms, 130; sentences, 75, 78, 85–86, 90–92, 95, 102–106, 114, 127–130, 139, 154, 160–167, 178–179; under the Vichy regime, 122, 129–130; work camps, 129, 138
procureur générale, 91, 131, 159, 163, 167, 207n31
property, 7, 56–57, 77, 79, 89, 129–130, 158, 160, 189
prostitution, 28, 111, 121
protests, 120–121, 134, 139, 153–157

race, 4, 96; and colonial policymaking, 130, 134; European racial hegemony/superiority, 2–4, 27, 110, 189–190; and policing, 41, 48–49, 110–113, 120–121, 124, 147; race riots, 99; racist discourse, 62, 120; segregation, 4, 110, 134; Vichy regime and, 118–120, 122, 129–130
Rassemblement national d'action sociale, 14, 23, 118, 120, 128–129
razzias, 78
reformism, 84–86, 132, 147, 150–152, 155–157, 161, 165–166, 182
Régis, Max, 62, 128–129
Regnier decree, 165–166
Renseignements généraux (RG), 15, 23, 132, 201n107; during the Algerian War of Independence, 185–186, 189; anti-communism, 151; anti-terrorism, 185; Arabic speakers, 43; duties, 22–23, 151, 185–186; recruitment, 39, 43–44; in France, 151–152; informants, 31; interagency relations, 26; and nationalism, 22, 152; operations, 126–127; and the

INDEX

Renseignements généraux (RG) (*continued*)
PPA-MTLD, 168, 176–179; promotions, 46–47; race and, 87; staffing shortages, 32, 122; torture of suspects, 176–186, 189; during World War II, 121–123, 126–127
riots, 77–78, 109–111, 119–121, 128–135, 156–158, 229n35
robbery, 28, 32–33, 62, 84, 88, 102; of Algerian property, 88–89; by allied soldiers, 141–142; armed robbery, 93, 102, 1111–113, 142, 171, 180; and banditry, 54, 61, 67–69, 74–78, 85, 170; burglaries, 73, 102; of Europeans, 87, 102, 190; food heists, 80; highway robbery, 61, 67, 72, 102; and murder, 106–107; and nationalism, 68; post offices, 67; the PPA-MTLD and, 170–171, 180; during World War II, 119, 134, 137–138

sabotage, 68, 71, 73, 78, 81, 87, 96, 108, 160
Sahara, 56, 58, 107, 119, 135, 168, 228n31
Saint Arnaud, 91, 97, 134–135
Salan, Raoul, 178
scouts, 85, 154–155, 160, 175
sénatus consulte (1865), 7, 9, 86
Service des liaisons nord-africaines d'Alger (SLNA), 179, 185
Service d'ordre légionnaire (SOL), 145–146
Service du travail obligatoire (STO), 124–125, 139
Service spéciale de documentation, 17, 122
Sétif, 18, 31–32, 35–37, 43–44, 47, 67, 70, 75, 91, 97, 106, 110, 130, 133, 149, 158–159, 168, 182
settlers, 4–7, 10–11, 14, 82, 147, 180; and 8 May 1945, 37, 43, 149, 158–159; during the Algerian War of Independence, 186, 188; anti-Algerian sentiment, 5, 150, 159, 161–162, 167; antisemitism, 127–132, 146; assaults on, 68–70, 84, 88, 94, 101–103, 143, 149, 152, 158, 169, 180, 189–190; and banditry, 60, 62, 67–70; colons, 7, 22, 24, 43, 70, 87, 91, 102–105, 115, 118, 159, 164; and crime, 90–91; and the criminal justice system, 108, 114–115; economic predominance, 68, 84, 107, 153, 157, 164, 190; and fascism, 117–118, 124, 126; land ownership, 35, 58, 152; militias, 149, 158–159, 182–183; murder of, 105–109; police and, 40, 51, 120, 144; politicians, 126, 150; and the PPA-MTLD, 179–180; property seizures, 7, 89, 149, 152; and race/colonialism, 10, 59, 86, 103, 147;

167; security concerns, 33, 59–60, 67–70, 87, 91, 95, 101–107, 123, 143, 155, 158–160, 179; settlement expansion, 6, 89; and the Vichy regime, 118–119, 124, 135–137, 144, 146; vigilante justice, 115; women, 103–104
sexual assault, 68, 70, 101–104, 143, 176, 186–189
Sidi-Aïch, 36, 66–68, 70–74, 120
Sidi-Bel-Abbés, 21, 38, 43, 118
smuggling, 90, 122, 137–140
Souk-Ahras, 53, 68, 106, 123–124, 175
Soummam, 67, 70, 72–75, 109
sous-préfets, 22, 31, 46, 78, 141, 169–170
Soustelle, Jacques (governor general), 184, 188–189
spahis, 4, 53, 57–60, 63, 70, 73–74, 95
Sûreté Générale, 20, 23, 29, 31, 41, 45, 67, 71, 105, 120, 187
surveillance spéciale, 53, 62, 78–79, 81, 114–115, 213n94

taxation, 68, 108–109, 136, 140, 153, 164, 168
Tébessa, 57–58, 74, 136–141, 163, 174
Territoires du sud, 1–2, 21, 26, 31, 172
Tiaret, 21, 32, 50, 146
Tirailleurs sénégalais, 63, 65, 75, 81, 104, 123, 216n44
Tizi-Ouzou, 32, 66, 73, 163, 168–170, 179
Tlemcen, 21, 47, 145, 163, 177
torture, 12, 115, 134, 165, 176, 182, 189, 191; during the Algerian War of Independence, 178, 184–189, 191; beatings, 144, 176, 186, 189; Chateau Germain, 176; courts and, 177–178; electricity, 144, 176, 188–189; of OS members, 188; paratroopers and, 178, 185–189; by police/gendarmes, 144, 175–177; of PPA-MTLD members, 161, 165, 175–179, 183, 186–189; sexual assault, 176, 186, 189; sleep deprivation, 189; starvation, 188; water, 144, 176, 186, 188–189; whipping, 176, 189
train derailments, 68, 94–95
trials, 75, 105, 113–114, 134, 158–160, 163–167, 177–179, 182
Tunisia, 35, 37, 43, 57, 64, 73, 130, 136, 163, 172, 187, 233n94

'Ulama, 100–101, 149, 151, 154–155, 171, 229n36
Union démocratique du manifeste algérien, 38, 50, 149–150, 156, 165–166, 171, 227n9

vagrancy, 21, 62
Vichy regime (Algeria), 14, 17, 22, 119, 124, 127, 144–146, 181; Algerians and, 42, 125, 133; anti-communism under, 42, 118–119, 126–127; antisemitism under, 42, 118–119, 127–130, 140; black market, 14, 17, 119, 121–123, 127, 129, 133–141; doctrine of, 117–118, 144; economy, 119–121, 125, 135; freemasons under, 42, 118–119, 121; and the Holocaust, 128–129; Jews and, 128–130; and nationalism, 133; police training, 38, 122, 146–147; policing in, 17, 25–26, 45, 120–122, 125–127, 136, 139, 143–145, 147; public criticism of, 119, 124–125, 135; purging of police/officials, 118, 121, 140; rationing, 133–136; resistance to, 121–127; settlers and, 118; shortages, 119–120, 133–135; STO, 124–125; and torture, 144
Viollette, Maurice, 85

Weygand, Maxime, 118
witnesses, 27–30, 67, 70, 105, 110–112, 125, 132, 163, 165, 167, 169, 176–178
women, 13–14, 77, 79, 103–107, 112, 121, 134–135, 142–143, 176
World War II, 86, 115, 122–125, 155, 168, 182; Algerian soldiers in, 173; anti-allied sentiment, 134; economy, 135; espionage, 122; gendarmes in, 123; Holocaust, 128; internment camps, 173; liberation, 145–146; nationalism and, 154–156, 182; Operation Torch/Allied landing, 17, 118, 123, 125–131, 137, 141, 144, 147; prisoners of war, 121, 139; resistance in Algeria, 124, 173

Zouaves, 53, 63, 73–74, 78–79

Milton Keynes UK
Ingram Content Group UK Ltd.
UKHW010922210224
438189UK00007B/79/J